John De Witt

The Psalms

A New Translation With Introductory Essay and Notes

John De Witt

The Psalms
A New Translation With Introductory Essay and Notes

ISBN/EAN: 9783337019617

Printed in Europe, USA, Canada, Australia, Japan

Cover: Foto ©Lupo / pixelio.de

More available books at **www.hansebooks.com**

THE PSALMS

A New Translation

WITH

INTRODUCTORY ESSAY AND NOTES

BY

JOHN DE WITT

D.D., LL.D., L.H.D.

SENIOR BIBLICAL PROFESSOR IN THE THEOLOGICAL SEMINARY AT NEW
BRUNSWICK, N. J., AND A MEMBER OF THE AMERICAN
OLD TESTAMENT REVISION COMPANY

NEW YORK
ANSON D. F. RANDOLPH AND CO.
1891

University Press:
JOHN WILSON AND SON, CAMBRIDGE.

INTRODUCTORY ESSAY.

IT may reasonably be expected that one who has lived in long and close contact with the Psalms as a translator, will contribute some thoughts at the beginning that shall be helpful to their intelligent and appreciative study.

The Psalms are unspeakably precious to all who call upon the one true and living God. This attachment, moreover, is very little, if at all, impaired by the fact that several of them contain much that seems inconsistent with the mild and forgiving spirit of the Gospel, if not absolutely shocking to Christian consciousness. These portions we learn to pass over, as belonging to different conditions and a period of inferior enlightenment, and not intended for us. Or else, going deeper than the words, we cast aside philological trammels, and ingeniously translate them into thought that is not incongruous with our later revelation. In spite of them, we all love the Psalms, and are more and more coming to regard them as of immeasurable importance in the worship of God.

What do they contain that has given them this permanent hold upon the hearts of men? What master spirits are these that can touch the deepest and most secret springs of feeling, and have expressed the transports of the soul in all its contact with evil so exquisitely that no other can surpass and supersede them?

The work of the translator is a matter of detail and microscopic examination. He takes up severally the words, clauses, and sentences of each Psalm by itself, for the closest scrutiny. If he be merely a cold-blooded philologist, provided that he have the requisite knowledge of the languages he handles, together with tact and skill in the application of sound exegetical principles, his efforts will be richly repaid, and he will perform thankworthy service for us all. But he may bring all this to his task, and much more, and may execute it with unimpeachable fidelity, yet know very little of the Psalms in their higher aspects. His necessary nearness to his work, arising from its peculiar nature, may have excluded him from any just conception of their glorious import, severally, or in their combination. So one may bring his eye so near a painting as to discern clearly every brushmark, and yet be in absolute ignorance of the conception of the artist in its breadth and fulness, and of the masterly execution by which he has achieved his grand success. Let us not become so absorbed in the correct translation of words and phrases in the Book of Psalms, as not to raise a question with regard to its contents in their unity, suitableness, and coherence, or as to whether their constituting elements have drifted together by chance, and have been clumsily or cleverly combined, or, on the contrary, have a common source and an inner principle of harmony that has attracted, and holds them together inseparably.

Any competent treatment of the Book will not neglect such consideration. Perchance we may find in it something like organic unity, and this animated by a spirit and a life, if inferior in potency, not different in kind from that which our Saviour claims for his own words. We may then come to see in the Psalms what we never saw before, and in their separate sentences a depth, a breadth, and a fulness of meaning that are splendidly illuminative, and shall prove to ourselves personally the affirmation, —

> " The unfolding of Thy words giveth light,
> To the simple it giveth discernment."

Two questions are before us with reference to the Book of Psalms: *the first* relating to *its contents*, including both substance and form; *the second*, to the *mode of its production*.

Most of the Psalms are direct addresses to God. The rest of them are devout meditations upon the Divine word, and the blessedness of those who receive it into their hearts, or varied expressions of spiritual life arising from the most intimate and inspiring relations with God, and suitable to the sanctuary. The central and ruling idea of the whole is *worship* in its most comprehensive sense, and is embodied in a single impressive sentence in Psalm xcv. : —

> 5. "Oh come, bowing down let us worship,
> Let us kneel before Jehovah our Maker;
> 6. For He is our God,
> And we are the people of His care,
> The flock of His hand."

Defining more particularly the word *worship* in the light of this invitation, it is the expression of all thoughts and feelings which man, in view of his complex relations with God, may suitably pour out before Him. It recognizes Him as the supreme and infinite personal Intelligence, from whom we have received our immortal nature, and on whose almighty and gracious care we are dependent, and it has regard to everything that affects our relations with Him, or in reference to which we may hopefully appeal to Him for sympathy and help.

We add here, in a word, that *the principle* in this worship is not constrained homage to a superior, enforced by arbitrary pains and penalties, but the cultivation of the higher nature in man by the encouragement of gracious affections in unreserved personal intercourse with God, and this as the only means of preserving him from utter moral deterioration and debasement.

The *leading elements* in acceptable worship are well understood by all who know these Psalms.

It begins with adoring recognition of the infinite perfections of God; of His wisdom, power, and other natural perfections without stint, as surpassing all thought or speech, and of the moral even more, — His holiness, justice, faithfulness, and love, each of them most comprehensive, and covering the whole ground of human aspiration and need. Although the main purpose of the Book of Psalms is not instruction, yet with respect to the person and nature of God it is a text-book, even fuller than the New Testament. In the latter, this previous revelation is assumed as not needing to be repeated. The knowledge of God that is imparted in these adoring appeals to Him in the Psalms is for the whole world and for all time.

Very closely connected with adoration, in the material for intelligent worship, is the conception of God as our Creator, and of consequent dependence on Him, as also of obligation, constantly accumulating, and which no gratitude of ours can cancel, for all Divine activities in sustaining us, and in filling our lives with good. This needs only to be mentioned.

Thus far, however, we are on the same footing before God as the angels, save in their different natural conditions. They are not constituted as we are, and the sphere of their existence is not the earth with its bountiful supplies. Yet alike, angels and men are dependent creatures, and in the same throng may bless and adore God for all His goodness and His wonderful works in their behalf.

But for our use a book of worship must be adapted to our special relations and circumstances under God's moral government. In this connection the first idea that will obtrude itself before some minds, is that of suffering; before others, that of sin. The recognition of both is indispensable, and they are inseparable. The thought of sin, when we approach a holy and just God, is entitled to the precedence as the originating cause. Yet man is liable to torture so intense that sometimes he can only wail in misery, and cry out for relief. These two elements are consequently intermingled. The early church fathers distinguished from the rest, as a class by themselves, seven Penitential Psalms. They are Psalms vi., xxxii., xxxviii., lvi., cii., cxxx., cxliii. But the incidental introduction of sin, and of feelings suitable to one who feels himself guilty before God, occurs in many of the others.

It is not necessary to dwell upon all that has place here, unless confession of sin before God is to be a mere mockery. There is a recognition of the heinousness of sin as an offence against the Divine purity, and a violation of the highest and most sacred obligations, and therefore as something which God's own grace must put out of the way by a free and absolute pardon, or it will forever separate between Himself and us. And there will further be combined with sincere confession an intelligent consideration of sin in the nature, as a deep-seated and fell disease, which requires a new act of creative power, restoring moral purity and love to the inner life; and besides these, surely some suitable expression of hearty loathing and abhorrence of sin as in contrast to the holiness of God, like the contrast between light and darkness, and of a turning away of the whole nature, in the act of renewing its fellowship with God, from that which as God He must necessarily loathe and hate. A truly penitent and regenerated soul will separate itself in its preferences, purposes, and practices, from all evil, and the separation will be most pronounced.

Here we are disposed to enlarge, and every one who has followed our thought through these commonplaces of practical religious truth, will surely follow us further, as we lead the way into a consideration of the most painful and perplexing problem that confronts us in the Book of Psalms. We allude to what are called the Imprecatory Psalms. It may be questioned by some what place they have in connection with penitence and a reinstatement in the Divine favour, as we now introduce them. But it is just here that we find their most satisfactory explanation, and we shall be thankful if we can suggest thoughts that will afford any measure of relief.

But first let us face the subject boldly. Here are Psalms that seem to be full of hatred and revenge for personal wrongs. Their imprecations seem in one place to pass into the unseen world, calling upon God to strike the name of an evil-doer out of the book of the living, and even include his progenitors and descendants. This cannot be overlooked, or dismissed, without an explanation, and one which shall commend itself to sound judgment. Not unfrequently it is asked, on the assumption that David was the author of these Psalms, how could a sincere and accepted worshipper of God, indulge such feelings of hatred against his enemies, and how can we in our worship make use of expressions so contrary to the spirit of the Gospel?

We cannot set aside as valueless, although it may not entirely relieve our perplexity, what is often said about the characteristic difference between the Old and New Testament dispensations. As a man, David, or whoever wrote these Psalms, is entitled to the plea that he could not be expected to express himself in accordance with a revelation so far distant in the future, and that feelings that would now be intolerable, are not discordant with the standard of right, in feeling and action, of the times in which he lived; and further, that even the inspiring Spirit did not detach him from his relations to those times, and the standard of moral propriety that he had in the only Scriptures of God he possessed. This is solid fact, and it is good so far as it goes.

It may further be said that these Psalms are poetry, and should not be read as prose. The language of poetry, and especially of Oriental poetry, is that of exaggerated passion. It must be judged by the conditions and rules that are peculiar to itself. This does not imply deception. No figure of speech is more common in the productions of Oriental genius, ancient or modern, than hyperbole, which is a rhetorical exaggeration, employed when language in its poverty must necessarily fail in expressing the fact in its full dimensions. Descriptions of this kind must not be pressed too literally. Instances of hyperbole can be found elsewhere, both in the Old Testament and the New, and are not confined to poetry. We need only refer to the people "like the sand upon the seashore," in Gen. xxii. 17, and to the books so many that "the whole world could not contain them" in the last verse of the Gospel of John. But there are no illustrations that will serve us so well here as those which are found in this very Book of Psalms, where *suffering* is the subject.

This David was a man of great personal heroism. The history of his persecuted life indicates wonderful endurance. He was ready to face any enemy, or to bear any privation, with undaunted courage and firm trust in God. Not an instance occurs of his having been unmanned by suffering, or the fear of suffering. The history to which we refer with confidence in this connection, which does not deal tenderly with his known moral weaknesses, is prose. Yet this fearlessness is sometimes expressed vehemently in the Psalms, for even poetry is not always hyperbolical. But in how many of them he appears in a quite different character, moaning, groaning, wailing, roaring, overwhelmed with grief day and night, making his bed to swim with tears, and through the hours of darkness calling aloud to God, — because evil-minded men were plotting against his life, or perhaps because some one man was persecuting him with vile slander. One would say, this is not manly, but childish. Such weakness is despicable. Surely neither David nor any man prominent in Israelitish history could have written these sentences.

But not more foreign to David's actual life was this cowardly spirit, than the revenge that seems to breathe out in others of the Psalms. We must not forget in any of them that we are in the fervid, impassioned, and demonstrative East, where to this day feeling of any kind is scarcely thought of as genuine, unless it is expressed extravagantly.

Another consideration occurs to us, as entitled to some weight. Those who draw contrasts between David's feelings toward his enemies and their own placid indifference, unfavourable to the former, do not consider that they know nothing of such enemies as he describes, — men that were the incarnation of treachery, cruelty, and diabolical malignity, who were seeking his life like veritable wolves and hyenas. It might be said that there is no Gospel against the extermination of wild beasts, and these were worse than wild beasts in their disposition and power to destroy. It is possible that in the presence of such enemies the equanimity and meekness of the critics would be disturbed, and they might so far forget the spirit of the Gospel as to long, and even to pray, for the destruction of men so savage and ruthless, not merely on their own account, but for the sake of the innocent lives that are exposed to the deadly arts of the malignant.

But in all this we leave out of view the actual problem to be solved, which pertains to these Psalms not merely as expressions of individual feeling, but as embraced in an inspired manual of worship. It is much more distressing. It is only those who believe them to be Divinely inspired that are seriously disturbed by the Imprecatory Psalms. Others indulge in flippant and captious remark, reflecting upon these fierce words as blots on the character of one who is claimed to be a man after God's own heart, or as strange inconsistencies in the Bible, one part of the book claimed to be Divine totally contradictory to another. They enjoy the difficulty that Christians find in reconciling them.

Such expressions of latent scepticism are most easily and thoroughly silenced, and our own perplexity soonest relieved, by stating the difficulty in its most formidable shape. It is not how a man, supposed to be sincerely religious, could deal in these strong denunciations. For we find them in a prayer-book which we believe to have been provided for us by the inspiration of the God whom we worship. The human penman now ceases to be responsible. We are arraigning the great Being who has distinctly defined in this book what worship will be acceptable to Him — unless we are prepared on account of the unworthiness of its contents to abandon our belief in its Divine origin. But we will surely not do this without the fullest consideration.

We then face the paradox, that the God of love has put into our lips words of hatred and wrath. Can we show it to be mere paradox, — an apparent contradiction to the actual, or even possible, which is really true and right and good? We find the relief by going back to our starting-point.

We have already alleged, that in coming before God as worshippers, we must confess our sins with penitent hearts, and must ask for pardoning mercy and renewing grace. This further point, also, we reached, and now resume: that God has the right to insist that the heart of the worshipper shall turn away with loathing and hatred from the falsehood, the injustice, and the malignity, that are desolating the world. These were not mild and inoffensive forms of evil that in God's name were denounced, but those most opposite to the light and love, the purity and truth, of His own nature. One loyal to God must hate them, and must declare himself on the Lord's side in the great battle against His person and government that was going on in the world. And this sin, so hated by God, was not an abstraction, an impalpable something floating in the region of the upper clouds, but an activity of deadly hate in the hearts and lives of men. If it were merely an abstraction, there need have been no Imprecatory Psalms. Then with the utmost composure it might have been consigned to oblivion. Whatever is harmless may be hideous, but we relieve ourselves simply by looking in another direction. But sin only exists concretely and in sinful men; and God, because he is the ideal and absolute love and purity and truth and goodness, must detest incarnate hatred, treachery, and malignity; and so must we, if we love Him. Perhaps in the earlier times, when men were less practised in abstract, philosophic thought than they are now, it was more difficult to separate the sin from the sinner than it is for us. This may have produced a tendency to clothe abstractions in an ideally personal and concrete dress. For the strong language of these hard sentences does not seem to reflect the actual feelings and conduct of the composer against living persons guilty of foul wrong. There is no evidence in the life of David, or of any good man of those times, that he was really malignant and revengeful. Rather the contrary. But the language of poetry is not that of philosophic thought. It does not deal in abstractions, but in vivid representations of human life as it is, and from this personality is inseparable.

Unquestionably most of these Psalms have their historic background in the conflicts and trials of the individual composer. But we have taken pains in some of the following notes (see on vii. 6, and ix. 1, 2) to show briefly that in adapting them to a higher and broader use by the assembly of God's people in their worship, the very license that distinguishes poetry from prose serves an admirable purpose. History is idealized. The individuals lose their own personality, and come to represent classes of men. Whatever personal hostility to leaders in persecution and injury may once have stirred in the heart of the poet, perhaps years ago, when great wrong was committed, now disappears in his higher thought. The identification with actual living persons he had once known as enemies, fades away, and the hostile feeling so strongly declared is only a more vivid and graphic expression of hatred to sin, as then and thereafter existent, rampant, defiant, triumphing over everything holy and good, and therefore accursed forever. Why, the man described and held up to detestation in Ps. cix. has become already a fiend, before descending into the pit, and is not one for whom a claim upon our charity and forbearance could be asserted, if he were now upon the earth. This fierceness of denunciation has its reason: —

> 16. " Because he forgat to show kindness;
> But the suffering and needy, and broken in heart,
> He pursued unto death.
> 17. The cursing he loved, it alighted upon him;
> Since from blessing he gathered no pleasure,
> It removed far away from himself.
> 18. He clothed him with cursing as a robe,
> And it entered his substance like water,
> And like oil it coursed in his bones.
> 19. Let it be like the coat he puts on,
> Like the belt which he ever girds about him.
> 20. This is the wage of my foes from Jehovah,
> Of those that plan harm to my life."

There may have been first in the poet's mind the countenances, called up from his earlier life, of those who had long before gone to their reward; and, so far as it related to them, the form of imprecation is only a graphic way of stating historic fact. The face before him may have been that of the crafty and malignant Ahithophel, responsible directly and indirectly for unnumbered lives, including that of Absalom, his father's idol; or, as in Ps. lii., that of Doeg the Edomite, the dastardly spy and informer, who occasioned the slaughter of eighty-five priests, with their families. But presently these features from the past fade away, and are replaced by the black face of Judas, " the son of perdition," with whose baseness this picture is connected in the New Testament, and to whom all thoughts turn as the ideal incarnation of evil. See John xvii. 12, and Acts i. 20.

This prepares us, with reference to some of these Psalms, to take higher ground. We note here a loftier than poetic inspiration. The pen, and harp, and voice that swept on in these stirring measures, were those of a *prophet*. What stands before his illuminated vision is not a personified principle, incarnations wrought by poetic fancy, to be dissipated presently into thin air. They are indeed persons, yet not as known individuals of our race, each standing for himself, against whom for personal wrong his darker human passions are roused, — but impersonations, standing for men always and everywhere, who crush innocent lives under their iron heel, who know neither pity nor kindness, justice nor truth, but with determined will identify themselves with evil of devilish stamp, hating men and defying God. It is no base human passion, but impassioned prophecy, in the name of Him to whom vengeance belongs, that calls down upon them a doom from which, if they repent not, there is no escape. And with whatever sadness, yet with firmness unflinching, let all people that are loyal to God pronounce their Amen !

A crucial instance of the relief afforded by the prophetic character of Psalms of this severe type is found in the closing verses of Ps. cxxxvii. : —

> 7. " Remember, Jehovah, to the children of Edom
>   The day at Jerusalem,
>   When they cried, Lay it bare, lay it bare,
>   Even down to its base.
> 8. O daughter of Babylon, doomed to destruction,
>   Blest is he that requites thee,
>   That does unto thee as thou didst unto us;
> 9. Blest is he that shall seize and dash down
>   Thy babes on a rock."

This may be thought of as poetic justice, not to be pressed too closely as fact. The precise act described is intensely realistic, yet not too shocking for Oriental taste, nor for high-wrought tragic poetry in any age. The slaughter of babes

in the most brutal manner is not the most horrid of the barbarities practised by conquering armies when cities with their
innocent inhabitants are given up to their wanton fury. In
this case the historic background is twofold: an earlier, in
the barbarity of the Chaldean invaders of Judea, seventy
years before, of which we have here a single representative
fact; a later, in the retribution inflicted at the capture of
Babylon by the Persian army, within a few years. It points
to Cyrus, who was raised up as the avenger of the sufferings
of God's people during their long and merciless bondage.
An old Israelite, just returned from the exile, is gazing with
a tortured heart on the ruins of the holy city and temple, and
the terrible past comes up freshly before him, as if actually
witnessing the savage act he describes. From this assumed
standpoint he speaks as a prophet of God, declaring of the
ruthless invader, that as he has sown even so also he shall
reap. But what is thus ideally exhibited for the sake of higher
poetic effect has already become historic fact. The judgment
has fallen, and the man who is felicitated as having redressed
the ancient wrong is the king of the Medes and Persians,
brought forward in the far-seeing providence of God for this
express purpose. As the representative of the King of kings,
in accomplishing a great deliverance, he has inflicted punishment in kind upon the desolators of Zion, so that all the
earth may stand in awe of Him that lives and reigns forever.
A repulsiveness remains; but it is the repulsiveness of fact,
in a world that is full of such horrid facts, which we must
make the best of, till the earth is delivered from its curse.
It could not have been omitted from a faithful picture of the
wrongs of Jerusalem and their reparation.

In this place alone the English Bible translates *'ashrē, happy*,
as of personal enjoyment, a meaning it never has. See note on
Ps. ii. 1. It expresses here emphatic approval of Divinely
ordered retribution. It would apply to a tender-hearted

judge, as once seen by the writer, with streaming eyes pronouncing the death penalty on one guilty of brutal murder.

The only questions that remain with reference to the Imprecatory Psalms are such as these: What are they to us? Can we use them in our worship without being faithless to the Divine spirit of love that irradiates the Gospel and is sometime to irradiate the world? Am I to unite with the great congregation in uttering these terrible sentences, and what is their meaning as issuing from my lips? Surely we are to use them; but whatever else they mean for us, they cannot mean that we are thus to express our hatred to the enemies of David, or of some unknown writer of sacred song, and to unite with him in praying for their extermination. He and they have passed from the earth long ago, and everything that relates to them is irreversibly settled. They exist here only in the images they suggest to the thoughts of men as shades of the past. Nor does our use of them mean that we are thus to denounce *our own* enemies. We have no such enemies as these, and they are never to be classed with the facts of our personal life. They stand before us as vivid representations of the hostility to God that is the black curse of the world, and which we, as born of God, must hate and denounce forever. The more I love God, and love my fellow-men in their actual personality, each and all, the more heartily and bitterly I shall detest and curse the principle of evil, incarnate or unincarnate, that, if it could, would blot out the light of the world, and leave us all in the blackness of darkness forever. This is the solution of our paradox. Love, because it is love, must hate hate. And God, because He is love, hates it. And we, if we have the love of God and man in our hearts, always and everywhere must hate it.

Closely connected with all that relates to *sin*, are man's appeals to God for sympathy and relief under *suffering*. This also is a universal experience, and one in which Divine aid is indispensable. Our worship recognizes God as gracious and full of compassion, and looks confidently to His great heart as directing His infinite power. How many Psalms besides the one hundred and thirtieth are *De profundis*, and how many that have misery as their key-note lie outside the few that are called " Penitential"! And these have touched a responsive chord in hearts wrung with anguish ever since they were written. We have alluded to them as abounding in hyperbole. To express our meaning more precisely, for *our* worship they describe not *more than* the literal fact, but *other than* the literal fact. They substitute the external for the internal, and so there is an underlying truthfulness. In actual use their most exaggerated expressions are hardly thought of as exaggerations needing apology. Like other hyperbole in Scripture they have their ground in the impossibility of describing in words the agonies of a tortured spirit. The nearest approach to truth that language can attain is found in the natural expression of extreme physical suffering, and so they deal in groans and tears, in wasting and faintness, in loud outcries and heart-rending complaints, which are understood to be figures of a wretchedness that none but God can know.

Some of these Psalms of the suffering have special interest and sacredness in their connection with the agonies of the great Sufferer who gave His life for the world. These too in their inception are founded upon the sufferings of the composer, but almost immediately he is carried away from them into the presence of woes such as he never experienced, and yet with which his personal being seems to be mysteriously blended. He becomes a typical representative, and so continues to speak of himself, and yet really of another identified with himself by prophetic laws. These descriptions are sometimes thought of as hyperbolical, and they come within the limits of what we have remarked on that subject. It may be said that the inspiring spirit of prophecy carries the poet into

what, as relates to himself, and perhaps in his own consciousness, is merely poetical exaggeration, but is intended by the
higher power that masters and sways his spirit to portray the
sufferings of One who by and by, using as His own language
borrowed from one of the most wonderful of these Psalms,
shall cry from the cross of agony and shame, " My God, my
God, why hast Thou forsaken me ? " It may be that in this
Psalm the poet intended to describe an ideal sufferer, typical
for all anguish and for all time, but he evidently finds his
starting-point in the persecutions of the malignant in his personal life. Yet the sufferings of Christ are inseparably bound
up with those of His people, or rather, theirs with His. Those
who preceded His own life on the earth prefigure Him that
suffered for us all, and they that come after " fill up what
was lacking of the afflictions of Christ." So all may find
comfort in the language of these sublime wailings of a deeper
than mortal woe, as including every throe of anguish they ever
endured.

We cannot dwell on all that the Psalms contain : their fervent
expressions of gratitude for God's saving mercy, of desire after
God, of delight in Him, of unfailing confidence and hope under
every apprehension of danger, and even in death itself. These
all belong legitimately to Old Testament times. Surely they
are not less suitable now.

Yet Judaism is not Christianity. Since the latest of these
Psalms were written a richer grace has enveloped the world,
and their utmost bound is too narrow for us. For worship,
in order to be adequate to its conditions and purpose, must
adapt itself to all new occurrences that materially affect man's
relations with God. From the time of the sacrifice and ascension of our Lord, prayer has assumed a new character,
joyfully recognizing these transcendent facts in all their significance. In the earlier time, His coming and kingdom were
only seen in the dim vision of prophecy. But since then,

His dying love is ever remembered, and His name ever urged before God, as the only ground of acceptance and blessing. A distinctively Christian office of prayer has a language of its own, rich, varied, and gracious. It could have no existence till the Son of God was revealed from heaven to give life to the dead. But all this is not a substitution, but simply an addition. Our primary relations with God are unchanged. We retain all that is permanent in the older worship, and enjoy it the more because its acceptance is secured through the grace of our glorified Redeemer; and we gratefully add to it the later, as bringing us still nearer to God, and giving us fresh hope in His mercy.

It must yet be observed, that intercession in behalf of the evil-minded scarcely appears in the Psalms. When the Crucified was enthroned, He immediately organized a " ministration of the Spirit," and set in operation the mighty agencies that by individual regeneration shall bring all nations into living fellowship with God. Our prophetic Psalms give charming glimpses of this in a far distant future; see notably Ps. lxxxvii. But they disclose no grace as then present, and available in answer to prayer, by which the savage natures that were regarded with horror might be transformed, and wolves become lambs. It is our rejoicing that for us this lacking element is abundantly supplied.

It was intimated at the beginning that a consideration of the *form and character* of the Psalms should not be omitted. We can notice only one or two of the more obvious points.

It has been incidentally stated that they are poetical, and that their main purpose is not instruction. The meaning of " poetical " in that connection is that the thought and diction are elevated. Under the impulse of strong emotion the imagination is set free, and the result must not be measured by prosaic rules. To this should be added that they are poetical *in form*, and intended for musical accompaniment.

David was a poet, not only lofty in thought, and able to stir the hearts of men by the beauty, the grandeur, or the tender pathos of his conceptions, but of no mean skill in constructing verse with due regard to the charm of song, and the most effective instrumental rendering. He was probably a magnificent harpist, and could lead an orchestra. All this was made subservient, by Him who created us with a susceptibility to be powerfully wrought upon by such means, to the principal purpose of the Psalms, which are not addressed to the intellect so much as to the emotional nature. The combined force of music and poetry is here employed to arouse man's sluggish nature in response to the tender appeals which the God of all grace, in deeds more than in words, is ever making to his heart. If this be so, how can we separate the inspiration of the Psalmist from the external form of his productions, including their adaptation to such audible enhancement as shall charm and soothe the hearts of men, and incline them to all gracious desires, purposes, and hopes, lifting them ever nearer to the centre of light and truth and love.

This result of inspiration cannot be literally transferred to another language. But it follows by necessary consequence that there can be no adequate rendering of the Psalms for the worship of God that does not aim at similar effects by similar methods. Their whole value for instruction may be enjoyed, and not without some deep effects in spiritual life, if they are translated into prose, to be quietly read. But the Divine purpose in providing them in this form would fail, were they not supplemented by the spiritual songs, only less directly inspired, that have since enriched the worship of the Church.

One consideration more seems worthy of mention that may not have appeared in anything that has been written upon the subject of Hebrew psalmody. It relates to the combination of words with musical expression, as requiring the strictest adjustment of one to the other. The more intense and impassioned of these songs are not to be judged as if intended to be read in soft, melodious voice in the contracted inner chamber with its shut door, or in the somewhat broader, yet narrow, family and social circles, or even for the subdued and solemn utterances, alternately by minister and people, to which we are accustomed in our modern worship of the sanctuary. Some of the Psalms, in their subject and their manifestly gentle intonation, remind us of the soft purling of the brook, or the sweet lay of the nightingale. They suggest the nablum and cithern, the softest and sweetest stringed instruments with which the solitary worshipper might accompany the flow from his heart before God. But some of them were composed and inwrought with suitable musical expression for the spacious courts of the temple, or for the open air. The elaborate cultivation of the art of music among the Hebrews should be remembered, and especially in connection with Divine worship. Large bands of the Levites were detailed for the service of song. Singers and players upon instruments were there in thousands, who devoted their lives to it. Besides the lute and the harp, or their nearest ancient equivalents, there was every instrumental device that genius could create, that could give loud and strong expression to strong feeling. The cry went forth to Israel in Ps. cl., the doxology of the whole Book: —

> 3. " Praise Him with blasts of the trumpet,
> Praise Him with the lute and the harp;
> 4. Praise Him with timbrel and dance,
> Praise Him on strings and the pipe ;
> 5. Praise Him with clear-sounding cymbals,
> Praise Him with cymbals loud clashing."

Yet not only in praise, but in every deep and intense emotion common to them all, while their hearts are throbbing before God as the heart of one man, there must be vehement expression. Not only must joy have its glad tumult, but fear its shriek, and agony its loud wail. Music, considered merely as sound addressed to the ear, must do its part, — producing vibrations upon the heart-strings of men, recalling them from their worldliness, rousing them from their torpor, and engaging them in the high service of God; and it must be allowed to produce its most intense effects by means best adapted to its principles and nature. To such music, language that is not impassioned, and that does not at times exhibit even violent emotion, would be altogether inappropriate. Witness the exaggerated expression in words and gesture in the dramatic accompaniment adapted to that modern masterpiece of musical genius, — the Italian opera. Such accompaniment, apart from the music, seems strained and grotesque; but with it, is felt to be suitable, and even indispensable to the finest impression. May it not be allowed that this is true in a measure of the Psalms? It accounts in some degree for expressions of suffering more intense than the known circumstances account for, but which utter only too feebly the secret sorrows of the heart before God.

We approach now the *second* principal question proposed at the outset: *How was this Book of Psalms produced?*

The key to the answer has already been furnished in the reference that has been made to their connection with the facts of individual life, whether of David or some later masters of sacred song. The royal poet, who calls himself in his last words (2 Sam. xxiii. 1) "the anointed of the God of Jacob, and the sweet psalmist of Israel," is the representative singer of the Old Testament. Others after him sang in like strains, after similar experience, and by inspiration of the same Divine Spirit; but he is the leader and type of them all. There is no good reason to doubt that he produced the grandest and sweetest of the Psalms, and probably the largest number; and, further, that they relate to the circumstances of his own history. This accounts for the tenacity with which those who know them hold them in deep affection, — that they are genuine, as having originated in an actual human life. Whatever imaginative activity they manifest, they are not, like much of our most charming poetry, mere fiction. We do not depreciate such poetry, but admire and enjoy it beyond measure. A true poet may hold men rapt and spell-bound by the creations of his own fancy. He moves them to shouts of joy or to tears on the hollow basis of simulated fact. Such productions are sources of refined and exalted gratification in ordinary life. But when we come to face the stern realities of human existence, with its conflicts and its woes, we must have truth. One who has suffered sore trouble, and found help in God, is the man whose words are seized with avidity by the suffering, and such words are these in the Psalms. They do not work upon our emotional nature by cunning counterfeits of genuine feeling. Their heroes are not those of the stage, exhibiting before us mock transports of grief and of joy. They lay bare their own bleeding hearts; they give us the outpouring before God of their actual hopes and fears, their struggles and conflicts, their dangers and deliverances. We see how and where they found comfort in their sorrow and hope in their despair, and on this basis they sway our hearts and control our lives. In approaching the Majesty on high we have solid ground under our feet in using words which sinful men like ourselves have used, and the Lord heard them, and saved them from all their fears.

We thus reach the very heart of the inquiry proposed. We believe that the Psalms have come to us by inspiration of God. But this does not reach the whole truth. Inspiration is very commonly thought of as a Divine power working mysteriously in the heart of some selected man, and producing in words spoken or written immediate results. If this only were true of the Psalms, if they came without human admixture right out of the mind and heart of God in some mechanical way, the man who wrote them would have passed out of mind, and we should have gloried in our Psalms as Divine, and doubtless should have found them very helpful and comforting.

But God designed something better for us, and long preparation had to be made. In order that our hearts might be more surely and effectively reached, as they are by the actual in the lives of men of like passions with ourselves, than by the purely ideal, even though Divinely produced, the fountains must be created out of which the healing streams shall flow. This at once carries us very far back of the time when the Psalms were composed, and of everything usually in our minds when we speak of inspiration. The story of the Psalms in their inception is somewhat like that of the Gospels.

It is comparatively recent in Biblical thought that the fourfold Gospel, on which we depend for our portraiture of the earthly life of our Saviour, was produced by men whose whole previous life had been Divinely ordered for this special purpose, and that these were brought into continued personal contact with our blessed Lord, that each might give us in a simple, truthful way the impression that had been made upon himself in the use of his own faculties. It was necessary that these witnesses should be typical men, who would fairly represent great classes of mankind to whom their story must be told. We cannot doubt that the individual traits of these men had been regarded, and their circumstances and surroundings arranged from their birth, so that each artless narrative should have the stamp of individuality and genuineness, and that in their combination the picture should be round and full, vivid and lifelike, and that the hearts of men might be seized by the conviction: This man actually lived upon the earth as here described, and he is the Son of the living God.

We pass back to David, the representative psalmist of the Psalter. There is no record in the Old Testament of the Divine ordering of a life more marked than we find here.

The prophet Samuel was sent to the house of Jesse to anoint, for the throne of Israel, the youngest of his sons, — the one his own father thought least eligible for high position. But we cannot believe that the Divine ordering began then. Already he had rich endowments for the future he was to attain. Not only were there excellencies of character, Divinely imparted, to be trained and developed as God best knows how, but he must have been a born poet. While his meditative and devout nature first responded to the claims of God during his shepherd life, it was then that his fledgling efforts at song were put forth. But in order that he might voice in poetic strains the most profound emotions of sinners and sufferers before God, he must become a pupil in their hard school. and not one stroke of the rod must be spared.

We are prepared now to fit what we have gotten into its place, and to speak emphatically. It was the gracious thought of God to provide for His people a book of worship which should cultivate their personal association with Himself, and thus lift them out of sin and misery, and one that should abide through all time, more clearly understood, and more highly prized with the advance of years. In order to accomplish this He first produced the men, appointed their circumstances of temptation and suffering, accompanied by such timely manifestations of His grace as should enable them to write Psalms that would stir the hearts of men to their depths, — Psalms on the face of which genuineness should be incrasably stamped. David, the father of all who cultivated sacred song in Israel, He brought up from the pastures and sheepfolds, to wear a crown indeed, foreshadowing the Messiah, but to find no comfort nor rest until he had been hunted like a wild beast through deserts and mountains, not until he had passed through a furnace seven times heated in the treachery of his friends and the malignity of his enemies, not until his own son, his pride and his joy, had basely turned against him,

and had driven him from his home and from the altars of
God, not until his heart had been wrung by the untimely
and violent death of that son, whom in all his wickedness
he had loved more than his own life, not until a combination of great powers had threatened to wipe him and his
kingdom off the face of the earth. David, the author of a
large number of these Psalms, so suffered that he might produce for the world this truly Divine book.

But there is a darker record in the life of the chief psalmist
than that of suffering, and even more important to us. The
man who shall furnish prayer of the right tone and quality for
us must have sinned grievously against his neighbour, and
even more against God. It has been a standing mystery and
marvel how a man like David could commit such foul wickedness, or, in a harder form, how one guilty of such sin could
be so near to God. We have our solution now. We must
have prayers that shall give voice to agonies deeper and more
terrible than those produced from without, by the pressure of
other men's sins. We must have the outcries of remorse, of
shame, of penitence most profound, of a broken heart and a
contrite spirit. We must have supplications for purity and
pardon, for all that it might seem the hardest for a holy and
a just God to give. We must learn, too, that the contrition
has prevailed, that the prayer has been granted, and that
peace is restored where all was uproar and confusion. We
must have a fifty-first Psalm, put always within reach for time
of need. For this is not the last man upon the earth that
shall come thus before God. At what time have there not
been many such as he, whose wretchedness might have been
voiceless and despairing without such a prayer as this? Not
so marvellous is the inspiration that enabled him, this royal
poet, long after he had sinned and received pardon, to repro-
duce truly and in suitable accents his pleadings before God,
as the far-seeing wisdom and grace that had brought him

up into a position of great temptation to indulge every evil passion of his nature, in the almost irresponsible power of royalty, and had then withheld the grace that up to that time had strengthened his heart in honour, and purity, and truth. How poorly furnished for us miserable sinners, our Book of Prayer would have been without the Penitential Psalms!

The Psalms were produced separately, but it was no accident that brought them together as here. We might almost say that it was a matter of natural attraction and cohesion. They could not be kept apart. But not less naturally, nor less surely, than if there were some occult law drawing together things that are in affinity, men of devout minds, recognizing their common suitableness for helping the utterance of sinful men when bowing in worship before God, without miracle, yet Divinely illuminated, have given us this Psalter.

It only remains to say something concerning the following version and its appendages. The thought of an independent translation of the Psalms had its beginning in connection with the Anglo-American revision of the Old Testament. In that revision conservatism and compromise were characteristic features and controlling principles. The revisers were bound by the rules they had heartily and wisely adopted, to respect the attachment of English-speaking people to the Authorized Version, and to confine themselves to the most necessary changes. This was adhered to most rigidly in the more familiar portions of Scripture, and most of all in the Psalms. It constituted the most delicate and difficult part of their work. They were continually reminded that they were merely revisers, and not independent translators, and often felt obliged to put aside manifest improvement, in favour of the more ancient and familiar rendering that had the ground. They were unanimous in acting on this principle, although they might occasionally differ about details.

Yet they knew very well how often by a delicate touch here

and there, a Psalm may be illuminated, and its beauty, as well as its clearness and power, immeasurably enhanced. The effect may be produced by bringing out an emphatic pronoun, by the change of a connective particle, by the closer observation of a misconceived tense, by the transposition of words into the Hebrew order for the recovery of lost emphasis, or by other like changes not affecting the substance of the Psalm. Singly they may seem of little consequence, but unitedly they often produce a wonderful transformation.

It was this that induced the attempt to translate the Psalms into language that should exhibit the thought of the original more faithfully, and yet more poetically; and those associated with the author in Bible revision in Great Britain and at home, have manifested their kindly interest and hearty approval. Some of our English Psalms are nearly faultless, while others fail in bringing out the spirit and rhythm of the old Hebrew bards, or are even prosaic, awkward in expression, and obscure. Why should not individual scholarship and taste be laid under contribution to perform for David and other masters of Hebrew song what so many gifted minds have done for the poetry of Homer? Many such translations might be made for private use, or in the interest of Bible study, with the greatest benefit. It is easy to distinguish between their use in public worship, where our grand old English Psalter, with comparatively little change, must hold its ground, and the less sacred use to which we now refer.

The first result of the author's efforts in this direction was published in 1884 under the title, "The Praise Songs of Israel," and a second revised edition in 1889. The promise was made with the former, and repeated with the latter, that when it should be practicable, explanatory notes would be given, having in view a further edition to which they might be attached. The promise of notes is herewith fulfilled, but the text has been so thoroughly rewrought that it may fairly be called a new translation. The kindly and generous comments upon the work in its first form produced no blindness to its imperfections. On the contrary, they occasioned a more severe scrutiny, in which every word was challenged anew, and the structure of every sentence and phrase carefully pondered.

Those who know how difficult it is to translate Hebrew poetry into a language so different in its idioms as the English, and at the same time preserve something of the poetic aspect, cadence, and flow of the original, will not wonder that this jealous re-examination suggested improvement. They will understand that one coming back to such work after a considerable interval, knowing well every difficult or doubtful point, remembering what renderings had been least satisfactory to himself, found many places where, by the change of a word, line, or couplet, a blemish might be removed, or some desirable effect produced, bringing out more distinctly the beauty, force, and impressiveness of the old inspiration, that had been at the best so imperfectly rendered. It was thought possible, by additional labour, to approach one degree nearer success in the attempt to weave into a fabric uniform in texture, colour, and all that produces impression upon the mind and heart, the various materials that compose these translated Psalms, Hebrew thought and English expression, renderings from the Authorized Version that can never be excelled, and fresher results that have been reached by masters in philological and exegetical science, together with some personal ventures where the sense is admitted to be doubtful.

In this fresh work special attention has been given to rhythmic effect. We cannot accept the views concerning the structure and rhythm of Hebrew verse which some Semitic scholars ardently insist upon, claiming exact measurement, — so many lines to the strophe, and so many syllables to the line. We strongly object to the temerity with which this is made the principle and basis of a new Textual Criticism, — making the fact conform to the theory, and freely omitting or inserting syllables or lines to bring the Massoretic text into harmony with the artificial *schema* of the restorationist. See our note at Psalm xlv. 6. But unquestionably this poetry has a free swinging rhythm, marked by the accents, which has sometimes been compared to the galloping of a horse. A Rabbi accomplished in reading Hebrew poetry will exhibit it charmingly; but the literal reproduction of this in English, syllable for syllable, beat for beat, and interval for interval, is not possible, or if it were, it would not be mellifluous to ears educated to different rhythmic expression. The nearest approach to it that could be read with pleasure is that of some of the most beautiful lines in our mother version, — indeed of a very large number with scarcely noticeable change. An instance occurs at the opening of that plaintive melody, Psalm cxxxvii. : —

> "By the rivers of Babylon, there we sat down;
> Yea, we wept, remembering Zion."

Its adaptation to varied and vehement emotion on a different key may be estimated in Psalms lxviii., lxxiv., and lxxxix. It comes nearest to the rhythmic cadence of anapæstic verse, yet perfectly free as regards the comparative length of lines and other requirements of such verse in metre and rhyme. The question had to be practically solved whether these features could be dispensed with without a feeling of loss, as if one were reading prose rather than poetry.

This last, however, was not the most important question to be encountered. It was whether one could yield himself to this rhythmic current without sacrificing faithfulness as a translator. The attempt has been made, with the most conscientious determination, to exhibit the thought truly, whatever else might have to suffer, and it is hoped not without some success. The translator bound himself to this at the outset, by resolving to attach to his rendering the exegetical notes he had largely prepared before his work was recast in the present form. It is believed in fact that in many cases he has come nearer to the original than in his first effort, as that represented it more nearly than the Authorized Version, and more nearly than the conservative rules of the Bible Revision Company permitted them even to attempt. It may be added that he could not have abandoned himself to this special verse movement, were it not manifestly the only one to which the most literal translation from the Hebrew easily accommodates itself. This is shown conclusively by the circumstance already referred to, that the early English translators so frequently fell into it unconsciously. The lines in the English Bible that exhibit it the most distinctly are most literal and exact as translations; and it is worthy of mention that it aids greatly in the intelligent and effective reading of the Psalms, throwing the emphasis on the accented syllable of each principal word in a sentence, and leaving the unaccented particles, or other short subsidiary words or syllables, to fill up the intervals.

The grammatical principles underlying this new translation are identical with those of the former work as exhibited and illustrated in the prefaces to the two editions. The most important of these relates to the use of the so-called Hebrew tenses. They were treated in the early grammars of the language as representing past and future time. The translators were confronted by the fact that the so-called *future* has almost the entire ground in historic narrative, and the so-called *past* in prophecy. They disposed of this ingeniously by attributing to the connective "and" a mysterious power of converting past into future, and future into past, calling it "vav-conversive." Having this, they did very well till they reached the poetical portions of the Bible, where they were helpless. They often found themselves compelled, in intelligent disregard of their grammar, to translate either form by the present tense. But their work exhibits no uniformity, and is often perplexing. Modern Hebrew scholarship has discerned that neither form of the verb properly represents either the past or the future. They are really *present* as respects either of the three conceptions of time, as indicated, adverbially or otherwise, outside of the form itself. In poetry they are continually intermingled. Very often both forms occur in the same verse as describing *present* emotion or fact under different aspects, and the same conception of time passes on without change from verse to verse, where translators confuse us by constant and needless variation.

As to the distinction between the two forms thus treated as present, the *perfect* tense, formerly called the *praeter*, includes with the act its completed issue in the present. It is something that lies in the mind of the writer or speaker as fully matured and permanent. The *imperfect* tense, formerly *the future*, exhibits the act in its inception and continuance until another act succeeds. The English language obliges us to render both aspects by the simple *present* tense. It should be always borne in mind that in the Hebrew, the imperfect tense is the natural and predominant expression of gracious affections in their active flow and succession — of love, trust, gratitude, joy in God, desire and praise as springing up responsively to the Divine touch upon the heart. The Revised Old Testament has recognized the true significance of these forms by giving us in Psalms xviii. 1, "I love Thee, O LORD, my strength," and in xxvi. 8, "I love the habitation of Thy house," where the Authorized Version has in the former, *the future*, and in the latter, *the past*. There are a thousand other cases where the same change might have been introduced with great advantage.

It will be noted that in Hebrew poetry nearly every verse is divided into two parts, called *hemistichs* (half-verses), indicated by a strong disjunctive accent at the close of the former. These principal lines are subdivided by minor disjunctives. Wherever in the following translation a line is thus subdivided, giving three or more lines to the verse, the beginning of the second half-verse is indicated by its being placed at the extreme left, the subordinate lines in either part being thrown somewhat forward.

Something should yet be said with regard to the material attached to the translated text, before and after. It required strong and constant repression to avoid increasing it, so as to make a very large book. A continued exposition, verse by verse, that might be called a commentary, was never intended. It was assumed that the translation had done all that lay in its province, leaving nothing obscure that it could legitimately clear up. In doing this it was sometimes obliged to be less mechanical than its wont, and to give the thought in its connection without adhering rigidly to the precise words, for to one unacquainted with Hebrew idioms, these are often hopelessly unintelligible. Yet more frequently our differences from the English Psalter arise from a closer adherence to the original. In determining what should be added or prefixed, it was designed to furnish in prefatory remark, in analytical outline, and in notes explanatory of words and phrases, or calling attention to the connection and drift of thought, whatever might be needed for the removal of obscurity. It was the combined purpose that the reader might be put, as nearly as possible, into the position of intelligent Israelites, who first sang these songs of Zion. Consequently the notes principally touch the points at which the true sense might not be readily discerned, or where it seemed hopeful that a few simple words would illuminate the Psalm in its unity of thought, and render the impression of the whole more vivid.

It was part of the plan, whenever it might be found necessary, for the sake of the just expression of the thought in

English, to depart slightly from precise mechanical literalness, to give in a note the Hebrew or its exact translation; and also, to avoid repetition by referring back to the explanation of a word or clause once given, whenever it should again occur. The former purpose has been executed as far as seemed necessary, and the latter to a considerable extent. It was found that a uniform system of back reference would needlessly overload the pages, for a single important word might require such notice ten, twenty, or a hundred times.

The translation of the Psalms by Prof. T. K. Cheyne, D.D., of Oxford, has been consulted with practical advantage. His renderings are usually excellent, often admirable. His critical material is important; partly, as indicating some necessary changes in the Massoretic text, but more, as proving its substantial correctness. His notes are able and suggestive, extending to matters not embraced in the practical purpose of this volume. It is impossible to do justice to the kindness of Professor Cheyne's frequent reference to " The Praise Songs of Israel," or to his generous deprecation of being supposed in rivalry with its author.

In this fresh effort to elucidate the Psalms the author has been encouraged by the hearty commendation of his former work by other Biblical scholars in Great Britain and America; such as the Right Rev. Edward Henry Bickersteth, D.D., Bishop of Exeter, the Very Rev. R. Payne Smith, D.D., Dean of Canterbury, Prof. A. H. Sayce, D.D., of Oxford, Principal David Brown, D.D., of the Free Church College at Aberdeen, Prof. John Dury Geden, D.D., of Didsbury College, and Prof. Alexander Roberts, D.D., of St. Andrews; and in the United States, the Rev. Drs. Howard Crosby, Charles A. Briggs, T. W. Chambers, and William Hayes Ward, of New York, and Professors G. Emlen Hare, D.D., of Philadelphia, George E. Day, D.D., of Yale, and J. Henry Thayer, D.D., of Harvard.

THE PSALMS.

THE PSALMS.

THE PSALMS.

BOOK I.

I.

THE RIGHTEOUS DISTINGUISHED FROM THE WICKED.

THE first Psalm is anonymous. It is supposed to have been written as an introduction to the First Book. But it is admirably fitted for its place at the head of the whole collection. For it touches the key-note of them all, unswerving loyalty in heart and life to God and His law, in contrast with faithlessness and disobedience. That in character and destiny there is "a difference between the righteous and the wicked, between him that serveth God and him that serveth Him not" (Mal. iii. 18), is a lesson that stands out in these Psalms in bold relief, like raised letters for the blind. In accordance with this difference our introductory Psalm is sharply separated into two strophes or stanzas, each consisting of three verses.

1. The righteous, his character, life, and happy lot (1-3). 2. The wicked, his character, light and worthless as chaff, and his condemnation before God (4-6).

  1 How blest is this man! —
      In the counsel of the wicked he walks not,
    Nor stands in the way of the sinner,
      Nor sits where the scoffing assemble;
  2 But delights in the law of Jehovah,
    And rehearseth His law day and night:
  3 As a tree planted in by the trenches of water,
      Yields fruit in due time,
        And its leaf does not fade,
    So in all that he does he shall prosper.

4 Not so are the wicked,
   But like chaff blown about by the wind ;
5 Therefore the wicked shall not stand in the judgment,
   Nor sinners where the righteous shall meet ;
6 For Jehovah knoweth the way of the righteous,
   But the way of the wicked shall perish.

(1) **How blest.** Heb. *'ashrē, O the happinesses of.* A noun absolute and exclamatory. The plural form intensifies and enlarges the conception, implying abundant and various felicity. This word is not to be confounded with the pass. participle of the verb *bārak, to bless,* as if the meaning were that God has blessed the man referred to, as in Jer. xvii. 7. The rendering *happy,* as describing an enviable condition, would convey the true sense, but not as necessarily including personal enjoyment. It is equivalent in this respect to the Greek μακάριος (see Matt. v. 3-11), and the Latin *felix.* The rendering *how blest* is less likely to be misunderstood, and exhibits the exclamatory emphasis of the Hebrew —The Hebrew verbs in this verse are in the perfect tense. But they are not to be translated by the English perfect (Cheyne and others), as if the felicity were confined to those who have never sinned. They rather describe the abandonment of sinful deeds and associations as now an accomplished fact, and steadfastly adhered to as a permanent characteristic. The so-called perfect tense in Hebrew often bears this sense and like the Greek perfect is to be rendered by our present. — **The wicked ... the sinner.** The terms most commonly employed to describe men of immoral life. Here the former seems to refer to character and principle, the latter to activity in evil-doing. — **Walks...stands ...sits.** *Walking* describes the life in its continuous activity. The man's conduct is not in accord-

ance with the "counsel," that is, the thoughts, purposes, and plans of unprincipled men (see xxxiii. 10, 11); *standing* represents brief intermissions in labor, when one may converse with those he likes best, here with "sinners"; *sitting,* the longer cessation at the close of the day's work, when he may seek out the places and companions which give him the greatest pleasure. — **Where the scoffing assemble.** Heb. *the sitting place,* that is, where they come together for free indulgence in blasphemous and corrupt conversation. See the same word in cvii. 32, as equivalent to *assembly.*

(2) **The law of Jehovah.** This is not to be confined to the Decalogue, but includes the whole body of Divine revelation thus far possessed, in its bearing on the life of man in his relations with God. The primary meaning of *tôrah* is *instruction.* See Is. ii. 3, 4, " He shall teach us of His ways, and we shall walk in His paths; for out of Zion shall go forth the law (*the instruction*) and the word of Jehovah out of Jerusalem."—**Jehovah.** This highest Divine name defines the *self-revealing* God. It is derived from *hāyāh,* often translated *to be.* But properly it does not affirm mere existence, as distinguished from non-existence, but *manifested* existence. Like the Greek γίνεσθαι it is used of events as occurring historically, and is well translated in the English Old Testament more than six hundred times, "*it came to pass.*" When used of persons it means *to come forward historically.* This presupposes existence, and the verb *to come,* that is,

into historic relations with men, more fully expresses the meaning than the verb *to be*. This is important in the explanation of the name Jehovah. It includes the ὁ ἐρχόμενος (*who cometh*) of Rev. i. 4, 8; iv. 8. It is also to be noted that the name Jehovah, properly *Jahveh*, is the imperfect tense of the verb *hāyāh*. It describes continuous activity. It is timeless, as belonging to all time, and in proper names it exhibits a permanent personal characteristic. Still further, the forms *I-come* ('*Ehyeh*) and *He-comes* (*Vahveh*) exhibit the personality of God. This is an element not found in any other Divine name. It is a standing protest against materialism and all idolatry. In addition to the light thrown upon the word by its derivation and form a special and delightful significance is thoroughly established in usage, which has its beginning in Ex. iii. 14, 15. God there designates the name Jehovah as an abiding pledge and memorial of *gracious* manifestation. It assures His people that He will always unfold and exhibit the properties of His holy, loving, and infinite nature in adaptation to their varying circumstances and need. The God of Revelation is also the God of Redemption. It is interesting to observe in Ex. iii. 14, that this name in its compressed form "*I-am*," or as above explained, *I-come*, which is one word (*Heb. 'Ehyeh*), was at its first announcement a clause, consisting of three words. The one word *I-come*, now virtually a noun, was repeated with the relative pronoun '*asher* (*who*) intervening. This implies the copula *is*, and gives us the full name, *I-come who* (is) *I-come ;* that is, the full significance of this name will be realized in the experience of all who trust and obey the God whose grace is so transcendently revealed. It is a revelation of assured fact. He will be found to be all that He calls

Himself. — **And rehearseth**. Heb. *hāgāh ;* A. V., *he meditateth*. See note on this word at ii. 1. It properly expresses low breathing or whispering, in soliloquy, in conning a lesson, or in speaking confidentially to another. It describes thought, not as vague and indefinite, but formed into words, and passing into the ear of God, though inaudible to man. See cxxxix. 4 : —

"When the word is not yet on my tongue,
   Lo, Jehovah, Thou knowest it all."

See also xix. 14: "the whispers of my heart in Thy presence."

(3) **As a tree**. Heb. *and becomes like a tree*, stating a consequence. But the close consecution indicates without the verb that the result of receiving the law of God into the spirit and life is like that of applying water to the roots of a tree, — strength, beauty and fruitfulness. — **Planted in**. Heb. *shathûl*, a poetical form that properly denotes deep planting. — **The trenches of water**. Heb. *palgĕ mayim ;* canals through which water is distributed in artificial irrigation wherever it is most needed. *Peleg* is never used of a natural stream. See Prov. xxi. 1 : —

"The King's heart is in the hand of Jehovah
   As the trenches of water;
He turns it whithersoever He will."

The value of the illustration consists in the absolute control that a man has over that which he has contrived for a given purpose. This would not apply to a river. See notes on xlvi. 4 and lxv. 9.

(4) **Not so** — turning to the opposite picture ; a negation of both parts of the preceding description. — **Like chaff blown about**, rather than *driven away* (A. V.) : for this verse refers to character, and not to destiny, and chaff is here the symbol of moral worthlessness. The resulting judgment follows in vv. 5 and 6. Otherwise the following "Therefore" would be without meaning.

II.

THE MESSIAH AS KING.

THE second Psalm, like the first, is anonymous, and its authorship cannot now be determined. It describes, as if present, a kingdom firmly established, in spite of the opposition of an ungodly world, whose permanence and universal extension are fully assured by the immutable purpose and promise of Jehovah.

It has its historic basis in the kingdom of Israel under the rule of David. Its full scope embraces the final glory of that kingdom when the grace of the Messiah shall pervade and dominate the whole earth.

The structure of this Psalm is very symmetrical, consisting of four strophes, each containing three verses.

1. The treasonable conduct and utterances of the heathen (1-3). 2. God scorns their efforts, and terrifies them by proclaiming the Messiah His own royal representative in Zion (4-6). 3. The Messiah speaks; God has greeted him as His son, and promised him universal dominion (7-9). 4. The poet counsels and warns the rebellious (10-12).

1 Oh why are the heathen in tumult,
   Why mutter the nations so vainly?
2 Earthly kings take their stand,
   The princes hold council together
      Against Jehovah and him that He anointed:
3 "Let us tear off their fetters,
   Their bonds cast away."

4 The Enthroned in high heaven derides,
   Yea, the Lord makes light of them all.
5 Then He speaks in His wrath,
   And His anger affrights them:
6 "As for Me, I have set up My king
   On My holy Mount Zion."

7 I proclaim the decree;
   Jehovah said to me, "Thou art My son,
      Whom I, this day, have begotten.

8 If thou ask, I will let thee inherit the nations,
  The earth shall be thine to its uttermost bound;
9 Thou shalt break them with a rod of iron,
  Shalt shiver them like ware of the potter.

10 And now, O ye kings, show your wisdom;
   Be warned, ye that rule in the earth.
11 Serve Jehovah with fear;
   Let your joy be with trembling:
12 Make peace with the son, lest His anger aroused,
     ye are lost from the way,
   For His wrath very soon will enkindle;
   How blest are all they that take refuge in Him.

(1) **Heathen.** Heb. *gôyim*, lit. *nations.* The word by association with historic fact suggests apostasy from God and the most shameful wickedness. This should be remembered in all Psalms containing imprecations against the nations of the earth. The subject here is the rebellion of heathendom against Jehovah and His Messiah. — **Are in tumult.** A. V., *rage.* The verb *rāgash* seems to be mimetic. It suggests external, rather than internal, commotion; not passion, but the confused rumbling and shuffling of a disorderly crowd. It is used only here in Biblical Hebrew. But in Psalms lv. 15, lxiv. 3, we find its derivatives, *régesh* and *rigshāh* (masc. and fem.), a *throng* or *crowd.* This is quite similar to *hhāmôn*, a *multitude*, from *hhāmāh*, *to hum.* In fact, for *rāgash* the Targums here use *hhāmôn*, which is also mimetic, but weaker. John Milton in his "Poetic Paraphrase" renders the line, "Wherefore do the Gentiles tumult," giving the meaning admirably. But *tumult* as a verb has become obsolete. — **Mutter.** Heb. *hāgāh;* A. V., *imagine;* so rendered elsewhere only in xxxviii. 13 The word 'imagine' is used in old English law of *conspiracy* or *plotting* (*Bouvier's* Law Dictionary), a sig-

nification that has become obsolete. The parallelism and context suggest a rendering more in accordance with the radical meaning and general usage of the word. This also is mimetic, and is used of the *murmuring sound* of the harp, the *cooing* of a dove, the *growl* of a lion, the *rumbling* of thunder, the *moaning* of distress, the low *breathing* or *whispering* of praise or entreaty, into the ear of God; also of the *muttering* of those practising incantations (Isaiah viii. 19). Especially notice Isaiah lix. 3, "thy tongue *muttereth* perverseness." It finely describes the murmuring of discontent, and the low tones in which conspirators discuss their plans.

(4) **The Enthroned in high heaven.** The picture before the poet's mind is that of God seated in the "heaven of heavens" as ruler over all, and looking down upon the puny and feeble mortals who are virtually proposing to dethrone him. The Hebrew word *shāmayim, heavens*, means literally *"the heights,"* and needs the descriptive adjective *"high"* to convey its significance in this connection. The allusion is to the fact that men seem like mere mites to one that looks down upon them from a great elevation. He who sees these poor insects in their

frantic madness, Himself so far out of their reach, may well deride them. See Isaiah xl. 22: "He that sitteth upon the circle of the earth (referring to the blue arch overhead), and the inhabitants thereof are like grasshoppers."

(6) **As for me, I have, etc.** The emphatic pronoun has its usual antithetic significance, as against the rebellious utterances (ver. 3) of these impious mortals, and introduces what God has done that ensures their discomfiture. — **Set up My king.** The primary meaning of the verb *nāsāh* is *to pour out;* never elsewhere used of *pouring upon,* or *anointing,* but of *pouring out* a libation (xvi. 4), of *casting* or *founding,* by pouring molten metal into a mould (Isaiah xl. 19), and then of producing something solid or firm. So in a passive form Prov. viii. 23, " I was set up from everlasting." Yet the emphasis is not upon the verb, but upon its personal subject; Jehovah Himself in His infinite majesty and might opposes their vain undertaking.

(7) **Thou art My son, whom I, this day, have begotten.** The emphatic pronoun lays stress upon the relation to God Himself, as securing by natural right the sovereignty of the world. At this point the Psalm touches historically 2 Sam. vii. 14: " I will be to him a father, and he shall be to me a son." The Epistle to the Hebrews (1. 5) recognizes the connection between the two, and establishes the typico-prophetical character of the Psalm. "This day," so far as relates to the typical king, Solomon, may refer to the time of the announcement by Nathan to David, or to the time when he became king. Solomon speaks of the promise as referring to himself (1 Kings i. 11). The sonship, like the sovereignty, applies to all who succeeded David as kings over Israel. They became thereby "sons of God" by adoption. In both respects their Messiahship was typical of one whose dominion was to be universal, absolute, and everlasting, and who, therefore, must be the son of God in a higher sense, "the effulgence of His glory, and the very image of His substance, and upholding all things by the word of his power" (Heb. i. 3, R. V.). As applied to Christ, the verb is to be taken declaratively, and the designation of time ("*this day*") points to his public recognition as the Son of God, and his entrance upon his eternal kingship, whether at his baptism, transfiguration, or resurrection. Decisive in favor of the last of these, we have Acts xiii. 33, and especially Rom. i. 4, "declared to be the Son of God with power by his resurrection from the dead."

(12) **Make peace.** Heb. *kiss.* But this meaning, as between subjects and the king on the throne, is not to be pressed in its literalness. It expresses homage (see 1 Sam. x. 1), and here cordial reconciliation. So the Greek προσκυνέω: prim. and in classical usage, *to kiss* (the hand) *to;* in New Testament, *to do homage to, to worship.* See Job xxxi. 27, of kissing the hand to the sun or moon in idolatrous worship. — **Very soon.** Heb. *like littleness;* the most minute particle. It is used both of *quantity* (so here in the A. V.), and of *time.* Here the latter is more suitable, as in Job xxxii. 22; Psalms lxxxi. 14; xciv. 17. (So R.V.) **Take refuge.** Heb. *hhāsāh, to hide from danger.* It occurs in the Psalms more than thirty times, and in the Authorized Version is uniformly rendered *trust,* except in lvii. 1, where the early translators were compelled to give its true meaning: "in the shadow of Thy wings will I make my refuge." The R. V. has this rendering in a few additional instances. The American Revisers would have preferred it everywhere. The more general idea of *trust* has its own special word *bātahh.*

III.

SORELY OPPRESSED, BUT CONFIDENT IN GOD.

THE third and fourth Psalms are companion pieces. They belong to the time of David's flight from Absalom. A disturbed life is finding a higher rest in God. His enemies are many, and his friends few and spiritless. But he maintains unfaltering confidence in the God of Salvation.

For the right appreciation of the former of these beautiful songs, composed in the midst of great peril, it is important to note that it was written under the inspiriting influence of the morning light, after a night of undisturbed rest. God, under whose protecting care he had slept safely, with danger all around him, could be relied upon for complete deliverance. As Ewald intimates, it may have been the morning after the night in which Ahithophel would have fallen upon him (2 Sam. xvii. 1). It is noteworthy that the Hollanders sang this Psalm according to their Version when they marched against the Belgians, Aug. 1, 1831.

There are four strophes, each having its own topic:

1. His enemies are many (1, 2)   2. Jehovah is his defender (3, 4).   3. He confides in Him (5, 6).   4. He addresses Him in prayer and praise (7, 8).

A PSALM OF DAVID, WHEN HE FLED FROM THE FACE OF ABSALOM HIS SON.

1 O Jehovah, how many oppress me;
   How many have risen against me;
2 How many are they that say of my soul,
   "He can find no salvation in God."   [Selah.]

3 But Thou, O Jehovah, art a shield round about me;
   Thou art my glory, and exaltest my head.
4 With loud voice I call on Jehovah;
   From His holy hill He answers my cry.   [Selah.]

5 It was mine to lie down and to yield me to sleep,
   I awaked for Jehovah sustained me;
6 I fear not the myriads of people,
   All around me in battle array.

7 O Jehovah, arise; my God, do Thou save me;
    For all my foes didst Thou smite on the cheek,
  And hast shattered the teeth of the wicked;
8 Jehovah gives victory;
  Oh, bless Thou Thy people.   [Selah.]

(2) **Of my soul**; not merely *of himself*, as a living, conscious, personal being (Cheyne), but, as the next line shows, with reference to his soul's unwavering trust in God. Often used in connection with some form of spiritual activity. See xiii. 2; xlii. 2. — **Salvation**; used here, as often elsewhere in the Psalms, of deliverance from the dangers that threatened his life.

(4) **With loud voice**. Heb. *with my voice;* an accusative of closer definition, indicating that the call was a loud one (Ewald, Moll).

(5) **It was mine**. Heb. *'ani, I.* The emphatic pronoun here with its beautiful significance has been overlooked by translators. It is antithetic to "Jehovah" following. Looking back to the preceding day, he could feel, when night came on, that he had done everything possible to human vigilance and strength. Excessive weariness demanded rest in preparation for another day of toil. He remembered that God needs no rest, and "neither slumbers nor sleeps," and realized that his own part was to commit himself fearlessly to Divine protection, — not only to lie down, but to dismiss unbelieving anxiety, and sleep. This is finely expressed in the Hebrew. The second verb (*vā'īshānah*) is in the

imperfect tense, with the *voluntative* termination *āh.* It is connected by *vav consecutive* with the preceding verb in the perfect tense. The two are thus closely united in time and purpose. He resolved that he must and would commit himself to sleep, leaving it to God to do His own gracious part in protecting him. A splendid lesson here, applicable to a multitude of cases. The antithetic clause following simply states that God accepted the trust and sustained him. See on iv. 8.

(7) **Didst Thou smite on the cheek, and hast shattered the teeth of the wicked**. Both verbs are in the perfect tense, and give the ground of his confidence in past deliverances from similar danger, referring to events in his own life which could never be forgotten. Delitzsch: "David means that an ignominious end has always come upon the ungodly who rose up against him, and against God's order in general, as their punishment. The enemies are conceived of as monsters given to biting, and the picture of their fate is fashioned according to this conception."

(8) **Victory**. Heb. *yeshūah*, usually translated *salvation*, but when it refers to the result of battle, *victory* is the better word.

IV.

FAITH TRIUMPHING OVER MALIGNITY AND UNBELIEF.

THIS Psalm, like the preceding, is in historical connection with the rebellion of Absalom. Most interpreters have recognized their striking similarity in thought and forms of expression.

But while that was a morning, this is an evening hymn. It may possibly relate to the evening of the selfsame day. It is the cry of one in the midst of great privations and perils, who has found safety, peace, and blessedness in Jehovah. Emboldened by his confidence in God, the righteous king denounces the sin of his persecutors, and counsels repentance and return to God in his appointed way of sacrifice.

Then, after expressing his joy in the light of God's countenance in contrast with the men who crave only an earthly portion, he commits his soul to Divine protection for the night.

The Psalm falls naturally into three parts:

1. An entreaty, based on God's righteousness and past goodness (1). 2. A warning addressed to his enemies, in two parts (2-5). 3. A calm expression of his peace and confidence in God (6-8).

FOR THE LEADER OF THE CHOIR. UPON STRINGED INSTRUMENTS.
A PSALM OF DAVID.

1 When I call, do thou answer, my God, who art righteous,
    Who in time of sore pressure hast freed me;
  In pity give heed to my prayer.
2 Men in power, how long ye are turning my glory into shame,
  Loving falsehood, and searching for lies.   [Selah.]
3 But know how Jehovah marks out as His own, him He loves;
  When I call, Jehovah will hear me.

4 Oh tremble, and cease from your sin;
  Thus admonish your heart on your bed, and be still; [Selah.]
5 Bring the offerings that are due Him,
  And trust in Jehovah.

6 There are many that say, "Oh that good might befall us!"
  Lift upon us, Jehovah, the light of Thy presence;

7 More joy Thou hast put in my heart than is theirs,
When their corn and new wine are increased.

8 I will lie down in peace, and forthwith I shall sleep;
For Thou, O Jehovah, were I left all alone,
Would'st make me to dwell without care.

(1) **My God, who art righteous** (so Hengstenberg, Moll, Delitzsch), or *God of my right*, that is, who maintainest my right (so Ewald, De Wette, Perowne). But the former sense involves the latter. It is God, as righteous, who maintains and vindicates the righteousness of His servants. A noun in construction with a qualifying genitive will take the possessive suffix in connection with the second noun when it belongs to the compound idea. So "God of my righteousness" is equivalent to "my righteous God." - **Who in time of sore pressure, etc.** Heb. *hast made wide for me in narrowness;* perhaps referring to the time when David was hemmed in at the fords of the Jordan (2 Sam. xvii. 16), and receiving word of Ahithophel's counsel, passed over the Jordan to a safe position. See xviii. 19, cxviii. 5.

(2) **Men in power.** Heb. *benê 'ish,* not *benê ādām;* the specific, not the generic; men individualized, or separated from the great mass; men of distinction, whether by noble blood, or by high office and dignity. See xlix 3; lxxxii. 7. The call is to the leaders in Absalom's rebellion. Absalom himself was only a tool in the hands of ambitious men. — **My glory,** referring to his royal dignity. The expostulation relates not only to his dethronement, but to slanderous assaults on his personal character. — **Falsehood.** Heb. *rîq.,* lit. *emptiness;* then, *moral worthlessness;* here, as shown by its parallelism with the following *hāzāb, lying;* statements that have no foundation in fact, slanderous falsehood. So

its equivalent *shāv, emptiness, falsehood,* xii. 2.

(3) **Marks out as his own.** Heb. *pālāh lô.* The verb *pālāh* describes a setting apart in which there is something wonderful. The royal poet probably refers to his elevation to the throne, followed by wonderful guidance and deliverance. — **Him He loves.** Heb. *hhāsíd, one beloved* (Hupf.), or *one who loves* (Del.); but neither is to be accepted exclusively. The English Bible gives *holy one* or *saint* nineteen times, and *godly* thrice, always following the misapprehension of the Sept. *Hhāsíd* is derived from *hhésed,* the love of God as practically manifested, especially to His faithful servants. See note on *hhésed* at xiii. 2. The derived word is properly passive. The active signification in nouns of this form is rare, and where it occurs is secondary. Since the love of God as expressed by *hhésed* is a Divine activity terminating on man, we might expect that the corresponding denomination of man would be passive, *beloved* rather than *loving.* Undoubtedly, however, it is active in xii. 1 and xviii. 25, and perhaps in some other instances. But the transition is easy. For it is the nature of love to excite its object to responsive activity, and the beloved becomes the loving, kindly, gracious. The connection must determine in any given case whether the active or the passive conception is uppermost in the mind of the writer. Here, as usually, the passive seems preferable. But from either the other may be surely inferred, as existent by natural sequence.

(4) **Thus admonish.** Heb. *'amerû, say ye;* implying words that are

spoken, and evidently referring to the admonition of the preceding line.

(6) There are many that say, etc. A probable transition to irreligious and worldly men in his own company. The camp of David during the rebellion under Absalom was, no doubt, poorly supplied with the means of sustenance, and expressions of discontent and despondency were freely and loudly uttered. But his own joy in God, notwithstanding his privations, exceeded the joy of the harvest festival, when the abundant products of the earth were gathered in.

(6) **Oh that good might befall us.** Heb. *who will cause us to see good.* The optative (*oh that*) is most frequently and strongly expressed in Heb. by using the interrogative pronoun (*who?*) followed by a verb in the imperfect tense. See liii. 6; lv. 6; 2 Sam. xv. 4, etc. It is a wish, not a prayer; and the good they crave is not the joy of God's presence, but the "corn and new wine," the product of the elements, of nature, chance, or any other wretched, impersonal substitute for God. It is the cry of the sordid, who had adhered to the king's standard because they imagined the rebellion would soon collapse, and they would thus better their own fortunes; and they are now disgusted with the miserable fare of the camp. It is only by apprehending this that we get the full force of the following address to God.

(8) This closing verse indicates the time of his meditation as the approach of night, when again (see iii. 5) he commits himself to peaceful sleep — **And forthwith I shall sleep.** The Hebrew connects the *lying down* and the *sleeping* by *yáhhad, together, at once* (Eng. Bible, *both*). The sleeping shall immediately follow, with no intervening period of anxious wakefulness. **Were I left all alone.** This clause is represented in the Heb. text by the single word *lebāãad* (*alone*). The Massoretic accentual division connects this with the preceding "Jehovah," as in the English Bible. All the ancient Versions connect it with the speaker. Modern opinions are almost equally divided. In usage, Deut. xxxii. 12 is quoted on the side of the former, and Deut. xxxiii. 28, of the latter. Riehm says, and Moll considers it decisive, " The thought that Jehovah is the only protection is without motive in the context, as it is not said that he lacked other protection, or that the 'many' sought protection anywhere else." But on either supposition may we not reasonably look for some " motive in the context?" What suggested the thought of being " alone," whether of God or himself? We find the answer in ver. 6. The worldly and irreligious men in his own company were impatient of continual hardship and danger, and almost ready to abandon the cause and leave their king to his fate. He contemplates the possibility, and faces it fearlessly. Though " left all alone," he will trust in Jehovah. This accounts for the indeterminates of the expression, and for its suspension between the two personalities, so as not to be severed from either. As if he had said, " Let them go; Jehovah does not need their aid to keep me in safety, and I do not need their presence to give me confidence." We have endeavored to express this by placing the adverb in a separate clause. — **Without care.** Heb. *lābétahh, confidently*, and so *securely*, rather than *safely.* In common usage these English words are treated as equivalent. But *secure* is from the Latin *sine cura, without care.* The Hebrew word and the context alike contemplate not only deliverance from danger, but from preceding anxiety and fear.

V.

MORNING PRAYER ON ENTERING GOD'S HOUSE.

THERE is no reason to doubt that David was the author of this Psalm as stated in the title. But there are no special circumstances in his life with which we can definitely connect it. Like the third Psalm, it is a prayer for the morning, but under different conditions. There, he was in banishment, and surrounded by open enemies. Here, he is in Jerusalem, and in full enjoyment of the privileges of the sanctuary, but is threatened by the secret plottings of impious and malignant men.

The Psalm is an earnest prayer for protection from the wicked, and is grounded upon the character of God as one who is righteous, and who therefore will surely protect and bless those that fear and serve Him.

1. Entreaty that God will hear his petitions (1-3). 2. Confidence in coming to God as to one who hates sin (4-7). 3. Prayer grounded on this confidence, —
(a) For personal guidance. (b) For the destruction of enemies. (c) For the protection and blessing of all who love God (8-12).

FOR THE LEADER OF THE CHOIR. WITH THE FLUTE. A PSALM OF DAVID.

1 Give ear to my words, O Jehovah;
   Heed my low whisper,
2 And regard my loud cry, O my King and my God,
   For to Thee is my prayer.
3 My voice shalt Thou hear at the dawn, O Jehovah;
   For Thee I prepare at the dawn, and look forth.

4 For Thou art not a God that has pleasure in sin,
   Nor shall evil be welcome with Thee;
5 The proud cannot stand in Thy presence,
   Those busy in wrong, Thou hatest them all;
6 And those that speak lies Thou destroyest,
   Bloodshed and fraud Jehovah abhors.

7 But I, through Thy great lovingkindness I come to
     Thy house;
   In Thy holy palace I worship and fear Thee.

8 In Thy righteousness guide me because of my foes;
   As a plain set before me Thy way:
9 For their mouth is not steadfast,
   A yawning gulf is within them;
   Their throat is a wide open grave,
   And they speak with smooth tongue.

10 Give them sentence, O God,
   By their plots let them fall;
   Thrust them forth in their many transgressions,
   Because they rebel against THEE;
11 That all that take refuge in THEE may rejoice,
   And may ring out their gladness forever;
   Give them shelter, and in Thee shall they triumph,
   That have love for Thy Name.
12 For Thou, O Jehovah, wilt the righteous man bless,
   Like a shield shall Thy favour surround him.

(1) **My low whisper.** Heb. *hăgîg*, from *hăgag* = *hăgăh*. See note on i. 2. It is not a "meditation " (A. V.), but a pouring out of the heart in prayer, clearly defined and earnest, though scarcely articulated to the ear of man; and presently it breaks forth into strong vocal expression (ver. 2). In the musical accompaniment the transition here from the faintest and sweetest murmuring of the cithern to the louder tone of the full orchestra would be most effective. See xix. 14.

(2) **My loud cry.** Heb. *qôl shav'ī* (שַׁוְעִי), lit. *the voice of my cry.* See note on iii. 4.

(3) **I prepare.** Heb. *'ărak* (עָרַךְ), *to put in order.* In the English Bible "*my prayer*" is supplied by the translator. But this verb is not elsewhere connected with prayer. In the Old Testament worship it is used of preparing and arranging the wood for the offering, and the pieces to be offered (Lev. i. 7, 8); so of the sacred lamps and the show bread. The preparation of the wood for the morning sacrifice was one of the first duties of the priest at the dawn of the day. The confinement to prayer is too narrow. With a probable allusion to the early sacrifice, the poet expresses his purpose to make all suitable preparation for the coming of one whose presence is anticipated with earnest longing. This preparation consists principally in putting away sin as always offensive to a holy God. Of this the morning and evening sacrifice was the appointed symbol. — **And look forth**, that is, expectantly. Heb. *tsăphăh, to look eagerly for*, with the primary idea of bending forward, as in *shăqaph* (see on xiv. 2). Remembering that this is a temple song, the thought of the poet is that the worshipper is in the house of God as an invited guest, who hopes for gracious reception and entertainment. The reason is then given for putting away sin from the heart and life by the means which God has graciously appointed.

(4) **Be welcome with Thee;** that is, as a guest. Heb. *yăgŭr.*

imperfect tense of *gûr, to sojourn,* as one receiving the hospitality of another. It refers here to visiting God's house for the enjoyment of His presence and grace. See xv. 1; lxi. 5; xxxix. 13.

(7) **Palace**. Heb. *hêkâl,* prim. *a spacious building;* then often, *a royal residence.* Here, the tabernacle is conceived of as the place where God is enthroned as King over Israel, and receives the homage of His subjects.

(9) **A yawning gulf**. Heb. *hā-vôth;* usually plur. *Evil desires* as insatiable and destructive; from *hāvāh, to yawn.* — **Within them**. Heb. *qirbām, their interior.* — **They speak with smooth tongue**. Heb. *they make smooth their tongue,* concealing their deadly purposes under flattering language.

VI.

A CRY FOR MERCY UNDER JUDGMENT.

THIS is the first of the seven Penitential Psalms (vi. xxxii. xxxviii. li. cil. cxxx. cxliii.), so called since the third century There are several occasions in the life of David to which it would be suitable, but we cannot determine upon either with certainty. It is the cry of a penitent, expressing great anguish in the opening sentences, becoming calmer as it proceeds, and ending in a burst of thanksgiving and triumph. The second strophe, ver. 4-7, is a transition from the first strophe to the third.

The Psalm seems to have been composed after severe suffering, which the sufferer recognizes as chastisement for sin. He has been brought to the verge of Sheol, the domain of death (ver. 5), probably by sickness. His physical sufferings have been aggravated by the taunts of his enemies (ver. 7, 10), but they are balked in their evil purposes by his unexpected recovery.

1. Cries of distress in suffering and terror (1-3). 2. He spreads out his misery before God, imploring deliverance (4-7). 3. He expresses his confidence in God, who has heard his prayers, and put his foes to shame (8-10).

FOR THE LEADER OF THE CHOIR.   UPON STRINGED INSTRUMENTS.

1 Not in Thine anger, rebuke me, Jehovah,
  Nor chastise me in wrath.
2 Have pity, Jehovah, for I wither away,
  And heal me, Jehovah, for my bones are dismayed;
3 Yea, my soul is exceeding dismayed;
  And Thou — O Jehovah, how long?

4 Return, O Jehovah; deliver my soul;
  Because of Thine own lovingkindness preserve me;

5 For in death, none will call Thee to mind;
  And who in the region of spirits will praise Thee?
6 I am weary of moaning;
     Every night my bed I dissolve,
  And water my couch with my tears;
7 Mine eyes are sunken with grief,
  Grown old through all mine oppression.

8 Depart from me, all that do evil,
  For Jehovah has heard my loud sobbing;
9 Jehovah has heard mine entreaty,
  Jehovah accepteth my prayer.
10 All my foes are ashamed, and exceeding dismayed;
   All at once put to shame they turn back.

(1) The sufferer is not to be understood as merely asking for some alleviation of his misery, which might be regarded as a correction in mercy. His chastisement has been so severe and protracted as to compel him to believe that he is the object of God's fierce and consuming wrath, and must soon perish unless it be wholly withdrawn.

(2) **Are dismayed.** A. V. *vexed*, as in ii. 5. Heb. *nibh'lû*, from *bāhal*, to be *convulsed with terror*, referring to the fear of death, as inevitable, unless God have mercy. The same word is repeated in ver. 3, with an intensifying adverb, *shaken greatly with terror*. His soul is even more shaken than his body. For the latter, represented by the bones, is firmer and less easily shaken. See Job iv. 14: "Fear came upon me and trembling, which made all my bones to shake."

(5) **The region of spirits.** Heb. *Sheol*. A difficult word to render into English, but the Hebrew conception of the condition of the disembodied dead is indicated by the derivation of *Sheol* from the verb *shā'al* to dig; a subterranean abode into which souls enter at death, which is represented in Job iii. 17 as a place where not only weariness and suffering, but the activities of the earthly life are at an end. By our present poet, the remembrance and praise of God are described as ceasing with death. What reason we have to rejoice in a later and fuller revelation in which "life and immortality are brought to light."

(6) Here, as in ver. 4, we have a remembrance of the night, indicating the time of composition as probably the morning. But there it was a night of refreshing rest, while here we find pain, weeping, and sleeplessness.

(8) **My loud sobbing.** Lit. *the voice* (noise) *of my weeping*, see note on iii. 4.

(10) **In their shame they turn back.** A. V. *they are ashamed, they turn back*. Heb. *yashûbû yēbôshû*. The alliteration (*paranomasia*) and inversion are noticeable. More important is the construction of two verbs with or without a connective *and*, where one qualifies the other adverbially. It is quite frequent in Hebrew, as it is also in the Greek, and might be called *hendiadys of the verb*. This is the first instance in the Psalms.

VII.

AN APPEAL TO GOD AS JUDGE OF ALL, AGAINST MALIGNANT AND DEADLY SLANDERS.

THIS is the first of eight Psalms that are assigned by their titles to the time of David's persecution by Saul (vii. xxxiv. lii. liv. lvi. lvii. lix. cxlii.). The Cush referred to in the title is otherwise unknown. As a Benjamite he was of the same tribe with Saul, and was probably a devoted adherent, and shared his bitterness against David. The protestation of innocence in verses 3 and 4, is very similar to David's language to Saul in 1 Sam. xxiv. 11, and the second line of ver 4 seems to refer pointedly to his magnanimity in protecting the life of Saul from his companions in arms.

The Psalm is much more irregular in arrangement of thought, strophical division, and rhythm, than most others, as if the poet's mind were intensely excited, and bewildered by opposite and contending emotions. Yet above all the turmoil and disquietude of a fugitive driven to great extremity, there arises a calm confidence in God, whose righteousness and power will prevail against all combinations of malignant evil.

1. Introductory. He seeks protection and deliverance (1, 2). 2. Protests his innocence (3–5). 3. Confidently appeals to God, as a righteous judge, for a just sentence, as between himself and his enemies (6–10). 4. Describes God's dealings with the wicked (11–16). 5. Anticipates with glad thanksgiving the success of his appeal (17).

SHIGGAION OF DAVID, WHICH HE SANG TO JEHOVAH CONCERNING THE WORDS OF CUSH THE BENJAMITE.

 1 Jehovah, my God, in Thee I take refuge;
     Oh save me, yea, snatch me from all my pursuers;
 2 That he tear not my soul like a lion,
     That he rend not, when no one can rescue.
 3 Jehovah, my God, if in this I am guilty,
     If iniquity cling to my hands;
 4 If I recompensed friendship with evil,
     I, that delivered my wanton assailant,
 5 Let an enemy chase and alight on my soul,
     Let him trample my life on the earth,
        And my glory bring down to the dust.   [Selah.]

6 Arise, O Jehovah, in anger;
    Lift Thee up 'gainst the wrath of my foes;
Yea, arouse Thee to meet me,
    With the justice which Thou hast ordained:
7 Call a concourse of nations about Thee,
Then return to Thy throne high above.
8 Jehovah is judging the nations;
Give me sentence, Jehovah, as Thou findest me righteous,
    As Thou knowest my freedom from guilt.

9 The ill deeds of the wicked, let come to an end,
    But establish the righteous,
God of justice, who triest the heart to its depths.
10 God beareth my shield,
The Saviour of the upright in heart.
11 God is righteous in judgment,
And a God that threateneth day after day.
12 If one will not repent, then His sword will He whet,
His bow He has bent and made ready;
13 He has aimed at the man the weapons of death,
And setteth His arrows aflame.

14 Behold, he that travails with evil,
He is pregnant with mischief, a lie he brings forth;
15 A hollow he digs, delving deep,
And falls down in the pitfall he makes.
16 The ill he had done comes back on his head,
Upon his own brow his outrage descends.
17 I will bring to Jehovah the thanks due His justice,
And on harps praise the Name of Jehovah Most High.

(1) **Take refuge**, as in ii. 12.

(4) **Friendship.** Heb. *shôlemî, my friend;* a participial noun connected with the Heb. *shālôm* and the *salaam* of the East, ancient and modern, as a friendly greeting, wishing health and prosperity. Here, one with whom I exchanged salaams. In such a case the conduct described would have been gross hypocrisy. So xli. 10. *'ish shalômî.* — **That delivered.** *'ahhallatsāh*, a *Piel* form. Cheyne translates *oppressed him;* Delitzsch gives *plundered mine enemy without cause;* making it refer to David's cutting off the hem of Saul's garment, affirming that it was not without cause, and therefore not an act of hostility. This is very strained and unnatural. It may be observed that while this verb in other forms may mean *to plunder,* it

never has that meaning in this *Piel* form, but always that of *delivering*. See 2 Sam. xxii. 20; Psalms vi. 4, l. 15, lx. 7, lxxxi. 8. The reference to David's magnanimity (see 1 Sam. xxiv.) is very clear.

(5) **My glory**; that is, his personal being as a living spirit, as in xvi. 9, xxx. 13, lvii. 9, lviii. 2; Gen. xlix. 6. It is indicated here by the parallelism in the two preceding lines. The "dust" is the dust of death. See xxii. 16, and Isaiah xxvi. 9. "They that dwell in the dust." The chief glory of man is his immortal nature.

(6) Here, as often in these sacred lyrics, the poet, in preparing a chant suitable for use by the great congregation in the long future, rises from the special to the general. Finding his starting-point in his personal experience of the hostility and gross injustice of those about him, presently he and his foes come to be symbols of a broader conflict between the people of God and the combined powers of evil, between the great Jehovah as the omnipotent Protector of the righteous on the one hand, and hostile nations on the other. It is the great battle between good and evil, which can have but one ending. The royal poet and his malignant enemy represent, on either side, the kingdoms of the world against Jehovah and His anointed. And now his language becomes prophetic of the utter collapse and discomfiture of falsehood and wrong, and he closes with a burst of praise. See on ix. 1.

(7) The host of the nations are summoned to stand before the Judge of all the earth, and after having executed judgment He will return to his rest on high.

(8) **Is judging.** Heb *yādin;* the prominent idea in this verb is that of *ruling,* but as including that of judging and determining; see lxxii. 2. In this it differs from *shaphat,* which follows in the next line. The

latter refers to judicial functions more exclusively, though these may be exercised by a king.

(9) **The heart to its depths.** Heb. *the heart and the reins.* In the Hebrew psychology, the *reins,* or kidneys, were regarded as the seat of the desires, affections, and passions; the *heart,* of thoughts and purposes, — though when standing alone the heart may be used in the former sense. According to modern conception, *the heart and the mind* would more nearly exhibit the thought of the Psalmist.

It seems hardly necessary to retain *kidneys* or *reins* in a translation, since the idea it represents has become thoroughly obsolete. See also xvi. 7, lxiii. 21, cxxxix. 10.

(10) Heb. *my shield is upon God,* that is, He has charged Himself with my protection.

(15) **A hollow he digs, delving deep.** Heb. *He digs a pit and delves it.* The two verbs *kārāh* and *hhāphar* are identical in meaning. See the latter alone in xxxv. 7, "*digged* [a pit] *for my life.*" It does not here describe a separate act, but qualifies the preceding word adverbially. Often as it occurs, our grammars and translations do not recognize *hendiadys of the verb.* See on vi. 10.

(17) **And on harps praise the Name.** Heb. *'āzammerāh, I will harp to the Name.* This verb seems primarily to be mimetic, imitating the vibration of harp-strings, and so means to *strike the chords* of a harp or other stringed instrument. Thence *to play* or make music (comp. Gr ψάλλω, of similar derivation and meaning); sometimes with mention of the instrument, xxxiii. 2, cxlv. 3, etc. In the English Bible usually rendered "sing." The music of stringed instruments, as a symbol of the high praises of God, is carried through the Bible to the visions of John in the Apocalypse, where we read of "harpers harping with their harps" Rev. xviii 22.

VIII.

THE GLORY OF THE HEAVENS, AND THE GLORY OF MAN.

THIS Psalm seems to belong to the time when David had charge of his father's flocks, rather than to any other period of his life. We may agree with Delitzsch and others that probably none of the Davidic Psalms in the Psalter were composed until after he was anointed king, and became "the sweet psalmist of Israel" (2 Sam. xxiii. 1, R. V.). But that does not forbid our finding here a vivid reminiscence of some brilliant night on the hills of Bethlehem, when the shepherd youth lifted up his soul to God, praising Him for the glory of the heavens, and, even more, for the honour He has bestowed upon man. It is probable that many of the Psalms were written in the tranquil old age of the royal singer, recalling the most remarkable events of his earlier life, and reproducing the thoughts and emotions that had then stirred mightily within him, and to some extent the very words in which they had found expression.

It is an evening song, the carol of the nightingale rejoicing in the sheen of the moon and the stars. Yet we may be sure that the soul of the singer was flooded with the sunlight of Divine grace and favour. It is a lyrical episode to the grand lyric of the creation, touching it at the story of the fourth and sixth of the creative days. There are several kindred songs, celebrating the wonders of nature, as exhibiting the perfections of God. But not one of them combines so marvellously the highest poetic beauty with inspiring suggestiveness. It touches the extreme points of God's self-attestation to man, uniting the glory of the beginning with the greater glory of the close, the light that flashed out when there was yet no human eye to behold it, with the light of the city of the redeemed.

The culminating point of the Psalm is the glory originally bestowed upon man in investing him with the sovereignty over all creatures upon the earth, alluding to the Divine ordinance in Gen. i. 28.

In working up to this point, the Psalmist enlists and holds our highest admiration. The opening Doxology is an adoring reference to the Name Jehovah, as suggestive of the grace of the personal God in coming into personal relations with men, and attracting them to Himself by entrancing manifestations of His power and kindness; and the emphatic repetition of this Doxology at the close is most suitable and impressive. Attached to it in the first verse, and not repeated in the last, there is a thankful recognition of the glory of God, as shining in the heavens, and so reflected to the earth that all may behold it, and bless His holy Name

The second verse refers to two classes of men who witness this exhibition: the enemies of God who deride, scoff, and deny: and children, even babes unweaned, the simple-minded, loving and sincere, whose grateful and unstinted praise scatters to the winds the aspersions of malignant scepticism.

We have now, in verse third, a delightful retrospection. The Divine work on the fourth day of creation, and the crowning work of the sixth, are brought vividly into the present, and in sharp contrast. The glory of the visible heavens with its flaming orbs seems to entitle them to higher estimation than any possible product of Almighty power. But upon man, in his insignificance and feebleness, even a greater glory was bestowed, and he is invested with the highest dignity. Under God, and yet but a little lower, he is made lord over all the earth. Every tenant of land, and air, and sea, is subjected to his power.

It is worthy of note that this is referred to as a permanent constitution. It not only belongs to the past, but to the present, and, by implication, to the future. Its foundation was laid in a creative act which even yet distinguishes the man from the brute, and the distinction is ineradicable.

Is this glorious Psalm *prospective*, as well as *retrospective?* By any legitimate interpretation, does it include within its sweep of space, and time, and power, God's redemptive, as well as His creative work? Does it contain any hint of a greater glory and a higher dignity in the future?

We think that it does most assuredly. If not distinctly in the thought of the sacred poet, it lay in the thought and purpose of God, as clearly as if already accomplished, that whenever the full glory of fellowship with God should be realized, whenever the germinal and immature living principle that he received by the Divine breath — his higher Divine nature — should attain its most perfect beauty and strength, he would indeed be *lord over all* in a loftier sphere. He was not made in the image of God that he might forever be a keeper of sheep and driver of oxen, or that he might subjugate the lion, and harpoon the whale. This "dominion over the beasts of the field, the birds of the air, and the fish of the sea" is a parable for the future, when more absolutely "all things shall be put under his feet." His rule over the brute creation was a fact in the then present. in accordance with his capacity in the first period of his existence. It comprehends a prophecy and pledge that in whatever position he shall hereafter occupy. when the glory of his nature reaches its fullest development, and he attains fitness for higher dignity and rule, he shall be lord paramount, none above him save God only.

The purpose of Jehovah seemed to be defeated when sin entered into the world, and the indispensable conditions of spiritual growth and pre-eminence ceased to exist, but it has never been abandoned. It is realized through Christ, as head of a new humanity, who, by uniting them to himself, as partakers of his own life, restores to men all they had lost, whether actual or possible. They become associated with him in the highest glory and honour.

In the light of these comments we can understand the effective use which the author of the Epistle to the Hebrews makes of the eighth Psalm in chap. ii. 5-10. The splendid significance which he attributes to it is quite within its legitimate scope and meaning, in its historic connection with the account in Genesis.

FOR THE LEADER OF THE CHOIR.   UPON GITTITH.   A PSALM OF DAVID.

1 Jehovah, our Lord,
     In all the earth how transcendent Thy Name,
  And what glory of Thine Thou gavest the heavens!
2 Of the praises of children, even infants unweaned,
     Hast Thou founded a stronghold because of Thy foes,
  To silence the hating and vengeful.

3 When I look on Thy heavens, the work of Thy fingers,
  The moon and the stars which Thou didst create,
4 Oh, what is weak man, that Thou dost not forget him,
  One born of mankind, that for him Thou shouldst care.
5 Little lower than God didst Thou place,
  And with glory and majesty crown him.
6 O'er the work of Thy hands didst Thou give him dominion,
  And all things put under his feet;
7 Of sheep and of oxen, these all,
  And also, the beasts of the field,
8 The birds of the air, and the fish of the sea;
  That which travels in paths of the seas.

9 Jehovah, our Lord,
  In all the earth how transcendent Thy Name!

(1) **Transcendent.** Heb. *'addīr.* The primary conception of the word is *breadth* or *expansion.* In usage it describes grandeur or immensity in persons or things. See its use in xciii. 4, of the billows of the sea. The adjective *excellent* of the A. V. is commonly used of things fairly, but not surpassingly good. As describing a name, the renderings *noble, honourable, splendid, eminent, distinguished, illustrious,* would ordinarily be suitable. But they are too familiar in connection with human greatness. The term *transcendent* alone seems fitly to express the infinite excellence of the name of God, as illustrated in His glorious works. — **Thou gavest.** The Hebrew form *t'nah,* which seems to be the second person Imperative of the verb *nāthan, to give,* is perplexing. Most exegetical authorities regard it as standing for *nāthattā,* the second person of the perfect tense, as rendered in the text.

(2) **Praises.** Heb. *peh, the mouth;* then, by metonymy *that which proceeds from the mouth,* as determined by the context. So *peh* is variously translated in the English Bible, *a command,* Gen. xlv. 21, *an*

appointment, Num. iv. 27, *a sentence*, Deut. xvii. 11, *sayings*, Psalms xlix. 14. No example of metonymy is more frequent in Heb. Here the context clearly suggests *praises*. The preposition *min* (*of*) is elsewhere prefixed to the material *of* which anything is made. Gen. ii. 19. — **Hast thou founded**. Heb. *yāsadtā*. A. V. *ordained*. The verb *yāsad* always signifies *to lay a foundation*, or by metonymy, *to build*. It suggests immediately that the following abstract form *'ōz* (עֹז) *strength*, is used for the concrete *mā'ōz* (מָעֹז) *a stronghold*, as in xxviii. 8 (R. V.); xlvi. 1; lxii. 7, — **Children, even infants unweaned**. Heb. *babes and sucklings*. The latter term by hendiadys defines the former, which is sometimes used of children more fully grown (Jer. vi. 11; ix. 20; Lam. iv. 4). In 1 Sam. xxii. 19, xv. 3, the two are expressly distinguished. Bickel ("*Carm. Vet. Test. metrice*" 1882), finding too many syllables in the line to suit his theory of Hebrew versification, must find some reason for discarding one of these words as a corruption of the text. He does this by a foot-note: "The addition by exaggeration destroys the sense; for sucklings cannot yet understand the glory of God as shown by His works." But the word *sucklings* in a warmer climate does not indicate an age so tender and unintelligent as with us. It was the Hebrew custom to wean a child when three years old or later. Samuel was not weaned till he was old enough to be helpful to Eli in the temple (1 Sam. i. 24).

(4) **Weak man**. Heb. *'enôsh* designating man as *feeble* and *frail*, *a mortal*, as in ix. 19, 20, x. 18 etc. — **Mankind**. Heb. *ādām* men described generically, — *the human race*, or any individual of that race.

(5) **Little lower than God didst Thou place**. All expositions of the eighth Psalm have assumed that this refers directly to Gen. i. 27: "So God made man in His own image." Probably most English readers, observing the verb "*made*" in the familiar rendering of the Psalm, as in Genesis, infer that they must equally describe man's creation, and consequently prefer that the translation *angels* (A. V.), incorrect as it is, should be retained, or some other substituted that shall not ignore the infinite distance that separates man from God. But is it certain that the poet refers here to the creation and nature of man? Does not his question in the previous verse imply that man already exists, not going back to the elements of his being, as Divinely produced and combined? The Hebrew text here contains no equivalent for the verb *made* in the English Psalter. It has only the transitive form of the verb *hhāsar, to be less*, and the most literal rendering would be, *Thou hast lessened him but a little from God*. We may then regard the following verses as explanatory of this, showing that the "glory and majesty" in the poet's mind are not in man's *nature*, but in his *position* relatively to the irrational world. To the brute, man is its supreme God, not even a little lower than the Creator of all things, inasmuch as in man it sees the only exhibition of personal intelligence and will that it is capable of apprehending. Undoubtedly it was on account of his superior nature that this dominion was assigned him, but the direct allusion in the Psalm is to the latter, and not to the former. That he was "made in the image of God," his spirit the breath of the Almighty, is the unmentioned solution of the perplexing question, why should God have conferred this honour upon man?

IX.

THANKSGIVING FOR SUCCESS IN WAR.

PSALMS ix. and x., by their structure, are very closely related. They are the first of the so-called Alphabetical Psalms. The plan proposed by the writer evidently was that the two unitedly should consist of twenty-two four-line strophes, corresponding with the letters of the Hebrew alphabet, and that each strophe should begin with one of the letters in their succession from Aleph to Tau. See cxix. The plan is regularly executed in thirteen strophes, in eleven partially so, but in the middle portion of Psalm x. (3-11) it is quite lost sight of. The other Psalms of this kind are xxv. xxxiv. xxxvii. cxi. cxii. cxix. and cxlv. Four of these, including the ninth, are ascribed by their title to David, in which most interpreters agree. This must include the Psalm following, for besides the above structural relation, there is striking similarity in language and style.

Yet there are convincing indications that they were not intended to be absolutely one. Their prevailing character is different; Psalm ix. is a thanksgiving Psalm, Psalm x. is supplicatory. In the former the personality of the poet is prominent; in the latter it is kept in the background. In the former he celebrates the defeat of foreign foes (Heb. *goyim*), the latter is directed principally against apostates and persecutors of his own nation (Delitzsch). Hitzig describes them as "two co-ordinate halves of one whole, which make a higher unity." In both Psalms God is exhibited as the omnipotent Ruler and Judge, who comes to the earth to execute His own righteous decisions.

In the ninth Psalm David speaks as the royal commander of the armies of Israel, and gives praise to God for signal victories over national enemies. The conflicts to which he refers are probably those recorded in 2 Sam. x. xi. xii.

1. Joyful thanksgiving; the defeat and ruin of enemies (1-6). 2. The Judge, worthy of all confidence and praise (7-12). 3. Prayer for himself personally, with renewal of praise (13-16). 4. A call for such complete discomfiture of the wicked that wrong and oppression may cease from the earth (17-20).

FOR THE LEADER OF THE CHOIR. SET TO "MUTH LABBEN." BY DAVID.

1 With all my heart I give thanks to Jehovah;
   I rehearse all Thy marvellous works:
2 In Thee I rejoice, yea, exult,
   To Thy name will I harp, Thou Most High.

 3 When my foes were repulsed,
     They stumbled and perished before Thee;
 4 Thou upholdest against them my right and my cause,
     Thou sittest enthroned, and wilt righteously judge.

 5 Thou rebukest the nations, destroyest the wicked,
     And forever and alway wilt blot out their name;
 6 Our foes come to nought in ruin enduring;
     Thou hast torn up their cities,
         Yea, of these has the memory perished.

 7 For Jehovah forever is King;
     And for judgment He set up His throne.
 8 He ever in righteousness judges the earth:
     With equity rules He the nations.

 9 That the troubled may find in Jehovah a refuge,
     A refuge in times of sore pressure;
10 And that knowing Thy name they may trust Thee;
     For Thy seekers, Jehovah, Thou wilt never forsake.

11 Strike the harp to Jehovah whose throne is in Zion;
     Tell the nations His glorious deeds;
12 For the Avenger of blood has remembered,
     He forgets not the cry of the suffering.

13 O Jehovah, have pity; behold how I suffer from my foes;
     For Thou broughtest me up from the portals of death,
14 That so I may tell all Thy praise
     In the gates of the daughter of Zion,
         And exult in Thy power to save.

15 The heathen are sunk in the pitfall they made;
     Their foot has been caught in the net which they hid;
16 Jehovah is known; He dealeth out justice;
     In the work of their hands are the wicked ensnared.
                              [Higgaion.   Selah.]

17 To the world of the dead must the wicked return,
     All the nations forgetful of God:
18 For the poor are not always forgotten,
     The sufferer's hope is not lost evermore.

19 O Jehovah, arise; let not mortals prevail;
   Let the nations have judgment before Thee:
20 Affright them, Jehovah,
   That the nations may know they are men.

(1, 2) The alphabetical type of this Psalm is most strongly marked at the opening. The four lines of the first strophe all begin with Aleph. It is not only the first letter of the alphabet, but of the personal pronoun *ani, I,* and as such it stands prefixed to each of the four verbs. The sufferer comes in his human personality before God, addressing Him by the Name which more than all others exhibits the Divine personality, Jehovah, the "I AM" (Ex. iii. 14). It is the highest privilege of man on the earth to enjoy the most elevating and strengthening personal relations and intercourse with the Father of spirits.

Yet it must be remembered that this Psalm, like most of the others, was prepared for the public worship of God in the great congregation, and that often, though originating in events distressing or joyful in the life of the individual composer, they immediately exhibit a broader scope, and describe conflicts and victories of the covenant people in its ideal unity. The apparent reference to a single man is maintained by the use of the personal pronoun, but it is a personified multitude that is speaking, with one heart and one voice. The perils and deliverances depicted are those of a people which God has taken under His almighty protection, against the hostile and crafty nations of the world. The sufferer is Israel, and the ruthless oppressor, at first a combination of Philistines, may come to stand from time to time for Nineveh, Babylon, or whatever heathen power shall become prominent, and then for all combinations of evil against the servants of God to the end of time. Mark the reference to nations and cities in ver. 4, which would be quite unsuitable if the subject were a contest of man with man. See note upon vii. 6.

(5, 6) These verses connect the recent interposition of God with similar judgments in the early history of Israel. They remind us especially of that upon the Amalekites (Ex. xvii. 14). "I will blot out the remembrance of Amalek from under heaven."

(6) **Torn up.** Heb. *nāthash, to uproot.* — **Yea, of these has the memory.** Heb. *their memory, they.* The emphatic pronoun *they* refers to the cities, which, though so firmly built as to be compared to a tree whose roots strike deep into the earth, shall be utterly destroyed.

(11) **Strike the harp.** See on vii. 17. — **His glorious deeds.** Heb. *'aliloth* (עֲלִילוֹת), lit. *doings,* but used elsewhere of God with reference to distinguished exploits as the omnipotent Leader of Israel (lxxvii. 11, lxxviii. 11, ciii. 7).

(12) **Avenger of blood.** Heb. *dôrēsh dāmīm, requiring* (satisfaction for) *bloodshed.* See Gen. ix. 5, xlii. 22 for the same expression. This was among the duties of the nearest relative (Heb. *gō'ēl,* the *redeemer*), who was hence called *gō'ēl haddāmīm,* the redeemer of bloodshed; Num. xxxv 19.

(17) **The world of the dead** Heb. *sheol.* See note at vi. 5.

(19) **Mortals.** Heb. *'enôsh, man in his weakness* (see on viii. 4), from *'ānash, to be sick* or *feeble,* in contrast with *geber,* man as *strong.*

(20) **Men.** The same word, *'enôsh, the mortal.* The frailty of men is here brought into contrast with the power of God that terrifies them.

X.

AN APPEAL AGAINST CRUELTY AND WRONG.

THIS Psalm, though structurally related to the preceding (see on ix.), is a distinct composition. There are several marked differences. In the former the writer's personal sufferings are prominent; here he makes no reference to himself. In that, we have, principally, thanksgiving; in this, outside the descriptive portion (ver. 3-11), supplication. Again, Psalm ix. relates distinctly to foreign enemies, Psalm x. apparently to apostates and persecutors at home. Yet in language and general characteristics of thought they are very similar. Though not strictly one, they were doubtless companion pieces. The tone of Psalm x. is that of deep and strong moral indignation against the enormities it describes, with a terseness and energy of expression that are hard to imitate in English.

The chief difficulty in translating this Psalm perspicuously is connected with its usual reference to the persecutor and his victim alike in the singular number, whether a noun is used or a pronoun. The antecedent of a pronoun is sometimes doubtful, especially when two of them occur in the same line and both are in the same number. See, for instance, ver. 3, where in the first line both nouns are in the singular, and in the second the pronouns that represent them are *they* . . . *they*, both in the plural. Inasmuch as the individual represents a class, it seems desirable to avoid confusion by retaining the singular number for the oppressor and using the plural for the oppressed.

1. The poet brings before God in a forcible description the cruelty and wrong that are ruthlessly practised by the arrogant and impious (1-11). 2. Jehovah is implored to rescue the suffering, and to show that He knows and abhors these infamous crimes (12-18).

  1 Why, O Jehovah, wilt Thou stand afar off,
     And why hide Thine eyes in times of sore trouble?
  2 Through the wicked man's pride are the lowly in anguish,
     And are snared by the wiles he devised.

  3 The wicked give praise for the greed of their soul;
     The despoiler contemning, yet blesses Jehovah.
  4 The wicked man says with an arrogant face,
        "He will not avenge;"
  "There is no God," is in all his devices.

5 Bold are his ways at all times,
        Thy judgments on high are out of his sight,
   His foes — he puffs at them all.

6 He says in his heart, " I cannot be shaken;
   Through age after age no mischance shall befall me."
7 Full of oaths is his mouth, of deceptions and grinding;
   On his tongue are sorrow and wrong.

8 He lies in the lookout of hamlets,
        In the coverts he slaughters the blameless;
   For the wretched his eyes are in hiding.

9 In ambush he lurks, like a lion in his lair,
        He lurks to take captive the lowly;
   He captures the lowly, drawn in with his net.

10 They are crushed, they sink down —
    So the wretched ones fall by his power.
11 He says in his heart, "God will not remember;
    He covers His face; He never will see."

12 Arise, O Jehovah; O God, let Thy hand be lift up;
    Forget not the suffering;
13 Why do the wicked hold God in contempt,
    And say in their heart, Thou wilt not avenge?

14 Thou hast seen; for Thou lookest on trouble and grief,
        To deal out with Thy hand;
    With THEE the wretched one leaves it,
        The orphan, whose help Thou becamest.

15 Break the arm of the wicked;
    And the evil, search out his ill deeds,
        Till Thou find them no more.
16 Jehovah is sovereign forever and alway,
    The heathen pass away from his land.

17 Thou hast heard, O Jehovah, the desire of the lowly;
 Thou wilt make their heart steadfast,
 And attentive Thine ear,
18 To redress the orphan and oppressed,
 That mortals of earth may strike terror no more.

(1) **Hide Thine eyes.** Heb. *hide.* The form is *Hiphil*, and transitive. It is only used elsewhere of hiding the *eyes* or *ears*, implying neglect, or refusal to help (Is. i. 15: Lam. iii. 56). In the text we supply the ellipsis.

(2) **Wiles.** Heb. *m'zimmōth*, crafty and destructive plots. The same word occurs in ver. 4, and is translated *devices.*

(3) **Give praise.** Heb. *hillēl.* A. V., R. V., etc., *boasteth.* But it is never elsewhere so rendered, except that in xliv. 8, we find boasting *in God.* The form is in constant use in the Psalms, and always of *praising God.* The ellipsis of the object presents no difficulty, since it is supplied after the parallelistic verb "blesses" in the following line. — **The greed.** Heb. *ta'avāh, desire;* here of *evil desire*, as in cxii. 10. But the *desire* is put by metonymy for the *object of desire*, as now attained, as in lxxviii. 29, etc. — **The despoiler.** A participial noun in the *qōtēl* form, in parallelism with *the wicked* preceding. See the same form as a concrete noun in Prov. i. 19, xv. 27. — **Contemning, yet blesses Jehovah.** Heb. *blesses contemns.* Other renderings are: Perowne, "He blesseth the robber, he despiseth Jehovah" — taking the first word of the clause as the object of the verb (so A. V. with Hupfeld, Moll, etc.); Delitzsch, "The covetous renounceth (and) despiseth Jehovah" (so R. V. with Ewald, Hitzig, etc.); Cheyne renders the whole verse, "For the ungodly praises for his soul's desire, and robbing he blesses (but contemns) Jehovah." This is nearer the mark, retaining the almost invariable meaning of the two principal verbs. Although the verb *bārēk* (usually, *blesses*), may apply to a parting salutation, and be translated *renounces* (as R. V. in Job i. 5, 11, ii. 5, and here), this signification is infrequent and doubtful, and it occurs nowhere else in the Psalms. It seems most improbable that the two words *hallēl* and *bārēk*, used often, and always in the Psalter, of acts of worship, should stand in parallelism in the same verse in a sense so different. Nothing but the most cogent exegetical necessity could warrant this. The language of the poet here reminds us that the worst men have often been hypocritical worshippers, covering up flagrant iniquity by their sanctimonious demeanor and long prayers. See in Zech. xi. 5 a description of wicked shepherds, who slay the flock, saying, "I am not guilty," and then make merchandise of them, and as they pocket their gains cry, "Bless Jehovah, I am rich." On the combination *blesses despises* see note at vii. 1, 2.

(4) **Thou wilt not avenge.** Heb. *wilt not require,* — that is, satisfaction in punishment. So in connection with crime the verb *dārash* comes to have the general sense of avenging or punishing. Used here and in ver. 13 with special reference to murder. See note at ix. 12.

(10) **They are crushed, they sink down** (of the oppressed); or, *He crouches, he cowers* (of the oppressor), as of a wild beast about to spring on his prey (so R. V.). This is on the supposition that the correction of the *K'ri*, which gives the active form, is to be preferred. The fatal objection is that even as so corrected the verb never means to *crouch*, but always to *crush*. — **By**

his power. Heb. *by his strong* (plur.), leaving the substantive to be supplied. A. V. and R. V., *by his strong ones.* Some refer the expression to the young of the lions. So apparently in the English Bible. Others, to the claws and teeth. So Gesenius. Ewald considers it an abstract plural noun meaning *strength.* So the Targum and Jerome. This we prefer.

(18) **Mortals.** Heb. *'enôsh.* Man as frail and feeble. See ix. 19 and 20, and the note there.

XI.

A REFUSAL TO FLEE IN TIME OF GREAT PERIL.

THIS Psalm, like the tenth, confidently assures the ungodly who are executing their murderous designs under cover of the darkness, that the all-seeing eye of Jehovah is upon them. The life of David, to whom even Hitzig and Ewald ascribe this Psalm, is threatened. The pillars of the state are shaken. The timorous friends of the king advise him to flee to the mountains. These are indications of the time when the rebellion of Absalom was secretly preparing. Everything indicated a speedy outbreak. The Psalm hurries on with a swift measure, and is clear in the principal thoughts, but it is not free from difficult points. In this respect it resembles all the Psalms that contain similar obscure allusions to the internal condition of Israel. The gloomy condition of the nation seems to be reflected in the very language. — *Delitzsch.*

1. The counsel of faint-hearted friends (1-3). 2. He justifies the confidence in Jehovah that he had expressed at the beginning (4-7).

FOR THE LEADER OF THE CHOIR. BY DAVID.

1 In Jehovah I hide me;
    How vainly ye say to my soul,
  " Like the birds make escape to your mountain;
2 For their bow the wicked are bending,
    And their arrow they fix on the string,
  To shoot from the darkness the upright in heart:
3 When the pillars are riven,
    Oh, what can the righteous man do?"

4 Jehovah in His palace most holy,
    Jehovah in heaven has His throne;
  With His eyes He beholds,
    With His eyelids He tries the children of men.

5 The righteous, Jehovah approves;
   But the wicked and lovers of outrage,
     He hates from His soul.
6 He will rain burning coals on the wicked,
   Brimstone with fire and a blast of fierce heat,
     Dealt out in their cup.

7 For Jehovah is righteous, and righteousness loves;
   His face the righteous alone can behold.

(1) **Take refuge.** See on ii. 12. —**How vainly.** Heb. *' êk, how;* an exclamation of surprise at the folly of the proposal, as of a thought that cannot be entertained for a moment. —**Like the birds**, or, *O ye birds.* The verb *nûsû* is plural, and the noun is a collective, the plural form never used. There is no particle to express resemblance, but the noun may be translated as an adverbial accusative, *bird-like.* The meaning, however, is substantially the same. Either rendering, by a formal comparison, or by the bold metaphorical vocative *Ye birds*, expresses the helplessness of birds, and their readiness to take flight at the slightest appearance of danger.

(4) **Palace.** See note at v. 7. Not the temple here, but the centre of majesty and power in heaven, where the King of kings is enthroned. See xviii. 6, xxix. 9.

(5) **Approves.** The verb is the same as that translated "tries" in the preceding verse. Both the righteous and the wicked pass under the scrutiny of God as Judge. But in the case of the righteous the testing proves value, and becomes an approving. They come forth from the trial as pure gold.

(7) **Can behold.** Heb. *y'hhezû.* This verb is the root of *hhâzôn* and *mahhazeh*, a *vision.* It is used only of *seeing God*, or of seeing *supernaturally*, and not of perception by the physical sense of sight.

XII.

HELP IN JEHOVAH WHEN FALSEHOOD AND OPPRESSION PREVAIL.

PSALM xi. is appropriately followed by Psalm xii., which is of a kindred character,—a prayer for the deliverance of the poor and miserable in a time of universal moral corruption, and more particularly of prevailing faithlessness and defiant oppression. The inscription points us to the time when the temple music was being established, — that is, the time of David.—incomparably the best age in the history of Israel, and yet, viewed in the light of the spirit of holiness, an age so radically corrupt. The true people of Jehovah were even then, as ever, a church of confessors and martyrs, and the sighing for the coming of Jehovah was then not less deep than the cry, "Come, Lord Jesus," at the present time.

This Psalm xii. (compare in this respect Psalm ii.) is a second example of the way in which the Psalmist, when under great excitement of spirit, passes over into the tone of one who directly hears God's words, and therefore into that of an inspired prophet. Just as lyric poetry in general, as being a direct and solemn expression of strong inward feeling, is the earliest form of poetry, so psalm-poetry contains in itself not only the *mashal*, the *epos*, and the *drama*, in their preformative stages, but prophecy also, as we have it in the prophetic writings of its most flourishing period, has, as it were, sprung from the bosom of psalm-poetry. It is throughout a blending of prophetical epic and subjective lyric elements. — *Delitzsch*.

FOR THE LEADER OF THE CHOIR. ON THE OCTAVE. BY DAVID.

1 Help, O Jehovah, for the loving are few,
   The faithful fail from the children of men;
2 Falsely they speak every man to his neighbour,
   With treacherous lips and a heart that deceives.

3 Jehovah destroy all the treacherous lips,
   The tongue that is speaking so proudly;
4 Those that say, " With our tongues we are strong;
   Our lips are our allies;
      Where find we our master?"

5 " The poor are oppressed, the needy are groaning;
   Therefore now will I rise," are the words of Jehovah,
      " The safety they pant for I give them."
6 The words of Jehovah are words without dross;
   They are silver the earth has assayed as a furnace,
      Refined seven times.

7 Yea, Thou, O Jehovah, wilt save them, —
   From this generation wilt ever preserve them;
8 Though the wicked on every side walk about,
   When the vile are raised high by the children of men.

(1) **The loving.** Heb. *hhasîd;* here used in its active signification as seen by its parallelism with " *the faithful*" in the following line. See note on this important word at iv. 3.

(4) **Are our allies.** Heb. *'ittânû, with us,* — that is, on our side as confederates.

(5) Heb *Because of the oppression of the poor . . . now will I arise.* Our rendering gives the precise logi-

cal equivalent. — **The safety they pant for I give them**. Nearly as the marg. of the R. V., where the text has "I will set him in safety at whom they puff." The verb here translated *puff* or *pant* is used in both senses. It expresses a violent emission of the breath,—of what kind is determined by the connection. We have had it in the former sense at x. 5. But there it is the bold and defiant puff of a proud and powerful oppressor against those who attempt to restrain him, and is not used as here in connection with relentless pursuit of feeble victims who are just ready to faint and expire. In this case a puff of proud rage is quite out of place and the other signification, adopted in the above rendering is more appropriate. (Similarly Ewald, Olsh., Hengst., Del., etc.) It is used of the panting of great haste at Heb. ii. 3, "*it hasteth toward the end*," where the marg. has Heb. "*panteth*." Compare the kindred verb *shā'aph*, Ecc. i. 5; of the sun as panting to complete its circuit round the earth.

(6) **Words of Jehovah**. Heb. *'amārōth*, the fem. plur. form of *'ōmer* (אֹמֶר), corresponding with the preceding verb *yomar* (יֹאמַר), *saith*. It is evident that the allusion is not to the word of God in general, as the sense is given in our English Bible, but to the promise just uttered that He will deliver the poor sufferer from the murderous rage of the ungodly. — **Words without dross**, — that is, without the dross of feebleness or falsity, the poor stuff that the promises of men are so often made of. — **They are silver tried in the furnace of the earth**. A. V. "*As* silver tried in a furnace of earth." R.V. "As silver tried in a furnace on the earth." The renderings of the A. V. and R.

V. exhibit the views of leading authorities. In the former "earth" is the *material* of which the crucible for refining silver is made. But the question is asked, Why should the material be mentioned at all? and a conclusive objection is that *'ĕrĕts, the earth*, could never be used to describe anything as earthen. The rendering of the Revisers exhibits the furnace as standing upon the earth. To this it is objected that the statement that a furnace for purifying metal is placed upon the earth, and not suspended in the air, seems so unnecessary as to be hardly possible. It is conceded by those who feel obliged to accept one or the other of these renderings, that the objections to both are very considerable.

The solution proposed in the rendering we have adopted is that Jehovah's promise of succour to His persecuted people is not *compared* to silver, but more boldly declared to be silver. The particle "*as*" is not in the Hebrew, but has been inserted by translators, and the figure is not *simile* but *metaphor*. This gracious promise of a faithful God is silver that has been tried in the fire, and found to be thoroughly trustworthy. It is not the trying of silver in a furnace of any special material, or in any particular position, that is before the mind of the poet, but the trying of the promises of God to His suffering people in a furnace seven times heated, and that furnace is the earth inhabited by men such as are described in vv. 3 and 4, and the testing fires are the fires of fierce persecution that they have kindled, out of which the precious words of grace have come forth thoroughly tried and proven to be worth more than "silver seven times refined."

XIII.

THE SUPPLIANT CRY OF ONE IN THE LAST EXTREMITY.

THIS Psalm, in contrast with Psalm xii., is personal. It seems to belong to the time when Saul, after long and unremitting persecution, set watchers to hunt David from place to place. 1 Sam. xxii. 22, 23, etc.

"The rapid transition of feeling, from a depth of misery bordering on despair to hope and even to joy, is very remarkable." — *Perowne.*

1. A complicated questioning ; hope struggling against despair (1, 2). 2. Calmer supplication, the heart already somewhat relieved (3, 4). 3. Joyful anticipation of a happy issue (5, 6).

FOR THE LEADER OF THE CHOIR.   A PSALM OF DAVID.

1 How long as if alway will Jehovah forget me?
   How long wilt Thou cover Thy face with a veil?
2 How long shall my soul lay its plans,
     Yet grief fill my heart through the day?
   How long shall my foes be exalted above me?

3 Look Thou, and answer, Jehovah my God,
   Give light to mine eyes, lest I slumber in death ;
4 Lest mine enemy say, " I am stronger than he,"
   Lest my foe should exult in my ruin.

5 And I, in Thy love is my trust,
   In Thy saving power my heart shall exult ;
6 I will sing to Jehovah,
   Because with His bounty he loads me.

(1) Heb. *How long dost Thou forget me forever ?* The apparent contradiction exhibits the conflict within between hope and despair. To the tortured soul during the period of suffering it seems as if its misery could never end. But hope still looks, at whatever distance of time, for a return of God's favour. As Prof. Cheyne suggests, it is virtually a quotation from his own despairing thought inserted in his prayer. Perowne says, "We might paraphrase 'How long wilt Thou make as if Thou wouldest forget me forever?'" adding the following from Delitzsch, "God's anger, the hiding of his countenance, cannot but seem eternal to

the soul that is conscious of it. Nevertheless faith still cleaves to the love which hides itself under the disguise of severity, and exclaims, 'Though He slay me, yet will I trust in Him.'" The same questioning is found in lxxiv. 10, lxxix. 5, lxxxix. 46. The wailing cry is drawn out and intensified in a four-fold "*how long?*" Shall this continue forever, forever, forever?

(2) **Lay its plans**. Heb. *How long shall I put* (that is, *set up*, or *propose*) *plans*. The mention of "plans," indefinite in number, connected with the preceding "How long," implies that plan after plan has been determined upon, and as yet all have been found unavailing.

One project after another has been abandoned, and their successive disappointment increases the anxiety. The following line, relating to his grief during the day, implies that his plans were made in the night.

(3) **Give light to mine eyes**,—not referring to cheerfulness and hope, arising from the light of God's countenance, but to the light of life (lvi. 13) in contrast with the darkness of death which seems to be impending. He is now walking "through the valley of the shadow of death" (see note at xxiii. 4), and prays that the darkness of the shadow may not end in the deeper darkness of the reality.

(5) **In Thy love**. See on xxiii. 6.

XIV.

PREVAILING CORRUPTION, AND LONGING FOR REDEMPTION.

THE lamentation again becomes general. "Both in this Psalm and in Psalm xii. the complaint is made that the wicked oppress and devour the righteous. In both, corruption has risen to its most gigantic height. But here the *doings* of bad men, there their words, form the chief subject of complaint. In form the ode is dramatic or quasi-dramatic. A great tragedy is enacting before the eyes of the poet. Sin is lifting itself up in Titanic madness against God, and God looks down upon its doings as once upon the builders of Babel. He sees utter apostasy (ver. 3); He speaks from heaven (ver. 4); and evil-doers are confounded at the word of His mouth (ver. 5). 'It would scarcely be possible,' says Ewald, 'for a great truth to be sketched in fewer or more striking outlines.'"— *Perowne*.

In Psalm liii. this Psalm is repeated with slight variation except in the substitution of the Divine Name Elohim for Jehovah.

1. Atheism, and resulting moral corruption, are universal (1–3). 2. The Divine indignation bursts forth, and the rapacious oppressors of innocence are smitten with terror (4–6). 3. A longing desire for the redemption of Israel (7).

FOR THE LEADER OF THE CHOIR. A PSALM OF DAVID.

1 " There is no God," saith the fool in his heart;
  They all are corrupt, yea, are vile in their deeds;
  There are none that do good.

2 Jehovah looks forth out of heaven
On the children of men,
To see whether any are wise,
Whether any are seeking for God.

3 They are all gone astray ;
All alike they are loathsome ;
There are none that do good,
No, not even one.

4 Do none of them know,
These whose works are so evil?
They feed on my people, as if feeding on bread ;
Jehovah, they call not upon Him.

5 They were there in great fear,
For the race of the righteous have God on their side.
6 Ye would fain bring to nought the plans of the
righteous,
But they hide in Jehovah, their refuge.

7 Oh that salvation for Israel might come out of Zion !
When Jehovah returns to His people in bondage,
Let Jacob be joyful, let Israel be glad.

---

(2) **Looks forth**. Heb. *shākaph*, lit. *to bend forward;* principally of leaning over from a height for closer observation of objects of absorbing interest; so of the men approaching Sodom, as looking down upon the doomed city (Gen. xviii. 16. xix. 28); so of the anxious mother of Sisera, as looking out from the lattice and crying, " Why is his chariot so long in coming?" (Judges v. 28). Most impressive is Ps cii. 19, of Jehovah, as "looking [lit. bending] down from His sanctuary to hear the sighing of the prisoner, and to loose those appointed to death." This graphic verb has its precise counterpart, both in the primary and the secondary sense, in the Greek παρακύπτω. See especially John xx. 5, of Peter at the sepulchre "stooping and looking in " (R. V.), where the two English participles are required to exhibit the meaning of the single Greek word; and 1 Pet. i. 12, of the angels as desiring to look into the revelation of grace in the Gospel, -- that is, to bend down with eager and observant eyes, that they may see and understand it all.

(4) **Do none of them know ?** or, *Do not they all know?* In Heb. usage *all*, as the subject or object of a verb accompanied by a negative particle, is often equivalent to *none.* Here the negative seems to connect closely with the verb: *are they all ignorant?* The question involves a burst of moral indignation, withering and blasting those who have commit-

ted these shocking enormities. It expresses surprise at their moral obtuseness, men whose lives are filled with injustice of the most flagrant and oppressive kind, apparently not able to distinguish between good and evil. The second line is subordinate, and descriptive of the wickedness referred to. They consume their daily food, and fatten upon acts of cruel rapacity, as if the two were equally innocent. Heb. *They eat My people, they eat bread*. It is not strange that such men, already described (ver. 1) as saying in their heart, " there is no God," should not worship Jehovah. This is a step beyond the hypocritical worship of x. 3.

(7) Returns to His people in bondage. Heb. *b'shûb Y'hovah sh'bûth 'ammō*. Lit. *returns to the bondage of His people*. The Heb. *shûb sh'bûth* occurs elsewhere in the Psalms at liii. 6, lxxxv. 1, cxxvi. 1, 4. In the earlier Books we find it only in Deut. xxx. 3 and Job xlii. 10, and in both figuratively, of misery of any kind. In the Prophetic Books it occurs twenty-four times, and always of literal captivity. The earlier instances are sufficient to show that its occurrence in this Psalm, or any other, does not prove it to have been written after the Babylonish Exile. In all the places the English Bible renders the verb transitively, usually *bring back* (or *again*) *the captivity* etc. In the plain meaning of the English phrase it can only describe the recurrence of captivity after having escaped from it. But this cannot be the signification of the Hebrew. Happily the context in most cases compels the reader to take it in the opposite sense, of delivery from captivity, which corresponds with historic fact, whatever be its merits as a translation. The explanation usually given, is that the abstract noun *captivity* is used by metonymy for the concrete *captives*, who are described

as brought back. This would suit most cases, but not the two earliest, which clearly refer to the *condition*, and not to the *persons* who are in that condition. No explanation that fails to cover all the instances can be admitted. The difficulty is serious, and can only be relieved by correcting the translation of the verb. The case is simply this. There are two principal forms of the verb; *shûb* (as here), which is intransitive, *to return*, and *hāshîb*, transitive, *to cause to return*, or *bring back*. The former occurs in the O. T. more than 800 times, and is always elsewhere *intransitive*, with the rarest, if any, exceptions. Hengstenberg (on Ps. xiv. 7, and in his *Beiträge*) maintains that there are none. The lexicons assign to it the transitive sense *bring back*, or *return*, only in Num. x. 36, Ps. lxxxv. 4, and Nah. ii. 2. But in these the intransitive *return to* is at least as suitable to the context, and much to be preferred. Schroeder claims that *shûb* occurs as transitive in Ezek. xlvii. 7 (so Briggs), but his grounds are insufficient, and the intransitive rendering of the A. V. is very properly retained in the R. V. The remark should be added, that while the prep. *'el* (*to*) might be attached, the form *shûb* is construed directly with the acc. in Gen. i. 14, Ex. iv. 20, Num. x. 36, and especially see Is. lii. 8, *b'shûb Y'hovah tsîyôn*, 'when Jehovah shall return unto Zion.' In all the places where the phrase under consideration occurs, Jehovah's return to His people under their sufferings, implies the restoration of His favour in all gracious manifestations, including their release from captivity. He had forsaken them in displeasure, and comes back to them in mercy. The meaning is broader and deeper than that afforded by taking the verb in its transitive sense. It suits Job xlii. 8, as well as the later passages, and the difficulty stated at the beginning of this note entirely disappears.

XV.

A WELCOME GUEST IN GOD'S HOUSE.

DAVID was no doubt the author.   A later date cannot be maintained, for the temple is not yet built.   The first verse brings us to Mount Zion, and exhibits the tabernacle (Heb. *tent*) as still standing.

This Psalm is very similar to Psalm xxiv., which was composed in connection with the removal of the ark to Zion.   The same question is there asked, but the answer is shorter, and more general.   Ewald suggests that this Psalm is later, and was composed with the express design of portraying the character of an acceptable worshipper more in detail and with greater impressiveness.

The description consists of eleven points, all contained in the Divine law, though not confined to that of Sinai.   They are such as might fairly be considered tests of moral worth, in view of the prevailing vices of that time.

There is no reference to sacrifice, or any ceremonial, as securing acceptance with God.   But these are not disparaged, nor is the conception of true religion in the mind of the writer confined to morality without ordinances of worship.   On the contrary, the opening question implies a place upon the Holy Mountain where God welcomes His guests to the enjoyment of these ordinances.   The question is raised in order to exclude men whose lives are wicked and hypocritical from coming to the sanctuary and altar, with the superstitious idea that these appointments of worship have some mystical virtue to secure impunity and acceptance for falsehood, impurity, and wrong.   It is a reiteration in other form of Ps. v. 4, " Thou art not a God that hast pleasure in sin, neither shall evil be a guest with Thee." It is implied that to the true, the pure, and the loving, God's holy court with its sacred rites, is a place of privilege, honour, and blessing.

God's favoured guest is described: 1. In his general character, the outward and the inward (2).   2. In his conduct toward his neighbour (3).   3. In his loathing of evil, and faithful performance of vows (4).   4. In his charity and integrity (5).

A PSALM OF DAVID.

1 Who may be a guest in Thy tent, O Jehovah,
   Or who find a home on Thy consecrate hill?
2 He whose walk is blameless, whose doings are right,
   And the thought of whose heart is the truth.

3 No slanderous word will he take on his tongue,
   No ill will he do his companion,
   No shame will he cast on his neighbour.
4 In his eyes the vile are contemned;
   Those that reverence Jehovah he honours;
   He may swear to his harm, but he swerves not.
5 His money he gives where he looks for no gain;
   He receives no bribe 'gainst the guiltless;
   He that doeth these things shall never be shaken.

(1) **May be a guest.** Heb. *ya-gûr.* See on v. 4.

(2) **Whose walk is blameless, etc.** In the Hebrew idiom, which is carried into the N. T., the *walk* is the life in its prevailing purpose, tenor, and direction, while the following term (*doings*) refers to single acts. — **The thought of whose heart.** Heb. *speaks truth in his heart.* What is said in the heart, in distinction from the utterance of the lips, is clearly defined thought (see x. 11, xiv. 1, xxxix. 1, 3). The language of the Psalmist here describes one whose thoughts and purposes are guileless and sincere, who is true to the centre and core of his nature. In his heart there are no delusions or subterfuges. He is honest to God and to himself, as well as to his neighbour. This is a deeper truthfulness than that which merely refrains from false speaking and fraudulent dealing, where the motive may be other than a genuine love of truth.

(5) **His money he gives where he looks for no gain.** Heb. *kaspô lô nathan b'neshek.* Lit. *his money he gives not on interest.* At this point in the Psalm the Anglo-American Revisers were in some perplexity. For *neshek*, rendered *usury* in the A. V., means *interest.* Originally this was no mistranslation, for in the time of King James the two words were equivalent. By the Jewish law it was forbidden, within certain limitations, to take interest, even at the lowest percentage. It was counted an unjust and oppressive exaction, as much so as unreasonably high rates are now. In the earlier passages this is clear from the context, but it is less so in the Psalm. Yet the Revisers were of opinion that the rendering of the English Bible fairly represents the spirit of the prohibition, and that more would be lost than gained by literalness. But a comparison of the parallel passages from the Pentateuch with the language of the Psalter, suggests a change here which not only allows, but requires, the plainest expression of the non-requirement of any interest whatever. The legal background of this item of the description is Lev. xxv. 35-37. This is a fuller statement of the earlier command in Ex. xxii. 25. and is therefore the principal passage. It refers distinctly to a brother that is "waxen poor." The positive side is given in ver. 35, "thou shalt surely uphold him;" that is, as immediately explained, give him money and food. The following direction is negative, but it implies the preceding positive, "thou shalt give him money, but not upon interest." It will be observed that the wording in Leviticus and in the Psalm are identical, except that the "thou shalt give" of Moses becomes "he gives" in David. There is a later law in Deut. xxiii. 19, 20, on the right of requiring interest, which expresses the same general idea, but in different language: "thou shalt not exact from (lit. *bite*) thy

brother, whether interest (*biting*) of money," etc. We infer that the Psalmist's mind was upon the former. It is really a quotation, with the slight change in person and tense required by the context. Every Israelite would think of it as referring to the relief of the poor, as an important characteristic of the acceptable worshipper. The Deuteronomic law forbade that interest should be required of any Israelite, but permitted it from foreigners. The difference lies in the agricultural life of the people. Trade was discouraged, as involving contaminating intercourse with the heathen. It was assumed, that in their simple domestic life, a loan would be asked only in connection with some temporary need. They must live in practical kindliness, not taking advantage of the necessities of a neighbour for their own enrichment. As to foreigners, they were usually traders who would borrow to enlarge their capital for greater gain, and might reasonably be expected to pay interest upon loans.

For these reasons it seems very clear that we have in the Psalm an extract from Leviticus, contining the reference to the poor, and that the change in position of the negative particle, glancing at the positive side of the obligation, is wholly warranted. This is one of the places where in justice to the material of which the text was constructed and which does not appear on the surface, the thought must be translated, rather than the words.

XVI.

JEHOVAH, HIS PORTION AND HIS JOY IN LIFE AND IN DEATH.

THIS Psalm is decidedly and in every aspect by David. It cannot be assigned with certainty to any special time in his life. Its profession of unlimited trust in Jehovah derives peculiar impressiveness from its having been written in imminent danger of death. " He rises to the grand thought of the immortality of the soul, and of the glory and blessedness that await the faithful in the unseen world. In the glory of this vision the language transcends the expectation of David, or any early king of the Jews, and awaits its fulness of meaning in the Messiah, the Lord's Anointed of the second Psalm, the true Son of God, and King of kings."

The Apostle Peter, speaking by inspiration, distinctly declares (Acts ii. 30, 31) that David here spoke as a prophet, and that he foresaw and testified of the resurrection of Christ.

There are three strophes: 1. An emphatic avowal of absolute confidence in God, and an earnest protest against idolatry (1-4). 2. The happiness and security of the man who has Jehovah as his portion (5-8). 3. An expression of joyous hope in the immediate prospect of death (9-11).

MICHTAM OF DAVID.

1 Preserve me, O God,
    For in Thee I take refuge:
2 I say to Jehovah, " Thou art my Lord;
    I have nought that is good beside THEE."

3 And I say to the holy tribes of the land,
   To the eminent nation in which I have all my delight;
4 " Many their woes that pay dowry to idols;
   I will not pour out their libations of blood,
      Nor lift up their names on my lips."

5 O Jehovah, dealt out as my portion and cup,
   By sure title I hold Thee mine own;
6 Amid pleasures the lines have determined my share,
   Yea, a goodly possession is mine.
7 I bless Jehovah who giveth me counsel,
   By night, too, my longings incite me.
8 I have set Jehovah before me forever,
   With Him at my right, I shall not be o'erthrown.

9 So my heart is rejoicing, my spirit exults,
   My flesh, too, abideth securely;
10 For Thou wilt not abandon my soul unto death,
   Nor let him whom Thou lovest consume in the grave.
11 Thou wilt show me the pathway to life —
   In Thy presence is fulness of joy,
      At Thy right hand are pleasures eternal.

(1) **Take refuge.** See note on ii. 12. He refers here to a past act that has resulted in present and permanent security. This first clause contains germinally the thought of the entire Psalm.

(2) **I say to Jehovah.** The verb is apparently in the 2d person fem., but is better taken as a defective form of the 1st person, *'amart* for *'amarti*, as in cxlii. 12, Job xlii. 2, etc. — **I have nought that is good beside Thee.** Lit. *My good* (that which I find and enjoy as good) *is not upon* (that is, in addition to, or beside) *Thee.* This is his reason for preferring Jehovah to all others who might be regarded as having a claim to his service and worship. There is a latent reference to idols and their worshippers, presently to be mentioned (ver. 4). He possesses in Jehovah the absolute and all-sufficient good, that satisfies the deepest cravings and the highest aspirations of his rational and immortal nature, which is itself the breath of the life of God (Gen. ii. 4), and can find its blessedness and rest only in Him.

(3, 4) The rendering of our text is an attempted solution of a recognized *crux interpretum.*

The first difficulty lies in the construction of *liqdôshîm* at the beginning of ver. 3. The principal views are the following: —

1. That the prep. *l* introduces an independent proposition and should be translated, " *with respect to.*" The principal objections are: (*a*) That it ignores any close relation between this verse and the preceding, such as we should certainly expect; (*b*) That it compels us to find as the new proposition, "All my delight is in them,"

which is surely too poor and flat to follow the grand avowal that precedes; (*c*) That it involves an insurmountable grammatical difficulty; '*addîrê* is in the construct state, which is here limited by a clause that in uniform Hebrew usage is relative, and can only be translated by the relative pronoun. See Is. xxix. 1; Ges. Gr. 116. 3. The *stat. const.* is never used for the *stat. absol.* It is true that this difficulty may be avoided by the translation, "They are the noble," etc. But the preceding "and," and the absence of the demonstrative pronoun, preclude this, as Delitzsch admits in his proposed alteration of the text. See below.

2. The second view of the construction is that the *l'* before *q'dôshîm* means *united to* or *associated with* the saints. (So Hengst., Hupf., Moll, etc.) But such association would not be so loosely and doubtfully expressed. No parallel case can be found.

3. The simplest and most probable view of the construction is that *liqdôshîm* and the preceding *laychovah* are coördinate, and both subordinate to '*amarti, I say;* the Psalmist first declaring to Jehovah that he looks to Him for all good, and then turning to his fellow worshippers with some appropriate declaration.

The principal difficulty lies in determining what the declarat'on is. Moll, who adopts No. 2, says that the construction now suggested is grammatically unassailable, but has little correspondence with the course of thought of the Psalm, and is foreign to its prevailing tone of prayer. This objection would be valid and fatal, if we were compelled to adopt his own view of the following context. Delitzsch finds the utterance sought for in the second line of the same verse. But, discovering no possibility of an adequate thought in the Hebrew text as it stands, he adopts a new text, transferring the conjunction "and" to the beginning of the preceding line, and changing the accentual division of the verse, so as to bring the pronoun *hemah* into this latter line. This enables him to extract the following translation: —

"And to the saints who are in the earth,
These are the excellent, in whom is all my delight."

But this could be said *of* the saints, rather than *to* them, and the suggested change in the text is not warranted by the result. For the sense thus gained does not seem sufficiently elevated and important to correspond with the preceding address to Jehovah. Nor does it fit in with the general tenor of the Psalm, which asserts throughout Jehovah's claim to the undivided homage and confidence of His favoured people.

It seems to be assumed by all, that a suitable utterance must be found in ver. 3, if anywhere. At least no one has proposed that the search be carried into the next verse. Ewald, indeed, makes ver. 3 subordinate to ver. 4. ("The saints who are in the land, and the nobles who have all my love, Many are their idols," etc.) But his exegesis of the latter fails to do justice to its contents, and he does not recognize its coördination to the declaration to Jehovah in ver. 2.

In the view embodied in our new rendering, ver. 3 is parenthetical, but very important as giving weight to the affirmation that follows it, as will presently be shown. The affirmation seems to be free from textual and grammatical difficulties and inherently more probable, and at the same time corresponds with the address to Jehovah and the scope of the Psalm.

In order to make the construction clearer, "I say" of ver. 2 is repeated in ver. 3. The connective *vav* at the beginning of the second line, which only attaches a further description of "the holy," is virtually appositional, as often elsewhere, especially in poetic parallelism. It might be translated "even," but it is as well omitted.

The scope of the section may be thus developed. The Psalmist first declares his personal confidence in Jehovah as the absolute good, and alone to be worshipped and adored; and then turning to his countrymen, who had been peculiarly distinguished by Divine favour, he protests against idolatry, as dishonouring God, and fruitful in misery to all that practise it, and expresses a determination, in which he might reasonably expect them to join, never to defile his hands or his lips with worship so derogatory to the God of Israel.

Surely this protest and declaration are grand enough to stand in this place, and they prepare the way for the fervid appeal in expansion of the leading thought, "I have nought that is good beside Thee," that sweeps through the Psalm to its very close.

A few words yet need to be said about the third verse. Why this parenthesis, postponing the expected utterance, and, some might think, encumbering the sentence by unnecessary words? On the contrary, it is full of meaning and force. It reminds them of two things, which should shame them out of every idolatrous thought, and bind them forever to God's service. First, the Israel he addresses is a "holy nation" (Ex. xix. 6, Deut. vii. 6, xiv. 2); a people set apart by the distinguishing favor of their covenant God, as His own. For the word "holy" here does not refer to individual purity and goodness, as if he were addressing the holy in distinction from the wicked among his own countrymen, but to the whole people as separated from and exalted above all the nations of the earth by their relation to God. He therefore has claims to their undivided homage that should never be forgotten. Secondly, they dwell in a goodly land, a rich heritage, for which they are indebted to his special favour. For the Hebrew is peculiar here. It is not simply *qedôshim ba'arets*, a lightly defining genitive, about equivalent to *my fellow-countrymen*, or (as Ewald) referring to those who were then at home, in distinction from himself, an exile. It forms a separate relative clause, with the subject *hêmah* (*these*) thrown forward under the heavy accent "who in the land these;" as if laying stress upon their exclusive and permanent possession of that land, in connection with God's claim upon them, which he now asserts. If they are a "holy people," this is a holy land. It is His gift, to be held by their descendants to the latest generation under special promise of His gracious presence and blessing. As sacred soil, to defile it by idolatry is simply monstrous.

The added expression of his personal delight in them comes in only incidentally, giving greater impressiveness and tenderness to the admonition, as prompted by his loving wish that they should not bring upon themselves miseries unmeasured by forgetting God their Redeemer.

If we are right, then the protest and plea that follow come out with tenfold cogency by this emphatic allusion to God's special claims, and the rhetorical and logical value of the interruption by parenthesis is very great. The solution proposed binds together the first four verses, and suggests the natural division of the Psalm into three strophes, 1-4, 5-8, 9-11.

(5) **Dealt out as my portion.** Heb. *my portion of lot*, that is, the portion that has fallen to me by lot. — **Sure title.** Heb. *possession of lot*. *Hhelqi* in the first line of the verse, and *gôrali* in the second line are synonyms, meaning primarily, *the stone* used in casting lots, and then *the lot* itself as a mode of distribution. The force and beauty of the poet's allusion are quite unintelligible under a literal rendering. Our translation gives a slight glimpse of the significance of the lot in connection with the ownership of property

in the rendering "*sure title*," rather than the literal "possession by lot." There is evident allusion to the distribution of land by lot at the first settlement of Canaan. Each family in Israel by the command of God received its portion by the casting of the lot. The result was not regarded as fortuitous, but as disposed and determined by God Himself. In each case the portion was accepted as a direct Divine gift. It was to be held in *inalienable possession through all time.* A creditor might establish a claim to temporary possession, but in the fiftieth year it must go back to the original owner. No title, therefore, could be stronger, no claim more sure and permanent, than that which was thus acquired. In the case of the Psalmist the property acquired and possessed as an inalienable gift was not a fair estate on the productive Israelitish territory, but the great God Himself, to be his own God forever.

(6) **Amid pleasures the lines have determined my share.** Heb. *the lines have fallen to me in pleasantnesses*, referring to the measuring lines by which the boundaries of each owner were defined. The common use of these words in connection with worldly success is a perversion of the thought of the Psalmist, which results from not observing the close connection between the fifth and sixth verses. — **Is mine.** This is emphatic, contrasting his own blessed portion with that of others who rejoice in pleasant homes and fertile fields, property of great value in the estimation of men. But what is their lot, if they have only this, compared with that of the man who can say, Thou art my portion, O God?

(7) **My longings.** Heb. *my reins.* In the Hebrew psychology the reins, or kidneys, were the seat of the deepest and strongest desires and affections that control our nature, which must now be otherwise expressed in order to be intelligible. It is not the reason, or the conscience, of which the poet is speaking, but that innermost function of his being that apprehends God as his portion and his joy, and longs after Him with intense desire. By night upon his bed this irresistibly impels him to express his confidence and hope in the living and faithful God. See Job xix. 27, where the reins are the seat of ardent desire and hope.

(9) **My spirit.** Heb. *my glory;* referring to his immortal nature, as in vii. 6.

(10) **Unto death.** Heb. *to Sheol,* the place into which the spirit passes when it leaves the body (see on vi. 5), and so it involves the broad idea of death as a condition. It is sometimes elsewhere personified as an evil power that gains the mastery over the man. See xviii. 5. — **Him Thou lovest.** Heb. *Thy hhāsīd.* See note at iv. 3. — **To consume in the grave.** Heb. *to see the pit.* As in xlix. 10, its equivalent is *to suffer death,* to have a full personal experience of the power of death and the grave. It therefore involves the idea of corruption, although the meaning *corruption* for the noun here used must be given up. The Septuagint rendering, as used by the Apostle Peter in Acts xiii. 35–37, is true to the thought, if not an absolutely literal rendering of the words. On the contrary, in Hebrew usage, as continued in the N. T., *to see life* is to experience and enjoy it; Eccl. ix. 9, John iii. 36.

XVII.

PRAYER FOR HELP AGAINST UNRIGHTEOUS PERSECUTORS.

ALL careful interpreters have noticed the striking similarity at many
points between this Psalm and the sixteenth. It touches not only
single characteristic words, but variations in style and structure, echoing
the writer's frame of mind. Especially the ruggedness and harshness of
the language, and difficult structure of sentences in parts where his soul
was wrought up in intense moral indignation, as for instance against idolatry in xvi. 3, 4, and against the flagrant profligacy of his enemies and of
the wicked in general in xvii. 13, 14. It is especially to be noticed that
these two Psalms express in their closing sentences the same blessed hope
of joy hereafter in the presence of God, and of beholding His glory.

The descriptions of the Psalm are in remarkable correspondence with
David's situation when persecuted by Saul, especially when pursued and
hemmed in by the forces of Saul in the wilderness of Maon; 1 Sam.
xxiii. 25.

*The prayer is threefold: 1. That God will hear the right (1-5). 2. That He will
defend the faithful (6-12). 3. That He will disappoint the persecutor (13-15).*

A PRAYER OF DAVID.

1 Hear the right, O Jehovah,
    Attend to my wailing, give ear to my prayer,
  For it comes not from lips that deceive.
2 Let my sentence go forth from Thy presence,
  And on deeds that are just let Thine eyes be intent.
3 Thou camest by night, and hast proven my heart;
  Thou hast tried me, and findest no planning of evil,
    And transgression is not in my mouth.
4 In the doings of men, by the word of Thy lips,
  I have noted the paths of the oppressor;
5 My steps have held firm to Thy footprints,
    I walk with unwavering tread.

6 And I, because Thou wilt answer me, call Thee, O God;
  Incline Thine ear to me, hear Thou my plea.

7 Show Thy marvellous kindness,
  Thou Saviour of those that take refuge
  In Thy right hand from all their assailants.
8 As one guardeth his eyeballs, protect me;
  In Thy shadowing wings let me hide
9 From my wicked destroyers,
  From the foes in their hate that surround me.

10 Their gross heart they have closed,
  With their mouth they speak proudly;
11 In our steps they are now round about us,
  Their eyes they have fastened upon us,
    And would fain bring us down to the earth.
12 Like a lion they are eager to raven,
  Like the young of the lion that lurk in the jungle.

13 Arise, O Jehovah, confront and subdue them;
  Save my life by Thy sword from the wicked,
14 From men by Thy hand, O Jehovah, the men of the world,
    Who in life have their portion:
    Thou fillest their greed with Thy treasures;
  They have sons and are satisfied,
    Wealth, too, they leave to their children.
15 But I on Thy face shall in righteousness gaze;
  When I awake, I will feast on Thy form.

(3) The text is somewhat doubtful. The sense given is obtained by a change in the accentual division of the verse, which is now generally admitted to be erroneous. If the Massoretic division is retained, the best rendering is that of Delitzsch, —
"Thou hast tried me,—Thou findest nothing
 If I think evil, it doth not pass my mouth."
The rendering of the A. V. cannot be maintained. The word translated "I am purposed" can only be a noun, and it cannot express an act of the will, but is always used of plotting or planning in an evil sense.

(4) **I have noted.** Heb. *shāmartī*, *I have kept* before me, that is, *noted* that I might avoid them. — **The oppressor.** Lit. *the violent man*, one whose life in the pride of his strength is full of outrage and injury.

(6) **And I, because, etc.** The emphatic pronoun; he founds his expectation of being heard on his personal experience in the past.

(10) **Their gross heart.** Heb. *their fatness;* fig. for a heart that is covered with fat, and that becomes insensible to all noble emotions; of those whose hearts are closed by their own selfish will; compare lxxiii. 7 and cxix. 70.

(14) **Greed.** Heb. *belly.* — **They have sons and are satisfied.** A. V. *who are full of children.* Heb. *yis-be'ū bānīm.* The primary signification of the verb is *to be full;* but when used of men, usually *to be sat-*

isfied, describing here the common desire of men of wealth to have heirs to their name and possessions.

(15) **But I.** The pronoun is emphatic, exhibiting the contrast in both members of the verse between himself and those he has been describing. — **Gaze**. Heb. *hhāzāh*, a fixed and eager look, as on an object fascinating and delightful; especially of seeing God. See text and note at xi. 7. — **When I awake,** — the awaking to a new life, as contrasted with the life in this world, in which the others have their portion (ver. 14). In the Old Testament, as in the New, death is a sleep, after which there must be an awaking to joy and blessedness. — **Will feast on.** Heb. *'esb'āh* (אשבעה), the imperfect tense with the voluntative termination *āh;* lit. *will fill myself with.* — **Thy form.** He anticipates a visible manifestation of the Divine glory, which shall constitute the brightness of heaven. The rendering of the A. V. retained by the R. V., *with thy likeness*, is ambiguous and misleading. It may mean, and many so understand it, with Thy likeness impressed upon myself, — *with being like Thee* (comp. 1 John iii. 2). But the parallelism forbids this. *Thy face*, in the first line, and *Thy form*, in the second, are equivalent. The same word is used of a manifestation of the Divine glory to men, referring to Moses, in Num. xii. 8: " The *form* of the Lord shall he behold," — alluding to Ex. xxxiii. 18-23.

XVIII.

A MEMORIAL HYMN, RECOUNTING GREAT DANGERS AND WONDERFUL DELIVERANCES.

THIS is a hymn of praise after deliverance from deadly perils. It is also found with slight verbal alterations at 2 Sam. xxii., in connection with that part of David's history that is mentioned in the title. The writer of the Books of Samuel found it already in existence as a song of David. Its composition probably belongs to his later life. It is evidently a thankful retrospect of God's wonderful dealings with him, referring especially to the time when his life was most beset with dangers, — his bitter and protracted persecution by Saul, his expulsion from his throne and kingdom by Absalom, and the fierce foreign wars that distracted him for a long time thereafter. But from all these he had been graciously delivered, and from a peaceful old age he now looks back with wonder and gratitude. He combines the whole of that stormy past in one idealized and glowing picture. In the imminent peril described, he gives us the concentration of many perils, and in his description of a gracious interposition, the concentration of repeated interpositions, brought to a common focus at which they are seen as one, with corresponding intensity. In the poet's imagination it is a Theophany, a visible exhibition of the presence and power of the great Jehovah in behalf of His servant, in such extremity that nothing less than this could have saved him. His style is majestic, his conceptions vivid, and his language graphic. It has been well said that this wonderful composition bears the marks of the classic age of Hebrew poetry. With the exception of the matchless sixty-eighth Psalm, it has no rival in this whole collection.

The constant shifting from one to the other of the two principal tense forms has given some trouble to translators, in their inclination to regard the perfect tense as relating to the past, and the imperfect to the present or future. The events depicted are all in the actual past, and might have been so presented. But the poet adds greatly to the intensity and interest of his picture by throwing himself into the midst of the stirring incidents of the past, and frequently describing them as if they were in the present. In the former part of his description he freely intermingles the two forms of the verb. But in transferring his conceptions to another language, we are compelled to avoid confusion, as between ideal and actual time, by using generally the historic tense. Yet even we, in animated narration, often so far idealize as to describe past events as if now passing before us in succession, and without creating the slightest embarrassment. This prepares us for the continuous use of our own present tense, as best representing the Hebrew imperfect, from ver. 24 to the close.

1. Affection and confidence growing out of personal experience presently to be described (1-3). 2. He is in peril, he cries to God and is heard (4-6). 3. God appears in his behalf in earthquake and tempest (7-15). 4. His deliverance, and its connection with his previous life as approved by God (16-23). 5. God is righteous and faithful (24-30). 6. A further recital of God's gracious aid against his enemies (31-45). 7. Fervent blessing for the help afforded, and vows of thanksgiving and praise among the nations (46-50).

FOR THE LEADER OF THE CHOIR. BY THE SERVANT OF JEHOVAH, BY DAVID, WHO SPAKE TO JEHOVAH THE WORDS OF THIS SONG WHEN HE DELIVERED HIM FROM ALL HIS ENEMIES, AND FROM THE HAND OF SAUL; AND HE SAID:

1 Dearly do I love Thee, Jehovah, my strength, —
2 Jehovah, my fortress, my cliff, my deliverer,
     My God, and my rock upon which I take refuge,
  My buckler, my tower, and the horn that has saved me.
3 I call on Jehovah, all worthy of praise,
  And He gives me escape from my foes.

4 The breakers of death raged about me,
  Destruction's strong torrents dismayed me;
5 The spirit-world's cords were engirdling,
  Confronting me, snares laid by death.
6 In my anguish I called on Jehovah,
     I cried to my God for His help;

From His palace He heeded my voice,
   For my cry to Him came to His ears.

7 Then the earth was sore shaken and trembled,
   The hills were convulsed to their base;
And because He was angry they swung to and fro.
8 A smoke mounted up from His nostrils,
   A fire that consumed from His mouth,
And thereby bright flames were enkindled.
9 He bended the heavens, and came down,
And thick darkness was under His feet.

10 He rode on a cherub and flew,
   Swept along on the wings of the wind;
11 He made darkness His covering,
   His screen round about Him,
Darkness of waters, dense clouds of the sky;
12 Out the darkness before Him,
   And through His dense clouds,
There came hailstones and flashes of fire.

13 Jehovah then thundered from heaven,
The Most High then uttered His voice,
   With hailstones and flashes of fire.
14 He shot forth His arrows and scattered them,
   Lightnings abundant dismayed them;
15 The deep bed of the sea could be seen,
   The base of the world was laid bare
      At Thy threatening, Jehovah,
At the blast of the breath of Thy nostrils.

16 He reached from on high, and He grasped me,
From great waters He drew me;
17 From my mightiest foe He delivered,
From mine enemies stronger than I.
18 In my day of sore pressure they faced me,
But Jehovah became my support;
19 He brought me forth into room unconfined,
For in me He delighted and saved me.

20 Jehovah rewards as He findeth me righteous,
   He regards my cleanness of hands in His sight;
21 For the way of Jehovah I kept,
   And I have not by sin gone astray from my God.
22 For all His commands were before me,
   His statutes I put not away;
23 And I thus became blameless before Him,
       I abstained from my sin.

24 So Jehovah rewards as He findeth me righteous,
   And seeth my hands to be clean;
25 With the loving, Thou showest Thee loving;
   With the perfect, Thou showest Thee perfect;
26 With the pure, Thou showest Thee pure;
   With the stubborn, Thou showest Thee firm;
27 For Thou, a lowly people Thou savest,
   But arrogant eyes bringest low.

28 For only through Thee doth my lamp give its light,
   Jehovah my God illumines my darkness;
29 For through Thee do I rush on a troop,
   Through the help of my God do I leap over walls.
30 As for God, without spot is His way;
       The word of Jehovah is tried as by fire;
   A shield He becomes unto all that take refuge in Him.

31 For who is a God save Jehovah,
   Or who is a rock save our God, —
32 The God that so girds me with strength,
   That I bound without harm on my way;
33 Gives me feet like the feet of a hind,
   And makes me stand firm on my heights.
34 My hands, too, He trains for the battle;
   And I bend the steel bow with mine arm.
35 Thou givest me also Thy shield of salvation,
   Thy right hand upholds,
       And Thy lowliness exalts me.

36 Thou makest beneath me full space for my steps,
   And my feet do not falter;
37 I pursue and come up with my foes,
   I return not before I destroy them;
38 When I smite them they cannot arise,
   But helpless fall under my feet.

39 Thou hast girt me with strength for the battle,
   Mine assailants Thou bringest beneath me;
40 Through Thee do I seize on my fleeing foe,
   And mine enemies wholly destroy;
41 They cry, but find no one to save them,
   To Jehovah, but He gives them no answer;
42 I crush them like dust in the wind,
   Pour them out like the mire in the street.

43 From the strife of the people hast Thou placed me in safety,
   At the head of the nations hast placed me;
     I am served by a people I knew not;
44 When first their ear hears they obey me,
   And men of strange lineage come cringing;
45 Men of strange lineage are withering away,
   They come forth from their strongholds with trembling.

46 Jehovah hath life, ever blessèd my Rock,
   And exalted be God, my salvation, —
47 The God who gives vengeance,
   And makes nations submit to my rule;
48 Who from enemies saves me,
     Yea, exalts me above mine assailants,
   My deliverer from violent men.

49 For this, O Jehovah,
     Midst the nations high praise will I give Thee,
   And the music of harps shall resound to Thy Name;
50 Who showeth His king His great power of salvation,
   And His kindness to David, His anointed,
     To him and his offspring forever.

(1) **Dearly do I love Thee**. Heb. *'erhhamkā*, imperf. of *rāhham*. This word in its intensive form (*Piel*), and its derivative noun *rāhham*, describe God's love for man in its most tender and gracious aspect. The radical meaning of the verb is *to be soft;* then, as in the Arabic, *to cherish, to soothe*, as a child. It so comes to describe *tender* and sympathetic feeling. It most nearly approaches the Greek στοργή, *natural affection*, the yearning tenderness of parent for child. Having its roots in deep sympathy, it takes its hue from the condition of its object. As expressive of God's tenderness for men as weak and suffering, it takes the form of *compassion*. It is used in ciii. 13, "as a father *pitieth*," and in Is. xlix. 15, "a mother *hath compassion*." It may well express the reflex filial affection, but so occurs here only. Yet not in the same intensive form does this child of God here use it to express his tender affection for his Divine Father. And here the conditions are changed. There is no room for compassion, for the Father is strong and blessed forevermore. But the yearning tenderness is there, and utters itself in this beautiful word. The verb "*love*," that has to serve for so many words that have no equivalent in Hebrew and Greek, is not sufficiently expressive here without an intensifying adverb. The rendering adopted above is that of the Geneva Bible.

(2) **My cliff**. Heb. *sēla'* (סֶלַע), a *cliff* or *crag*, formed by *cleavage*, and consequently *steep, precipitous*, — usually the reference is to *inaccessibility*, and so *safety*, as lifted above danger (see xl. 2), but sometimes to a *cleft* or a hiding-place in the high rock. — **And the horn that has saved me**. Heb. *my horn of salvation*. The "horn" is an image of victorious strength, derived from animals that depend on their horns for protection; see Deut. xxxiii. 17; 1 Sam. ii. 1. Frequent in the Psalms.

(4, 5) **The breakers**, as in 2 Sam.

xxii. 5; unquestionably the original text, suiting "torrents" in the parallelism and avoiding the improbable occurrence of "cords" in two successive verses. — **Destruction**. Heb. *beliyäal* (בְּלִיַּעַל); usually of moral, but here of physical, worthlessness; death as destroying the substance. Comp. Is. xiv. 9: "Sheol stirreth up the *Rephaim*." A. V. *the dead;* lit. *the weak ones, the shades;* also xlix. 14: "Their form shall be for Sheol to consume." "Destruction" here, and Sheol, the spirit-world in ver. 5, are both in parallelism with "death" as a condition into which men pass when they cease from the earth, and its nearest equivalent. In ver. 5 death and Sheol are personified as hunters capturing their prey.

(6) **His palace**. See note at v. 7; also at xi. 4, where, as here, the reference is to God's dwelling-place in heaven.

(8–10) The appearance of Jehovah for the deliverance of His servant is here symbolized by the activity of great natural forces, earthquake and tempest, the heavy clouds sinking toward the earth, and from them burning flames leaping forth, as symbols of the hot wrath of God, the consuming terrors of the Almighty.

(10) If by a comparison of passages like civ. 3, and Is. lxvi. 15, we understand David according to the description of Ezekiel, He rides upon the cherub as His living throne-chariot. The throne floats upon the cherubim, and the cherub-throne sweeps forward upon the wings of the wind. The manager of the chariot is God Himself, hidden behind the thick thunder-clouds. — *Delitzsch*.

(12) **Flashes of fire**. Heb. *fiery coals*, that is, the lightnings flashing like blazing coals

(13) **Thundered**. The thunders represent God's voice speaking from the clouds in threatening tones. See Job xxxvi. 2, Ps. xxix., and lxxvii. 18.

(15) **The deep bed of** the sea. Heb. *'appiqē ma-im*, lit. *the channels* (or *deep cuttings*) *of waters*.

See the same in Ps. xlii. 1, of *deep pools* in the bed of torrents; here of the lowest depths of the sea.

(16) **He reached**. Heb. *He sent forth* (His hand). See 2 Sam. vi. 6. — **From the depths of the waters**. Connected with laying bare the bed of the ocean in ver. 15, and a reminiscence of ver. 4.

(19) **Room unconfined**. Heb. *a broad place*, that is, the opposite to the "sore pressure" (Heb. *narrowness*) of the preceding verse.

(21) Heb. *have not done wickedly from my God*. The idea of separation from God by wickedness is conveyed by the preposition "*from*." Indulgence in sin is in itself separation from God.

(30) **Tried as by fire**. Heb. *tsâruph*, from *tsaraph, to melt;* literally of refining metals. See the same word in xii. 6, "Silver the earth has tried as a furnace." Here as there in allusion to the promise of God to deliver His people as tested and proved in the hot fires of persecution.

(32) **The God**. Heb. *'El, the Mighty One*, preceded by *'Elohim* in ver. 31. The change is required here; the power of God strengthens man for combat and victory, under the figure of putting on a girdle in preparation for successful activity. See the same in ver. 39, with the addition "for the battle." — **That I bound unharmed on my way**. (So Ewald.) Heb. lit. *maketh perfect my way* (as A. V.).

But the poet's thought is quite lost sight of, unless we remember that we have before us a warrior so fully equipped for battle that as he rushes forward into the thick of the fight he receives no wound. The reference is to physical perfection, as against being cut down and disabled.

(34) **The steel bow**. Heb. *n'hhôsheth*. A. V. here and elsewhere *brass*. The metal seems to have resembled *copper* rather than brass. It must have had the hardness and elasticity of steel, which best represents the meaning here.

(40) **Through Thee do I seize on my fleeing foe**. Heb. *Thou givest me the nape of the neck of my foes*. This literal rendering hides its full meaning somewhat below the surface. The "nape of the neck" indicates that the foe is fleeing from him, and by the help of God he is enabled to overtake and grasp him.

(44) **When first their ear hears**. Heb. *at the hearing of the ear*, that is, at the report received by the ear, or when they received tidings of his victories, they did not wait for his coming, but in terror hastened to submit. — **Come cringing**. Heb. *lie to me;* their professed submission was not honest; at heart they were rebels still.

(45) **Men of strange lineage**. Heb. *sons of foreignness*, that is, foreigners by birth.

XIX.

THE GLORY OF GOD IN NATURE AND SCRIPTURE.

MODERN criticism finds in the nineteenth Psalm two fragments, the former incomplete at the close, the latter at the beginning, without relation or coherence. It is suggested that long after their composition by different authors, by blunder or chance they have come together as one under the name of David. The difference in subject is emphasized in proof of this, also the difference in structure and rhythm; and it is mentioned as decisive, that in the earlier portion the only Divine name mentioned is *'El*, the Mighty, and in the latter Jehovah.

But admitting the difference in subject between the two, they only present different aspects of the one God in His self-revelation to man.

It seems not improbable that the same poet, having before him his description of the glory of God in the heavens, may have added, perhaps after a lapse of time, a description of the revelation of the Divine glory in His holy law. It has been remarked, too, that the difference in tone and rhythm corresponds with the change of subject. Moreover the transition from the one Divine name to the other is quite in harmony with the use of *'Elohim*, a developed form of *'El*, in connection with the creation of the world in Gen. i., and of *Jehovah 'Elohim*, in connection with God's dealings with man in Gen. ii. As Moll has observed, " the identity of the God of revelation with the Creator is the fundamental principle of the Theocracy, and is expressly testified to by the Old Testament from the earliest times."

Nothing of importance can be adduced against the Davidic authorship of the Psalm. Hitzig has pointed out strongly marked features indicating its antiquity, and particularly that David wrote it.

The following sentence from Professor Briggs is of interest: " This Psalm may be compared with the eighth, an evening psalm similar in its contemplations to this morning psalm. In both the contemplation of the Divine glory as declared in the heavens begets a feeling of humility in the soul of the Psalmist, which rises in Ps. viii. 5 into the expression of faith and confidence in God, in Ps. xix. 11–14 into prayer for forgiveness, preservation, and acceptance."

1 *The glory of God is set forth in the universe (ver. 1), and especially in the alternation of day and night, as connected with the circuit of the sun (4–6). 2. The excellency of the law of God (7–10). 3. A prayer to the God of nature and grace (11–14).*

FOR THE LEADER OF THE CHOIR. A PSALM OF DAVID.

1 The heavens are telling the glory of God,
 The skies showing forth the work of His hands.
2 Day to day pours out speech,
 Night to night utters knowledge;
3 There is no speech and no language
 Where their voice is not heard.
4 Into all the earth their line is gone forth,
 Their words to the end of the world,
  Where God pitched a tent for the sun;
5 And he like a bridegroom comes forth from his couch,
 Like a warrior he springs on his path;

6 From heaven's extreme he comes forth,
   His circuit extends to its bounds,
  And nothing can hide from his heat.

7 The law of Jehovah is perfect,
   Refreshing the soul ;
  The witness of Jehovah is faithful,
   Making wise the untaught ;
8 The precepts of Jehovah are right,
   Rejoicing the heart ;
  The commands of Jehovah are faultless,
   Enlightening the eyes ;
9 The fear of Jehovah is pure,
   Enduring forever ;
  The judgments of Jehovah are true,
   And all of them righteous ;
10 They are more to be wished for than gold,
  And sweeter than honey as it drops from the comb.

11 By these, too, Thy servant is warned,
  And great the reward of those that observe them.
12 Who can discover his errors?
  Absolve me from those that I know not ;
13 And keep back Thy servant from sins of presumption ;
   Let them not rule me ;
    I then shall be upright,
  Found free from the greater transgression.
14 Let come with acceptance the words of my mouth,
   And my whispers of heart in Thy presence,
  O Jehovah, my Rock and Redeemer !

"The heavens" and "the skies" in the first verse, and "day" and "night" in the second, are personified. "All the host of them," the moon and the stars, are to be included. There is no reference to the Pythagorean music of the stars, of which the Hebrews knew nothing, but these creations of the wisdom and power of God are ideally vocal, and there is no discord. The participles in the first verse express permanent occupation. They are really concrete nouns, in accordance with the most frequent use of the pres. act. part. in Hebrew. The heavens are the narrators, the skies the exhibitors, of God's glory in creation, as if appointed to their office from the beginning; and they never weary of their task.

(1) **Telling.** Heb. *m'sapp'rim,*

from *sāphar*, *to tell* or *count* numbers; then to *tell*, to *recount* or *narrate* incidents in detail. — **God**. Heb. '*El;* the primary idea is that of power, from '*ûl* (אול), *to twist*, then *to be strong* (see note on v. 4); especially appropriate in a description of the works of creation. — **The skies**. Heb. *rāqia'* (רקיע), Eng. Bib. *firmament*. This clumsy rendering, which cannot very well be displaced from the text in use, is derived from the "firmamentum" of the Latin Vulgate, and this last from the *stereōma* of the Septuagint. Both are founded upon a misconception of the radical meaning of the word, as if it were from *rāqa* (רקע), in the sense *to beat* into a solid mass, whereas by common consent it means *to beat out*, or expand by beating. It embodies the idea of the great spread of the arch over our head. The revisers could find no suitable English word to substitute for it. *Expanse* is too abstract and unfamiliar. There is no better word than *sky*, especially in the breadth it acquires in the plural *skies*. Some liberty has been taken in cl. 1, in substituting for " Praise Him in the firmament of His power," " Praise Him in the skies spread out by His power."

(2) **Pours out**. Heb. *nāba* (נבע), *to gush out with, pour forth copiously*, of a fountain in Prov. i. 23. This with the following "utter," properly *breathe*, indicates the free, smooth expression of what they have to tell. In eloquent silence they move on and shine on, through all their appointed seasons and years.

(3) **There is no speech and no language where their voice**. According to Hebrew usage the third negative, in the second line, is not a repetition of the preceding *'ēn, there is not*, but *b'lī*, one that belongs only to relative, or privative clauses. The *relative* rendering of the A. V. " *where* their voice;" that is, in which their voice, recognizes this. So the same negative is rendered very properly in lxiii. 1, " where no

water is;" that is, in which there is no water. Or the negatives may all be *privative*, and depend on ver. 4: " Without speech, and without language, etc., into all the earth " (Ewald, Heb. Synt.). But we should expect strong emphasis on these utterances as being universally intelligible. That they are voiceless is so manifest as to need no mention, and is comparatively unimportant.

(4) **Where**. Heb. *bāhem, in them,* referring to the preceding nouns of the verse, especially the last, "the end " (extreme limit) of the world.

(5) **And he**. The pronoun is here emphatic in the Hebrew, calling attention to a new object singled out from all the rest for fresh personification. — **Comes forth**. The Hebrew conception of the "rising" and " setting" of the sun is a "coming out" and "going in." — **Couch**. Heb. *hhuppah*, properly a *screen* or *canopy*, a bed with curtains. Often at sunset we can see the gorgeous curtains behind which the sun retires to rest, or in the morning we can see them flaming with his rays as he again bursts upon the world and hastens upward, as if exhilarated by sleep.

(5) **A warrior**. Heb. *gibbôr*. Sometimes used as an adjective, *mighty*, but most frequently, as here, it is a noun; but always of a military *hero, champion*, or *chieftain*. See xxiv. 8, xxxiii. 16, xlv. 3, cxx. 4, cxxvii. 4, etc. — **Path**. Heb. *'ōrahh*. The word is usually translated *path*, and is very frequent in the Psalms. It is never used in connection with *racing*, and there is nothing to indicate that sense here. Evidently it is the war-path.

(7) **Refreshing the soul**. Heb. *m'shībath nephesh*. It is an idiomatic expression of recovering from faintness and languor. See 1 Sam. xxx. 12, Lam. i. 11. The *soul* is the individualized personal life. *Conversion* (A. V.) cannot be referred to, but the re-animation of one who loves the Divine law, and feels him-

self through its communications ever revived and inspirited for duty and trial. So the same word in xxiii. 3.

(10) Heb. *the droppings from honeycombs*.

(12) **Errors**. The Hebrew term covers all sins of ignorance, inadvertence, and infirmity, for which special sacrifices were provided in the Levitical law; Lev. iv. 2.

(13) **Sins of presumption**. These were the deliberate, high-handed, and daring transgressions which were excluded from mercy; Exod. xxi. 14; Deut. xvii. 12.

(14) **Whispers**. Heb. *hegyôn*, from *hāgāh*. See on i. 2, ii. 1.

XX.

PRAYERS FOR THE KING ON THE EVE OF BATTLE.

THIS Psalm and the one that follows it are connected with the same events, and very similar in style and structure. We have here a prayer for Divine assistance in a war with foreign enemies who are provided with horses and chariots (ver. 6), and thus had apparently an advantage over the Israelites, who were forbidden to keep many horses, Deut. xvii. 16. It is probable that the king referred to is David, and that he was the author. For by Solomon and his successors the above restriction was no longer observed; 1 Kings x. 26-29. The Psalm was carefully prepared for use in connection with the sacrifices commanded before going out to battle, and is intended for a responsive service.

The opening verse presupposes sacrifices and vows by the king himself. The assembled congregation invoke for him safety and success. The Psalm is smooth and flowing in style, but very spirited, and expresses strong confidence in God.

The historic occasion is probably the war with the mighty host of the Assyrians recorded in 2 Sam. x. 18, 19.

1. An intercession by the people in behalf of the king, who is offering his sacrifices (1–5). 2. A solo by a priest, expressing confidence in the saving power of God (6–8) 3. A closing invocation by the people in chorus (9).

FOR THE LEADER OF THE CHOIR. A PSALM OF DAVID.

1 Jehovah respond in Thy day of distress,
  The Name of the God of Jacob protect thee;
2 From His holy hill send thee help,
  Out of Zion sustain thee;
3 Thine oblations, remember them all,
  And thine offerings by burning accept;   [Selah.]
4 As thy heart shall desire may He give thee,
  And all thy purpose fulfil.

5 Thy salvation is ours, and we joyfully shout ;
   A banner we lift in the Name of our God ;
      "All thy prayers will Jehovah fulfil."

6 I now know that Jehovah will save His anointed ;
   From His holy heaven will He answer
      In deeds of power by His saving right hand.

7 In their chariots some glory, and some in their horses,
   But we in the Name of Jehovah, our God :
8 As for them, they sink down and they fall,
   It is ours to rise up and stand firm.
9 Save the king, O Jehovah ;
   May He hear us when we call.

(1) **Distress.** Heb *tsārāh, hard pressure ;* the stress of battle when the foe is pressing hard, and confident of victory. — **The Name of the God of Jacob**, a probable reference to Gen. xxxv. 3. "The Name of God of Jacob " is the self-manifesting power and grace of the God of Israel (Del.). It is equivalent to the Name Jehovah, the Divinely appointed symbol of gracious manifestation to Israel. — **Protect thee.** Heb. *set thee on high*, but figuratively, put thee out of danger. So lxix. 29 : lix. 1, etc.

(3) **Oblations.** Heb. *m'nāhhōth, meal offerings*, a part of which, mingled with incense, was placed upon the altar to be consumed with the burnt offering, and was called *'azkā-rāh, memorial*, and the sweet odour of which, ascending, was supposed to commend the worshipper to the remembrance and favour of God. There is probably reference to this in the "remember." — **Accept.** Heb. *make fat*, that is, may He find it fat, and so approve it, as rich, nourishing food.

(5) **Thy salvation is ours.** A transition here from prayer for Divine help to the joyful recognition that God has come for deliverance. He is now more directly addressed

as the God of salvation. It is assumed that the heart of the king has gone up with the heart of the people, and now the prayer is heard, as if fire from heaven had consumed the sacrifice. The banner is triumphantly unfurled. — **A banner we lift.** Heb. *nidgōl*, from the noun *dègel, a banner*. The passive participle *nigdāl* occurs in Cant. vi 4. "Terrible as a bannered army." — "**All thy prayers will Jehovah fulfil.**" Eng. Bib. "The LORD fulfil all thy petitions." The sudden recurrence from exulting confidence to the supplication that preceded it is unaccountable, especially as it is immediately followed by a more emphatic assurance of acceptance and deliverance in ver. 6. It can hardly be that the distress and anxiety that prompted the preceding prayer so suddenly returned, to be as suddenly dissipated. (So Del. and others) Ewald does better in translating as future, "Jehovah will fulfil." Taking it in connection with the triumphant display of the banner, it may be taken as a motto or absolute profession of faith in Jehovah with reference to the impending conflict, and possibly as the inscription on the banner now unfurled.

(6) **I now know.** A solo by some Levite in the temple, who

may perhaps personate the king. It grows immediately out of the preceding, and is upon the same key.

(7) In their chariots some glory. A historic reference that proves that the Psalm belongs to the time of David. See Deut. xvii. 16, where it was forbidden that a king should multiply horses. This was not transgressed till Solomon. See 1 Kings x. 26–29. The emphatic pronouns in ver. 6 and 7 express forcibly a twofold contrast between them and their enemies. See, with reference to the army now arrayed against Israel, 2 Sam. x. 18.

(9) The chorus, in which the whole people unite. The pointing of the Massoretic text makes the king the subject. "Jehovah save; may the king answer us when we call." The versions and interpreters are all against it. The subject of the whole Psalm is that God will save His anointed king. It is scarcely possible that the word *mélek, king*, should immediately follow the verb, except as its object.

XXI.

THANKSGIVING FOR VICTORY, AND CONFIDENCE FOR THE FUTURE.

THIS Psalm in its subject is a companion to Ps. xx., and resembles it in being constructed for responsive worship. The Divine blessing and aid there implored with reference to the approaching conflict were granted; and the victorious king has returned, and with his people again visits the house of God, that they may offer their united thanksgiving.

1 A grateful acknowledgment by the congregation of God's goodness in bestowing bodily and spiritual blessings upon the king in answer to prayer (1-7). 2. An address to the king, perhaps by a representative priest, expressing confidence of further Divine blessing upon his sons and his kingdom (8-12). 3. A chorus, calling upon God to manifest His power, that His people may praise Him the more (13).

FOR THE LEADER OF THE CHOIR. A PSALM OF DAVID.

1 How glad is the king in Thy strength, O Jehovah;
Because Thou hast saved him, how great is his joy!

2 The wish of his heart hast Thou granted,
The desire of his lips Thou hast not denied.   [Selah.]

3 For with blessings of good didst Thou meet him,
A crown of fine gold hast Thou set on his head.

4 He asked of Thee life, and life didst Thou give him,
Even days long extended, forever and aye.

5 His glory is great because Thou hast saved him;
   Grandeur and power hast Thou lavished upon him

6 Thou grantest him blessings enduring,
   And the joy of Thy face gives him cheer.

7 For the king puts his trust in Jehovah,
   Through the love of the Highest he cannot be shaken.

8 For Thy hand shall find out all his foes,
   Thy right hand shall find those that hate him.

9 When Thy face shall appear,
       As a furnace of fire wilt Thou make them;
   Jehovah in wrath will consume,
       And a fire shall devour them.

10 Their fruit wilt Thou sweep from the earth,
   And their seed from the children of men.

11 Because they think evil against Thee;
   They have planned an ill purpose, but cannot perform;

12 For their back wilt Thou force them to turn,
   When Thine arrows are aimed at their face.

13 In Thy might be exalted, Jehovah;
   We will sing with the harp to Thy power.

(2) **The desire.** Heb. *'arésheth*. This word occurs only here, but the meaning is fully established from the Arabic. Delitzsch gives *longing*.

(3) **A crown of fine gold.** This may be figurative, meaning that by His recent grace God had confirmed him in his royal dignity, as if now newly crowned; or it may be anticipative of what occurred after the conquest of the royal city Rabbah, when the crown of the Ammonitish king was set on his head. See 2 Sam. xii. 30.

(4) **Days long extended.** See note at xxiii. 6. — **Forever and aye.** See note at xlv. 6.

(7) **Cannot be shaken.** Heb. *bal yimmût*. The verb *mût* means *to shake or totter* by violent convulsion. Here, and often elsewhere, it implies a shaking down, a complete overthrow. The usual rendering. "moved," of the English Bible is always inadequate. See at xlvi. 2.

(12) **Their back.** Heb. *the shoulder.* — **Thine arrows are aimed at.** Heb *Thou preparest Thy bowstrings against.*

(13) **Sing with the harp.** Heb. *nashirû v'zammerû.* Hendiadys of the verb. See note at vi. 10; and for the verb *zimmer*, at vii. 17.

XXII.

ELI, ELI, LAMA SABACHTHANI.

A PSALM peculiarly sacred and precious, as portraying typically the sufferings of Christ. No other is so frequently quoted in the New Testament, as fulfilled in him. The reasons assigned by some for referring it to a later time than the life of David, especially for putting it after the captivity, are most unsubstantial. This is proposed on the assumption that the sufferer of the Psalm is not an individual, but the nation, and that we must look for the historic background to some great national calamity. But much more probable is the reference to special sufferings of the writer, which are there idealized, sublimated, intensified. * His mind is so wrought upon by the Spirit of prophecy as to pass consciously beyond the limits of his sharpest personal experience of anguish to the sufferings of a greater king upon the same throne, whose kingdom, as had been promised, should be everlasting. It would not seem strange to him, in view of the determined and malignant hostility which he encountered for a long time after he ascended to the throne, that his most glorious successor, in whom Israel's hopes should be realized, must fight his way against fiercer opposition, more bitter hatred, and more excruciating personal suffering. There is no indication, however, in this Psalm of an apprehension of the deeper significance of these sufferings in connection with the priesthood of the Messiah and the forgiveness of sins.

There are three principal divisions: 1. Anguish and lamentation, struggling through to some faint hope, and renewal of prayer (1–11). (a) A cry of distress, continued but unavailing (1, 2). (b) Yet God is holy, and when the fathers cried he helped them (3–5). (c) In contrast with this he himself is despised and scoffed at (6–8). (d) Yet he remembers God's goodness in his earliest years and will pray (9–11). 2. He spreads out his misery anew and in detail (12–21). (a) His peril from enemies raging like fierce beasts (12, 13). (b) Its effects upon his person (14, 15). (c) Indications that the end is near (16–18). 3. Thanksgiving and hope (22–31). (a) Praise for his deliverance in the congregation of his brethren (22–24). (b) He will bring his thanksgiving, when others will unite in praising God (25, 26). (c) A forecast that all the earth will turn to Jehovah and serve him forever (27–31).

FOR THE LEADER OF THE CHOIR. SET TO "'AYELETH HASHAHAR."
A PSALM OF DAVID.

1 My God, O my God, why forsakest Thou me?
    Why so far from my help are my outcries of suffering?
2 O my God, in the daytime I call Thee,
      And Thou givest no answer,
  And by night, but I get no relief.

3 Yet holy art Thou,
   Enthroned on the praises of Israel.
4 Our fathers were trustful in Thee,
   They were trustful, and them Thou deliveredst;
5 Unto Thee they cried out, and were rescued,
   In Thee did they trust, and were not put to shame.

6 But I — am a worm, not a man,
   Am reviled by mankind, am despised by the people;
7 All that see me deride me,
   They thrust out the lip, and the head toss about:
8 They say, "Roll on Jehovah.   Let Him give him help;
   Let Him rescue the man He delights in."

9 Yea, in truth, for through Thee did I come to be born,
   On the breast of my mother Thou mad'st me to rest.
10 Upon Thee was I cast from my birth;
   Thou wert my God when my breath was first drawn.
11 Oh, be not far off, for sore trouble is near,
   And there is no one to help me.

12 Mighty bulls are about me,
   The strong ones of Bashan surround me;
13 Against me their mouth opens wide,
   As if lions were rending and roaring.
14 I am poured out like water;
        All my bones are disjointed;
   My heart is like wax,
        It is melted within me.

15 My strength is dried up like a potsherd,
   My tongue cleaves fast to my jaws;
        In the dust of death dost Thou lay me.
16 For dogs come about me;
   A band of ill-doers hems me in;
        They mangle my hands and my feet.
17 All my bones I can number;
   Mine enemies gaze at me gloating,
18 Distribute my garments among them,
   Cast lots on my vesture.

19 But Thou, O Jehovah, remove not far off,
 My strength, oh come quick to mine aid;
20 Snatch my life from the sword,
 My one only life from the power of the dog;
21 From the mouth of the lion, oh, save me,
 From the horns of wild cattle —
  Thou hast answered my prayer.

22 I will herald Thy Name to my brethren,
 In the midst of the church will I praise Thee.
23 Praise Jehovah, ye that fear Him;
 Give Him glory, all ye offspring of David;
  Stand in awe, all ye offspring of Israel.
24 For the pain of the sufferer He despised not, nor spurned,
  And concealed not His face,
 But heard when he cried for His help.

25 From THEE comes my praise in the great congregation;
 Before those that fear Him my vows will I pay.
26 The lowly shall eat and be filled,
 They that seek for Jehovah shall praise Him;
  May your heart get new life evermore.

27 All the bounds of the earth
  Shall remember and turn to Jehovah;
 All the families of nations
  Shall worship before Him;
28 For Jehovah is King,
 And He governs the nations.
29 All the rich of the earth shall eat and bow down,
  And before Him shall kneel,
   All those that go down to the pit —
 Even he that cannot preserve his own life.

30 An offspring shall serve Him,
 And speak of the Lord to the next generation;
31 They shall come and His righteousness herald,
 People yet to be born shall be told what He wrought.

(1) **My God, O my God.** The Divine Name here twice used is '*El, the Mighty.* See on xix. 1. His appeal in suffering and peril is to Omnipotence as alone adequate to his deliverance from the malignant human power into whose grasp he has fallen. — **Why.** Heb. *lāmāh, for what* reason, here accented as emphatic in connection with what he knows of God; why will not He whose power is infinite, and whose love and truth are unquestionable, interfere in my behalf? The question is not one of impatience, faultfinding, and arraignment, but of grief and entreaty. Further, this *lāmāh,* although not repeated in the Hebrew, like the same interrogative at x. 1, covers the whole verse. It binds its two portions together as containing virtually a single question. The second line is an explanatory development of the first. — The construction exhibited in our rendering, which makes "far" the predicate, placed before the subject, "my outcries of suffering" (Ges. Gr. § 148.2), corresponds with the margin of the R. V. The rendering of the text in A. V. and R. V. cannot be fairly extracted from the Hebrew. (So Delitzsch, Moll.) — **Forsakest Thou me?** The tense is the perfect, but describes conditions that continue in the present. The meaning of the verb is defined by the following parallelism, "Far from my help"— that is, far from bringing me Thy help — "are my outcries of suffering." This thought has further expansion in the following verse, — my unceasing prayers are unavailing: I still suffer unrelieved. Like the question, "Why standest Thou afar off?" in x. 1, the words must not be pressed as if God were actually far off, or might ever withdraw from any person or place. God is said to come to a place when He manifests His power there, and to depart from it when He ceases to do so. In the case before us the cry is that of one in great agony under the pressure of injustice and cruelty. The question is not of the personal presence or absence of God, as affecting the comfort of the sufferer, but of helping or not helping. He addresses God as within hearing, though by His inaction it might seem as if He were far away: and he still appeals to Him as his own God, who has not cast him off. Will He not be moved to deliver him from his foes? The meaning of the verb here is that of the same verb in xvi. 10, "Thou wilt not abandon my soul unto Sheol;" that is, Thou wilt not let it remain there in suffering, and not, Thou wilt not leave it without Thy presence. We add that elsewhere in the use of this verb, when God is said to *forsake* any one, the meaning is to withdraw or withhold His help from him. Gen. xxviii. 15, Josh. i 5, Ps. xxvii. 9, lxxi. 9; so of a people, Ps. ix. 11, Is. xlii. 16, liv. 7; of a land, Ezek. viii. 12, ix. 9.

This outcry is entitled to special attention in its connection with the sufferings of our blessed Lord upon the cross. In the supreme moment of anguish, He expressed in these words the intensity of His woe. He is supposed also to indicate a kind of suffering of which we get no glimpse elsewhere, not even in the dark hour of Gethsemane. It touches the mystery of the atonement at its most mysterious point, introducing an element which is as painful as it is incomprehensible. In what intelligible sense could the infinite Father forsake His only begotten Son, leaving Him alone in absolute darkness in His dire need? It is easy to say that this was part of the penalty of sin which He suffered vicariously as the representative of man. But the chief and constituting element in that penalty is the wrath of God. There are some who are quite ready to speak of Christ as the object of Divine wrath in some putative and representative sense, — a thought painful beyond expression. But surely, never for a moment can this Divine sufferer have been the object of the Father's displeasure, — He that came from heaven to do His will, to execute the purpose of infinite love in the redemption of a ruined world, at whatever personal cost. Never, on the contrary, was the thought of the Father fixed on the Son with more unqualified approbation and intense affection: "Therefore my Father loveth me, because I lay down my life, in order that I might take it again." Never can He have been more thoroughly conscious that He is doing the Father's will, and must be approved, and could never be forsaken of Him, than now.

But if language have a clear and definite meaning, how can all this be reconciled with the cry? Simply upon the sound exegetical principle that language cannot be legitimately interpreted outside of historical and contextual relations, which constantly affect the meaning of words.

In this terrible outcry our Saviour is giving vent to His anguish under the torture of the cross, in an expression that came from the lips of a sufferer who centuries before had represented Him typically. The echo, in aught that is doubtful, must be interpreted from the original cry, the true significance of which we have attempted to give. The Divine sufferer must have used the words in accordance with the thought of the Psalmist. How important then is the application of sound principles here.

(3) **Holy**. Lit. *separated* from all evil, only and in all things to be adored: imputing to God absolute perfection, never to be disparaged, but always to be loved and trusted. —**Enthroned**, etc. A reference to God's exaltation as King. Holiness is enthroned. So evil must and will be put down, and goodness, truth, and purity will triumph at last. This is recognized in Israel's songs of praise. It may be that as these,

with clouds of incense, rise toward heaven, they are contemplated as a royal pavilion, within which in holy majesty He exalts Himself against unrighteousness and oppression.

(6) **Not a man**. He is degraded in the estimation of others of his kind, and no longer treated as one of them. Comp. Is. lii. 14.

(8) **They say, Roll on Jehovah**. Spoken ironically to the sufferer by some of the persecuting crowd, who then turn with mocking faces to their fellows; but the scoffing words addressed to them are intended to reach his ears.

(9) **Yea, in truth**; suggesting an intermediate unexpressed thought. The sufferer confirms, as actual truth, what has been said tauntingly. Indeed God delights in him, for He has graciously sustained him from the first moment of his life.

(11) **And**. Heb. *for*. In Hebrew as in Greek the causal conj. *for* is sometimes repeated before a further reason assigned, as it would not be in English.

(16) **They mangle**. Heb. *ka'ari*. The form is precisely that which would usually be translated, *like a lion*, and some insist upon that meaning here. But the sense given is unsuitable to the context, and the oldest Greek translators have given it as a verb. It seems an irregular form, either participial or the perfect indicative, of the verb *kûr*, *to dig into*. Prof. Cheyne translates *they have digged into*, and remarks, "Few now maintain the reading *like a lion*, which is too short a phrase to be intelligible, interrupts the lifelike description of the dogs, and seems at any rate to assume that the lion specially attacks the hands and the feet."

(17) **Gaze at me gloating**. Heb. *yabbîtû yir'û bî, they stare, they look on me*. Hendiadys of the verb; see on vi. 11. The former verb describes a fixed gaze; the latter is the ordinary word for seeing, but when followed as here by the prep.

b', upon, it means *to look with delight, to gloat upon.* Comp. Eng. *to feast the eyes upon.* See xxxvii. 34, liv. 7, cvi. 5, cxii. 8, cxviii. 7, Job iii. 9, xx. 17.

(20) **My one only life.** Heb. *y' ḥidi, my only one,* implying *preciousness,* as one that cannot be replaced; like an only child. So xxxv. 17.

XXIII.

JEHOVAH MY SHEPHERD.

A PSALM so simple, familiar, and precious, scarcely needs introduction or comment. There is no good reason for separating from the general current of opinion that ascribes it to David as its author. It is so like Ps. iii. iv. xxvii. lxiii., and others that are connected with David's outcast life during Absalom's rebellion, and it fits in so well with the incidents of that period, that we look in vain for a more satisfactory historic coincidence. Especially in reading ver. 5, we may think of Mahanaim, and of the bountiful provision brought out by Barzillai and his companions for the refreshment of David and the faint and weary that were with him (2 Sam. xvii. 27–29). It may be remarked here, as at v. 7, that the mention of the house of Jehovah by no means implies that the temple was already built. In the earliest Semitic usage any place of lodging was called *Bēth* (a *house*); and any place where God is worshipped and manifests His presence would be so designated, see Gen. xxviii. 17. Consequently the tabernacle (Heb. *tent*) is repeatedly called so; Josh. vi. 24. 2 Sam. xii. 20, etc.

The characteristic feature of the Psalm is calm and untroubled confidence in God, and unfaltering expectation of a blissful future in His presence.

1. He is under the care of Jehovah as his shepherd (1–4). 2. He is a guest at a royal banquet, and what he now enjoys is the earnest of richer grace in the future (5–6).

1 Jehovah is my Shepherd,
    I suffer no want;

2 In pastures of verdure He makes me lie down,
    By the rest-giving waters He leads me.

3 He refreshes my soul,
    And along the right paths
        For His Name's sake He guides me.

4 Yea, e'en when I walk in the valley of the shadow
of death,
No ill do I fear, for Thou art beside me,
Thy sceptre and staff are my comfort.
5 A table Thou spreadest before me,
In front of my foes;
My head Thou anointest with oil,
And alway my cup is o'erflowing.

6 There only shall follow me goodness and love
All the days of my life,
And for days long extended,
I shall dwell in the house of Jehovah.

(1) **I suffer no want.** The so-called tense is the *imperfect;* and all the verbs that follow, till the last verse, are in the same form. With no adverbial or other designation of time, this form represents the English present in the continuous flow of vivid description. This includes ver. 4.

(2) **Verdure.** Heb. *dĕshe', freshly sprouting grass.* — **Rest-giving,** not *still,* which might be stagnant, waters. Heb. *m'nŭhhŏth,* lit. *waters of resting-places;* that is, by the side of which there are inviting places of rest, with perhaps a reference to the soothing sound of a running stream.

(3) **Refreshes.** Heb. *y'shŏbĕb, brings back* to the animation and vigour it has lost by the heat and hardness of the way. See on xix. 7. — **The right paths.** Lit. *straight* or *level paths.* But in his poetic conceptions he never loses sight of the higher relations they illustrate. Paths smooth and safe for the sheep represent, on the plane of spiritual life, activities directed by the holy and righteous will of God. He has a higher "Name" to be glorified than that of "Shepherd."

(4) **Yea, e'en when I walk.** Heb. *gam ki 'elek.* The present (Heb. *imperfect*) tense, preceded by the particle *when* (not the hypothetical *though*), must exhibit an actual experience. In the shepherd life "the valley of death-shade" represents a dark and perilous defile through which the timid flock may have to pass (Briggs). The Psalmist refers to those deep wadies, or wild and gloomy ravines, which abound in the mountains of Palestine, the rocky sides of which are filled with caverns, the abode of beasts of prey. It is often necessary for the shepherd to lead his flocks through these wadies and across these ravines, and it is always perilous, even to the shepherd himself. There is no reference here to death itself, but to the *peril* of death, so often experienced in life. — **Thy sceptre and staff.** The latter of these words (*mash'ān*) is always *a staff* for support. The former (*shĕbet*) may be *a club* for protecting the flock from wild beasts (Cheyne), or the shepherd's crook, a symbol of guidance. But the two staves in Zech. xi. 7 (Briggs), will not help us here, for each staff in the shepherd's hand has a special, defined significance for that place. It seems more probable that just at this point of transition to a royal banquet, in which he is to be the guest of Jehovah, the Psalmist remembers that his Divine Shepherd is also a *King,* a conception eminently suited to the confi-

dence just expressed, as well as to what follows. So *shêbet* in ii. 9, xlv. 6, cxxv. 3, etc.

(5) **A table Thou spreadest.** Probably referring to 2 Sam. xvii. 27–29.—**My head Thou anointest.** Anointing the head of a guest with richly perfumed oil is a symbol of honour, welcome, and joy (xlv. 7, Luke xi. 46).—**My cup.** The cup represents refreshment, blessing, and gracious fellowship (xvi. 5, 1 Cor. x. 16).—**Is always overflowing.** Heb. *r'vâyâh, overflowing fulness;* from *râvâh, to be drenched* or *sated* with drink. The word here is neither verb nor adjective, but a noun. The cup is named by its permanent characteristic, always filled to the brim and running over.

(6) **And love.** Heb. *hhésed;* it sometimes expresses kindness between men, but more frequently the kindness of God to men, in feeling and act. Often translated in the English Bible (after Coverdale) *lovingkindness;* much oftener, and less happily, *mercy.* It is the active principle in a moral nature that is most opposite to selfishness, — love, not so much a passion as an energy, ever working out beneficent results. Prominently it is God's steadfast interest in His covenant people (Hupfeld), but not necessarily restricted to this. Its deepest and richest significance is confined to gracious spirits, who yield themselves to God's will in loving obedience. As for others, it is excluded from their inner being by their own moral repulsion, and can only produce some exterior and temporary effects. Yet in its inherent quality, tendency, and

capability, it is the same. Just as the same sunlight that falls upon an opaque substance and brightens only the outer surface, leaving darkness within, may fall upon one that is thoroughly transparent, and meeting with no obstruction, it penetrates and irradiates its innermost depths. —**For days long extended.** Heb. *for length of days.* We have already had this expression in xxi. 4, followed by *ôlâm vâ'ed, forever and alway.* The present life only may have been in the mind of the Psalmist, but it is scarcely possible in view of his relation of grace and favour with the eternal and unchangeable Jehovah, as just described, that he should not have regarded this relation as necessarily permanent. It may be that he used this in preference to either of the usual expressions of everlasting continuance, because his mind was fixed on his residence in God's house, not so much with reference to its having no end, as to its being a life of protracted and continual enjoyment. Every day and every hour must have its own peculiar sweetness, which might be extended to eternity without weariness. Assuming that he shall never again be cast out into the wilderness, he brings out more fully all that lies in the last word of the familiar combination "forever and alway." See note at xlv. 6. The same expression, "extension of days," is found in xci. 16. —**I shall dwell,** or *I shall return,* depending on a doubtful form; but if the latter is the true meaning, a subsequent *abiding* is implied.

XXIV.

THE GLORIOUS KING COMES TO ZION.

THIS Psalm celebrates the removal of the ark from Kirjath Jearim to the ancient citadel of Zion; 2 Sam. vi. 17; compare xi. 11, and 1 Kings i. 39. It is similar to Ps. xv., which was perhaps a later amplification of the first six verses. This former part is strongly marked, as distinct in subject and character from the following four verses, and each portion seems complete in itself. Some have inferred from this that two Psalms originally separate have here been combined. But it is in the highest degree probable that in preparing a liturgical Psalm for the occasion referred to, the service would be divided for use at different stages of the advance of the solemn procession toward the spot where the sacred burden should be deposited. The former section (1–6), like Ps. xv., would be suitable when they reached the foot of Mount Zion or during the ascent, and the latter when they reached the gateway of the citadel.

"Incorporated in Israel's hymn-book, this Psalm became, with regard to its original occasion and purpose, an Old Testament Advent hymn in honour of the Lord who should come into His temple, Mal. iii. 1; and the cry, 'Lift up, ye gates, your heads,' obtained a meaning essentially the same as that of the voice of the crier in Is. xl. 3. 'Prepare ye Jehovah's way, make smooth in the desert a road for our God.' In the New Testament consciousness, the second appearing takes the place of the first, — the coming of the Lord of Glory to His Church, which is His spiritual temple ; and in this Psalm we are called upon to prepare Him a worthy reception." — *Delitzsch.*

1. A general chorus, praising the God of the whole earth (1, 2). 2. The question, perhaps of a single voice, "Who may ascend," etc., the place chosen for the ark, already by anticipation regarded as "holy" (3). 3. The response, perhaps also a solo, "He whose hands are clean," etc. (4, 5). 4. The voice of the general chorus, "This is the race," etc. (6).

The second part, sung at the gates of Zion: *1. A general chorus, calling upon the citadel to open its gates to Jehovah (7). 2. The response of a single voice, describing Jehovah as the King of glory (9). 3. The general chorus takes up the question and replies with emphasis (10).* (So Briggs, following Delitzsch.)

BY DAVID. A PSALM.

1 The earth is Jehovah's, and the fulness thereof,
   The world with all that are dwelling therein;
2 For by Him was it based on the seas,
   It was He made it firm on the floods.

3 Who may ascend the hill of Jehovah,
In His holy place, who may rise up?
4 He of innocent hands, and a heart that is pure;
Who lifts not his soul unto evil,
And takes no oath with deceit.

5 Blessing is his from Jehovah,
And righteousness, given by his God of salvation;
6 Such is the race that inquireth to know Him;
It is Jacob, O God, that seeketh Thy face.
7 Lift your heads, O ye gates;
Be lifted, ye doors of old time,
That the glorious King may come in.

8 Who is He — this glorious King?
Jehovah, the Strong One, the Champion,
Jehovah, the Champion in battle.
9 Lift your heads, O ye gates,
Be lifted, ye doors of old time,
That the glorious King may come in!

10 Who is He — this glorious King?
Jehovah of hosts
Is Himself the glorious King.

6) **It is Jacob, O God, that seeketh Thy face.** The construction here is peculiar, and the meaning not obvious. It is possible that *Elohai* has been lost from the text, and that the true reading is "that seek Thy face, O God of Jacob" (so the oldest Syriac, and most commentators) or, "the face of the God of Jacob" (so the Sept., Cheyne, and others). But Hengst., Delitzsch, and Hitzig accept the text as correct. It seems clear that God is addressed, and in our rendering we insert the Divine Name, not as a correction, but for greater perspicuity. The name Jacob evidently refers to the descendants of the patriarch, especially those who show the same believing and obedient spirit. It is in explanatory apposition with the descriptive phrases in this and the preceding line. The name, as suggestive of Jacob's faith and piety, sums up the whole, and stands in the Hebrew in the emphatic place at the close of the verse. Those who worship God sincerely are true children of Jacob.

(8) **The Champion.** Heb. *gibbôr*, *a mighty man, warrior, hero.* See xix. 6, xlv. 3.

XXV.

PRAYER FOR DELIVERANCE AND GUIDANCE.

THIS Psalm cannot be identified with any special events in the life of David, or in the history of Israel. Nothing decided can be said to prove or disprove its authorship by David. It is one of the nine Alphabetical Psalms, in this respect resembling the ninth and tenth, and also in the fact that the alphabetical arrangement is not rigidly carried out. But this artificial structure by no means proves that it is of late origin.

The fundamental thought, carried steadily through, is that God favours and helps those that seek and serve Him.

1. The Psalmist asks for deliverance, instruction, and forgiveness (1-7). 2. The didactic element prevails, one verse of prayer (ver. 11) being preceded and followed by three on the advantages of meekness and obedience (8-14). 3. Seven verses of entreaty for personal deliverance, followed by a single intercession for Israel (15-22).

BY DAVID.

1 Unto Thee, O Jehovah, I lift up my soul;
2 In Thee do I trust, O my God;
    Let me not come to shame,
And give me not up to the triumph of foes.
3 Yea, let none that are hoping in Thee come to shame,
Let those come to shame who are wantonly faithless.

4 Thy ways, O Jehovah, make me know,
Teach me Thy paths;
5 In Thy faithfulness guide me and teach me,
For Thou art my God of salvation,
    I wait for Thee all the day long.

6 Bear Thy mercies in mind, O Jehovah,
    And Thy manifold kindness,
For these are of old;
7 And bear not in mind the sins of my youth,
    Nor my many trangressions;
But bear me in mind in Thine own loving-kindness,
    For the sake of Thy goodness, Jehovah.

8 Good and upright is Jehovah,
  He will, therefore, teach sinners His way;
9 The humble He guides in right doing,
  The humble He instructs in His way.
10 All the paths of Jehovah are kindness and truth,
  To those keeping His covenant and precepts.
11 For Thy Name's sake, Jehovah,
  Mine iniquity pardon, because it is great.
12 What man is he that revereth Jehovah?
  Him will He teach in the way he should choose.
13 In blessing his soul shall abide,
  And his offspring inherit the land.
14 In close bonds with Jehovah are they that revere Him,
  And His covenant He gave to instruct them.
15 Mine eyes ever look to Jehovah,
  For my foot He will free from the net.
16 Turn toward me with pity,
  For loneness and suffering are mine.
17 Relieve the distress of my heart;
  Bring me forth from my troubles.
18 Behold me in suffering and anguish,
  And forgive all my sins.

19 Behold, too, my foes, for they are many,
  And the hatred they bear me is cruel.
20 Oh, keep me, and deliver my soul;
  Let me not come to shame,
    For I hide me in Thee;
21 Let integrity and uprightness keep me,
    For in Thee is my hope.

22 Redeem Israel, O God,
  Out of all his distresses.

(3) **Faithless**. Heb. *bogedīm, the treacherous;* here having reference to their relations with God. Sin is treachery to solemn obligations. — **Wantonly**. Heb. *rēgām,* lit. *emptily;* that is, without cause: not even the poor excuse of provocation, or of personal advantage, but from sheer wantonness: all things being equal, they prefer evil to good.

(14) **In close bonds**. Heb. *sôd;* prop. *a conclave* or *divan* for consultation on important affairs. It implies the most confidential relations,

in which personal feelings and purposes are freely interchanged. It is used of the secret association of wicked men in Gen. xlix. 6. Here of familiar converse with God in which the knowledge of things hidden from others is imparted; "Shall I not tell Abraham?" To be in such fellowship with God is the result of covenant relations. Hence what follows in the same verse in Genesis and here. See lv. 14.

XXVI.

THE PLEA OF THE UPRIGHT SURROUNDED BY INFAMY AND OUTRAGE.

THIS Psalm resembles the preceding at various points. Perowne observes the following difference : "There are wanting in this Psalm those touching confessions of sinfulness, and pleadings for forgiveness, which in the other are thrice repeated. Here is only the avowal of conscious uprightness,—an avowal solemnly made in the sight of the Searcher of hearts, and deriving no doubt much of its intensity and almost impassioned force from the desire on the part of the singer to declare his entire separation from and aversion to the worthless and evil men from whom he here distinguishes himself."

1. He appeals to God as the witness of his sincerity and integrity (1–3). 2. He describes his own life in his separation from the wicked (4, 5), and in his delight in the sanctuary and its worship (6–8). 3. An entreaty that he may be distinguished from sinners, and enjoy the loving favour of God (9–11). 4. The prayer is changed into rejoicing and praise (12).

BY DAVID.

1 Give me justice, Jehovah,
  For my walk has been blameless;
 With unwavering trust I look to Jehovah.
2 Search me, Jehovah, and try me,
 And prove Thou my spirit and heart.
3 For THY lovingkindness I keep in my sight,
 And I order my way in Thy truth.
4 I sit not in council with men that are false,
 With dissemblers I go not;
5 The assembly of transgressors I hate,
 With the wicked I will not combine.
6 My hands I in innocence wash,
 And will compass Thine altars, Jehovah,
7 To proclaim with the voice of thanksgiving,
 And to tell all Thy wonderful works.

8 I love, O Jehovah, the house where Thou dwellest,
The place where Thy Glory abides.

9 Do not gather my soul with the wicked,
My life with the men that shed blood;

10 Who have crime in their hand,
Full of bribes is their right hand.

11 But I in integrity walk;
In Thy pity redeem me.

12 On a plain have my feet come to stand;
Jehovah will I bless in the choirs.

(4) **Sit . . . in council.** Heb. *yâshab*. In ver. 5 the same word is rendered *combine*. Prop. *to sit*, yet not confined to sitting as a bodily posture, but modified by the connection. Sometimes, on a throne, *to be enthroned*, or in a house, *to dwell.* Here of association for evil purposes; sitting in conclave or consultation about some wicked enterprise in which they combine. Notice the parallelism in both verses, and see the notes on the derived noun *moshâb*, prim. *a seat*, at i. 1, and at xxv. 14.

(8) **Where Thy Glory abides.** The parallelism with "Thy House" in the preceding line shows that he refers to the manifestation of God's presence in the Holy of Holies.

(12) **On a plain have my feet come to stand, etc.** Delitzsch: "The Epilogue. The prayer is changed into rejoicing, which is certain of the answer that shall be given. Hitherto shut in, as it were, in deep trackless gorges, he even now feels himself to be standing upon a pleasant plain, commanding a wide range of vision, and now blends his grateful praise of God with the song of the worshipping congregation and its full-voiced choirs." The Heb. *maghêlim* (prop. *convocations*) is sometimes used, in connection with singing praise, of the organized band of singers, Ps. lxviii. 26.

XXVII.

DEVOUT CONFIDENCE IN GOD.

WE connect this Psalm, like the preceding, with the rebellion of Absalom and David's separation from the privileges of the sanctuary. In the midst of danger we see the same confidence in God, and the same courageous spirit that cries in Ps iii., "I fear not the myriads of people that surround me on every side." This, however, applies only to the first seven verses. From that point the subject and style change, and the authorship by David is more questionable. The portion 7–14 may have been added at a later date by another hand; yet possibly by David himself in a different mood.

1. Fearless confidence in the grace and power of God (1-3). 2. Longing for the house of God with anticipated satisfaction (4-6). 3. Prayers for Divine favour, help, guidance, and deliverance (7-12). 4. Self-encouragement to fuller confidence (13, 14).

BY DAVID.

1 Jehovah is my light and salvation ;
     Then whom shall I fear?
  Jehovah my stronghold of life ;
     Before whom shall I tremble?
2 When the wicked assailed me,
     To feed on my flesh,
  My oppressors and foes
     Then stumbled and fell.
3 Though a host camp against me,
     My heart shall not fear ;
  Should war rise against me,
     Even then would I trust.

4 This one thing I asked of Jehovah,
     And still do I seek ;
  To dwell in the house of Jehovah
     All the days of my life,
      That with joy I may gaze on Jehovah's fair grace,
       And make search through His royal abode.
5 When the evil day comes,
     In His bower will He hide me ;
  In His tent out of sight will conceal,
     On a rock will exalt me.
6 And higher shall now be my head
     Than my foes that surround me ;
  In His tent shall mine offering be jubilant praise,
     With the harp will I sing to Jehovah.

7 Hear my voice when I call, O Jehovah,
  Show me pity and answer ;
8 When Thou saidst to me, " Seek ye My face,"
  From my heart came response,
    " O Jehovah, Thy face will I seek."

9 Conceal not Thy face from my sight;
  Reject not Thy servant in anger;
Cast me not off nor forsake me,
  O God, my salvation.
10 For forsaken by father and mother,
Jehovah Himself will receive me.

11 Teach me Thy way, O Jehovah;
In plain paths do Thou lead me
  Because of my foes;
12 To the will of mine enemies yield me not up,
For false witnesses rise up against me,
  And cruel the words they breathe out.
13 Oh, had I not hope of enjoying
  The goodness of Jehovah in the land of the living —
14 Look to Jehovah;
Hold fast, let thy heart be courageous,
And look to Jehovah.

---

(4) That with joy I may gaze. Heb. *hhāzāh, to gaze upon;* see on ix. 11, xvii. 15. Like *rā'āh, to see,* and other verbs of sense, when followed by the preposition *beth* (ב), it means *to see with pleasure, to feast the eyes upon.* So also the verb that follows, *biqqēr, to search out, to explore,* having the same preposition, implies an object of desire, and great satisfaction in finding. — **Fair grace.** Heb. *sweetness* to the taste; then *pleasantness* to the eye. It refers to all gracious manifestations. See xc. 17.

(6) Shall my offering be jubilant praise. Lit. *I will sacrifice sacrifices of loud sound;* Heb. *terū'ah* (תרועה), comp. *zibhhē tôdāh, sacrifices of praise,* Ps. cvii. 22. "The context decides whether. the sound is that of a trumpet (Num. x. 10), a voice singing (xxxiii. 3), or a voice shouting (lxxxix. 16)." — *Cheyne.* — **With the harp will I sing.** Heb. *I will sing and will harp.* On the second of these verbs (*zimmēr*) see note upon vii. 17.

(10) For forsaken by father and mother. This is not hypothetical as in the A. V., but a statement of fact. It does not imply wilful desertion by parents, nor their recent loss, and does not oblige us to attribute the Psalms to some other than David. It only asserts that in great trouble all help from man fails him; he has no father or mother on earth, but the all-sufficient God has gathered him into His own household, and protects him from all harm. The former verb is in the perfect tense; the forsaking is a thing of the past. The latter is in the imperfect, a continuous parental kindness.

(13) Oh, had I not hope, etc. In his strong feeling he leaves the sentence incomplete. It implies that his faith in God has sustained him, and virtually says that if it had not he must have perished.

XXVIII.

CRY FOR HELP, AND THANKSGIVING.

THERE is nothing in this Psalm that indicates positively its historic connection. Yet there are points of resemblance to several of those that seem to belong to the time of Absalom's rebellion. There is no good reason for setting aside the title which ascribes it to David.

1. He prays for deliverance and judgment (1–5). 2. He gives thanks for both (6–9).

BY DAVID.

1 Unto Thee, O Jehovah, I call;
    Turn Thee not from me in silence, my Rock;
Lest if THOU shouldst keep silence,
    I become like men that go down to the pit.

2 Hear my suppliant voice when I cry for Thy help,
When I lift up my hands to Thy holy retreat.
3 Oh drag me not off with the wicked,
    With those busy in wrong,
Who greet kindly their friends,
    But have evil at heart.

4 Give them wage for their work,
    For the evil they do;
As their hands have wrought do Thou give them;
    Let them have their desert.
5 Because they regard not the deeds of Jehovah,
    The work wrought by His hands,
He will therefore destroy,
    And will not rebuild them.

6 Jehovah be blessed,
    For He heard my suppliant voice.
7 Jehovah, my stronghold and shield,
    In Him my heart trusts and He helps me;
With my heart full of joy,
    In my song will I praise Him.

8 To His people is Jehovah a stronghold,
   To His anointed a fortress of safety;
9 Deliver Thy people, Thy heritage bless;
   Be their Shepherd, and bear them forever.

(2) **Cry for Thy help**. Heb. *shava* (שׁוע), distinctly *to cry for help*, and not merely to express suffering by an outcry. — **Retreat**. Heb. *d'bir*, properly the hinder or inner part. In 1 Kings vi. 19, 22, the inner sanctuary of the tabernacle and temple; the holy of holies.

(3) **Who greet kindly**. Heb. *dibrē shālôm, speaking peace*, but with all the breadth of the Oriental salaam, wishing health, prosperity, and blessing.

(9) **Be their Shepherd**. The Heb verb *rā'āh* (רעה), *to tend a flock*, embracing all that is included in the work of a shepherd. The feeding is a small part of it. The active participle of this verb means *a shepherd*. This verse is delightfully suggestive of Is. xl. 11, which was probably in the poet's mind: "He shall feed His flock like a shepherd, He shall gather the lambs in His arm, and bear them in His bosom."

XXIX.

THE THUNDER-STORM.

THE occasion of this Psalm is a thunder-storm. It is not, however, limited to the outward natural phenomenon, but therein is perceived the self-attestation of the God of the history of redemption. Just as in the second part of Psalm xix., the God of the revelation of salvation is called Jehovah seven times, in distinction from the God revealed in nature, so in this Psalm "the voice of Jehovah" is repeated seven times, so that it may be called the Psalm of the seven thunders (Rev. x. 3).

Between two verses of introduction, and two of conclusion, there are seven verses celebrating the voice of Jehovah.

1 Give Jehovah, ye sons of the mighty,
   Give glory and strength to Jehovah;
2 Give Jehovah the glory of His Name;
   Oh worship Jehovah in holy attire.

3 On the waters the voice of Jehovah!
   It is God in His glory that thunders;
     Jehovah is on the great waters;
4 The voice of Jehovah with power!
   The voice of Jehovah in grandeur!

5 The voice of Jehovah is rending the cedars,
 The cedars of Lebanon Jehovah is rending;
6 And he makes them to spring like a calf,
 Lebanon and Sirion like young of the deer;
7 The voice of Jehovah hews out flashes of fire!

8 The voice of Jehovah convulses the desert;
 Jehovah convulses the desert of Kadesh.
9 The voice of Jehovah brings hinds to their **travail**.
 And the forest strips bare,
 While all in His palace cry, " Glory ! "

10 Jehovah sat enthroned at the flood,
 And Jehovah forever sits enthroned;
 Jehovah gives strength to His people;
 Jehovah is blessing His people with peace.

(2) **In holy attire.** Heb. *b'ha-drath qōdesh*, properly *in holy decoration;* that is, clothed in the vestments worn on the great festivals. So xcvi. 9, and the masc. form *hadrē qōdesh* in cx. 3. It refers here to the dress of the priesthood, and implies with it all the solemn rites of worship as Divinely instituted.

(3) **On the waters.** Not the waters of the sea, but those suspended in the black masses of cloud, xviii. 12, Jer. x. 12.

(7) **Flashes of fire.** The lightnings that dart from the cloud, as if they were produced by the thunder, hewn off from the great mass, and themselves cloven as by some sharp instrument.

(8) **Convulses the desert.** Not perhaps of an earthquake accompanying the thunder-storm (Delitzsch), but of the tremulous motion as of some heavy concussion that accompanies the loudest peals of thunder.

(9) **His palace.** Heb. *hēkāl*. See v. 7. Throughout the Psalm Jehovah is presented in His royal majesty, and every burst of thunder that echoes through His stately abode proclaims His omnipotence, and is a signal to the whole heavenly host to give glory to His holy Name.

XXX.

A THANKSGIVING AFTER RECOVERY FROM DANGEROUS SICKNESS.

EVERYTHING here indicates that David was the author, and that it relates to a personal experience of God's favour in his recovery from almost fatal illness. There is no apparent allusion to the dedication of a house, whether his own palace or the temple, such as we should expect from the title. The Psalm is mentioned in the Jewish Ritual as the song for the Dedication, — referring to the feast instituted in the time of Judas Maccabeus (165 B.C.) to commemorate the purification of the temple from its desecration by Antiochus Epiphanes. Riehm suggests with strong probability that the original title was "A Psalm. By David," and that it was enlarged when it came to be used as just mentioned.

The poet feels impelled to make known God's gracious dealings with him, and to urge all others to the same high confidence that glows in his own heart.

1. Thankful recognition of Divine power and grace in delivering him from imminent peril of death (1–3). 2. A call to others to praise God for His long-suffering and compassion (4, 5). 3. He reviews more specifically his past experiences: (a) his former self-confidence; (b) his delusion dispelled; (c) his expostulations and entreaties (6–10). 4. A final burst of thanksgiving for the great change in his life through God's gracious interposition (11, 12).

A PSALM. A SONG AT THE DEDICATION OF THE HOUSE. BY DAVID.

1 I extol Thee, Jehovah,
    That Thou liftedst me up,
And no joy in my ruin
    Hast Thou given my foes.
2 O Jehovah, my God,
    I cried out for Thy help,
And Thou sentest me healing.
3 From the world underneath
    Hast thou brought up my soul ;
Thou hast called me to life
    From the depths of the grave.
4 O ye men of His love,
    Strike the harp to Jehovah ;
Sing praise to His holy memorial Name.

5 He is wrathful a moment,
　　But gracious a lifetime;
　Though weeping come in at the evening to lodge,
　　Glad shoutings are heard at the dawn.
6 But I said, self-confiding,
　　" I shall never be shaken."
7 Through thy favour, Jehovah,
　　Hadst Thou made my mountain stand strong;
　When Thou hidedst Thy face
　　I quailed in dismay.
8 Then to Thee, O Jehovah, I called,
　　I entreated Jehovah:
9 " What wilt Thou gain by my death
　　And descent to the grave?
　Can the dust give Thee thanks,
　　Or speak of Thy truth?
10 O Jehovah, give ear,
　　Let Thy pity be shown;
　Oh help me, Jehovah."
11 A glad change hast Thou wrought,
　　Giving dancing for sorrow;
　Yea, my sackcloth hast loosed,
　　And hast girt me with gladness;
12 That my soul may sing songs,
　　That it may not be silent;
　O Jehovah, my God,
　　I will praise Thee forever.

(1) **Liftedst me up.** Heb. *dillî-thani, hast drawn me up,* as of one sunken in the depths of suffering and horror that are described in the following verses (comp. xviii. 16, lxxxviii. 4, Jon. ii. 3).

(3) **The world underneath.** Heb. *sheol.* See on ix. 15.

(4) **Ye men of His love.** Heb. *hhasîdim,* His *beloved.* See on iv. 3. — **Strike the harp.** Heb. *zamm'rū,* properly, *strike the strings* of a musical instrument; sometimes more general, to *make music.* See on vii. 17. — **Holy memorial Name.** Heb. *zēker qōdesh, holy memorial.* Delitzsch: " Instead of 'the Name of Jehovah,' we find the expression 'memorial' in this instance and in xcvii. 12, after Ex. iii. 15. Jehovah by revealing Himself renders Himself capable of being both revered and remembered, and that in the most illustrious manner. The history of redemption is as it were an unfolding of the name of Jehovah, and at the same time the setting up of a monument, the establishment of a memorial, and in fact of a *holy* memorial, because all God's attestations

flow from the sea of the light of His holiness."

(5) Come in . . . to lodge. Heb. *yalin*, from *lûn*, *to pass the night*, implying merely the night, in distinction from permanent abiding.

(6) But I. Heb. *and I;* the pronoun, otherwise unnecessary, emphasizes the foolish thought of his own heart in contrast with the reality. This emphasis and contrast require the conjunction "*but*" for their expression. — **Self-confiding.** Heb. *b'shalvi*, in *my tranquillity*, arising, as the following words show, from confidence in being able to maintain his position, irrespective of Divine support and blessing. **Be shaken.** Heb. *mût*, *to totter*, as by violent shaking. It anticipates the "mountain" of the following verse. See xxi. 8, xlvi. 2.

(7) My mountain; that is, Mount Zion as representing figuratively the kingdom of David in its promised stability.

(9) Perowne: "The truth seems to be that whilst the *faith* of the Old Testament saints *in God* was strong and childlike, their *hope* of immortality was at best dim and wavering; brightening perhaps for a moment when the heart was rejoicing in God as its portion, and then again almost dying away."

(11) See the counterpart to this verse in Jer. xxxi. 16 — **My sackcloth hast loosed.** Clothing of sackcloth (see Esth. iv. 2) was fastened to the body by a cord as an expression of sorrow and humiliation before God. Comp. "girding of sackcloth," Is. iii. 24.

(12) My soul. Heb. *kābôd* for *kābôdî*, *my glory*, as in vii. 5, xvi. 9, cviii. 1.

XXXI.

ONE SORELY PERSECUTED SURRENDERS HIMSELF INTO THE HAND OF GOD.

THIS Psalm is attributed by Hitzig and Ewald to Jeremiah, on account of some resemblance in thought and language. Moll says to the contrary: "If partly the elegiac softness, and partly the character of the language remind us of Jeremiah, yet as Hupfeld states, there is no evidence in this for the composition of the Psalm by Jeremiah, especially as there are frequently found in this prophet expressions and turns of thought from more ancient books, particularly from the Psalms." This important remark furnishes a reply to many opinions of the modern critical school, assigning to a later date on similar grounds.

1. Prayer for deliverance (1, 2) based on confidence in the grace of God (3–5), especially as previously exhibited to himself (6–8). 2. Description of present trouble, rising anew to protestations of trust, and assurance of being heard (14–18). 3. Thankful praise, with exhortation to believing hope in God (23, 24).

A PSALM OF DAVID.

1 In Thee I take refuge, Jehovah,
    Let me ne'er come to shame ;
    In Thy righteousness grant me an escape.

2 Bend Thine ear and make haste to my rescue;
  Let me find Thee a stronghold of rock,
      A fortified dwelling to save me.
3 For my cliff and my refuge art THOU;
  For the sake of Thy Name Thou wilt lead me and guide me;
4 Bring me out of the net they have hid,
  For from THEE my deliverance must come.

5 Into Thy hand I yield up my spirit,
  For Thou Jehovah, God of truth, hast redeemed me;
6 Those that hope in vain idols Thou hatest;
  But I, in Jehovah I trust.
7 Let me joy and exult in Thy kindness,
  Who hast seen mine affliction,
      Hast known the distress of my soul,
8 And hast not shut me up in the enemy's power,
  But my feet hast Thou set in broad space.

9 O Jehovah, have pity, for I suffer sore pressure;
  Withered through grief are mine eyes,
      Yea, my soul and my body;
10 For my life wastes in sorrow,
      My years pass in sighing;
  Because of my sins has my strength fallen off,
      And my bones are consumed.
11 All my foes make me a mark for reviling,
          Most of all to my neighbours;
      Mine acquaintance behold me with fear;
  Those that see me abroad flee away.
12 Forgotten, like the dead out of mind,
  I become like a thing left to perish;
13 For I hear the sly creeping of many defamers,
      All around there is horror;
  In their plotting against me,
      They would fain take my life.

14 But I, O Jehovah, in Thee do I trust,
  I say to Thee, Thou art my God.

15 In Thy hand are my times;
   Snatch me away from the hand of my foes,
      And from those that pursue me.
16 Make Thy face to shine on Thy servant;
   In Thy great lovingkindness, oh save him:
17 Let me never come to shame, O Jehovah,
      For on Thee do I call;
   Let the wicked come to shame,
      In the world of the dead put to silence;
18 Stricken dumb be the lips that speak lies,
   Those whose words of the righteous are insult,
      With pride and contempt.

19 How great is Thy goodness, stored up for Thy servants;
   Dealt out unto all that take refuge in Thee,
      In sight of the children of men.
20 As a covert Thy presence shall hide them
      From the wranglings of men;
   In a bower Thou wilt screen them
      From contention of tongues.

21 Jehovah be blessed,
   Who shows me His marvellous kindness
      In a city with walls.
22 But I, in my peril I said,
      I am cut off from the sight of Thine eyes;
   Yet surely Thou heardest my suppliant voice
      When I cried for Thy help.
23 Love Jehovah, all that share in His kindness;
      For Jehovah preserveth the faithful,
   But repayeth the proud in full measure.
24 Hold fast; let your heart be courageous,
      All ye that hope in Jehovah.

(2) **Let me find Thee.** Heb. *become to me;* that is, *manifest* or *prove Thyself such.* This does not contradict the claim upon which the plea is founded in ver. 6, which is connected with past manifestations of faithful grace. Virtually, "Let me find Thee now what Thou hast always been in the past."

(5) **Into Thy hand I yield up my spirit.** Memorable and sacred forever are the words in which our

Saviour breathed out His life. Perowne: "*My spirit* (*rûahh*) is more than *my soul* or *life* (*nephesh*). It is not only from sickness and death, but from sin and all ghostly enemies that the man of God would be kept, and therefore he commends to God, not his body or his bodily life alone, but the life of his spirit, which is more precious (comp. Is. xxxviii. 16, 'life of my spirit'). I commend; that is, place as a *deposit, entrust*."

Delitzsch: "The language of the prayer lays hold of life at its root as springing from God, and as also living in the believer, from God and in God; and this life it places under His protection, who is the true life of all spirit life.

"The period of David's persecution by Saul is the most prolific in types of the Passion; and this language of prayer, which proceeded from the furnace of affliction through which David passed, denotes, in the mouth of Christ, a crisis in the history of redemption in which the Old Testament receives its fulfilment. Like David, He commends His spirit to God, not that He may not die, but that dying He may not die; that is, that He may receive back again His spirit,— corporal life in imperishable power and glory."

(6) Thou hatest. The Hebrew text has *I hate*, but the Sept., Vulg., Arabic, and Syriac Versions give the 2d person, which best corresponds with the antithesis that follows.

(7) Who hast seen. This verb and the three following are in the perfect tense, and refer to a past experience of God's mercy.

(8) In broad space. Heb. *bammerhâb*, in contrast with the preceding *tsâroth, distresses* (lit. *straits*).

(11) Most of all. Heb. *m'ōd* (כראד), *especially*. Assuming that this must be a noun, Delitzsch renders it *a burden*, and proves satisfactorily from the Arabic that this meaning is possible. Cheyne translates it *a shaking of the head*. But there is no sufficient reason for departing from the otherwise uniform rendering: lit. *and especially to my neighbours*. The conjunction *and* presents no difficulty. It attaches a clause of further specification.

(12) A thing. Heb. *k'li*. Eng. Bible, *vessel*. But the Hebrew *k'li* is the name for any article whatever that is used for any purpose, and must sometimes be translated *thing;* as in Lev. xiii. 49, 52, 53, 57, 59. Here it is followed by the participle *'obēd, perishing,* or *about to perish*.

(13) The sly creeping of many defamers. Heb. *dibbath rabbīm*. The former from *dâbab*, a mimetic word imitating the tapping of the feet of those going softly about destroying character, and the following line describes the horror of those who hear and believe the base charges of these cowardly slanderers.

XXXII.

THE FORGIVENESS OF SINS.

THIS is the second of the Penitential Psalms (see Ps. vi.). As compared with Ps. li., which belongs to the same class, it shows an advance in the order of gracious experience. There we have the penitent in a tumult of remorse under the burden of fresh sin, crying to God for mercy. Here the storm has subsided. He has been pardoned, and peace has taken possession of his soul, and adoring gratitude for the grace that has been shown. With comparative calmness he can tell the whole story of his personal experience. The key-note, forgiveness of sin, as the only foundation for comfort and hope, is sounded in the first verse.

1. The blessedness of the justified sinner (1, 2). 2. A twofold experience: (a) pain and distress, while he refused confession; and (b) pardon, following immediately upon the penitent acknowledgment of his guilt (3–5). 3. Encouragement of others to seek similar relief, and his personal confidence, on the same basis, of future protection from all evil (6). 4. Exhortation (8, 9) and warning (10, 11).

A MASKIL. BY DAVID.

1 How happy is he
  Whose transgression is pardoned,
 Whose sin is forgiven;
2 How happy the man
  Unto whom Jehovah imputeth no guilt,
 In whose soul no deceit can be found.

3 While I spake not,
  My bones were worn out
 By my outcries all the day long;
4 For Thy hand day and night lay heavy upon me,
 My moisture was turned into midsummer drought.

5 Then to Thee I acknowledged my sin,
   I concealed not my guilt;
  I said, " I confess my ill deeds to Jehovah,"
 And THOU didst lift off the guilt of my sin. [Selah.]

6 For this every man in Thy love
  Shall implore Thee in the time set for finding;
 And when the great waters sweep by,
  He shall surely be out of their reach.
7 Thou art my refuge,
  Thou wilt guard me from evil,
 And with songs of deliverance surround me. [Selah.]
8 Be ye not like the horse or the mule,
  That have no understanding;
 Whose mouth must have bit and bridle to hold them,
  Or they will not come near thee.

> 9 Be glad in Jehovah, rejoice, O ye righteous,
> And joyfully shout, ye upright in heart.

(1, 2) We have three terms expressive of sin under different aspects. They all occur again in ver. 5. — **Transgression.** Heb. *pésha* (פֶּשַׁע), *a breaking loose, a tearing away* from God. — **Sin.** Heb. *hhatta* (חַטָא), *missing the mark;* that is, of Divine approbation. — **Guilt.** Heb. *'avôn* (עָוֹן); primarily *twisting* or *perversion* of the nature and life. In its etymology the second (*hhatta*) corresponds with the Greek *hamartia* from *hamartano.* But in usage the prevailing sense of this word in the New Testament, and of *'avôn* (No. 3 above) is sin in its evil nature and desert, as against the Divine law, as an act to be pardoned or punished, best represented by the word "guilt." So we read in ver. 5 *the guilt of my sin.* It carries with it so strongly the idea of ill desert apart from the act itself that it is sometimes to be rendered *punishment.* Especially see Gen. iv. 13; Is. liii. 6.

We have also in these verses three terms expressive of forgiveness most frequent in the O. T.: *lifting off,* Heb. *nāsā'; covering,* Heb. *kāsāh,* as by atonement; *not reckoning* or *imputing* guilt. Heb. *lô hhāshab.*

(2) **No deceit.** Heb. *lô remîyah.* This refers to "the deceit which denies and conceals, or extenuates and excuses, this or that favourite sin. Any such sin designedly retained is a secret curse, hindering justification" (Delitzsch).

(5) **And Thou** ... Heb. *attā nāsāthā.* The pronoun is emphatic, *Thyself,* and no other. The matter of sin and forgiveness lies between the individual sinner and God. It cannot be disposed of by any other.

XXXIII.

THE GOD OF CREATION, PROVIDENCE, AND GRACE.

THE close relationship between this and the preceding Psalm has been noted by Ewald and others. Its opening strain is similar to the close of the former. There are several other remarkable coincidences with this difference. Psalm xxxii. is based on a personal experience of forgiveness of sin and maintains the character of individual testimony. Whereas the present Psalm moves throughout in the tone of a hymn *for the congregation as such,* expressing the happiness and security of a people chosen as His own and guided by the Creator and Ruler of the whole world (Moll). Its fundamental thought appears in ver. 12, which ascribes the same blessedness to the people under God's special guidance and protection as was ascribed to the individual in xxxii. 2.

The Psalm is remarkably symmetrical. It begins and closes with strophes of three couplets each. The intermediate portion, containing the matter of praise, is broken into two principal parts, each consisting of eight couplets.

1. God worthy of all praise in general aspects ; introductory (1–3). (a) As the God of Revelation in the kingdom of grace (4, 5). (b) As the Creator of the world in the kingdom of nature (6–9). (c) As the irresistible Ruler in the history of man (10, 11). 2. God to be praised in view of all that His people possess in Him as the omniscient, almighty, and immutable Jehovah, their only and all-sufficient reliance (12–19).

1 Sing for joy in Jehovah, ye righteous,
　It is comely for the upright to praise Him.
2 With the harp give ye thanks to Jehovah,
　Sound the lute of ten strings to His praise.
3 Sing a new song to His Name,
　Play with skill and joyfully shout.

4 For the word of Jehovah is upright,
　And faithful is all He has done ;
5 He delights to be righteous and just,
　The earth is full of the kindness of Jehovah.

6 By the word of Jehovah the heavens were made,
　All their hosts by the breath of His mouth ;
7 He gathers the waters of the sea as a heap,
　And in treasuries hoards up their depths.

8 Let all the world stand in awe of Jehovah,
　All that dwell in the earth, let them tremble ;
9 When He spake it was done,
　His commandment stood fast.

10 Jehovah annuls the counsel of kingdoms,
　He defeats the thoughts of the nations ;
11 But Jehovah's counsel shall stand for all time,
　The thoughts of His heart to the uttermost age.

12 How blest is the nation whose God is Jehovah,
　The people He chose for possession ;
13 Jehovah looks forth out of heaven,
　He beholds all the children of men ;

14 From the place where He dwells He looks forth
　Upon all that inhabit the earth —
15 He that fashions the hearts of them all,
　And all they are doing considers.

16 A king is not saved by vast armies,
   Nor a nation set free by great strength;
17 All in vain is the horse for salvation,
   Though great is his strength he cannot deliver.

18 But Jehovah's eye is on those that revere Him,
   Those resting in hope on His kindness,
19 To deliver their soul from death,
   In famine to keep them alive.

20 Our soul waits for Jehovah,
   He alone is our Helper and Shield.
21 For in Him our heart shall rejoice,
   Because in His holy Name is our trust.
22 Let thy favour, O Jehovah, be upon us,
   Forasmuch as our hope is in Thee.

(3) **A new song**, implying some new mighty deeds of Jehovah and a fresh impulse of gratitude in the heart (xl. 3, and frequently in the Psalms). This and other expressions indicate that the occasion of the Psalm was some new deliverance of the nation from heathen oppression, but without war (Delitzsch).

(7) **As a heap.** Heb. *nēd;* of a *heap of sheaves* in the harvest, Is. xvii. 11, reminding us of Ex. xv. 8; Josh. iii. 15, 16; Ps. lxxviii. 13. Here we have an abiding and characteristic action described. "The idea is called forth of the waters of the *high* sea, swelling up above, yet firmly held together by Omnipotence" (Moll). The knowledge of some convexity of the earth seems to be implied.

(10) **The counsel**; that is, the schemes and projects determined upon.

(16) **Vast armies.** Heb. *berōb hháyil.* Lit. *by great power*, but often translated *a host* or *army*, referring to power for war; R. V., *the multitude of a host.*

XXXIV.

THANKSGIVING AND INSTRUCTION IN VIEW OF GREAT DELIVERANCE.

THE title connects this Psalm with David's escape from the wrath of Saul by feigning madness. There seems to be no sufficient reason for setting aside the tradition on which this is based, and finding some other authorship, with Hupfeld. It is one of the Alphabetical Psalms,— each verse beginning with a letter of the Hebrew alphabet. Dr. Moll thinks (with Hengstenberg) this artificial construction, together with the calm and didactic character of the Psalm, sufficient to show that it was not a lyric effusion produced under the warm impulses of gratitude at the time of the deliverance, but prepared for general purposes of devotion at some later and vivid recollection of his remarkable preservation. The course of thought is in favour of this.

1. His resolution and vow of continued praise to God, with a call to others to join him (1–3). 2. His personal experience, and its application to the religious life of his companions in the service of God.

BY DAVID, WHEN HE FEIGNED MADNESS BEFORE ABIMELECH; AND HE DROVE HIM AWAY, AND HE DEPARTED.

1 Jehovah will I bless at all times,
　And have alway His praise in my mouth.
2 My soul makes her boast in Jehovah,
　The suffering shall hear and rejoice.
3 Come, join me in extolling Jehovah,
　Together exalting His Name.
4 When I sought for Jehovah, He answered,
　And freed me from all that I feared.
5 They look unto Him, and are beaming,
　And never let their face yield to shame.
6 When this sufferer called, Jehovah gave ear,
　And saved him from all his distress.
7 Around those that fear Him Jehovah's angel encamps;
　Out of danger he plucks them.
8 Taste ye and see that Jehovah is good;
　How blest is the man that takes refuge in Him.
9 His holy ones, fear ye Jehovah,
　They that fear Him shall suffer no want.
10 The young lions do lack and are hungry,
　But those seeking Jehovah shall want no good thing.
11 Come, ye children, and hearken to me;
　Let me teach you the fear of Jehovah.
12 Where is the man that desires long life,
　That loves to see prosperous days?
13 Put a guard on thy tongue to withhold it from evil,
　On thy lips that they utter no guile;
14 Turn away from the evil, and practise the good;
　Inquire after peace and pursue it.

15 The eyes of Jehovah are fixed on the righteous,
   And His ears give heed to their cry.
16 But the face of Jehovah is against evil doers,
   To cut off from the earth their remembrance.
17 The righteous cry, and Jehovah hears them,
   And frees them from all their distresses.
18 Jehovah is near the broken in heart,
   And the crushed in spirit He saves.
19 Many are the sufferings of the righteous,
   But Jehovah delivers from all.
20 He preserves all their bones,
   That not one can be broken.
21 Evil doing brings death to the wicked;
   Held guilty are the foes of the righteous,
22 But Jehovah redeemeth the soul of His servants,
   And none are held guilty that take refuge in Him.

(5) **They look.** Heb. *hibbitū*, from *nābat*, an intense look of confidence, desire, and expectation. — **Are beaming.** Heb. *nāhārū*. Lit. *they shine*, as in Is. lx. 1, "Arise, shine; for thy light is come, and the glory of the Lord is risen upon thee." Here as there it is shining by reflection of the Divine glory. We are reminded of the shining of Moses' face when he came down from the mount (Ex. xxxiv. 29, 30, 35). But a different word is used there, and it describes a visible supernatural brilliancy, whereas here it is figurative. Comp. *bālag*, also *to shine*, xxxix. 14. — **Never let their face yield to shame, etc.** Heb. *'al yahhpārū*, from *hhāphar*. The neg. particle *'al* is properly prohibitive (like the Greek μή). In poetry, occasionally, it stands for *lō*, in emphatic declaration of what shall not be, as if prohibiting it. Here it expresses the permanency of the impression that should be made by any special experience of God's gracious power. Let those that have received such favour not sit in gloom, yielding to doubt, fear, and shame. The verb *hhāphar*, lit. *to blush*, in contrast with the bright and hopeful look just spoken of. On the other hand, *bōsh, to be ashamed*, means, lit. *to be pale;* as in sudden disappointment the blood may be drawn to the heart, or rush to the face. For confirmation of this, see Is. xxiv. 23, where the moon is called, poetically, *l'bēnāh, the white one*, and the sun, *hhāmāh, the ruddy one*, and we read literally, "Then the pale one shall blush, and the ruddy one shall blanch," for "The moon shall be confounded, and the sun ashamed," of the English Bible. These poetical names for the sun and moon are used only elsewhere in Is. xxx. 26, and Cant. vi. 10. Here we might read, "Never let their face blush for shame."

(6) **When this sufferer called.** This does not necessarily refer to himself, but to any individual near at hand, whose countenance is beaming with joy, emphatically illustrating the preceding verse.

(7) **Encamps around,** — enclosing them like a wall of fire, so that no enemy can force his way within the circle so effectually guarded.

For a remarkable parallel see Zech. ii. 5, ix. 8.

(9) **His holy ones** — in the sense of "a holy nation" in Exod. xix. 6, 1 Peter ii. 9, and "holy" in Ps. xvi. 3. They are those that He set apart from all others as belonging peculiarly to Himself, and who may be expected to recognize that high distinction in all practical ways.

(14) **Peace.** Heb. *shālōm*, in the full round meaning of the word in the O. T. from *shālēm*, *to be whole, sound*, including salvation from sin, and all blessing, as resulting from right relations with God.

(21, 22) **Held guilty.** See the same verb, *'āsham*, in Is. xxiv. 6, A. V. *desolate*, R. V. *found guilty*.

XXXV.

A CRY OF TORTURE AGAINST MURDEROUS INJUSTICE.

THIS Psalm is a rhythmical and agitated appeal to God for help when most sorely needed. The same three elements recur in the three chief divisions, vv. 1-10, 11-18, 19-28, but always with different forms, references, and figures. These are, (1) *Prayer that Jehovah will interfere without delay* for the protection of His servant, that his righteous cause may be maintained and his enemies ruined; (2) *Description of the wickedness and unthankfulness of these enemies*, who have previously received sympathy and tokens of love from him whom they now persecute without cause; and (3) *Vows of thankfulness*, which the delivered man will publicly offer to the Lord in the great congregation of Israel. The movement of these thoughts around in a circle corresponds throughout with the deeply felt experiences of a heart that is shaken *to its foundation* by intense and protracted suffering, and the disappointment of cherished hopes. He can become master of his own emotions only gradually, and indeed only by urgently *clinging to God*.

In the life of David the most suitable time for the composition of this Psalm is found during his persecution by Saul, and it is most nearly related to Ps. xl. and lxix. It is a lyrical carrying out of the words used by David, 1 Sam. xxiv. 16, and probably owes its place in the collection of Psalms to the circumstance that the Angel of Jehovah is mentioned here in the singular, as in the preceding Psalm (Moll).

BY DAVID.

1 Assail, O Jehovah, mine assailants,
  Give battle to those that give battle to me;
2 Grasp the shield and the buckler,
  And arise to defend me.
3 Draw the spear, and shut off my pursuers;
  Say to my soul, " It is I that will save thee."

4 Put to shame and confusion those seeking my life,
  Those bent on my ruin, drive back in disgrace:
5 As the wind drives the chaff,
      Let the Angel of Jehovah disperse them;
6 Let their way become dark, and in slippery paths,
      Let the Angel of Jehovah pursue them.

7 For they hid for me snares unprovoked,
  Unprovoked digged a pit for my life.
8 Let ruin overtake him unawares,
  Let the net which he hid catch himself;
      In the same destruction let him fall.

9 Then my soul shall rejoice in Jehovah,
  Shall exult in His power to save;
10 My bones shall all say,
      "Who, O Jehovah, with Thee can compare,
  Who deliverest the oppressed from one stronger than he,
      The oppressed and the poor from his spoiler?"

11 Malignant accusers are risen against me,
  Who charge me with that which I know not;
12 They reward me with evil for good,
  Bereavement is come on my soul.

13 But I — in their sickness my clothing was sackcloth,
      My soul I humbled with fasting,
  And my prayer — to my bosom let it turn.
14 As if for my friend, for my brother, I wandered about;
  As one mourns for a mother,
      In garments of woe I bowed down.

15 But they, when my weakness came on,
      Were glad, and they gathered against me,
  They gathered with smiting, I knowing not when;
      Without ceasing they rent me;
16 Like sycophants vile,
  They beset me with gnashing of teeth.

17 How long Thou beholdest, O Lord;
   Recover my life from the ruin they wrought,
     My one only life from the lions;
18 And thanks will I bring in the great congregation,
   To a host in full strength will I praise Thee.

19 Let my foes not rejoice in the lies that malign me,
   Nor those wink the eye that causelessly hate me;
20 For they speak not with peaceful intent,
   But frame plots 'gainst the quiet in the land;
21 Yea, against me with wide-open mouth they cry out,
   "Aha, with our eyes we have seen."

22 Thou beholdest, Jehovah, keep not silence;
   Be not far from me, Lord;
23 Awake, yea, arouse Thee for justice,
   My God and my Lord, in behalf of my cause.

24 In Thy righteousness judge me, Jehovah, my God;
   Let them never exult in my ruin,
25 Nor say in their heart,
     "Aha, what we wished we now have."
   Let them not say, " We have swallowed him up."
26 Let those that rejoice in my sufferings
     Be ashamed and confounded;
   Let those that swell proudly against me
     Be clothed with contempt and disgrace:

27 But let those that rejoice in knowing me righteous
     Shout aloud and be glad;
   And ever let them say, " Give Jehovah the glory,
     Who delights in the good of His servant;"
28 Then shall my tongue of Thy righteousness speak,
     All the day long of Thy praise.

(1) **Assail, O Jehovah, mine as-sailants.** Heb. *ribāh 'eth y'ribū.* Usually of ordinary strife of words, or of a legal contest. Here there is reference to a violation of rights which God as judge must decide. But the injustice complained of is too defiant to yield except to the compulsion of Omnipotence, and God is invoked to arm Himself for

battle. Perowne: "An amplification of the figure occurring already in the Pentateuch where God is spoken of as a man of war, Ex. xv. 3, Deut. xxxii. 41. The bold anthropomorphic working out of the figure is, however, remarkable. It shows the earnest desire of the poet's mind to realize the fact that God not only taught his fingers to fight, but mixed in the battle, fighting as it were by his side, and assuring him of victory." See also Ex. xiv. 24, 25; Judg. v. 20.

(3) **Shut off.** Heb. *shut against.*

(5) **The Angel of Jehovah** (twice). The "angel of Jehovah" in xxxiv. 7 was an angel of protection, but here he is an angel of judgment. In both instances a manifestation of God's personal presence and power in redemption, and to be connected with the fundamental passages, Ex. xxiii. 20-23 (where notice the expression, "My name is in him"), xxxii. 2, and elsewhere in the Pentateuch, beginning with Gen. xvi. 7.

(11) **Malignant accusers.** Heb. *'êdê hhāmās.* See Ex. xxiii. 1. There as here, and generally, *hhāmās* expresses more than untruthfulness. It is false testimony with the express purpose of inciting to violence and outrage.

(12) **Bereavement is come on my soul.** Delitzsch: "My condition is that of being forsaken by all who formerly showed me marks of affection; all these have, as it were, died off so far as I am concerned. Not only had David been obliged to save his parents by causing them to flee to Moab, but Michal also was torn from him, Jonathan removed, and all those at the court of Saul who had hitherto sought his favour and friendship were alienated from him. ... In ver. 13 he contrasts himself with the ungrateful and unfeeling ones."

(13) **In their sickness, etc.** He refers to some special instance of suffering in which he had shown the sincerest sympathy, not elsewhere noted. **My prayer, to my bosom let it turn.** The meaning seems to be that his prayer was such as he would wish under like circumstances offered for himself. It may be illustrated *per contra* by the familiar proverb, "Curses, like chickens, come home to roost."

(14) **Wandered about.** Heb. *hithhallêk*, lit. *went about.* Here, of the slow aimless roving of one absorbed in deep grief.

(15) **When my weakness came on.** Heb. *at my stumbling*, or *fall*, not referring to moral delinquency, but to the beginning of the present calamities.

(16) **Like sycophants vile.** Heb. *like the vilest of cake-jesters;* a term that seems to describe those who made sport at the tables of the great for the sake of dainty fare; it refers to those who turned against David with malignant derision for the sake of favour with Saul.

(17) Heb. *y'hhîdî, my only one.* See on xxii. 20.

XXXVI.

A SHARP CONTRAST.

THIS Psalm seems quite general in its reference. It will apply to the condition of things during almost any part of David's reign. Even the prayer at ver. 11 may not be connected with any special emergency.

There are three principal parts: 1. Description of a wicked man, representing a class whose character and life are utterly perverted (1–4). 2. Description of the manifested perfections of God (5–9). 3. Prayer for further exhibitions of these perfections to others as well as to himself, with a prophetic glance at the ruin of all combinations of iniquity (10–12).

BY DAVID, THE SERVANT OF JEHOVAH.

1 Sin's oracle voice possesses the wicked man's heart,
  And his eyes have before them no God to be feared;
2 For his eyes it so cheats with its flattering words,
  That they see not his guilt as proven and hated.
3 The words of his mouth are iniquity and falsehood;
  He has ceased to do wisely and well.
4 Iniquitous deeds he plans on his bed;
  In ways not good he has taken his stand,
    And evil abhors not.

5 Thy kindness, Jehovah, extends to the heavens,
  Thy faithfulness reaches the skies;
6 Like the mountains of God, Thy righteousness towers,
    Thy judgments are vast like the deep;
  Thou, Jehovah, art guardian of man and of beast.

7 How precious is Thy lovingkindness, O God.
  The children of men may hide in Thy shadowing wings;
8 On rich viands they feed in Thy house,
  And Thy gift for their thirst is Thy river of joys.
9 For in Thee is the fountain of life;
  It is ours to see light in the light that is Thine.

10 Continue Thy kindness to those that revere Thee,
  Let Thy righteousness bide with the upright in heart.
11 The footstep of pride, let it not overtake me,
  And the hand of the wicked not fright me away.
12 Behold where they that work evil are fallen,
  Are thrust down, and cannot arise.

(1, 2) There are few passages in the Psalter about which interpreters differ more widely than they do about the first two verses of this Psalm. But the key to the whole seems to lie in the first two words of the first verse.

(1) **Oracle voice.** Heb. *ne'um, an oracle,* is a noun in the form of the pass. participle of the verb *nā'am.*

to mutter. The conception is borrowed from the obscure utterances of heathen oracles in pretended revelations from the gods. The verb is used but once, and there followed by this noun, of false prophets claiming Divine inspiration, Jer. xxiii. 31, *nā'emū ne'um;* Eng. Bible, *they say, he saith.* Elsewhere *ne'um* is regularly followed by the genitive of the person uttering the oracle. This is always Jehovah, except in Num. xxiv. 3, 4, 15, 16, of Balaam, 2 Sam. xxiii. 1, of David, and Prov. xxxi. 1, of Agur, as speaking by inspiration. It occurs in the Prophetical Books, with Jehovah as its subject, more than 300 times. In the instance now under consideration the genitive following is *pésha* (פֶּשַׁע), sin as *rebellion, a breaking away* from God. It is here personified as assuming a *quasi* Divine authority and control over the man who has yielded himself to its power. Always, except here and in Jer. xxiii. 31, the words of the oracle precede or follow. Olshausen would supply them as part of the original text (so Cheyne), from xiv. 1, *'ēn 'Elohim,* "There is no God." But this is unnecessary, since the purport of the oracle is clearly implied in the following description. It boldly denies God's effective justice, and produces practical atheism. The oracle is addressed to the wicked, and is inward and not outward. The Massoretic text reads " in *my* heart." (So the A. V.) But this gives no intelligible sense. We cannot conceive of an oracle of personified sin addressed to the wicked in the heart of the Psalmist. The Sept., Syriac, and Arabic Versions, with Jerome and some MSS., for *libbī* (לִבִּי), *my heart,* substitute *libbō* (לִבּוֹ), *his heart,* and this must be the true reading, involving in the unpointed text merely the slight lengthening of the letter *Jod.* (So Hitzig, Hupfeld, Böttcher, Moll, Perowne, and others.) The personification of sin is found elsewhere in the O. T. at Gen. iv. 7, and in the N. T. in Rom. v. vi. vii.

and a personification of falsehood in the lying spirit of 1 Kings xxii. 21–23. It is noteworthy, however, that in our passage we have not a personification of rebellion, as an evil power or principle dominant in the world, but the man's own active rebellion is personified as objective to himself, prompting him to further defiance, or even denial of God. The seat of the oracle is *in the interior* of his heart; *qéreb* (קֶרֶב) is to be distinguished from *tôk* (תּוֹךְ), as describing not *the centre,* but all within the circumference. The thought is that the man is fully occupied and controlled by the false revelation to the exclusion of every message from God. It is virtually demoniac possession. — **No God to be feared.** Heb. *no terror of God.* The principal word here is *pahhad,* the fear awakened by approaching judgment. His oracle, which is the echo of x. 4, has effectually disposed of all that.

(2) **It so cheats.** The first question relates to the subject of the verb. *Hehheliq,* prim. *to make smooth,* or *deal smoothly,* then *to flatter.* The A. V. understands it reflexively of the wicked man, " he flattereth himself." This is elaborately, but not conclusively, defended by Moll. Hupfeld, Hoffman, and Perowne translate, *"He* (that is, *God) deals smoothly,"* but each has a different opinion about the continuation. Delitzsch finds the subject in *pésha, rebellion,* of the preceding verse, but considers this a malignant principle or power, hiding from him the sure consequences of his folly, and inciting him to the hatred of God and man: as if a lying spirit had come to him from without, determined to accomplish his ruin. But what is more evident than that this personification is nothing external to himself, but simply an idealization of his own evil nature? The wicked man, blinded and hardened by every sinful act, and persisting in rebellion and wrong, endeavours with fatal success to escape from the horrible consciousness

of wrath to come, by declaring it all a delusion.

"The wicked man says with an arrogant face,
 'He will not avenge;'
'There is no God' is in all his devices."— x. 4.

Our English Bible gives us the substantial, prosaic fact. But in the exhibition of that fact by the Hebrew poet, the second verse is bound closely to the first, and the personification continues.

In commenting upon the second line of this second verse the leading interpreters are widely apart, and have suggested various emendations of the text. The ancient versions differ very much from each other, and from the Hebrew. The R. V. substitutes another rendering for that of the A. V., with an alternative in the margin that differs from either, to which it adds a rendering marked Heb., that differs from all. These differences, however, arise mainly from various opinions about the preceding line, and about the general conception that underlies the whole. If the view embodied in our rendering above is correct, this last line gives simply the ultimate point which the idealized self-deception touches; namely, the future exposure of monstrous wickedness to punishment and detestation. The spirit of rebellion that animates and rules him, ignores and derides every such thought.

A precise literal translation of the second verse will show that the view we adopt imposes no strain upon the language; "For it makes smooth to him in his eyes, as to finding his guilt for hating." Here as elsewhere the verb *mâtsâ'* (מָצָא), *to find*, describes the judicial ascertainment of the man's guilt, by satisfactory proof.

Two more verses in this Psalm complete the description of one whose character and life are thoroughly perverted. The following strophe (5–9) describes the manifested perfections of God that are most opposite to the preceding exhibition of moral perversity, evidently drawn from a precious personal experience. It is in the form of direct and adoring address to Jehovah.

Prof. Cheyne thinks that we have here parts of two Psalms that have come together by accident or mistake. He claims that the connection suggested between ver. 4 and 5 "is somewhat forced." But surely nothing is more natural, than that the eye that has become wearied by the contemplation of evil in its shocking details, should be lifted for relief to the transcendent excellency of God. And nothing is more common in the Psalms, than contrast between man in his shame, and God in His glory.

XXXVII.

HOPE ON, AND WAIT FOR THE END.

THIS Psalm falls into line with ix. x. xxv. xxxiv. in its alphabetical arrangement, but with some irregularities, such as occur in several of the others. It is didactic and sententious, resembling somewhat a collection of proverbs, yet flowing and elegant in style. Its repetitions are intended for emphasis upon important thought. Ver. 25 connects it with David's advanced life. It differs from most of his Psalms in having no reference to his personal self, other than results of his own observation in ver. 25 and 35, 36. The key-note of the whole composition is sounded in the first verse. Do not be disturbed by the present prosperity of the wicked, and the depression of the righteous. The future will exhibit their actual standing in the sight of God.

It is made up of pleasing contrasts between the righteous and the wicked, with appropriate injunctions interspersed, but no clear order of thought can be traced.

BY DAVID.

1 Do not rage at ill-doers,
   Nor be jealous against the unjust;
2 For like grass they must soon be cut down,
   Like herbage must wither away.

3 Put your trust in Jehovah, and do that which is good;
   Abide in the land, and in faithfulness find thy delight;
4 Seek Thy pleasure in Jehovah,
   The desire of thy heart will He give thee.

5 Commit to Jehovah thy way;
   Be trustful in Him, and He will accomplish —
6 As the light will He make thy righteousness shine,
   Thine uprightness clear as the noonday.

7 Be at rest in Jehovah, and hold to Him firmly,
   And rage not at him that prospers his way,
     At the man that performeth his evil devices.
8 Desist ye from anger; be wrathful no more;
   And rage not, thus only doing evil.

9 For the wicked shall perish ;
   Those that hope in Jehovah shall inherit the land.
10 Yet a little while and the wicked shall cease,
   When thou observest his place he is gone.
11 But the lowly in heart shall inherit the land,
   And delight in abundance of blessing.

12 The wicked man plots 'gainst the righteous,
   He beholds them and gnashes his teeth ;
13 But Jehovah derides him,
   For He sees that his day is approaching.

14 The wicked — the sword they have drawn,
    And their bow they have bent,
  To bring down the suffering and needy,
    To murder the upright in life;
15 But their sword shall pierce their own heart,
  And their bow shall be shivered.

16 Better a little that a righteous man hath,
  Than the multiplied wealth of the wicked;
17 For the arm of the wicked is shattered,
  But Jehovah upholdeth the righteous.

18 Jehovah observeth the days of the upright,
    Their heritage dureth forever;
19 They are not put to shame when the evil time comes,
  But in days of sore hunger are filled.

20 But the wicked shall perish; like the glory of the
    meadows the foes of Jehovah
Shall vanish away, like smoke shall they vanish away.

21 The wicked shall borrow, and cannot repay,
  But the righteous show kindness, and give;
22 For those that God blesseth inherit the land,
  But those that He curseth shall perish.

23 A man's steps are made firm by Jehovah;
  He delights in his way:
24 He may fall, but he shall not lie prostrate,
  For Jehovah lays hold of his hand.

25 I was young, and have now become old,
    Yet I never have seen the righteous forsaken,
    Nor his seed begging bread;
26 All the day long he shows kindness and lends,
    And his offspring are blessed.

27 Turn away from the evil, do that which is good,
    And abide evermore.

28 For Jehovah delighteth in justice;
>> Those He loves He forsakes not,
>> He guards them forever;
> But the seed of the wicked shall perish.
29 The righteous inherit the land,
> And therein they have always a home.

30 The righteous man's mouth utters wisdom,
> And his tongue speaketh justice;
31 In his heart is the law of his God,
> And his feet shall not falter.

32 The wicked lie in wait for the righteous,
> And are seeking to slay him;
33 Jehovah will never yield him up to their hand,
> Nor in judgment condemn him.

34 Hope in Jehovah, and keep thou His way;
>> He will exalt thee to inherit the land;
> When the ungodly are cut off, thou shalt see it.

35 I have seen a wicked man haughty and fierce,
> Like a thrifty tree in its native soil he was spreading;
36 I passed by, and behold he was gone;
> When I sought him he could not be found.

37 The perfect man mark, and the upright behold;
> There is hope for the man that seeks peace;
38 But transgressors shall all be cut off,
> The hope of the wicked has perished.

39 From Jehovah is the safety of the righteous,
> Their stronghold in times of distress;
40 Jehovah will help and deliver,
>> Will deliver from the wicked and save them,
> Because they take refuge in Him.

(1) **Do not rage.** The reflexive form of *hhārāh, to burn,* of fierce passion. The rendering " fret " of the A. V. is feeble, and far below the burning wrath expressed by this Hebrew verb. — **Jealous against.** Nearly equivalent to the preceding verb. It describes *indignation* rather than *envy.* See at lxxiii. 2.

(3) **Do that which is good.** The

rendering "do good" of the A. V. is literal and exact. But it has come to be used in a narrow sense of practical benevolence, or doing good to others. Whereas the word *good* here implies *all virtue*, or obedience to the will of God, under the general distinction between good and evil in the life and conduct of man. So in ver. 27. — **In faithfulness find thy delight**. Heb. *rĕ'ĕh* (רעֵה) *ĕ'mūnāh*. Lit. *feed on;* that is, *to enjoy*, perhaps with reference to their relations by covenant with God; find your pleasure in His faithfulness, and in serving Him faithfully. But it is not to be confined to this.

(35) **Haughty and fierce**. Heb. *'ārīts* (ערִיץ), usually translated *violent*. The primary idea is *fear-inspiring*, a combination of wickedness with pride, strength, and fierceness.

— **Like a thrifty tree, etc.** Heb. *'ezrahh ra'anān*. The former word of a tree that has never been transplanted; used of persons, *native*, in distinction from foreign (Lev. xvi. 29, xviii. 26, etc.) and *ra'anān, putting forth leaves*, vigorous and flourishing; as in xcii. 14.

(36) **I passed by**. Heb. *he passed by*, which may be impersonal, *some one* (they). (So Luther, Delitzsch, etc.) Here the Sept. and Syriac render "I passed by," which is probably correct. Comp. Prov. xxiv. 30. Observe the parallelism. "I sought him."

(37, 38) **Hope**. Heb. *'ahharīth*. Lit. *futurity*. See Prov. xxiii. 18 (R. V. text and marg.), xxxiv. 14, 20. The probable reference is to posterity. Comp. ver. 28.

XXXVIII.

"IN WRATH REMEMBER MERCY."

THIS is the third of the Penitential Psalms. The opening words are almost identical with those in the first of the series, Ps. vi. It describes great distress of body and mind. Worn out by some terrible and painful disease, his sufferings are intensified by consciousness of guilt. When we reach the second half of the Psalm a third element of misery is added in his desertion by friends and the presence of deadly enemies, who use his bodily condition to injure and ruin him. In all this trouble he yet calls hopefully on God.

There are three principal parts, each of which commences with a fresh appeal to God.

1. He describes his suffering, aggravated by consciousness of guilt (1–8). 2. From desertion and persecution with growing confidence he casts himself upon God (9–14). 3. Despairing of his own power, and of all other aid against this fearful combination, he waits for an answer (15–22).

A PSALM OF DAVID. TO BRING TO REMEMBRANCE.

1 Correct me no more in Thine anger, Jehovah;
   No longer chastise me in wrath;
2 For Thine arrows have pierced me,
   Thy hand bears me down.

3 Because Thou art wrathful, my flesh has no soundness,
  My bones have no health on account of my sin;
4 For my head is overwhelmed by my guilt,
  My burden is heavy, too heavy to bear.

5 My stripes are corrupt and are loathsome,
  Because of my folly;
6 I writhe, I am brought very low,
  All the day long I go mourning.

7 For a burning, deep in, fills my loins,
  And my flesh has no soundness;
8 Benumbed and sore bruised
  I cry out with disquieted heart.

9 My longing is all before Thee, O Lord,
  And from Thee my sighs are not hid.
10 My heart is fluttering, my strength is all gone,
  And the light of mine eyes, even this is not left me.

11 My friends and companions hold aloof from my woe,
  My kinsmen, too, stand afar off;
12 Those that seek for my life have laid snares;
      Intent on my ruin, they speak deadly words,
  And all the day long whisper falsehood.

13 But I, like the deaf, shall not hear,
  Shall be like the dumb men that ope not their mouth;
14 Yea, am now like a man without hearing,
  From whose mouth there come forth no replies.

15 For to Thee, O Jehovah, I look;
  O God, mine own God, Thou wilt answer;
16 For I cry, " Let them not be exultant;
  When my foot giveth way, let them not rise proudly
      against me."

17 For, indeed, I am ready to fall,
  And ever my grief is before me;
18 Yea, my guilt I confess,
  I think of my sin and am fearful.

19 For strong are my foes without cause,
   And many by lies show me hatred;
20 They pay evil for good;
   They rise up against me,
      Because I still seek after good.

21 Forsake me not, Jehovah;
   Be not far off, O my God;
22 Haste Thee on to mine aid,
   O God, my salvation!

(2) The same verb is in both lines (*nāthath, to come down*), with change of preposition, "*Thine arrows . . . into,*" "*Thy hand . . . upon.*"

(12) **Whisper.** Heb. *hāgāh.* See i. 2, ii. 1 (note), and xix. 14.

(19) For *hhayyim, living, hhinnām, without cause,* should be read, as in the parallel passages, xxxv. 19, lxix. 4. So most textual critics and interpreters.

XXXIX.

IN GREAT SUFFERING BUT SUBMISSIVE.

THIS "Psalm of David" is elegiac, and as Ewald says, "the most beautiful of all the elegies in the Psalter." It was written under great suffering, apparently during painful and wasting illness, which he feared would terminate fatally. This does not appear in the former half of the Psalm, but it gives its colouring to the whole. The exemption of others around him from such sufferings, the ungodly in their success and pride, may have embittered him at first; and possibly if he had not put a curb on his mouth he might have uttered complaints similar to those of Ps. lxxiii. But there is nothing in the language of the Psalm that implies that this was his principal grief and the burden of the Psalm (Delitzsch), or that connects his present sorrow with the historic occasion that lies back of Ps. iv., or with persecutions such as are described in Ps. lxii. So much as this, however, appears, that there were near him those who were ready to rejoice in his sufferings, and would charge him with some great wickedness that had justly subjected him to the severest punishment. See xli. 5-8, xlii. 3. There was scarcely any time in his life when he was not liable to such misconception by the envious and malignant.

1. Strong repression of complaint against God in the presence of the wicked (1, 2). 2. Unable to maintain silence he humbly addresses God: (a) He prays that he may be impressed by the shortness of life (4, 5). (b) In view of the vanity of life, he looks to God as his only hope (6, 7). (c) He accepts the stroke as the just desert of his sins, but prays that in the Divine mercy his life may be spared (7-14).

FOR THE LEADER OF THE CHOIR. FOR JEDUTHUN. A PSALM OF DAVID.

1   I said in my heart, "My ways I must heed,
     Lest I sin with my tongue;
  With the wicked before me,
     I must bridle my mouth."
2   I was speechless and dumb,
     In silence held off from relief,
  And my sorrow was painfully stirred.
3   My heart became heated within me;
     While I brooded there flamed up a fire,
  And I spake with my tongue;

4   "Teach me, Jehovah, mine end,
  And what is my measure of days;
     Make me know how fragile I am.
5   Lo, the days Thou hast given me are handbreadths,
     And my lifetime is nothing before Thee;
  Yea, all men are only a breath,
     Even when standing most firmly.
6   For only a shadow each goeth about,
     For only a breath is their turmoil;
  One gathers, but knoweth not who shall enjoy. [Selah.]

7   And now, Lord, whither shall I look?
  My hope is in Thee.
8   Deliver me from all my transgressions,
  Let me not be the scorn of the vile.
9   I am dumb, I ope not my mouth,
  Because it is Thou that hast done it.
10   Oh spare me Thy stroke;
  By the blow of Thy hand I must perish;
11   For he whom thou scourgest, correcting for sin,
     His beauty melts away, as if eaten by moth;
  Yea, all men are only a breath.   [Selah.]

12   Hear my prayer, O Jehovah, give ear to my cry;
     When I weep, be not silent;

For I am with Thee a guest,
   And a tenant at will, as my fathers all were.
13 Let Thy frown pass away, that my gloom may be scattered,
   Before I go hence and have vanished.

(1) **In my heart** is supplied in translating, in order to distinguish this from the speaking out in ver. 3. The simple *'āmar, to say*, is frequently used of thought, prayer, or purpose, not audibly expressed. — **Must** (twice). The voluntative termination *āh* sometimes expresses obligation, or some internal constraint.

(2) **Held off from relief.** Heb. *mittôb*. Lit. *from good*. Delitzsch forces too much into the word when he makes it mean turning away from the prosperity which he saw the wicked enjoying. It seems rather to mean that he separated himself from enjoyment in the good things of this life, which under other circumstances he would most highly value, or, in sharper connection with his silence, that he denied himself the good (the relief) that would have resulted from the free expression of his grief. This is often the only comfort that sufferers have. — **Painfully stirred.** Heb. *'ākar* (עָכַר). Lit. *to make turbid*, of water; then, of persons, *to trouble, to afflict* (Gen. xxxiv. 20; Josh. vi. 18, etc.). Here, of suffering as made more intense.

(4) **Teach me, O Jehovah, mine end.** When at last he speaks, while his sufferings by repression have a sharper sting, he has become more patient and submissive. The pious feeling that before prevented him from speaking at all, has had its effect. There is now no complaint, nor a word that even the wicked might not hear. — **Fragile.** Heb. *hhādēl, ceasing*, or *liable to cease*; a verbal adjective.

(5) **Standing most firmly.** Heb. *nitsāb, when he stands* (sound and firm), Zech. xi. 16.; that is, at his very best.

(6) **Each.** Heb. *'ish, a man*, is here distributive, the individual. — **Their turmoil.** The plural has reference to men in the mass in their sharp competitions and jealousies; ever jostling against one another rudely. The same word is used of tumultuous nations in ii. 1, from *hāmāh, to hum*.

(7) **Whither do I look?** Heb. *mah qivvīthī*. The verb does not mean *wait* in the ordinary sense of *delay*, but *ardent and exclusive desire and hope*, in the sense developed at xl. 1; and the preceding *mah* is not *for what* reason, but *for what* relief, or better, *in what* direction. This is confirmed by the parallelism, "My hope is in Thee." The rendering of the A. V. is ambiguous.

(10) **Spare me.** Heb. *remove from me*.

(12) **A guest .. a tenant at will.** Heb. *gēr ... tôshāb*. For the former see v. 4, xv. 1. The latter is from the verb *yāshab, to dwell*, and used of one who dwells in a place by sufferance of the owner, and during his good pleasure, but who has no legal right. The term "tenant at will," well known in English and American law, best expresses it. In both words he disclaims all inherent right of occupancy, casting himself on the merciful kindness of God, as the sovereign proprietor.

(13) Lit. *look away from me that I may brighten up;* implying gloom and distress produced by the frowning countenance of an inexorable judge. See margin of the R. V., and the same verb in Job xiv. 6: "Look away from him that he may rest." — **And have vanished.** Heb. *'ēnennī, I am not;* but it refers to disappearing from the earth, as in Job vii. 8-10, not to absolute non-existence.

XL.

SALVATION, SELF-SURRENDER, AND SUPPLICATION.

THIS Psalm is closely related to Ps. lxix. Various points of resemblance indicate the same authorship. Its contents connect more suitably with the life of David in the deadly persecution that preceded his second anointing as king over Israel, than with that of any other. This is rendered more probable by the prominence everywhere assigned to David as a type of the Messiah, and the use made of this Psalm in the Epistle to the Heb. ch. x. 5–10. Delitzsch: "The words of David, the anointed one, who is now on his way to the throne, are so moulded by the Holy Spirit, the Spirit of prophecy, that they sound at the same time like the words of the second David, passing through suffering to glory, whose offering up is the end of animal sacrifices, and whose person and work are the very kernel and star of the roll of the law."

The last five verses appear separately with slight alteration in Ps. lxx. But neither this, nor the difference in tone and contents between the several parts of the Psalm, is opposed to their being by the same author and originally connected. Transition from thanksgiving to prayer, with corresponding difference in style, is very common.

1. Looking to the past: (a) Praise for a great deliverance (1–4); (b) Consecration, obedience, and public acknowledgment (5–12). 2. Prayer for further Divine assistance against enemies (13–17).

FOR THE LEADER OF THE CHOIR. BY DAVID. A PSALM.

1 For Jehovah I anxiously waited;
His ear He inclined, heard my cry for His help,
2 Brought me up from the pit of destruction,
From the depths of the mire;
Set my feet on a cliff,
And my footsteps made firm;
3 And He put a new song in my mouth,
Even praise to our God;
There are many that see it, and fear,
And trust in Jehovah.

4 How blest is the man, who, making Jehovah his trust,
Neither turns to the proud,
Nor to lying apostates.

5 And Thou, Jehovah my God,
     How many the wonders Thou wroughtest,
      And Thy thoughts for our welfare —
  There is none that with Thee can compare —
    I would utter and speak them,
      But they cannot be told.

6 Slain beasts and oblations are not Thy desire,
    But mine ears didst Thou open ;
  For offerings by burning and offerings for sin
    Do not meet Thy demand:
7 Then I said, " Lo, I come,
  With the roll of the volume enjoined me ;
8 O God, I have pleasure in doing Thy will,
  In mine innermost heart is Thy law."
9 I as herald of righteousness spake
    To the great congregation ;
  Lo, my lips I restrained not,
    O Jehovah, Thou knowest,
10 Nor Thy righteousness hid in my heart;
    But Thy faithfulness told,
      And Thy power to save ;
  I concealed not Thy kindness and truth
    From the great congregation.
11 And Thou, O Jehovah,
    Restrain not from me Thy merciful deeds ;
  Let Thy kindness and truth protect me forever ;
12 For ills without number beset me ;
    My sins overtake me,
      I can no longer see ;
  They are more than the hairs of my head,
      And my heart has forsaken me.
13 Be pleased to deliver me, Jehovah ;
  Oh haste Thee, Jehovah, to help me.
14 Let them all come to shame and confusion
     That hunt for my life ;
  Let those be repulsed in disgrace
     That desire to destroy me.

15 Let those be struck dumb by their shame
   That say to me, Aha!

16 But all those that seek Thee,
       In Thee let them joy and be glad;
   All that love Thy salvation,
       Fore'er let them say,
           " Jehovah be greatly exalted."
17 And I, in my suffering and need,
       Make haste to me, O Lord ;
   Thou art my help and deliverer,
       Delay not, O God.

(1) **Anxiously waited.** Heb. *qavvāh qivvīthī.* A. V. *waited patiently.* In the Heb. the indicative form is preceded by the infinitive of the same verb (*I waiting waited*), a common method of expressing intensity. The verb *qāvāh* is usually elsewhere translated *to wait.* But it implies great ardour and earnestness in desire and hope, and the rendering "patiently waited" is too passive to give the right conception. It is used here of one in imminent peril and great misery, who is crying loudly and most importunately to God. It should be intensified to express the meaning of the accompanying infinitive, but the adverb selected should intensify the vehemence that lies in the word. It is often used elsewhere in connection with *yāhal, to expect,* or *hope,* as its equivalent; as in xxxix. 7, lxii. 5, and especially in cxxx. 5, a passage that best defines the meaning of the word, and suggests irrepressible anxiety, rather than patience: "My soul waiteth for Jehovah, and *my expectation* is from Him." " My soul waiteth for Jeho-

vah more than they that watch for the morning, more than they that watch for the morning."

(2) **Depths of the mire.** Heb. *mud of the mire,* — two equivalent words, implying depth of mire, and consequently great danger.

(6) **Mine ears didst Thou open.** Heb. *ears didst Thou dig for me.* Open ears are the symbol of obedience, in contrast with the preceding mention of various sacrifices (comp. 1 Sam. xv. 22), and in accordance with the following reference to the impartation of knowledge. The ears stand by synecdoche for a body furnished with all the faculties called into exercise by the Divine law. The Septuagint gives the general idea in its rendering, "a body hast Thou prepared me." The passage thus rendered is quoted in Heb. x. 5, as prophetic of Christ.

(12) With the confession of personal guilt in this verse, the typical reference to Christ falls into the background, and does not appear again in this Psalm.

XLI.

THE COMPLAINT AND PRAYER OF ONE SICK AND PERSECUTED.

INTERNAL evidence supports the title, "A Psalm of David." He is lying upon a bed of painful and dangerous sickness, and surrounded by malignant enemies, who came to him under pretence of friendship, but upon leaving spread calumnious reports about the desperate nature of the attack, and its connection with gross wickedness. One of these is conspicuous as having grossly abused the friendship and mutual confidence which had subsisted between them. In addition to the general typical relation of all Psalms descriptive of a suffering servant of God to the suffering Christ, our Saviour Himself speaks of his betrayal by Judas as a fulfilment of Scripture, quoting David's mention in ver. 9 of the treacherous friend who had "lifted his heel" against him.

In contrast with this, the Psalm opens with an invocation of the richest Divine blessing upon some friend who had been faithful and tender in his greatest distress. This personal reference is one of the most touching pictures of the Psalm. In the first three verses David prays God that if the man who has shown such loving sympathy should ever come under similar pressure of calamities, God will abundantly reward him by such seasonable help as is only possible for almighty power and infinite love.

He then and not before prays for himself; humbly spreading out his troubles, he confesses himself a guilty sinner before God, but implores Divine grace and help, with strong confidence that even by his sins he has not forfeited his place in the Divine favour. He is still substantially "blameless." His heart is yet sound and true in its allegiance to God.

1. He invokes the blessing of God upon one who had treated him with sympathy and kindness (1-3). 2. He confesses his sins, and complains of malignant slanders, especially of the treachery of a trusted friend (4-9). 3. He prays that being restored to health by God's mercy, he may be able to punish the treason from which he had suffered, and expresses his confidence in God (10-12).

FOR THE LEADER OF THE CHOIR. A PSALM OF DAVID.

1 How blest is the man who cares for the suffering;
  Jehovah protect him when evil days come.

2 Jehovah preserve him, and let him live on,
    "A happy one" called in the land,
  And give him not up to the greed of his foes.

3 On the couch where he pineth, Jehovah give strength;
  In his sickness his bed Thou wilt wholly transform.

4 I pray for myself, Jehovah have pity;
    Give health to my soul, for I sinned against Thee.
5 For mine enemies say of me, wishing me evil,
    " How soon shall he die, and his name be no more?"
6 If one come to see, he speaks falsehood;
        His heart gathers slander,
    And going abroad he proclaims it.

7 United against me, my foes are all whispering,
    They meditate evil against me ;
8 "A deed of baseness has fastened upon him,
    From the place where he lieth he shall rise not again."
9 Yea, my friend whom I trusted, that ate of my bread,
    Has lifted his heel as my foe.

10 But Thou, O Jehovah, in pity,
    Raise me up to requite them.
11 By this shall I know I have pleased Thee,
    That my foes shall not triumph against me;
12 And myself Thou upholdest as blameless,
    And hast placed in Thy presence forever.

13 JEHOVAH, THE GOD OF ISRAEL, BE BLESSED
    THROUGH THE AGES EVERLASTING: AMEN AND AMEN.

(1) **The suffering.** Heb. *dallim*, prop. *the feeble*, from *dālal, to hang down*, as a bucket in a well, or the slender branches of trees ; then, of the weakness of men, as shown by the limbs hanging down feebly. It is often used of *the poor*, in distinction from the rich, as powerless. But here the primary sense is most suitable, with reference to the Psalmist's prostration by dangerous illness, as described in the following verses.

(3) **In his sickness his bed Thou wilt wholly transform.** Heb. *his whole bed in his sickness Thou wilt turn.* There is no reference to a mere change on the surface for the temporary refreshment of the sufferer, as appears in the Eng. Bible, but a change in his whole condition.

The bed of sickness shall be exchanged for a bed of healthful rest. The perfect tense of the verb does not refer to past time, but what is anticipated as sure is seen as an accomplished fact.

(10) **To requite them.** " The requital meant is that to which David as lawful king was bound, and which he actually rendered in the strength of God, when he overcame Absalom's rebellion and asserted his authority in opposition to faithlessness and baseness." — *Delitzsch.*

(13) The doxology in this verse does not belong to the original Psalm, but concludes the First Book of Psalms. -- **Through the ages everlasting.** See note on xc. 2.

BOOK II.

XLII.

THIS Psalm and the following were no doubt originally one. At some unknown time the part constituting the present Psalm xliii. was detached for separate use. They are very similar in tone and tenour to the eighty-fourth Psalm, and have reference to similar circumstances of enforced absence from Jerusalem, and the worship of God as there established. It is not improbable that they are by the same author.

In its style and allusions this duplex Psalm seems best fitted to the time of David, and his circumstances during Absalom's rebellion. Though attributed by the title to the sons of Korah, it would seem to be the royal exile himself who is here represented as speaking, by companions who knew so well what thoughts agitated his mind and heart during that cheerless wandering. " These two Psalms were used together in the Hebrew synagogues at the great Festival of Tabernacles. Psalm xliii. is appointed in the Gregorian use for Good Friday, and in the present Latin Church for Easter Eve." — *Wordsworth*.

CRITICAL NOTE. In the Hebrew text the refrain in xlii. 5 differs from that in verse 11, and xliii. 5, in the absence of *'Elohai, my God*, at the close. There is the strongest probability that they were originally alike. The probable solution has been suggested, and is generally approved, that in the transition from the very ancient continuous writing to the present division into words and verses, *'Elohai, my God*, the first word of the following verse in the present text, should have been included in verse 5. (So Sept., Syr. and Vulg.) Perowne suggests as probable, but his view has no support from versions, that in the oldest text *'Elohai* occurred at the end of verse 5, as well as at the beginning of verse 6, and that while they were not yet separated by verse division or intervening space, one *'Elohai* was omitted in correction of a supposed error, and that in the subsequent verse division the remaining *'Elohai* was given to verse 6, which needed it the least.

The apparent difference in the possessive pronoun is easily disposed of. If *'Elohai* had remained at the end of verse 5, in accordance with either of the above suppositions, the Massorites must have pointed the preceding letter *vav*, which makes the difference between "his countenance" and "my countenance," as the connective *and*. We should then have had in verse 5, as at the close of the following strophes, "my countenance and my God."

1. Longing after God, and tender reminiscence (xlii. 1–5). 2. Description of his own misery (6–11). 3. Prayer for deliverance, and joyful anticipation (xliii. 1–5). Each strophe ends with a refrain remonstrating with his own soul, and inciting himself to courage and hope.

FOR THE LEADER OF THE CHOIR. A MASKIL. BY THE SONS OF KORAH.

1 Like the hind when she pants
    For the brooks that have water,
  Is my soul, O God, in its panting for Thee.
2 My soul thirsteth for God, for the God that has life;
  Oh when may I come and appear before God?
3 My tears are my food day and night,
  While all the day long they say to me,
    " Where is thy God? "
4 I must call this to mind, and within me will pour out my
    soul,
  How I led on the crowd with slow step to God's house,
    With clear singing and praise, a festival throng.
5 Oh, why art thou downcast, my soul,
    And why art thou moaning within me?
  Still hope thou in God, for e'en yet I shall praise Him;
    He whose presence will save is my God.

6 My soul, O my God, lies prostrate within me;
  In the land of the Jordan I therefore recall Thee,
    On the Hermons, and highland of Mizar.
7 At Thy voice in the cataracts, wave calls to wave;
  All Thy breakers and billows o'erwhelm me.
8 Yet His own lovingkindness
    Jehovah by day will command;
  In the night, too, a song shall be with me,
    A prayer to the God of my life:
9 I will say unto God, my high-lifted rock,
    " Oh, why put me out of Thy mind,
  And why go I mourning, oppressed by the foe? "

10 As if crushing my bones mine enemies scoff,
        While all the day long they say to me,
            " Where is thy God? "
11 Oh, why art thou downcast, my soul,
        And why art thou moaning within me?
    Still hope thou in God, for e'en yet I shall praise Him ;
        He whose presence will save is my God.

XLIII.

1 Give me justice, O God,
        With a merciless nation contend for my right ;
    Oh, save me from crafty and violent men.
2 For Thou art my refuge, O God ;
        Then why dost Thou spurn me,
    And why go I mourning, oppressed by the foe?
3 Thy light and Thy truth,
        Send them forth that they lead me ;
    To Thy holy hill let them bring me,
        To the place where Thou dwellest.
4 Then will I come to the altar of God,
        Unto God, my most joyful of joys ;
    O God, my God, on the harp will I praise Thee.
5 Oh, why art thou downcast, my soul,
        And why art thou moaning within me?
6 Still hope thou in God, for e'en yet I shall praise Him ;
        He whose presence will save is my God.

(1) **Like the hind.** Heb. *'ayil.* The noun is feminine, as shown by the feminine form of the following verb. This may be partly to correspond with *nephesh, the soul,* which is feminine in Hebrew; but the male deer with its horns, a standing symbol of strength, would be less suitable in a picture of helpless suffering, appealing to our sympathy; especially since this noun *'ayil* in its primary meaning signifies *strength.* — **Pants** . . .

The word expresses intense and irrepressible desire. Moll : " Its application here to the relation of the soul of man to God, and in Joel i. 20. to the beasts of the field, is explained by the fact that the living God is often set forth as a spring of living water for the refreshment of the thirsty ; Ps. xxxvi. 8, lxxxiv. 3 ; Jer. ii. 13, xvii. 13." — **The brooks that have water.** Heb. *'appiqe mayim.* The noun *'appiq* is used in Is. viii. 7 and

Ezek. xxxii. 6 of the *channel* or *bed* of a stream; and in Ps. xviii. 15 of the *bed* or *lowest depths* of the sea. Elsewhere simply of a *brook* or *torrent;* cxxvi. 4; Job vi. 15, etc. The added *máyim, water,* suggests streams that have water, in distinction from those that have failed in the summer heat. Most of the streams in Palestine are torrents, flowing only in winter. The combination *'appîqê mayim,* occurs elsewhere only in Joel i. 20, in a description of extreme drought, when the beasts are said to "pant toward God," because even *the channels of water,* that is, those in which on account of their depth it may usually be found, are dried up.

(2) The soul's longing is now a *thirsting,* not for water, but for *the living God* (Heb. *'ēl khay),* as in lxxxiv. 3,—not merely of God as living, in contrast with dead idols, but as elsewhere, of God as having in Himself the absolute, potential life from which all life proceeds. Compare xxxvi. 9, "the fountain of life." So Job xix. 25, "my Redeemer liveth" (Heb. as here, *hhay)* as the ground of the hope of life in the future then confidently expressed. This is the "life in Himself," the life-producing Life, possessed by the Father and given to the Son, John v. 26, to which our Saviour in ver. 25 directly attributed the resurrection of the dead. — **Oh, when may I come and appear before God.** The Psalmist hopes for some new infusion of this life from God through the ordinances of the sanctuary. Notice the concurrence of the two Divine names, *'Elohim* and *'El.* The former exhibits God as *one to be worshipped,* the latter as the Strong. Where the two come together, and often elsewhere there is express reference to Divine power. See xix. 1, xxii. 1, and especially l. 1, where they both occur in combination with Jehovah, founded on Josh. xxii. 22, where they are twice repeated. One might almost weave the identical

Hebrew words *'El, 'Elohim, Jehovah* into our English rendering, as R. M. McCheyne has given us *Jehovah Tsidkēnu,* for "the LORD our Righteousness," in a delightful hymn.

(3) **My tears are my food;** that is, they take the place of my food. (See Job iii. 24.) In his daily life he is weeping when he should be eating, as in lxxx. 5, cii. 9: 1 Kings xxii. 27; Is. xxx. 20. In connection with this verse and vv. 9 and 10, we are not to suppose that malignant enemies had followed him into this far off wilderness. On the contrary they must have remained at home to enjoy the fruits of their treason. The poet here idealizes, as if his subject were possessed of a double personality, one in Jerusalem enduring ignominy and insult, compared to the crushing of his bones, and the other a fugitive in the far North. The idealization is founded upon the fact that he had vividly before his mind the scoffs, slanders, and imprecations from which he well knew that his enemies did not desist even during his absence, and they produced the keenest suffering.

(4) **I must call this to mind.** Heb. *'ēleh, these,* referring to what follows, his former condition of privilege in the sanctuary. The verbs in this line are in the *voluntative* form. He yields himself to the sad, yet comforting recollection. The imperfect tenses that follow describe what was habitual in the past, now called up vividly into the present. — **Led on the crowd with slow step.** The principal verb *'eddaddēm,* from *dādāh, to go softly* or *slowly,* either of an individual alone (see Is. xxxviii. 15), or as here, of a solemn procession with reverent step. The objective suffix *ēm* shows that the verb is transitive, and that the poet was director, not necessarily that he was leader of the choir (Ges., Del., etc.), but that as king, after singers and priests, he occupied the principal place in the procession. The preceding verb *'ebar, I pass on,* blends by

Hendiadys with that which follows, imparting the onward motion to the slow leading. — **Crowd.** Heb. *sak*, from *s.ikak. to interweave;* this noun form occurs only here ; prop. *a thicket* of trees, then poet. *a dense crowd* of men. — **A festival throng.** Lit. *a feast-keeping throng,* the part. *hhôgêg,* prop. *moving in a circle;* then, *celebrating a festival,* as it comes round in its turn every year. Eng. Bible, *keeping holyday.*

(5) **He whose presence will save is my God.** Adopting, as seen in the critical note above, a change in the Hebrew text that unifies the refrain here with ver. 11 and xliii. 5, the more literal rendering would be, "My salvation by His presence and my God."

According to Hebrew usage, the noun "salvation" and its limiting genitive, "*of countenance,*" form a compound. In such cases, if a defining article or possessive pronoun is required, it must always be attached to the second noun, yet belongs to the first as limited by the second. In several hundred instances of the use of this Hebrew word as noun or verb, with mention of its object, never elsewhere is the idea presented of saving a man's countenance. Moreover, no instance can be given of *the countenance* being used for the man himself in his personality, except the very unsatisfactory one cited by Dr. Moll, Is. iii. 15, "Ye grind the faces of the poor."

But *salvation, help,* or *victory,* as the word *yeshûahh* is variously translated, is often ascribed to God's face or countenance. In fact, by common consent, if the received text of xliii. 5 be the true reading, "the help of His countenance," or "the salvation of His presence," is the correct translation, and the "countenance" or "presence" that saves, is God's. Every one recognizes the genitive here as a genitive of origin and not of object. But in ver. 11 and in xliii. 5 it has been assumed without question that in the construction "salva-

tion," "help," or "health" of "face," "countenance," or "presence," we have a genitive of object and not of origin, — that it is not God's countenance that saves, as before, but man's countenance that is saved.

Now these refrains, admitting an original difference in the text, can hardly be so wide apart in meaning as this. If in the first of them we may or must read, "the health (Am. Rev. *help)* of His countenance," or more literally "His help of countenance ; " then lower down in the same Psalm we should, in consistency, read " He is my help-of-countenance and my God," or " He whose presence saves me, and my God."

It was probably in their feeling that the expression *help,* or *salvation of my countenance,* for *my personal salvation,* was hard and inadmissible, that the early English translators have given *yeshûahh* the rendering *health,* here alone in more than one hundred instances of the use of this very familiar word. The explanation they would have given is probably that it refers to deliverance from great trouble under the figure of the restoration of a sick man to health, as indicated by his countenance. This surely is not the meaning of the Hebrew. The American Revisers prefer "the help of my countenance." This is neither English nor Hebrew. It must be said, however, that their very conservative rules did not allow them to change materially a passage like this. They could do no more than to suggest the insertion in the text of the marginal "help," which is certainly a better translation of the word.

We only now give a few instances in which salvation or help for man is represented as originating in God's countenance or presence, sometimes beautifully and grandly of the light of His presence as dissipating the darkness of misery and ruin. In the Psalms consider xxxi. 16, xliv. 3, lxvii. 1, 2, lxxx. 3, 7, 19. These and their like, together with many expressions of wretchedness and suffering experienced or apprehended through the hiding of God's countenance, have their origin in the *loci classici* on this subject; Exod. xxxiii. 14, 15, and Num. vi. 26.

(6) **On the Hermons and highland of Mizar.** The plural "Hermons" does not refer to the peaks so called, but is to be understood in a broad sense as covering the whole northeastern corner of Palestine on the slopes of Hermon. With the country over the Jordan it includes the whole ridge of Anti-Libanus running southeasterly (Delitzsch).

Mount Mizar cannot be identified. The name means *littleness*. There is no apparent allusion to this here. But the mountain probably was small, and therefore very little known then or since. Perhaps the poet himself gave it the name, to mark it in his own recollection, and in the story of his wanderings. Have we any hint of its importance in the story as here told? It would seem to lie in the next verse. Crossing the Jordan at the "fords of the wilderness" (2 Sam. xvii. 16, 22), the fugitives pass through the country east of the river till they strike the northern mountain region in sight of the snowy peaks of Hermon, and reach at last a mountain insignificant in itself, but ever memorable from its position, and all it suggested to the mind of their leader. From the height overlooking some unknown body of water, they see a raging storm. Added to the fierce sweep of the winds, and the tumult of the waves, they hear the roar of the mountain torrent pouring down the sharp declivities. The sound of the cataracts, which to the poet, like the roll of the thunder in Ps. xxix., is the voice of Jehovah, is giving the signal for the wildest commotion, and exciting the waves to greater fury. One great swelling mass of water calls to another, and now, what he sees becomes a para-

ble of his tempest-tossed life. His own soul, in helplessness and terror, seems to be struggling amid the billows, and unless God please to deliver, will be hopelessly overwhelmed. — **At Thy voice in the cataracts.** Here the Septuagint gives *kataraktoi*. The Hebrew word seems to mean a *pipe*, or *orifice*. It probably refers to the narrow channel in the rock out of which the water was leaping into the gulf below. Coverdale has, "At the noyse of thy whystles," thinking of a wind pipe, through which God was giving the signal as a trumpet. Here, as in the refrain above (see on ver. 5), the possessive pronoun belongs to the first of the words in a genitive construction, and we have "At thy cataract voice." It is impossible to identify the body of water upon which the storm was seen. The most probable of the conjectures connects it with the Lake of Muzerib, "the outflow from which into the Meddan forms a magnificent waterfall of sixty to eighty feet, the only one in Syria" (DeWetstein's Appendix to Delitzsch on Job).

(7) We have here, literally, "breakers and rollers," the descriptive words that are yet often applied to the great surges of the sea.

(9) **My high-lifted rock.** Heb. *sela* (סֶלַע), *a cliff*, as a place on which one is lifted out of danger. See note at xviii. 2.

(xliii. 3) **Thy light and Thy truth.** The light of God's saving grace shining upon the night of misery, and His truth in the fulfilment of His promises, are here personified as Divine messengers, who would surely lead him back to all he had lost.

(4) **My most joyful of joys.** Lit. *my joy of exultation*. The notion of joy is put in the superlative by uniting two nearly synonymous words. This is often done in Hebrew by repeating the same word.

XLIV.

A LITANY OF ISRAEL, HARD PRESSED BY THE ENEMY AND YET FAITHFUL TO ITS GOD.

THE counterpart of this Psalm is Ps. lxxxv., both being plaintive and supplicatory Psalms of a national character, by the sons of Korah. Of the same general tenor are lx. lxxx. and lxxxix., all contrasting the present with former times, and lamenting the failure of the promises of God to His chosen people. This differs from the others in the expression of conscious innocence. As to its historical background, there are some coincidences with the time of the Maccabees, but by other important considerations this reference is precluded (Del.). The solemn assertion of Israel's covenant faithfulness (ver. 17, 18) is conclusive against all suppositions except that which assigns it with the Ps. lx. to the time of David and the Syro-Ammonite war, the result of which is given in 2 Sam. viii. 1–14. Before the first onset, when mighty hosts were advancing against them, there were probably great anxiety and dejection. The burial of the many in Israel that were slain, and Joab's fearful revenge are mentioned incidentally in 1 Kings xi. 15, 16. (So Hengst., Keil, Del., and Moll.) Perowne objects that "the language of the Psalm is too large to be applied to a sudden attack. It describes a more serious and lasting calamity." But it is just here that we must expect some difference between poetic representation and historic fact. It is quite characteristic of the Psalms to idealize the circumstances to which they relate, seeing deeper and darker evils and sufferings in natural sequence to those existing, which are inevitable unless God graciously interposes. The imagination of the poet transports him into the midst of calamities fearfully anticipated, which he describes as if present and actual.

1. God's power and kindness as shown to their fathers (1–3). 2. Confidence that He will now give them victory (4–8). 3. The contrast of this hope to their recent overwhelming defeat (9–12). 4. And their consequent disgrace among the nations (13–16). 5. Yet they have not been unfaithful to their covenant (17–19). 6. But can appeal to the omniscient God that they are suffering on account of their fidelity to Him (20–22). 7. And entreat His help in their great distress (23–26).

FOR THE LEADER OF THE CHOIR. BY THE SONS OF KORAH. A MASKIL.

    1 O God, we have heard with our ears,
        Our fathers have told us,
      What work Thou didst in their days,
        In the days of old time;

2 That Thine was the hand that uprooted the heathen,
       And themselves planted in;
   That broke up the nations,
       And themselves spread abroad.
3 For not by the sword did the land become theirs,
       And their arm did not save them;
   But Thine the right hand, and the arm also Thine,
       And Thy presence gave light,
           For Thy favour was with them.

4 Do Thou, the same God, who Thyself art my King,
   Command victories for Jacob.
5 Through Thee do we push down our foes,
   Through Thy Name trample down our assailants.
6 For not in my bow do I trust,
   And my sword cannot give me the victory;
7 But Thou from oppressors didst save us,
   And by Thee were our foes put to shame.
8 All the day long do we triumph in God,
   And Thy Name will we praise evermore.   [Selah.]

9 Yet Thou puttest us from Thee disgraced,
   And goest not forth with our hosts;
10 Thou hast made us turn back from the foe;
   They that hate us take spoil at their pleasure;
11 Like sheep hast Thou given us for food,
   In the lands of the heathen dispersed us;
12 Thou sellest Thy people for nought,
   And hast not gained wealth by their price.

13 Thou hast made us a scorn to our neighbours,
   A scoff and a jeer to those round about us.
14 Thou hast made us a by-word to heathen;
   The nations toss the head in contempt.
15 All the day long my disgrace is before me,
   And the shame of my face overwhelms me,
16 At the voice of blaspheming revilers,
   At the sight of the hating and vengeful.

17 Though all this came upon us, we do not forget Thee,
Nor yet are we false to Thy covenant.
18 Our heart draws not back,
Our steps have not swerved from Thy path,
19 That so Thou shouldest crush us,
In the place of the jackal,
With the shadow of death shouldst enshroud us.
20 If forgetting the Name of our God,
We spread forth our hands to the God of the alien,
21 Would not God search this out?
For He knows the deep thoughts of the heart.
22 But for Thee are we slain all the day long,
We are reckoned as sheep for the slaughter.

23 Arouse Thee; why sleepest Thou, Lord?
Awake; do not spurn us forever.
24 Oh, why hast Thou hidden Thy face,
Forgetting our suffering and pressure?
25 For our soul is bowed down to the dust,
And our body cleaves close to the earth.
26 Oh, arise for our aid;
For the sake of Thy great lovingkindness redeem us.

(3) Thine the right hand, etc.; strengthening the preceding subject "*Thou;*" God's right hand being the symbol of His power in its highest activity.

(4) Do Thou, the same God, etc. Heb. *Thou, He, my King, O God;* "Thou" is emphatic, — Thyself and no other. The pronoun "He" is not an independent predicate, as in cii. 27, but it strengthens the subject, and contains an emphatic reference to the past as just related. It identifies the God who now rules, with Himself in former deliverances. See Neh. ix. 6, 7, for precisely similar use of the pronoun. — **Jacob.** The personal name of the patriarch identifies his descendants now living with those whom God had formerly befriended so signally.

(14) The nations toss the head in contempt. Heb. lit. *a headshaking among the nations.* See xxii. 7.

(19) In the place of the jackal. The most lonely and terrible wilderness. The cry of the jackal, resembling the wailing of human beings is suggestive of the greatest distress.

(22) But for Thee are we slain, etc. St. Paul quotes these words in Romans viii. 36, as descriptive of the sufferings of the N. Test. Church.

(23) Why sleepest Thou? God is said to sleep when He does not interfere in whatever is taking place in the outward world here below, for the very nature of sleep is a turning in into one's self from all relationship to the outer world, and a resting of the powers which act outwardly (Delitzsch).

XLV.

THE MARRIAGE SONG OF AN INCOMPARABLE KING.

IT is doubtful to what king this Psalm refers. He was evidently of the house of David, and about to be married to a foreign princess. It is assumed in the Epistle to the Hebrews (i. 8) that it describes the Messiah, and the Messianic interpretation is very ancient. But back of this there was undoubtedly the espousal of a king of Israel cotemporary with the poet. As Delitzsch remarks, except on the presupposition of its prophetico-allegorical sense, we cannot understand its admission into the sacred canon. This meaning and interpretation are founded on the typical character of the whole royal line in Israel on the one hand, and on the other, the frequent representation of the relation of the chosen people, in its organic unity, to Jehovah as a marriage. "To the kingship of David according to 2 Sam. vii. 8–17, there were attached great promises applying to an unlimited future, and, therefore, also all the anticipations of Israel's future blessedness and glory." — *Delitzsch.*

It is not strange that an inspired poet should seize on the occasion of the marriage of an illustrious scion of this line to compose a hymn for all time, depicting on the historical basis of the event then celebrated, the glories of the Messiah whose dominion should be everlasting, and the regenerate Israel of the future brought into permanent relations of love and blessedness with her anointed king.

The allegory, however, must not be pressed too closely in its poetic details. Many of them belong to the drapery of the poem in its connection with the customs of the time, and have no prophetic significance.

It cannot be certainly determined whether we are to find the historic origin of this song in the marriage of Jehoram, the son of Jehoshaphat, to Athaliah, a princess of the royal house of Tyre (Del.), or of Solomon to a daughter of Hiram king of Tyre (Hupf.), or to a daughter of the king of Egypt, as most interpreters.

1. The praise of the royal bridegroom, his beauty, his eloquence, his might and prowess in war, his divine majesty, and the righteousness of his sway (1–9). 2. The description of the royal bride, her gold-inwoven garments, the virgins in her train, the music and songs of the bridal procession (10–15). 3. Anticipations for the children by this marriage who shall perpetuate the dynasty of the monarch, so that his name shall be famous forever (16, 17).

FOR THE LEADER OF THE CHOIR. SET TO "SHOSHANNIM." BY THE SONS OF KORAH. A MASKIL. A SONG.

1 My heart overflows with good words,
      For I, and I only, can say,
         "My song is in praise of the king;"
  Be my tongue the pen of swift writers.

2 Thou art fairer by far than the children of men,
    And grace is shed forth on thy lips;
  God surely had blessed thee forever.

3 With thy sword on the thigh, mighty champion,
  Gird about thee thy splendour and glory;
4 In thy splendour press forward, ride on,
    In the cause of truth, and the right of the lowly,
  And thy right hand shall guide thee to terrible deeds.
5 Thine arrows are sharp,
    And under thee nations shall fall,
  The king's enemies pierced to the heart.

6 Thy throne is forever and alway, O God,
  And a sceptre of right is thy sceptre of rule.
7 Since justice thou lovest and hatest oppression,
  With oil of rejoicing above thy companions,
    God, thine own God, doth anoint thee.

8 Thy robes are all myrrh,
    And the wood of the fragrant agalloch,
  And from ivory palaces harps give thee joy;
9 Among those in thy favour
    Are the daughters of kings,
  And in gold, brought from Ophir,
    The queen has her place on thy right.

10 Hearken, O daughter, and see,
    Let thine ear be attent;
  Thy people forget and the house of thy father,
11 That the king may have joy in thy beauty;
  For he is thy lord, and worship thou him;
12 And the daughter of Tyre shall bring gifts,
  The rich of the people shall sue for thy favour.

13 All glory is the royal maiden abiding within,
  Her raiment inwoven with gold;
14 And on fabrics embroidered is led to the king,
  With her virgin companions that follow —
    To thee are they brought;

15 They are led with rejoicing and gladness,
   To the king in his palace they come.

16 In place of thy fathers thy sons shall appear;
   Thou wilt set them as princes to rule the whole earth.
17 I will publish thy name to all generations,
   That forever and alway the people may praise thee.

(1) **Overflows.** Heb. *rāhhash, to boil over*, as boiling water, or a fountain. The expression denotes intense excitement and exuberant fulness. — **I, and I only, can say.** Heb. *'ōmar 'ani.* The emphatic pronoun becomes doubly emphatic by being put after the verb, and under a heavy accent, and the emphasis is exclusive. It is his special and peculiar honour and privilege. He is the poet laureate, and the thought stirs up his whole nature to do its best work. — **My song is in praise of the king.** Lit. *my works are for*, that is, the *constructions* or *creations* of his mind and heart, tongue and pen, as seen in this poem. — **Be my tongue the pen, etc.**; as if he were improvising, or as he composes were chanting to a suitable melody, and a rapid writer were taking down the words from his lips.

(2) **Thou art fairer by far.** Heb. *yoph-ya-phī-thā*, a form of the verb *yaphāh, to be beautiful*, intensified by reduplication of the consonants. This produces an alliteration that is echoed in our rendering. — **God surely had blessed thee forever.** Heb. *'al-kēn Elohim.* The usual rendering "*therefore*" would here be misleading. The poet does not state *a result;* as if God had blessed him on account of his beauty and gracious utterances. But he infers from them an antecedent cause. What he now sees and hears is the manifestation and proof that God has blessed him; consequently the tense is the perfect, preceded by a statement in which the ruling verb is in the *imperfect* (virtually the *present* tense). This

use of the tenses, like our pluperfect, gives the near and the remote their proper perspective. See Driver's *Heb. Tenses,* p. 19.

(3) **Mighty champion.** Heb. *gibbōr, a strong man*, but always of a warrior, hero, or champion distinguished in military affairs. See on xix. 5, xxiv. 7, 9. Here a champion or defender of truth and righteousness.

(4) **The right of the lowly** Heb. עַנְוָה צֶרֶק, *meekness-righteousness.* Two nouns apparently in apposition. Perowne: "*righteous meekness.*"

(5) Lit. *In the heart of the king's enemies.*

(6) **Thy throne, O God.** Modern criticism until very recently has pressed hard for a translation which shall avoid rendering '*Elohim (God)* as a vocative, advocating either "Thy throne of God," that is, thy Divine throne; or, assuming an ellipsis, "Thy throne is (a throne of) God;" or, "Thy throne is God." But it is now fully conceded that any translation of the present Hebrew text, other than that of the Septuagint, which our English Bible follows, is harsh, unsatisfactory, and most improbable. The claim is substituted, that the Hebrew text is corrupt. This is based, however, solely on subjective and conjectural grounds, and has no support from any manuscript or version. See Cheyne *in loc.* and Toy's *Quotations from the O. T.* under Heb. i. 8. Cheyne, adopting Bickel's restoration (?), translates as follows, the supplied words in italics : —

"As for thy throne, *firm is its foundation,*
   God *has established* it forever and ever."

This is a fair example of the dangerous temerity of some modern leaders in textual criticism. — **For-ever and alway**, — not the more usual repetition 'ōlām v'ōlām, but the frequent 'ōlām v'ad (עַד וְעֹלָם); 'ad from 'ādāh, *to pass along;* 'olam gives us time in the mass — the great cycle whose farthest bound is hidden from sight; but 'ad (עַד), that endless time in *detail, duration, continuity;* somewhat like the Greek ἄχρι, in distinction from μέχρι. This is of value in the full conception of eternity.

(8) **All myrrh.** Not *like* myrrh; a bold metaphor, as if myrrh, etc., were the material of his clothing. — **The wood of the fragrant agalloch.** Heb. 'ahhālōth qetsīōth. The two words are without the intervening connective *and.* The 'ahhalāh is also mentioned as a perfume in Prov. viii. 17 and Cant. iv. 14. There as here the form is plural, and is translated as plural in the Eng. Bible. It is not to be identified with the bitter and nauseous drug bearing the name "*aloes*" (always plural), nor with the aloe proper, a plant or tree found in various parts of the world. It is the agalloch, a very large tree growing in India and Cochin China, and of great value for its perfume. The name is not of Semitic but of Indian origin. Sanscrit *aguru.* Hind. *aghīla.* The misleading name "aloe" probably came into use from its similarity in sound to the word in the Indian dialects. See the Lexicons. *Ahhalōth* is directly followed by *qetsī'ōth.* It is a word not found elsewhere in the O. T., *qiddāh* being the "cassia" mentioned in Exod. xxx. 24 and Ezek. xxvii. 19. Here, too, the translation of the word by "cassia" may have originated in similarity of sound, in addition to the suitableness of this well known aromatic bark in connection with the two fragrant productions already mentioned. But its direct connection with 'ahhalōth, and its similar feminine plural termination, as if in grammatical agreement, besides its evident relation to the verb *qātsāh, to cut off* or *out,* in the *qātil* form of the passive participle (like 'āsir, *imprisoned,* and *māshiahh, anointed*), suggest as far more probable that it describes the preceding 'ahhalōth not as trees, but as wood cut up into blocks or chips; for in this form the perfume was brought from far-off regions with other precious things in the time of Solomon and thereafter. Dr. Royle of the Royal Asiatic Societies of London and Calcutta, an eminent authority, gives a very full and satisfactory account of the agalloch under "*Ahalim,*" in Kitto's Encyclopædia. He describes the wood, the *bois d'aigle* (eagle-wood) of commerce, as gorged with fragrant resin. It is obtained by the natives by cutting into the body of the huge tree until the dark-coloured veins which contain the perfume are reached, and pieces charged with it are taken away. Specimens may be seen in the Museum of the East India House at Calcutta.

The opinion that the reference here is not to the trees, but to pieces of the wood obtained by incision, is confirmed by the absence of all fragrance from the bark, branches, or leaves of this tree, and perhaps somewhat by the plural form *ahhālōth,* remembering that the Heb. word 'ēts (עֵץ), *tree* (coll.), in the plural form 'ētsīm, often means not *trees* but *sticks of wood, boards, timber,* or wood in pieces for any purpose whatever.

(8) **Harps.** Lit. *strings of harps.* So all later authorities.

(12) **Shall sue for thy favour.** Lit. *shall stroke thy face.*

(14) **On fabrics embroidered;** usually taken as descriptive of the clothing. But the queen's dress has already been mentioned twice (vv. 10, 14), and this verse relates to the marriage procession to the palace. The Hebrew expression is general: embroidered material for whatever

purpose designed.   Besides, the
preposition is not, as in ver. 13, *min*,
of the material of a fabric, nor *b* (ב),
of that *in* which one is clothed, but

the more indefinite *l* (ל), *as to*, or
towards, which is used in Hab. i. 6,
of walking on or over (Maurer, Perowne).

XLVI.

OUR GOD IS A STRONGHOLD.

THERE can be little doubt that the historic occasion of this Psalm is
the sudden destruction of Sennacherib's army before the gates of
Jerusalem, in the days of Hezekiah.   The confidence and insolence of the
Assyrian invaders are vividly portrayed in Is. xxxvi. xxxvii.   The leader
of the mighty host seemed fully warranted in his contemptuous and defiant
boasting by indisputable facts: "Let not Hezekiah deceive you, saying,
'the Lord will deliver us;' hath any of the gods of the nations delivered
his land out of the hand of the King of Assyria?"

But Israel is now to enjoy a manifestation of Divine power in her behalf,
second only to the deliverance from Egypt.   By a blow direct from heaven,
the pride of the conqueror is humbled, and he retreats in dismay.   " The
fall of so great a worldly power at so unexpected a time, and in contrast
with such slight external resources as Judah possessed, was bound to
awaken in every way joy and exultation, as well as profounder reflection."
— *Ewald*.

It would seem as if the poet had idealized recent historic events, as
connected with great Divine forces, that are working in defence of truth
and right against the evil and wrong that have so long been defiant and
dominant in the world.   This wonderful deliverance is before his mind as
suggestive of the final deliverance of the church from oppression and suffering. of a time under the reign of the Messiah, when evil shall be forever
vanquished, righteousness and peace covering the whole earth.   In this
aspect this song of praise is permanently precious.   It is the inspired
basis of Luther's magnificent choral, "Ein feste Burg ist unser Gott."

The *first strophe* brings out the general truth of the safety of those who
are under God's protection, even amidst the wildest commotions, and most
appalling dangers (1-3).

The *second strophe* exhibits more particularly the safety of Zion, as God's
dwelling place; from which all gracious influences descend in living
streams, and which He will maintain in beauty and strength, while under
His judgments opposing kingdoms shall tumble into ruin, and in the heat
of His wrath the solid earth shall be dissolved (4-7).

In the *third strophe* the completed result of the recent Divine interposition is celebrated in joyful song.   The uproar has ceased.   The enemy,

before the pride of whose power the chosen people had so lately trembled
in deadly fear, is put to silence, the instruments of war are destroyed, and
peace is restored to the wearied and exhausted earth (8–11).

FOR THE LEADER OF THE CHOIR.   BY THE SONS OF KORAH.   UPON
ALAMOTH.   A SONG.

1 We have God on our side, a refuge and fortress,
   A help in distress to be found without fail;
2 Therefore we fear not when the earth is all changed,
   And the mountains are shaken in the heart of the sea.
3 Let its waters roar and boil up,
   Let the mountains quake with their swelling.   [Selah.]

4 In the holy pavilion of God, the Most High,
      A river is flowing,
   Whose streams fill His city with joy;
5 She has God in the midst, and cannot be shaken,
   For God gives her aid at the earliest dawn.
6 The nations roared, the kingdoms were shaken,
   When He uttered His voice the earth was dissolved.
7 Jehovah Sebáoth is with us,
   The God of Jacob our refuge.   [Selah.]

8 Come, behold what Jehovah has done;
   What stillness He brought on the earth.
9 He silences war to the bounds of the earth;
   He shivers the bow, breaks asunder the spear,
      And burns up the chariot with fire.
10 Cease ye, and know, I am verily God;
   Above nations exalted, I am high in the earth.

11 Jehovah Sebáoth is with us,
   The God of Jacob our refuge.   [Selah.]

(1) **God on our side.** Heb. '*Elohim lānu.* The emphatic position
of *lānu* and its evident reference to
antagonistic powers favour our translating as in cxxiv. 1, 2. So *Jehovah
li* in cxviii. 6, " Jehovah is on my
side "—**Without fail.** Heb. *me'ōd,*
usually rendered *exceedingly.* It here
strongly confirms the whole preceding affirmation. Perowne renders,
"A help in distress He is very surely
found."

(2) **When the earth.** The prep.
b (2) before the infinitive is uniformly *temporal,* meaning *in the
time of,* and it cannot properly

be represented by the contingent "*though*" (A. V.). The early translators failed to see that the Psalmist is not drawing upon his imagination for possible convulsions in the frame of nature, in which should they occur, he would maintain his trust in God. But he is describing in figurative language actual events. A comparison of vv. 2, 3 with ver. 6 identifies the "change" of the earth with the desolation of war, the roar of the waves with the roar of excited nations, and tottering mountains with tottering kingdoms, — all among the palpable facts of recent history. **All changed**. Heb. *hāmîr*, a word meaning *exchange*, or the bartering of one thing for another, and so it describes a complete change in appearance or condition. — **Shaken**. Heb. *mût*. Here the R. V. substitutes "*moved*" for "*carried*" (A.V.), to correspond with the rendering of the same verb in verses 5, 6, and uniformly elsewhere. But this is a feeble and always inadequate rendering. The Heb. word always means *to shake* or *totter*, except where the context suggests the stronger idea of *falling*, or absolute overthrow. This latter may be the meaning here: the mountains overthrown (toppling over) into the heart (the depths) of the seas; or, according to our rendering, shaken to their very roots, which are regarded as spreading under the seas. This is affirmed here of mountains, and of the kingdoms of the world; but Zion, sustained by Almighty power, cannot be shaken.

(4) The exact order of the words in the Hebrew text would give us "A river (is flowing) whose streams make glad the city of God, the holy sanctuary of the Most High." The first Hebrew word, *nāhār, a flowing stream*, is from the root *nāhar, to flow*, which supplies a verb for the otherwise imperfect sentence. The second word *pelāgîm, streams,* —

that is, the conduits for conveying water in artificial irrigation. See note on i. 3. The question remaining relates to the last clause, "the holy sanctuary," etc.; whether it is in apposition with "the city," identifying the two (so A. V.), or an adverbial accusative, the place where the river is seen, and from which its waters are conveyed to the dwellings and inhabitants of the city. This is exactly consistent with grammatical usage. It gives clearness and beauty to the description, connecting the spiritual refreshment and blessing provided for the people at large with the institutions of worship as the appointed means of grace, as if streams were flowing from the heights of Zion to the lower levels of human life.

(7, 11) **Jehováh Sebaoth**. Jehovah *of hosts*, or *armies*, as in xxiv. 10. *Sebáoth* first appears as an addition to the highest Divine Name in the prayer of Hannah, 1 Sam. i. 11. It exhibits the omnipotence of God, as having all things created under His control as a vast army. The angels and the stars are called *His hosts* in ciii. 21, cxlviii. 2. Of the former see Gen. xxxii. 2. "He said 'This is God's host;'" of the latter, Jud. v. 20, "The stars in their courses fought against Sisera." Compare Joel iii. 11.

(8) **Stillness**. (A.V.) *desolations*. Heb. *shammôth*, lit. *silences*, from *shāmam*, prim. *to be struck dumb;* then the silence of a place deserted and desolate, in contrast with the noise and turmoil of inhabitants. The word seems to refer here not to *desolations*, whether wrought by war or more immediate Divine judgment, but more graphically to the *hush* that prevails when the tumult of war and the shouts of battle have ceased. This is confirmed explicatively by the following verses, "He silences war," etc.

XLVII.

ALL NATIONS WORSHIP JEHOVAH AS THEIR KING.

THE subject of this Psalm is the joyful acknowledgment by all nations of God's absolute sovereignty in the world. It embodies, therefore, the Messianic idea of the fulfilment of the promise to Abraham that he should be the father of nations, and so points forward to the time when this idea and promise should be fully realized in the ascension and exaltation of our blessed Lord.

Its position between Psalms xlvi. and xlviii. seems to embody a very ancient tradition that connects it with the same historic events. As already intimated in connection with the former of this triad, the invasion of Judea by the Assyrian army, and its defeat by special Divine intervention, as related in Is. xxxvii., seem best to correspond with the allusions of these Psalms. Hupfeld calls Ps. xlvii. a practical expansion of xlvi. 10, "I am exalted among the nations, I am exalted in the earth."

There are two strophes, — the first consisting of four verses, the second of five.

1. All nations called upon to rejoice in the subjugation of the earth to Jehovah as its rightful King (1-4). 2. Jehovah's assumption of the sovereignty, and ascension to the throne (5-9).

FOR THE LEADER OF THE CHOIR. BY THE SONS OF KORAH. A PSALM.

1 Clap your hands, all ye peoples ;
  Shout unto God with loud triumph ;
2 For Jehovah, Most High, is one to be feared,
  Over all the earth a great King.

3 He makes peoples submit to our rule,
  And nations puts under our feet ;
4 For us doth He choose the land we inherit,
  The pride of Jacob, the people that He loved.

5 Our God is gone up amid shoutings,
  Jehovah with sound of a trumpet ;
6 Strike the harp unto God, strike the harp,
  Strike the harp to our King, strike the harp.

7 For God is the King who rules the whole earth,
   Strike the harp with a song wisely wrought.
8 God governs the nations as King;
   On His holy throne is God seated.

9 The princes of peoples assembled,
       As a people of Abraham's God ;
   For God's own are the shields of the earth,
       He is greatly exalted.

(3, 4) The tenses here are present. There is reference, indeed, to the grace by which at the beginning of their national history the Canaanitish nations were conquered, and the chosen people put in possession of the goodly land. But that wondrous grace is here "idealized and generalized" (Del.). Every victory over invaders who would have robbed them of their inheritance is a confirmation, and virtually a repetition, of that ancient grace. It stands before the poet's eye as a new choice and gift by the immediate act of their covenant God.

(5) **God is gone up.** The display of God's power on earth in special judgments upon men is described as a descending from His throne; so when His designs have been accomplished, He is said to return to it; Gen. xvii. 22; Judg. xiii. 20; Ps. vii. 7, lxviii. 18.

XLVIII.

MOUNT ZION UNDER THE PROTECTION OF HER ALMIGHTY KING.

THIS Psalm is connected historically, and by internal sequence, with the two that precede it.

1. God praised, and Zion admired in its beauty and strength (1–3). 2. The defeat and dispersion of invading enemies (4–8). 3. The thought of 1–3 amplified ; God to be praised in all the earth, Israel to rejoice, and the glory of Zion to be recited to all generations (9–14).

A SONG. A PSALM BY THE SONS OF KORAH.

1 Jehovah is great and all-worthy of praise,
   On His holy mount, in the city of our God.
2 A beautiful rise, the joy of all earth,
   Is Mount Zion at the northernmost bounds,
       The city where dwells the great King;
3 God has made Himself known
   As a tower on her fortified heights.

    4 For, lo, when the kings set their time,
          They together came on;
    5 Even they, when they saw, were struck dumb,
          They were greatly afraid and they fled;
    6 Then shuddering seized them;
          They writhed like a woman in travail:
    7 With winds from the east,
          Ships of Tarshish Thou breakest in pieces.

    8 As we heard, even so have we seen,
              In the city of Jehovah of Hosts,
                  In the city of our God;
          God Himself upholds it forever.
    9 We have pondered Thy great lovingkindness, O God,
          In the midst of Thy palace;
   10 As Thy Name, even so is Thy praise;
          It reaches, O God, to the bounds of the earth,
              And righteousness fills Thy right hand.

   11 Let Mount Zion be glad,
              Let the daughters of Judah rejoice,
          Because of Thy judgments.
   12 Walk about Zion, the full circuit complete,
          Take account of her towers;
   13 Set your mind on her walls,
              And consider her fortified heights;
          That so ye may tell the next generation;
   14 For this God is our God, forever and alway,
          It is He that will guide us evermore.

(1) **All worthy of praise**. Heb. *m'hall³l me'ôd, to be praised exceedingly.*

(2) **At the northernmost bounds**: that is, of the city, or of the elevated plateau on which it was built. There can be no longer a doubt that the ancient hill of Zion is near the northern extremity of the more westerly of the two ridges into which the city was anciently divided. The temple hill was opposite on the eastern ridge. The crest of Zion was much the higher. On account of its elevation it was the characteristic feature of the Holy City, but by immense labour it was removed by the Maccabees, so that no hill higher than the Temple and the Upper City might be occupied by an enemy, as this had been by the Macedonians (Warren's " *Underground Jerusalem*," p. 52). On the eastern, western, and southern sides Jerusalem was bounded by impassable ravines, the valley of Hinnom on the west, and the valley of

Kedron on the east, with their steep declivities, forming a junction at the south, rendering the city almost impregnable except on the northern side, where strong fortifications were needed. Inside the wall, having the deep gorge on its easterly side, the massive citadel of Zion towered above everything around it.

The topographical features connected with the northern elevation of the fortress, furnish the simplest explanation of the phrase *yarkethē tsāphōn*. *Yarkethē* is a fem. *dual* form ; properly the *two haunches* or *hips* of an animal, at the back, and not at the *front*. The fem. form was reserved for *things* that round backward, having two sides; the part of a building farthest away from the front entrance ; in 1 Ki. vi. 16, the *back* of the temple (R.V.); in Is. xiv. 15, the *deepest recesses* of a pit, where the two sides converge.

The added *tsāphōn*, the *north*, gives the trend of the valleys on the two sides of Mount Zion, or the direction of the part referred to from the principal entrance of the citadel, which was probably on the southern exposure, facing the Upper City. It was *the hinder part* that presented itself most formidably to an invading army. We must assume the position of one approaching the city from a direction that gives a full view of the northern elevation. The description of the front may be more thoroughly appreciated in the light of the following sentences from Dean Stanley: " There is an approach to the city which is really grand, — namely, from Jericho and Bethany. It is the approach by which the army of Pompey advanced, — the first western army that ever confronted it, — and it is the approach of the Triumphal Entry of the Gospels. . . . The beauty consists in this, that you there burst at once on the two great ravines which cut the city off from the surrounding table-land, and that there you have a complete view of the Mosque of Omar. From whatever

point that graceful dome with its beautiful precinct emerges to view, it at once dignifies the whole city" (*Sinai and Palestine*, p. 157). We have only to substitute for the army of Pompey the confederate kings, whose consternation, flight, and ruin are described in verses 4–7, and for the Mosque of Omar the lofty ramparts of Zion, and we understand the Psalm. In " *the two sides*," or *thighs*, of the Hebrew text, there is probably an allusion to the two great converging ravines.

(3) **Fortified heights**. Heb. '*armôn, a fortress*, or *castle*. See 1 Ki. xvi. 18, 2 Ki. xv. 25; but the primary idea from the root '*aram* is *height*. The plural form refers to the mass of buildings included in the citadel; so in ver. 13. See 2 Sam. v. 10.

(4) **Set their time**. Heb. *yā'ad*, (יָעַד), *to appoint a place or time*. The Niphal form is reciprocal, — to agree upon a time, etc. It includes all preliminary arrangements for a united attack.

(5) **Even they**. The emphatic pronoun referring to their strength, self-confidence, and usual fearlessness.

(7) **Ships of Tarshish**. These in their size and strength are symbols of the powers of the world in their opposition to God. See Is. xxxiii. 21, 23. An expression of comparison, *as*, or *like*, might have been used. But the poet is bolder. Ideally he sees before him, in these enemies of Zion, strongly built ships of Tarshish foundered by the east wind. Yet there is possibly reference to an actual disaster at sea, similar to that related in 1 Ki. xxii. 48.

(8) **As . . . so**. Here the terms of comparison are used, characteristic of the concluding strophe. The poet's mind labours to express adequately the splendour of Zion, as glorified by the presence of her Divine King. " As we have heard " refers to what they have heard from their fathers of ancient deliverances; see xliv. 1.

—**God Himself.** The position of the Divine Name is emphatic.

(9) **Pondered.** Heb. *dammīnū, we have compared,*—of putting two things side by side, as in the preceding verse, in order to form a correct estimate. The result is reached in the *as* and *so* of the verse following.

(10) **As Thy Name, even so is Thy praise.** God's Name, as encouraging hope in His faithful love, and the praise of that love as realized, are equal, and both immeasurable.

(11) **The daughters of Judah.** A personification of the cities and villages of Judah that had suffered by the invasion.

(14) **Forever and alway.** See on xlv. 6. —**Evermore.** Heb. *'al-mūth.* Lit. *upon death.* Engl. Bible, *until death.* But this preposition never means *until,* and if it might, the thought is unsuitable here, as limiting the preceding assurance of eternal blessing to the present life. There are two explanations. The two words may be united, giving the meaning *eternities.* But this would be a feminine form which is never used elsewhere. Or, the *'Al-mūth* is a musical designation, belonging to the title of the next Psalm, as in the title to Ps. ix. The vowel pointing of the text is adapted to this view, but to no other. If it be correct, the Psalm properly ends, " It is He that will guide us." It is implied, however, that the guidance will continue " evermore," in the close connection of this line with the preceding, and the sense is not materially affected whether we insert or omit the word that expresses it.

XLIX.

THE VANITY OF EARTHLY AGGRANDIZEMENT.

PSALM xlix. is didactic, and contains no national or historic allusions. It is addressed to all men without distinction. " It discusses the problem of temporal happiness and the prosperity of the ungodly, and is therefore related to xxvii. and lxxiii." (Moll). It exhibits the transitoriness of the success and joy of the wicked, and the sure hope of the upright resting upon God. Its character is in harmony with the title which ascribes it to David as the author.

1. An introduction, exhibiting the general character and source of the communications that follow (1–4). 2. A description of the rich and ungodly, proud of their wealth and splendour, but surely passing away from the earth (5–12). 3. The lot of the righteous hereafter, contrasted with that of the wicked (13–20).

Each of the principal divisions is followed by a refrain, differing in a single word.

FOR THE LEADER OF THE CHOIR. BY THE SONS OF KORAH. A PSALM.

1 Hear this, all ye nations,
  Give ear, all that dwell on the earth,
2 Both low born and high,
  The rich and the poor all alike.

3 My mouth utters wisdom,
  And the thought of my heart is sound judgment;
4 Mine ear I incline to deep sayings,
  And my riddle disclose with the harp.

5 Why should I fear when the evil days come,
  When my guilty pursuers surround me?
6 They that trust in their riches
  And boast their abundance of wealth,
7 Not one can at all redeem his own brother,
  Nor make payment to God of his ransom, —
8 For the purchase of life is too costly,
  And forever must they let it alone —
9 That he may alway live on,
  And never go down to the grave.
10 For he seeth that wise men must die,
  The fool and the brutish, alike must they perish,
      And give up their riches to others.

11 It lies in their mind that their houses continue forever,
      Their dwellings to age after age;
  To their lands they give their own names.
12 But man in his grandeur abides not;
  He becomes like the beasts that must perish.

13 This is their course in their folly,
  With those coming after
      That delight in their sayings;   [Selah.]
14 They are gathered like sheep into Sheol,
      With Death as their Shepherd;
  In the morning the just tread them down,
      And their form shall Sheol consume,
          Till it have no place of abode.
15 But my soul God redeemeth from Sheol,
      For He will receive me.   [Selah.]

16 Have no fear when a man is made rich,
  When the glory of his house is increased.
17 For he dies and takes nothing away,
  His glory descendeth not with him.

18 Although in his lifetime he blesses his soul, —
   And others will praise thy good deeds for thyself, —
19 To his fathers' generation it goeth,
   Who eternally see not the light.
20 Man in his grandeur abides not,
   But resembleth the beasts that must perish.

(4) See the same combination of *māshāl, proverb*, and *hhīdāh, riddle*, in lxxviii. 2; Prov. i. 6.

(5) **Guilty pursuers**. Heb. *guilt at my heels*. See lvi. 6. "They watch my heels," — that is, my steps. The reference here is to evil-minded men who have been following in his track, and have overtaken and now are all about him.

(9) **That he may alway live on**. This connects with ver. 7, and ver. 8 is parenthetical.

(12) **It lies in their mind**. Heb. *b'qirbām, in their interior*. The intentional and admirable vagueness of the word has puzzled translators and interpreters. The poet is giving an inference from the outward to an unuttered and undefined inward. The "houses" mentioned are those they inhabit, and the "lands" (Heb. *'adāmōth, grounds*, land as cultivated), are those they occupy during their lifetime. The solidity of the former seems to embody the idea of resistance to the ravages of time, and possible convulsions of nature, and the acquisition of an everlasting home. This appears to have lain in the mind of the builder, not as an opinion, nor an expectation, nor a wish (Hengst., Del., Hitz.), and scarcely even as the ghost of an impression. In fact, while it has a certain activity and effectiveness, it is mainly negative. It ignores the dread certainty of death, and impels a man without thought or questioning to build as if for eternity. The Hebrew has no word to express this, or to fix its location in the human mechanism in the psychological significance of its several parts, and the poet takes refuge in the indeterminate *qirbām*. It is inside of him, somewhere in the circumference of his personal life. Our best name for it is perhaps instinct. It is the *simulacrum*, the spectre of his forfeited immortality that will not be laid to rest. The Targ., Sept., and Syr. versions translate here as if they had before them in the text *qebārām*, "*their graves are their houses forever*." This is probably a conjecture occasioned by the singular use of *qirbām* in such a connection. It has been followed by Olsh., Ew., Riehm, Cheyne, and others. Perowne does not adopt it, yet says, "It gives a good sense, and is the simplest reading." But whatever we gain here is more than counterbalanced by the difficulty in finding an intelligible sense for the closing line, and especially of finding a new subject for the verb "they give" (Heb. *qare'ū*. Lit. "they call"), after having put the owners of the land into their graves. Cheyne confesses this when he says, "Something must be supplied; rhythm and sense require it," and still more when he gives the following bold rendering, in palpable disregard of the Hebrew text, the versions, and all other authority, "(Forgotten are) they whose names men spoke with honour in the lands." The poet reminds us here of "the kings and counsellors of the earth" in Sheol (Job iii. 14), "which builded up waste places (Heb. *hharāboth*, marg. R. V., *desolate piles*) for themselves," referring to their palaces, as given up to desolation.

(13) From this point the style labours, as if oppressed by the gloom of the subject, and the sense here and there is obscure. — **Their course**. Heb. *their way*, of life in its future, as in xxxvii. 5, referring to the description in verses 14-19.

L.

THE NATURE OF TRUE WORSHIP DECIDED JUDICIALLY.

THIS is the first of twelve Psalms that bear the name of Asaph. The others, lxxiii.-lxxxiii., are the first eleven of the Third Book. Asaph and his sons were leaders of four out of the twenty-four classes into which the musical service for Divine worship was divided by David: 1 Chron. xxiii. 2-5. As a writer of Psalms Asaph is mentioned with David in 2 Chron. xxix. 30, where he is also called " the seer." The Asaphic Psalms have several characteristics in common. They are distinguished by loftiness of tone, combined with spirited and picturesque expression, and especially by their frequent exhibition of the sovereign judgment of God as determining the future.

While Ps. l. was probably composed by the elder Asaph, some Psalms of the group bear evidence of later origin. It is not unlikely that Asaph is here a family designation. The Asaphites are mentioned as late as the time of Nehemiah; Neh. vii. 44, xi. 22. Here, as in lxxv. and lxxxii., God appears as Judge, and addresses judicially those arraigned before Him.

The claim that in this Psalm the sacrifices of the Mosaic ritual are repudiated is without foundation. The only service repudiated is the substitution of the externality of sacrifice for the claims of the moral law, and for spiritual worship.

1. A Theophany, similar to that on Sinai, and a call on the covenanted people to stand before God for judgment (1-6). 2. An exposition of the Divine law, as against those who imagine that God is to be honoured only by sacrifice (7-15). 3. The ungodly are judged for their gross violations of the second table of the law, and appropriately warned (16-23).

A PSALM. BY ASAPH.

1 El Elóhim Jehovah
    Speaks and summons the earth
  From the rise of the sun to its setting.
2 Out of Zion the perfect in beauty,
    It is God that shines forth; .
3 He that comes is our God,
    He will not keep silence ;
  Consuming fires are before Him,
    And around Him fierce tempests.

4 He summons the heavens on high,
And the earth to attend,
    While He judges His people;
5 " Bring before me the people I loved,
Who accepted my covenant with sacrifice slain ; "
6 And the heavens proclaim Him the Righteous,
For God, and He only, is Judge.

7 " My people, oh hear, let Me speak ;
I must witness against thee, O Israel,
    I am God, and as God I am thine.
8 I do not arraign thee for sacrifice due,
For thine offerings by burning are ever before Me ;
9 No bullock I ask from thy house,
Nor he-goats from thy folds.
10 For all beasts of the forest are MINE,
And the kine on a thousand high hills.
11 I know every bird of the mountains,
And with ME is the brood of the plain.
12 Not to thee would I speak were I hungry,
For Mine is the world and its fulness ;
13 Do I feed on the flesh of your bullocks,
Or drink of the blood of he-goats?
14 Offer God thy thanksgiving,
And pay to the Highest thy vows ;
15 And call upon Me in the day of sore trouble,
I will come to thy rescue,
    And then thou wilt give Me the glory.

16 But God saith to the wicked,
    How darest thou utter MY statutes,
And my covenant take up on thy lips,
17 Thou that hatest instruction,
And behind thee art casting My words?
18 When thou seest a thief,
    With him thou hast pleasure,
And hast shared the adulterer's sin ;
19 Thy mouth hast thou loosened for evil,
And thy tongue frames deceit ;

20 Against thine own brother thou sittest and speakest,
    Yea, thou slanderest the son of thy mother.

21 These were thy doings, and because I kept silence,
      Thou thoughtest Me wholly like thee;
    I accuse thee and array them before thee.
22 Consider this, ye that put God out of mind,
    Lest I rend you asunder when none can deliver.

23 From him have I honour who offers thanksgiving;
    And to him that gives heed to his way,
      I will show the salvation of God.

(1) **El Elóhim Jehovah.** The three principal Divine Names grouped together, as only elsewhere in Josh. xxii. 22, to give impressiveness to the august majesty of God as now to appear for judgment; *El*, the oldest, God as *strong*; *Elóhim*, God as *feared and worshipped*; *Jehovah*, God as *manifested* in the history of redemption, especially as the God of Israel: see note at i. 2.

(5) **The people I have loved.** Heb. *hhāsīdī, my beloved*, referring to his gracious choice of Israel, as the object of special favour; see note at iv. 3.

(16) **How darest thou.** Heb. *what here for thee.*—that is, what right hast thou here? in severe questioning and reproof.

(23) **And to him, etc.** Or, *and prepareth a way where I show him the salvation of God* (Delitzsch).

LI.

THE SUPPLICATION OF A PENITENT.

THIS is the fourth of the Penitential Psalms (see on Ps. vi.), and one that has been used by the Church in song and prayer oftener than any other in the Psalter. We cannot doubt that its historic root is to be found in David's great sin. But as prepared for the worship of Israel, some of its expressions imply a consciousness of many sins. It is claimed to be proven by the last two verses that it was written during the captivity in Babylon. To this it is replied that these verses may have been a later addition. Or, if they are considered as belonging to the original Psalm, the phrase "build Thou the walls of Jerusalem" does not necessarily imply that the walls were actually prostrate, but only David's consciousness that the stability of his kingdom was imperilled by his sin (Perowne), and it is virtually a prayer that the walls of the city may be permanently established. Comp. Ps. lxix. 35. The Psalm includes—

1. Prayer for pity and pardon (1, 2). 2. Penitent confession of sinful deeds, and of a sinful nature (3-6). 3. Renewed prayer for deliverance from sin (7-9). 4. For renewal of heart (10-12). 5. For complete restoration, including grace to offer God acceptable sacrifices (13-17). 6. Intercession for Israel (18, 19).

FOR THE LEADER OF THE CHOIR. A PSALM OF DAVID, WHEN NATHAN THE PROPHET CAME TO HIM, AFTER HE HAD GONE IN TO BATHSHEBA.

1 Show me pity, O God, in Thy great lovingkindness,
   As Thy mercies abound, my transgressions blot out;
2 From my guilt wash me throughly,
  From my sin make me clean.

3 For I, oh I know my transgressions,
  And alway my sin is before me;
4 Against Thee, Thee alone, have I sinned,
    And this evil have done in Thy sight;
  That Thy charge may prove just,
    And Thy judgment be faultless.

5 Lo, in guilt was I born,
  And in sin did my mother conceive me;
6 Lo, Thy pleasure is truth deep within;
  In the part that is hid give me knowledge of wisdom.
7 With hyssop branch cleanse me, I then shall be pure;
  If Thou wash me, I thus shall be whiter than snow.

8 Joy and gladness again let me hear,
  That the bones Thou hast crushed may rejoice.
9 Hide Thy face from my sins,
  And all my guiltiness blot from Thy book.

10 Create for me, Lord, a pure heart,
   Yea, renew a right spirit within me;
11 And cast me not off from Thy presence;
   Thy Spirit of holiness, take Thou not from me.
12 My joy in Thy power of salvation restore,
   Let a willing spirit uphold me;
13 Then will I teach transgressors Thy way,
   And the sinner to Thee shall return.

14 Deliver me from bloodshed,
    O God, my God of salvation;
  Let my tongue of Thy righteousness sing.
15 Lord, open my lips,
  And my mouth shall publish Thy praise,
16 For sacrifice slain is not Thy delight,
    Or this would I bring Thee;
  Burnt offerings can give Thee no joy:
17 A broken spirit is sacrifice pleasing to God;
  A heart broken and contrite,
    O God, Thou wilt not despise.

18 In Thy favour do good unto Zion,
  And build Thou Jerusalem's walls;
19 Then shall right sacrifice please Thee,
    Burnt offerings, burnt offerings entire;
  Then shall bullocks be led to Thine altar.

(1, 2) **Transgressions, guilt, sin.** See note on these words at xxxii. 1, 2.

(6) **Truth deep within.** Heb. *battûhhôth, in the reins*, or kidneys; *tûhhôth* is equivalent to *kilyôth*, Ps. xvi. 7, where see note. Comp. xl. 8; God's law *in the midst of my bowels*. Truth in the reins signifies the firm establishment and rule of truth and right in a man's deepest and most inward experiences and emotions, in his most secret life, the life of his conscience and heart (Del.). See xv. 2, "the thought of whose heart is the truth," and consult the note there. — Parallel to this, **the part that is hid.** Heb. *sâthûm.* A most appropriate prayer here follows that the depths of his heart, the most secret springs of thought, purpose, and action, may be occupied and held by that Divine wisdom which is truth, and which expels all falsehood and delusion. The man who has it walks in the light as God is in the light; 1 John i. 9.

(7) **With hyssop branch cleanse me.** This is virtually a prayer for forgiveness. But not with any superficial view of the real situation, but with a deep consciousness of a moral impurity, which separates him from God, and which He only can remove. His expression of this cannot be understood except by referring to Lev. xiv. 4–7, and Num. xix. 18. A bunch of hyssop wound around with scarlet wool must be dipped and saturated for the sprinkling of the leper, and of those who had become unclean by contact with the dead. The reference is not to external and physical sprinkling by human manipulation, but to the Divine act which the sprinkling prescribed in the law symbolizes.

(16) **Sacrifice slain is not Thy delight.** This is not to be understood in disparagement of sacrifice, as if God had not appointed it, or it had ceased to be acceptable. It only declares the insufficiency of sacrifice as an *opus operatum*, and quite separate from the state of the heart described in the next verse. Elsewhere in similar connection prayer, sacrifice, and all observances of the cere-

monial law are declared offensive to God. See Is. i. 13-15. But what follows in the Psalm shows that such language must not be strained as implying the abrogation of the law of sacrifice: "Then shall right sacrifice please Thee," etc. See also at xl. 6.

(12) **A willing spirit** is one that obeys the Divine law, not by constraint, nor for the sake of reward, nor from fear of punishment, but spontaneously. His will, in all its impulses and inclinations, is in harmony with the will of God.

(19) **Burnt offerings entire**. There are no sacrifices in the Levitical law that are known specifically as "whole burnt offerings." The expression is elsewhere found only in Deut. xxxiii. 10, which also is poetical. The burnt offering as such was entirely consumed by fire; Lev. viii. 16, 17. It is probably only intended here to emphasize the disposition of one who has received pardon and special favour from God, to abate nothing from the most complete fulfilment of the law of sacrifice. His offering shall indeed be a holocaust, which shall symbolize the absolute surrender of his whole being to God his Redeemer.

LII.

THE PUNISHMENT OF THE MALIGNANT.

VARIOUS attempts have been made to find some other probable occasion for this Psalm than that mentioned in the title. But they have all failed. It is connected with the dastardly act of Doeg, the keeper of Saul's asses, informing the king of Ahimelech's kind treatment of David, as related in 1 Sam. xxii. 9. It resulted in the slaughter of eighty-five priests, with many men, women, and children in a priestly city. In fact, by the command of Saul he slew these defenceless ones with his own hand, and so merited the scornful salutation, " O hero ! "

It is a remarkable feature of this Psalm that God is not invoked in any part of it. The poet begins with direct address to the infamous offender, and severe arraignment and castigation, as representing the Almighty, in whose Name and by the inspiration of whose Spirit he speaks.

1. Denunciation (1–4). 2. Announcement of the Divine retribution (5–7). 3. Contrast between those who trust in wealth and wickedness, and those who rely upon God (8, 9).

FOR THE LEADER OF THE CHOIR. A MASKIL BY DAVID: WHEN THE EDOMITE CAME AND TOLD SAUL, AND SAID TO HIM, "DAVID IS COME TO THE HOUSE OF AHIMELECH."

  1 Why wilt thou glory in evil, O hero?
     Our God's lovingkindness endures through all time.
  2 Thy tongue, that devises engulfing destruction,
     Is a whetted razor, thou dealer in guile.

3 Thou hast pleasure in injury more than in kindness,
     And preferrest a lie to right speech;
4 All words that devour give thee pleasure,
     Thou false-speaking tongue.

5 God Himself will in turn destroy thee forever;
     He will seize, — from thy tent will He pluck thee,
        Rooted out from the land of the living.
6 The righteous shall see it and fear,
     And shall hold him to scorn:
7 " Lo, the man that refused to take refuge in God,
     But abundance of wealth was his trust,
        Yea, his greed was his strength."

8 But I, in God's house,
        Like an olive tree, thrifty and strong,
     Forever and alway God's love will I trust.
9 I will thank Thee forever for what Thou hast done,
     And will hope in Thy Name because it is gracious,
        In the presence of those whom Thou lovest.

LIII.

PREVAILING CORRUPTION AND LONGING FOR REDEMPTION.

A REPRODUCTION of Ps. xiv. with some variations. These are
   principally in ver. 5, as compared with xiv. 5, 6, and the substitution
here of Elohim for Jehovah.   See the prologue to Ps. xiv.

*1. Atheism, and resulting moral corruption, as universal (1–3).   2. The Divine
indignation bursts forth, and the oppressors of innocence are smitten with terror (4, 5).
3. A longing desire for the redemption of Israel (7).*

FOR THE LEADER OF THE CHOIR.   SET TO MAHALATH.   A MASKIL OF
                              DAVID.

1 " There is no God," says the fool in his heart;
     Corrupt they became, yea, in wickedness vile,
        There are none that do good.

2 It is God that looks forth out of heaven
       On the children of men,
   To see whether any are wise,
       Whether any are seeking for God.

3 They are all gone astray,
       All alike they are loathsome;
   There are none that do good,
       No, not even one.

4 Do none of them know,
       These whose works are so vile?
   They feed on my people as they feed upon bread;
       Jehovah, they call not upon Him.

5 They were there in great fear,
       Where nought had been feared;
   For God scatters the bones of those that besiege thee;
       Thou hast put them to shame,
           Because God has abhorred them.

6 Oh that salvation for Israel
       Might come out of Zion;
   When Jehovah returns to His people in bondage,
       Let Jacob rejoice, let Israel be glad.

(2) It is God that. He whose existence they deny sits above them as judge. The position of Elohim before the verb is emphatic. Ps. xiv. has here "Jehovah."—**Looks forth.** Heb. *shākaph*. See note on xiv. 2 for an account of this very remarkable word.

(5) Where nought had been feared. These impious men had been absolutely confident of their power to maintain themselves against all opposition. Not recognizing the power of God to sweep away every combination of evil, they had come forward in perfect fearlessness, and the ruin that befell them was a terrible surprise. This verse corresponds with Ps. xiv. 5 only in the first line, after which another verse is there added that has no counterpart here. But here, even more distinctly than there, some overwhelming calamity is referred to which cannot be identified historically.

(6) Returns to His people in bondage. See note on xiv. 6.

The question may be asked, here or at Ps. xiv., whether the poet is speaking of the race at large, in general terms, and without historic connection, or has in mind some special Divine interposition in behalf of the victims of oppression. His language in verses 2 and 3 seems to describe humanity, as such and everywhere, as evil and not good. But such absolute ungodliness, and utter abandonment to gross moral corruption as his words indicate, can never have been universal. There was always a holy seed, a people of God, who worshipped and served Him. Even this dark picture of crime is lighted up by more than one glimpse of an Israel quite distinct from the infamous world in the foreground. The seventh verse, with its pointed allusion to time and place in the adverb "there," shows clearly that the writer had before him a manifestation of peculiarly atrocious wickedness on the one hand, and of Divine justice in appropriate severity on the other. We have here an instance of judgment on a limited scale in the past, as symbolizing the complete and final overthrow of evil in the future. But in being idealized it is generalized, and brought into the present, as belonging to all time, an object lesson for the world. This is the poet's true position in dramatic representation. The historic basis is found, if possible among the occurrences of his own lifetime. Having chosen this, it is easy to recall the past most vividly, and to describe it as an eye witness of events in their succession. David had a large store of such material, accumulated during the hard experiences of his early manhood, and giving profitable employment to his serene old age.

LIV.

CONFIDENCE IN THE PRESENCE OF MURDEROUS ENEMIES.

HERE, as in lii., the title is the best guide to the occasion. It points to the account given in 1 Sam. xxiii. 19–29, and xxvi. 1. A connection with the preceding Psalms may be found by comparing ver. 3 with liii. 2, and ver. 6 with lii. 11.

1. Prayer for help (1-3). 2. Thankful acknowledgment of the answer (4-7).

FOR THE LEADER OF THE CHOIR. WITH STRINGED INSTRUMENTS. A MASKIL OF DAVID, WHEN THE ZIPHITES CAME TO SAUL AND SAID, "DOTH NOT DAVID HIDE HIMSELF WITH US?"

1 Save me, O God, by Thy Name,
 By Thy power defend me.
2 Hearken, O God, to my prayer,
 Give ear to the words of my mouth;
3 For aliens are risen against me,
 Oppressors are seeking my life,
  And God they set not before them.

4 Behold God is my helper,
 The Lord has upholden my life;

5 He requites the ill deeds of my foes;
   Blot them out in Thy truth.
6 I bring Thee mine offering, a gift of free will;
   I give thanks to Thy Name, O Jehovah,
       Because it is gracious;
7 For from all my distress it has freed me;
   Mine eye can now gaze on my foes.

(5) **In Thy truth.** This refers to God's faithful promise of help and deliverance in time of extreme peril. He now entreats for the fulfilment of that promise.

(7) **Can now gaze on my foes.** That is, without fear, or even with joy. The verb *rā'āh, to see*, when followed by the preposition *beth* (ב) im plies looking intently, and with pleasure. See note on xxvii. 4. In xcii. 11 hearing is included with sight in the same construction and sense. So Is. xi. 3, lit. "He shall smell in the fear of Jehovah;" which Delitzsch happily translates: "The fear of Jehovah shall be fragrance to him."

LV.

PRESSED BY MALIGNANT ENEMIES AFTER BETRAYAL BY A FALSE FRIEND.

A COUNTERPART to Ps. xli., which refers to the same intrigue and hatred of enemies, and to the same treacherous friend. It belongs to the time just before David's dethronement by the partisans of Absalom under the crafty lead of Ahithophel. The latter is undoubtedly the person whose faithlessness is complained of, and who is well called "the Old Testament Judas." See 2 Sam. xv.

1. His distress described (1-8). 2. The condition of the city, and special exposure of the aggravated perfidy of Ahithophel (9-15). 3. Refuge sought and found only in God (16-23). Sorrow prevails in the first part, anger in the second, and confidence in the third (Delitzsch).

FOR THE LEADER OF THE CHOIR. ON STRINGED INSTRUMENTS. A MASKIL OF DAVID.

1 Give ear, O God, to my prayer,
   And hide not away from my suppliant cry;
2 Oh regard me and answer;
   While I pour out my grief,
       I sway to and fro, and must moan,

3　Because of the enemy's voice,
　　　Because of the oppression of the wicked;
　　For they load me with evil,
　　　And fiercely withstand me.
4　My heart is in anguish within me,
　　The terrors of death overtake me;
5　Fear and trembling have seized me,
　　And horror o'erwhelms me.
6　I say, Oh had I wings like a dove!
　　Then away would I fly and find rest;
7　Surely then would I flutter far off,
　　I would lodge in the wilds;
8　I would haste to my refuge
　　From storm-blast and tempest.

9　Consume, O Jehovah, confuse Thou their speech;
　　For outrage and strife have I seen in the city.
10　Day and night they go around on its walls,
　　And within it are evil and sorrow;
11　Yawning gulfs are within it,
　　Oppression and fraud never leave its broad street.
12　(For it is not a foe that reviles me —
　　　I then could endure it;
　　Nor mine enemy he that comes proudly against me—
　　　I could hide myself from him;
13　But thou, a man in my circle,
　　　My companion and friend;
14　In fellowship sweet we were living,
　　And went to God's house with the festival throng.)

15　Let death fall upon them unawares,
　　　In full life may they sink into Sheol;
　　For the ill of their dwellings, it lodges within them.
16　As for me, I will call upon God,
　　　And Jehovah will save me.
17　Evening, morning, and noon, do I moan and lament,
　　　And He heareth my voice.

18 My life He preserveth in safety
    That they cannot come nigh me;
For many are they that assail me.

19 God will hear them and answer,
    He that sits King from of old,
Even these that are changeless,
    And without fear of God.   [Selah.]

20 He puts forth his hand 'gainst his friend,
    And his covenant profanes;
21 His mouth is smoother than butter,
    With war in his heart;
Soft as oil are his words,
    But are swords without sheath.
22 Cast thy burden on Jehovah,
    It is He will sustain thee;
He will never let the righteous be o'erthrown.

23 But Thou, O God, into the abyss wilt Thou cast them,
    The bloody and deceitful
        Shall die ere the midst of their days;
But I, in Thee will I trust.

---

(9) **Confuse Thou their speech.** Heb. *divide their tongue.* Alluding to the confusion of tongues at Babel; Gen. xi. 9. The tongue being the means of conversation, the meaning is, break up their intercourse, separate them in thought and purpose, and so frustrate their iniquitous projects.

(11) **Yawning gulfs.** See note on v. 9 — **Its broad street.** Heb. *r'hhōbāh, a broad place;* that is, the public square, or market place, where magistrates sat in judgment, men came together for consultation on interests in common, and most business was transacted. It was usually near the entrance or principal gate of the city, for the convenience of those living outside the walls; Neh. viii. 1, 2.

(13) **In my circle.** The renderings, *mine equal, of my rank, of mine order,* will not serve here, for they imply that the man referred to, like David, was royal. The word means *arrangement* or *estimation.* The preceding and following clauses indicate here an arrangement of men into two classes, — his enemies, and his friends. This man had belonged to the latter class, at least in social intercourse and general estimation.

(15) **Lodges within them.** Heb. *b'qirbām, is within them;* that is, in their hearts. See v. 9. and note on xlix. 11.

(19) **That are changeless;** referring to the pursuit of evil, that which has become a permanent characteristic of their lives. They never desist from it.

LVI.

THE CHEERFUL COURAGE OF A FUGITIVE.

HERE again the title is a sufficient guide. The Psalm is connected with the seizure of David by the Philistines, and his presentation to Achish, the king of Gath, as the champion of Israel; 1 Sam. xxi. 10-15. "It is a characteristic possessed in common by the Psalms of this period, that the prospect of the judgment that will come upon the whole of the hostile world, is combined with David's prospect of the judgment that will come upon his enemies; vii. 8, lv. 8, lix. 5."—*Delitzsch.*

1. The malice of men, and the faithfulness of God (1-4). 2. A more detailed description of the activity of his enemies, ending in imprecation (5-7). 3. Confidence in God's special and watchful care, ending in a refrain which repeats verses 3 and 4 with greater emphasis (8-11). 4. Thanksgiving and hope (12, 13).

FOR THE LEADER OF THE CHOIR. SET TO "JONATH 'ELEM REHHOQIM." A MICHTAM OF DAVID, WHEN THE PHILISTINES TOOK HIM IN GATH.

1 Pity me, O God, for men pant for my life,
   All the day long they fiercely pursue me;
2 Mine enemies pant for me all the day long,
   For many war proudly against me.
3 In the day I might fear,
   With trust do I cleave unto Thee.
4 In God (I give praise for His word),
   In God do I trust, and am fearless;
     What can flesh do to harm me?

5 All the day long do they torture my words,
   All their thoughts are against me for evil;
6 They gather in bands, they set spies;
   These watch at my heels, for they seek for my life.
7 Shall they escape for the evil they do?
   Cast down in Thine anger the heathen, O God.

8 Thou hast numbered my wandering steps,
     And my tears hast Thou put in Thy bottle;
   Are they not noted down in Thy book?

9 In the day that I call, my foes shall fall back,
     This I know, having God on my side.
10 In God (I give praise for His word),
     In Jehovah (I give praise for His word),
11 In God do I trust, and am fearless;
     What can man do to harm me?

12 Thy vows, O God, are upon me;
     The thankofferings due, I now pay Thee;
13 For my soul hast Thou rescued from death,
         And my feet kept from stumbling,
     In the light of the living to walk before God.

(3) **With trust do I cleave unto Thee.** Heb. *unto Thee I trust.* After *bātahh, to trust,* the prep. *'el,* as elsewhere, indicates a clinging to the object of trust. In verses 4, 11, 12 the preposition is changed, with a change in the form of the verb from the *imperfect* tense, expressing present active emotion, to the *perfect,* of established confidence, growing out of the past.

(4) **In God (I give praise for His word).** The rendering of the English Bible, " In God will I praise His word," is unmeaning. Such a combination occurs nowhere else. But nothing is more natural, in connection with an avowal of fearless trust in God's mercy and power in great peril, than a thankful reference to His faithful promise of deliverance; see text and note at xii. 5, 6. The ejaculation included in the parenthesis, with the repetition of the Name of God required after it, gives great emphasis to the avowal. This emphasis is greatly increased at the recurrence of the refrain in verses 10 and 11, by a repetition of the ejaculation of praise, with the Divine Name Jehovah, and followed by the exact echo of the closing line here, " In God do I trust, and am fearless." Immense weight and power are thus gained, in preparation for the thankful sentences that close this beautiful hymn.

LVII.

A CRY FROM THE CAVE.

THIS Psalm also belongs to the time of David's persecution by Saul. The cave mentioned is more probably the cave of Adullam to which he made escape from the sharp pursuit of Saul (1 Sam. xxii.), than the cave in the wilderness of Engedi, where later on he sojourned for a time (1 Sam. xxiv.). There are various resemblances in style and expression in this group of Psalms that indicate the same time and authorship.

*It contains: 1. Supplication (1-5). 2. Thanksgiving (6-11). Each of these
principal divisions ends with a refrain (5, 11). The last five verses occur also at the
beginning of Ps. cviii.*

FOR THE LEADER OF THE CHOIR. "AL-TASHHETH." BY DAVID, WHEN
HE FLED FROM SAUL IN THE CAVE.

1 Show me pity, O God, show me pity,
  For my soul takes refuge in Thee;
 In Thy shadowing wings I take refuge,
  Till these yawning gulfs pass away.
2 I will call unto God, the Most High,
 Unto God who in all things befriends me.
3 He will send forth from heaven, and will save me,
  From revilers that fain would devour; [Selah.]
 God will send forth lovingkindness and truth.
4 With my soul amidst lions,
  I must needs lay me down with the fiery, —
 The children of men, their teeth spears and arrows,
  And their tongue a sharp sword.
5 Even higher than the heavens be exalted, O God,
 And above the whole earth be Thy glory.

6 They made ready a net for my steps,
  And my soul was bowed down;
 They opened a pitfall before me,
  Into which they are fallen themselves. [Selah.]
7 And now steadfast, O God, is my heart,
  Yea, steadfast my heart;
 I will sing, and make melody on the harp.
8 Arouse thee, my glory,
  Arouse, lute and harp;
 I will rouse up the dawn.

9 Midst the peoples will I praise Thee, O Lord,
 And to Thee strike the harp midst the nations;
10 For Thy great lovingkindness reaches up to the heavens,
 And Thy truth to the clouds.
11 Even higher than the heavens be exalted, O God,
 And above the whole earth be Thy glory.

LVIII.

AN OUTCRY AGAINST THOSE WHO PERVERT JUSTICE.

"THIS Psalm belongs to the time of Absalom, who made the administration of justice a means of stealing from David the hearts of the
people.   The incomparable boldness of the language does not warrant us
to deny it to David.   In no Psalm are there found together within a similar brief space so many transcendent figures.   To a certain extent, however, Ps. lxiv. and cxl. are a guarantee that David speaks here.   These
three Psalms, whose similar closing verses of themselves challenge comparison, show that the same David who usually writes so elegantly, tenderly, and transparently, can soar in a great variety of transitions to a
sublimity in which his language, especially where it implores (lviii. 7) or
announces (cxl. 10) God's judgment, rolls on like deep thunder through a
gloomy mass of dark clouds." — *Delitzsch*

*1. An address to unjust judges and rulers (1, 2).   2. Description of the wicked
then dominant, in their falsity, malignancy, and obduracy (3-5).   3. The judgment
of God upon them (6-9).   4. The results of the judicial interposition of God (10, 11).*

FOR THE LEADER OF THE CHOIR. AL-TASHHETH. BY DAVID. A MICHTAM.

  1 Are ye verily dumb that should speak for the right,
     With equity judging the children of men?
  2 Yea more, ye devise base deeds in your hearts,
     And weigh out in the earth
        The violence wrought by your hands.

  3 Estranged from the womb are the wicked,
     From birth they stray off speaking lies;
  4 They have poison like poison of serpents;
     They are deaf as an adder that closes its ears,
  5 That hears no voice of enchanter,
     Of a charmer that charmeth with skill.

  6 O God, break their teeth from their mouth,
     Crush the fangs of these lions, Jehovah!
  7 Let them melt away like the running of water;
     When one bendeth the bow, let his arrow be blunt;
  8 Let them be like the snail that dissolves as it goes,
     As the untimely born that see not the sun;

9 As thorns, ere your pots feel the heat,
  Whirled away by the tempest,
      The green and the burned all alike.

10 Let the righteous be glad having vision of vengeance,
   In the blood of the wicked his steps shall he bathe.
11 Men shall say,
      "Of a truth there is fruit for the righteous,
   There is truly a God, who is Judge in the earth."

LIX.

THE INNOCENT MAN IN GREAT DANGER.

THIS Psalm seems to belong to the period in the pursuit by Saul described in 1 Sam. xix. 11 ff. There is no reason to limit it to the single night in which Michal aided his escape. There may have been several preceding nights in which his house was closely beleaguered. "Considering that the description of the ongoings of his foes by night is repeated in a refrain verse, and that in v. 17 the poet sets his believing and joyous anticipations with regard to the coming morning over against the vain eagerness with which these patrols spend the night. Ps. lix. seems to be an evening song originating in those perilous days that he lived through in Gibeah."

There are two principal parts (1-9, 10-17), each subdivided into two. 1. Prayer for help; the movements of the enemy; judicial interposition invoked (1-5). 2. Further description of the enemy and confidence in God (6-9). 3. Fear has passed away, hope prevails, and God is invoked to maintain His sure rule over Israel and the whole earth (10-13). 4. With the same beginning as at verse 6, the enemy is described; but now in their unsatisfied hunger, in contrast with his own deliverance and abundant joy (14-17).

FOR THE LEADER OF THE CHOIR. AL-TASHHETH. BY DAVID. A MICHTAM.
   WHEN SAUL SENT AND THEY WATCHED THE HOUSE TO PUT HIM TO
   DEATH.

1 Set me free from my foes, O my God;
  Make me safe from those that assail me:
2 Set me free from those busied in crime,
  Oh, save me from bloodthirsty men.
3 For lo, on the watch for my life,
      The fierce band together against me;
  Yet not for my fault, O Jehovah, and not for my sin.

4 Without guilt of mine, they run and prepare;
  O arouse Thee to meet me, and see:
5 And do Thou, O Jehovah of Hosts, God of Israel,
  Bestir Thee to visit all heathen,
        Do not spare all iniquitous traitors.

6 They return at evening, and snarling like dogs,
  Go the rounds of the city;
7 Lo, they foam at the mouth,
        On their lips there are swords,
  For they say, "Who can hear us?"
8 But Thou, O Jehovah, wilt deride them,
  Thou wilt hold all the heathen in scorn.
9 In Thee I have hope, O my Strength;
  For God is my fortress of safety.

10 My God in His kindness will meet me,
   God will give me to see the defeat of my foes.
11 Let them live, lest my people forget;
        But our God and our Shield,
   Disperse by Thy power and subdue them.
12 For the sin of their mouth for the words of their lips,
        Be they snared in their pride, —
   For their cursing and lies that they speak.
13 Consume them in wrath,—yea, consume out of life;
   Let them know that the God who is Ruler in Jacob,
        Bears rule to the bounds of the earth.

14 They return at the evening, and snarling like dogs,
        Go the rounds of the city;
15 They wander up and down to devour,
   And with nothing to fill them are spending the night.
16 But I, of Thy power will I sing,
        And of Thy lovingkindness will sing at the dawn;
   For Thou art become my safe tower,
        A retreat in my day of distress.
17 Unto Thee, O my Strength,
        I bring music of harps;
   For God, my safe tower,
        Is the God that has loved me.

LX.

AFTER A LOST BATTLE.

THIS Psalm seems to be founded upon a defeat of the Israelites by the Edomites during the Syro-Ammonitish war. The lamentation with which it begins refers to the laying waste of the land by the Edomites before the victories recorded in 2 Sam. viii. and 1 Chron. xviii.

1. Prayer for Divine help in great national distress (1-5). 2. The appropriation of a Divine oracle promising victory (6-8). 3. Renewed supplication, but with confidence in God (9-12).

FOR THE LEADER OF THE CHOIR.   SET TO SHUSHAN-EDUTH.   A MICH-
TAM OF DAVID: WHEN HE FOUGHT WITH ARAM OF THE TWO RIVERS,
AND ARAM OF ZEBAH; AND JOAB RETURNED, AND SMOTE IN THE
VALLEY OF ABIMELECH TWELVE THOUSAND MEN.

1 O God, Thou hast spurned and dispersed us;
  Thou wert sore displeased, but restore us again.
2 Thou hast shaken the land, and rent it asunder;
  Its breaches rebuild, for it totters.

3 Thou afflictest Thy people with hardship,
  The wine of reeling Thou makest us drink:
4 To Thy servants Thou gavest a banner,
  That now they may flee from the bow!   [Selah.]
5 To deliver Thy beloved,
  Let Thy right hand save us, and answer our prayer.

6 It is God in His holiness who promised,
    I therefore will triumph;
  I will portion out Shechem,
    And distribute the valley of Succoth.
7 Gilead is mine, and mine is Manasseh,
    With Ephraim the shield of my head,
  And Judah my sceptre of rule.
8 My washpot is Moab,
    I cast off my shoe upon Edom;
  Over me, O Philistia, shout aloud.

9 Who to the fortified city will bring me,
  Who can conduct me to Edom?
10 O God, hast Thou not cast us off,
  And no longer, O God, goest forth with our hosts?
11 Oh give us Thy help from the oppressor,
  For vain is deliverance by man.
12 Through God we shall conquer;
  It is He that shall stamp on our foes.

(5-7) **Shechem, Succoth, Gilead, Manasseh, Ephraim, Judah.** The Divine oracle promising victory confirmed David in the possession of the whole of Canaan, in accordance with its original geographical distribution. Shechem represents the east, and Succoth the west side of the Jordan. Gilead was the portion of the tribes of Reuben and Gad, and so in conjunction with a part of the tribe of Manasseh covered the territory first reached after the journey through the wilderness, while Ephraim and Judah were the principal tribes between the river and the sea. — **My sceptre.** Heb. *m'hhōqēq.* An allusion to the promise of royal dignity to Judah in Gen. xlix. 10, where the same word is used. It is not the "lawgiver," the person invested with supreme authority, but his staff, or sceptre as its symbol. So Rev. Old Test. in both places.

(8) **Moab, Edom, Philistia.** These were the earliest enemies of Israel on the east and south. — **My washpot.** He who aspired to the mastery shall be a servant of the lowest grade; comp. Is. xxv. 10. — **Cast off my shoe.** In the eastern world casting the shoe on a piece of land was an assertion of absolute ownership. — **Shout aloud.** This must here mean a scream of terror and pain. Hupfeld adopts a change in the pointing of the word, conforming to the recension of this verse in cviii. 9, and renders it, " over Philistia is my exultation," a reading that has much in its favour. So Cheyne.

LXI.

AN EXILED KING RETURNS TO HIS THRONE.

THE general tenor of this Psalm indicates that it belongs to the period of David's flight from Absalom. But the danger is now past. The royal army has smitten the rebels in the forest of Ephraim (2 Sam. xviii. 6-8), and the king has his face toward Jerusalem. The king referred to in verses 6 and 7 is evidently himself. He probably uses the third person because his thought embraces the royal line that God had promised should descend from him, and rule in righteousness forever. Under this aspect the Psalm is Messianic.

There are two strophes, each containing four verses :

1. Confident supplication for continued Divine favour (1-4). 2. Acknowledgment of prayers already answered, as a ground of hope for all the future (5-8).

TO THE LEADER OF THE CHOIR.   ON A STRINGED INSTRUMENT.
BY DAVID.

1 O God, hear my cry,
   Attend to my prayer.
2 From the bounds of the earth unto Thee do I call,
       When my heart is o'erwhelmed;
   Lead me up on the rock too high for my climbing.
3 For Thou art my refuge,
   A tower of strength away from the foe.
4 In Thy tent give me welcome forever,
   In Thy sheltering wings let me hide.   [Selah.]

5 For Thou, O God, hast heeded my vows,
   And hast given me share with those fearing Thy Name.
6 Thou wilt add further days to the days of the king,
   And his years wilt for ages continue;
7 Forever enthroned before God,
   Lovingkindness and truth be Thy gifts to preserve him.
8 Thus the harp will I sound to Thy Name evermore,
   That I daily may pay Thee my vows.

(2) **From the bounds of the earth.** In his separation from the privileges of the sanctuary, the extreme borders of the land seemed to him at an immeasurable distance from Zion, the home of his heart. Delitzsch remarks that from the earliest times the country east of the Jordan was distinguished from Canaan, and regarded to a certain extent a foreign country. See Num. xxxiii. 32.

(4) **Give me welcome forever.** Heb. *'agûrâh 'ôlāmîm*. The verb *gûr* lies at the basis of *gēr, a guest,* and carries with it the same meaning. See v. 4, xv. 1. It implies protection and gracious entertainment. In ordinary life both verb and noun are used with reference to one who takes up his abode in a foreign land, and does not possess or acquire the rights of a native. The *gēr* was a "stranger," not a native, nor possessed of the full rights of citizenship, yet under certain legal obligations, and by the Divine statute entitled to be treated with kindness, as guests from abroad. See Lev. xix. 33, 34, where this word is used. Hence in the Psalms the verb, as well as noun, describes those who are welcomed to the house of Jehovah, and live under His special care.

LXII.

THERE are decided marks of relation between this Psalm and xxxix. which indicate that David wrote it, and that it relates to the times of Absalom.

1. He declares his strong confidence in God, and expostulates with his oppressors (1–4). 2. Continued expression of confidence in God as his strong refuge (5–8). 3. The worthlessness of man, contrasted with the power and goodness of God (9–12).

FOR THE LEADER OF THE CHOIR.   UPON JEDUTHUN.   A PSALM OF DAVID.

1 Only be silent toward God, O my soul,
  For from Him my salvation shall come.
2 Only He is my rock and salvation,
  Having him my defence I can ne'er be o'erthrown.
3 How long ye all rush on a man to destroy him,
  Like a leaning wall, like a tottering fence!
4 They only consult from high station to thrust him,
    Having pleasure in falsehood;
  In each mouth there is blessing,
    But they inwardly curse.

5 Only be silent toward God, O my soul,
  For from Him what I hope for will come;
6 Only He is my rock and salvation;
  Having Him my defence I cannot be shaken.
7 In God have I safety and glory,
  For God is my fortified rock and my refuge.
8 Confide in Him alway ye people,
    Pour your heart out before Him;
  We have God as our refuge.   [Selah.]

9 Only a breath are the low-born, and nobles a falsehood,
  They go up in the balance, they all are of breath;
10 Put no trust in oppression, and boast not of spoil,
  If wealth should spring up do not heed it.
11 This one thing God spake, these two have I heard:
  That power belongs unto God,

> 12 And to Thee lovingkindness, O Lord;
>   For Thou givest to each the reward of his work.

(2) **Can ne'er be o'erthrown.** Heb. *cannot be greatly shaken.* See note upon xxi. 8. The verb *mût* standing alone may describe a complete overthrow. In ver. 6, which is a repetition of this verse, the adverb "greatly" (Heb. *me'ôd*) is omitted. This implies a difference in thought: "I cannot be shaken;" that is, not at all.

(4) **They only consult, etc.** This exhibits their profession, as distinguished from their deadly purpose. Their words are smooth, plausible, even complimentary. They only desire a change in administration, and would not harm the good man. But their hearts are full of venom. See v. 9 and lv. 21, relating to the same period.

(9) **The low-born and nobles.** The Hebrew words are *'ish, a man,* individual, and *'ādām, man,* generic. When thus occurring together the former is one entitled to special consideration, *a man of rank,* and the latter one of the mass, *a common man.* So in xlix. 2; Is. ii. 9, v. 15.

(10) **Do not heed it.** Heb. *set not the heart,* or more properly, *the mind;* for in this Hebrew phrase the reference is not to *the affections,* but to *the thoughts;* 1 Sam. iv. 20; Prov. xxiv. 32; Job ii. 3.

LXIII.

A MORNING SONG FROM THE DESERT.

THE contents of this Psalm fully verify its title. Like lxi. and lxii. it belongs to the time of Absalom's rebellion. More specifically it is connected with the sufferings of David and his followers while he tarried near the fords of the wilderness (2 Sam. xv. 23, 28), in the region lying between the plain of Jericho and the northern shore of the Dead Sea. This is described as barren and desolate in the extreme. While here the band of exiles endured weariness and thirst; 2 Sam. xvi. 2, comp. xiv. 15, 28, xvii. 19. In connection with verse 2, Delitzsch quotes Furrer's article *Wüste* in Schenkel's *Bibel Lexikon :* "Not a strip of grass refreshes the eye here upon the wide plain, not a brook ripples, except during the rainy season." The title is in accordance with the direction which the historian relates that David's flight took. "It throws light upon the whole Psalm and is verified by it. The poet is a king. He longs for God in Zion, where he has so gladly beheld Him who is there revealed. He is persecuted by enemies, who have aimed at his destruction. The assertion that he finds himself in the wilderness is no mere figure of speech; and when he anticipates for his enemies that they shall become 'a portion for jackals' (ver. 11), we can easily discern the impression that the wilderness has had upon the shape taken by his thoughts."

There are three principal parts: *1. Thirsting for God (1–4). 2. Satisfaction in God (5–8). 3. A contrast between the rebels and their banished king (9–11).*

A PSALM OF DAVID, WHEN HE WAS IN THE WILDERNESS OF JUDAH.

1 O God, Thou art my God; I earnestly seek Thee;
  For Thee my soul longs, for Thee my flesh pines,
    In a desert land without water, and faint.
2 Even so, in the sanctuary intently I looked,
  To behold Thy power and Thy glory.

3 For Thy lovingkindness is better than life,
  And therefore my lips shall extol Thee;
4 Even thus while I live will I bless Thee,
  And lift up my hands in Thy Name.

5 My soul shall be filled as with marrow and fatness,
  And my mouth shall praise Thee with lips full of joy;
6 When I call Thee to mind on my bed,
  Through the watches of night, my thoughts are of Thee.

7 For Thou camest to help me,
  In the shade of Thy wings I joyfully shout;
8 My soul, while pursuing, cleaves closely to Thee,
  And Thy right hand upholds me.

9 But they, to their ruin, while seeking my life,
  Shall enter the depths of the earth;
10 Given up to the power of the sword,
    And a portion for jackals.

11 And the king shall be joyful in God;
  Let every one glory that sweareth by Him,
    But the mouth that speaks lies shall be stopped.

(8) Heb. *my soul cleaves (adheres) after Thee.*

(11) **That sweareth by Him;** that is, by Jehovah. Every word of the persons referred to is in sacred adherence to **truth, as if attested by** the solemnity of an oath, — in contrast with the malignant falsehood so justly denounced in the closing words of this Psalm, and described with graphic power in the Psalm that follows.

LXIV.

PROTECTION FROM THE WICKED.

THERE are no special features that connect this Psalm with either of the two great periods of suffering in the life of David.

1. Prayer for deliverance from the malicious (1-4). 2. Their crafty devices are described (5, 6). 3. God's judgment upon them (7-10).

FOR THE LEADER OF THE CHOIR.   A PSALM OF DAVID.

1 O God, hear my voice, as I tell of my grief,
   Guard my life from the fear of the foe;
2 From the league of the wicked conceal me,
   From the fellowship banded in wrong;
3 Who sharpen their tongue like a sword;
   Who level their arrows, their slanderous words,
4 From their hiding to shoot at the upright;
   They suddenly shoot and are fearless.

5 They strengthen their purpose of evil,
     By speaking of snares they have hid;
   " Who can see them?" they say:
6 They devise schemes of wrong;
     " We are ready with plans well conceived:"
   Deep is all that is in them, every one,
     And deep is his heart.

7 But God thrusts them through;
   With an arrow they are suddenly wounded,
8 And they fall; their own tongue wrought their ruin;
   All that see shake the head with exulting.
9 Yea, all men shall fear,
   And shall tell of God's doing:
     His work they will wisely consider.
10 Let the righteous be glad in Jehovah,
     And take refuge in Him;
   The upright in heart, let them all give Him glory.

LXV.

A HARVEST SONG.

IT is difficult to decide whether this Psalm has reference to an approaching harvest, or to one just past.   Probably to the latter, and the vow
mentioned in ver. 1 is a special thanksgiving for the wealth of gracious
provision with which the land was then teeming, as described in the last
strophe.   The early and the latter rain are principally before the poet's
mind, preceded by a grand and beautiful reference to the power of God as
variously manifested in nature and in the affairs of men.

*1. Thankful recognition of God's grace in the sanctuary, especially in accepting
worship and pardoning sin (1-4).   2. Praise to God for His power and goodness in
nature and history (5-8).   3. Praise for abundant rain in preparation for harvest
(9, 10).   4. Thankful description of the earth as laden with abundant increase
(12, 13).*

FOR THE LEADER OF THE CHOIR.   A PSALM OF DAVID.   A SONG.

1 Loud praise to Thee, O God, breaks the stillness of Zion,
   As to Thee our vow we perform.
2 O Thou Hearer of prayer,
   Unto Thee all mortals shall come.
3 The guilt charged against me, I cannot withstand,
   But our sins Thou Thyself wilt absolve.
4 How blest is the man Thou wilt choose and bring near,
      To dwell in Thy courts;
   May we enjoy to the full the good of Thy house,
      Of Thy palace most holy.

5 With terrible deeds, our God of salvation,
      Dost Thou righteously answer our prayer;
   In Thee put their trust all the bounds of the earth,
      And the sea afar off;
6 Who by strength holdest firmly the mountains,
   Being girded with power;
7 Who stillest the noise of the seas,
      The roar of their billows,
   And the tumult of nations.

8 They that dwell at the uttermost bounds,
    Stand in awe at thy tokens;
  The lands of the morning and evening sun,
    To glad shouts Thou inspirest.

9 Thou hast come to the land, and hast made it o'erflow, and
    its wealth to increase, —
  Full of water are the cisterns of God;
  Thou providest their grain from the ground thus prepared;
10 Its furrows Thou drenchest,
    Dost level its ridges,
  With showers dost soften,
    Its sprouting dost bless.

11 Thou crownest the year with Thy goodness;
  Thy footsteps are dropping with riches:
12 They drop on the grass in the wilds,
  And the hills are all girdled with joy;
13 The meadows have clothing of flocks,
    And the valleys are mantled with grain;
  They are shouting for joy; yea, they sing.

(1) **Loud praise to Thee, O God, breaks the stillness of Zion.** Heb. *l'ka | dûmiyâh | tchillâh | 'Elôhîm | b'tsiyôn; to-Thee | stillness | a-song-of-praise | O God | in-Zion.* All authorities agree that the meaning " waiteth " of the English Bible cannot legitimately be extracted from the second of these words. The Septuagint, on the basis of a different vowel-pointing that connects it with the root *dâmâh, to be like,* gives for it πρέπει, *it is suitable.* This Cheyne adopts: " Meet for Thee, O God," etc. The rendering *stillness is praise to Thee in Zion* makes a complete sentence, but does not yield a thought in harmony with the scope of the Psalm, nor even with the immediate context. For " stillness " can only mean submission and patience under suffering expressed by silence. This is the view of Hup-feld and others, quoting Ps. xxxix. 9, " I am dumb, I open not my mouth, because Thou didst it." But this is a song of joyful thanksgiving for great prosperity, and the vow the singers are performing is that bringing an offering from the fruits of the earth with loud and cheerful praise. It would be possible to understand here the sudden burst of song with instrumental accompaniment in the place where up to that moment profound silence had reigned, as if the very silence could no longer contain itself, and breaks out in loud praise. It is better to regard the stillness as simply descriptive of the usual quiet of Zion, except when interrupted as now by the coming of worshippers.

(2) **All mortals.** Heb. *all flesh;* men as earthly and perishable. The line seems to express confidence that the time will come when all men will

look in their need to the Hearer of prayer for comfort and help; but the form may be understood as potential, recognizing thankfully the grace of God in admitting mortals into His presence; "unto Thee all mortals may come."

(3) The guilt charged against me. Lit. *words* (or *matters*) *of guilt-inesses*, the plural referring to the many sins that must separate men from God, if not forgiven.

(8) At Thy tokens. The manifestations of Divine power in the course and order of nature before which men tremble, yet fill them with confidence and joy. — **The lands of the morning and evening sun.** Heb. *mūtsāoth, the places of outgoing of the morning and evening.* The term evidently refers to the sun as *going forth*, which is the Hebrew equivalent for *rising* in idiomatic English, but leaves to be supplied before the word "evening" the *coming in*, or *setting*. For the former see Gen. xix. 23; Ps. xix. 5; for the latter, Gen. xv. 12; Ps. civ. 19. The line refers to the extreme east and west, the regions on which the first and last rays of the sun rest in his full circuit from horizon to horizon.

(9) The cisterns. Properly a trench for conducting water from a reservoir, for irrigating the soil. See note on i. 3. It stands here by metonymy for the whole system of irrigation in nature by means of the clouds, as wafted by the wind, and pouring out their treasures upon the thirsty earth. God is represented in this and the following verses as actively engaged in tilling the soil for the sustenance of His great family. In this the supply of water is the first consideration, and the clouds are mentioned here by a term familiar in oriental cultivation. A similar term is found in 2 Kings xviii. 17, and Is. vii. 3: "the conduit of the upper pool." See the mention in 2 Kings xx. 20 of the "conduit" and "pool," as made by Hezekiah. But the conduit in these places, from its etymology, is the pipe by which the water is lifted from the stream to the reservoir, whereas *peleg*, used here, is the trench or channel by which it is conveyed to the gardens and fields. The whole conception of a most successful process of agriculture on a vast scale, carried on methodically by the wisdom and power of God, is very grand.

LXVI.

NATIONAL AND PERSONAL DELIVERANCE COMMEMORATED.

THERE are no certain indications of the authorship or historic reference of this Psalm or the one that follows it.

There are two principal parts, ver. 1-12 relating to national history, 13-20 to personal experience.

In the former: 1. All the earth is called upon to praise God (1-4). 2. The mighty deeds of God in the deliverance of the infant nation from Egypt are recounted (5-7). 3. A more recent deliverance from suffering and danger is thankfully acknowledged (8-12).

In the latter part, the poet speaks of his personal obligations: 1. He resolves to bring to the house of God the sacrifices he had promised in his vows (13-15). 2. He acknowledges publicly God's goodness in answering his prayer (16-20).

FOR THE LEADER OF THE CHOIR. A SONG. A PSALM.

1 Shout for joy unto God, all the earth;
2 Strike the harp to His glorious Name,
Give Him glory in songs to His praise;
3 Say unto God, " How fearful Thy deeds!
In the might of Thy strength,
    Thy foes come cringing before Thee.
4 Let all earth strike the harp and bow down, —
Strike the harp to Thy Name."

5 Come and see what God has accomplished,
How fearful His deeds to the children of men;
6 Before Him the sea became land;
    We passed through the river on foot,
And rejoiced in Him there.
7 In His might He forever bears rule,
    His eyes keep close watch on the nations;
Let rebels lay aside their proud bearing.

8 Bless our God, O ye peoples,
Let your voices be heard in His praise;
9 For our soul He preserveth in life,
And our feet doth not suffer to stumble.
10 For, O God, Thou hast proved us,
Thou hast tried us as silver is tried;
11 Into the hunter's toils didst Thou bring us,
And heavy the burdens Thou laid'st on our loins.
12 Thou mad'st mortals to ride o'er our heads;
Through fire and through water did we go,
    Yet Thou broughtest us forth,
      And our blessings abound.

13 I enter Thy house with burnt offerings;
    I pay Thee my vows,
14 Which my lips have pronounced,
And my mouth has spoken in trouble.
15 Burnt offerings of fatlings I bring Thee,
    With the incense of rams;
I bring bullocks with goats.

16 Come and hear, I will tell,
    All ye that fear God,
  What He did for my soul;
17 I called with my mouth,
  With my tongue I extolled Him;
18 If my heart had delighted in evil,
  The Lord would not hear me;
19 But in truth the Lord heard me,
  He gave ear to my suppliant voice.
20 Blessèd be God,
    Who turns not my prayer away from Himself,
      And from me He withholds not His kindness.

(3) **Come cringing.** Heb. *lie;* that is, falsely profess submission. See on xviii. 44.

(17) **With my tongue I extolled Him.** Heb. *exaltation beneath my tongue.* Ever there, and ready for utterance; as if stored up for use on every suitable occasion. Comp. x. 7, 7, *under his tongue are* trouble and wrong.

LXVII.

THANKSGIVING FOR A BOUNTIFUL HARVEST.

" EACH plentiful harvest is to Israel a fulfilment of the promise given in Lev. xxvi. 4, and a pledge that God is with His people, and that its mission to the whole world shall not remain unaccomplished."— *Delitzsch.* It lies in direct connection with the promise to Abraham in Gen. xii. 3, and in this broad sense is Messianic.

1. The priestly benediction from Num. vi. 24-26, followed by a prayer that the saving knowledge of God may spread over the whole earth (1-2). 2. The prospect exhibited of the entrance of all nations into the kingdom of God (3, 4). 3. The conversion of the nations is shown in its connection with the present joyful event. Every fruitful season is an earnest of further blessing up to the full measure of God's promise.

FOR THE LEADER OF THE CHOIR.   ON STRINGED INSTRUMENTS.

1 God have compassion and bless us,
  And grant us the light of His presence ;
2 That Thy way may be known in the earth,
  Thy saving power to all nations.

    3 Let the peoples, O God, give Thee praise,
         Let the peoples all give Thee praise;
    4 Let the nations be glad, let them joyfully shout;
         For with justice Thou judgest the peoples,
             And guidest the nations of the earth.

    5 Let the peoples, O God, give Thee praise,
         Let the peoples all give Thee praise;
    6 The earth yields her increase,
         And Jehovah our God gives us blessing;
    7 God gives us blessing,
         Let the bounds of the earth all revere Him.

LXVIII.

JEHOVAH TRIUMPHANT.

THERE is a wide difference of opinion among critics as to the time and occasion of the sixty-eighth Psalm. But all agree that it is the grandest of these sacred odes. In its description of the wonderful achievements of Jehovah, as King and Protector of Israel, there is an intermingling of epic stateliness and grandeur with lyric simplicity and elegance. It is greatly enriched by frequent allusion to more ancient songs commemorative of signal deliverances. It is the most elaborate and artistic of the Psalms, but incomparably bold, rugged and abrupt in its style and transitions. The last mentioned features are decidedly in favour of assigning it to a very early date. In its extensive sweep it covers the whole history of Israel, from its birth as a nation under the sovereign rule of Jehovah, till His final triumph over all the kingdoms of the earth in the reign of the Messiah. "The fundamental thought is as clear as the arrangement and rhythmical organization, namely: the celebration of an entrance of God into His sanctuary after a victory, and His rule over the earth, extending itself from thence." — *Moll.*

The central historic fact with which the song of triumph is connected is probably the close of the wars recorded in 2 Sam. x. xi. against the Ammonites, and the immense gathering of mercenary Syrian soldiers from beyond the Euphrates, whose aid they had purchased against the armies of David. See ver. 30, and 2 Sam. x. 6, 15–19. The ark, representing the Divine Majesty (Ps. lxxviii. 61), had been carried before the host of Israel, and after a decisive victory is now borne back to Zion in a festal procession.

The Psalm consists of two principal parts: the former (1-17) is vividly descriptive of preceding events; the latter (19-35), of the present and future.

1. God comes forth in His might to the ruin of His enemies. The righteous are called to rejoice over His victorious advance through the desert, and its rich results to the miserable (1-6). 2. A similar march, after the exodus from Egypt, is recalled, and the Theophany at Sinai, very terrible, but accompanied by special kindness to the feeble and dependent (7-10). 3. The recent victory is described, — a vivid narration of passing events in their succession (11-14). 4. The return of the triumphant host, with the ark before them, to the sacred hill of Zion (15-18). 5. A doxology to God, as the God of salvation, who will surely destroy those that defy Him (19-23). 6. The triumphal procession to the sanctuary is described (24-27). 7. Prayer that God will fully accomplish His merciful purpose, that all men may yield to His sway, and that the whole world may glorify Him (28-35).

FOR THE LEADER OF THE CHOIR.   BY DAVID.   A SONG.   A PSALM.

1 God arises, His enemies scatter,
   They that hate Him are fleeing before him:
2 As smoke is driven dost Thou drive them;
   As wax melts away before fire,
     The wicked come to nought before God.
3 But the righteous are glad, they rejoice before God,
   Yea, exult in their gladness.

4 Sing ye to God; strike the harp to His Name,
     A highway cast up for the Rider through deserts,
   In Jah as His Name, exult ye before Him.
5 The Defender of widows, and Father of orphans,
   Is God in the place where His holiness dwells:
6 The exiled and lonely He brings to a home,
     And the bound, He sends forth to abundance;
   But rebels abide in a land parched and dry.

7 When with Thee before them Thy people went forth,
   In Thy march, O God, through the waste,   [Selah.]
8 The earth was convulsed; yea, the skies fell in drops
     before God;
   Before God yonder Sinai was shaken,
     Before Israel's God.
9 A free-flowing rain didst Thou send us, O God;
   It was Thine to refresh Thy drooping possession:
10 For there were Thy living ones dwelling,
   In Thy goodness, O God, Thou hast care for the poor.

11 When the Lord gives command,
   A great host are the women that herald the tidings;
12 "The kings of the armies are fleeing — are fleeing,
   She that bideth at home shall distribute the spoil;
13 When ye camp midst the sheepfolds,
      Covered with silver are the wings of the dove,
   And her pinions with glistening gold;
14 For yonder the Almighty has scattered the kings,
   Like the snow upon Zalmon."

15 Mountains of God are the mountains of Bashan,
   Many peaked mountains, the mountains of Bashan;
16 Why gaze ye with envy, ye mountains with peaks,
   At the mount God desireth to dwell in?
      Yea, Jehovah will dwell there forever.
17 The chariots of God are myriads twice told,
      Upon thousands are thousands;
   The Lord is among them,
      In His holy place now, as on Sinai.
18 Thou ascendest on high, leading captive the captives
      Thou receivedst as gifts among men;
   And even with rebels Jehovah our God is to dwell.

19 Ever blessèd be God, who daily is bearing our burdens,
   Even God who has saved us.
20 God on our side is a God of salvation,
   Through Jehovah our God escape we from death.
21 Yea, God smites asunder the head of His foes,
   The hairy crown that stalks on in his sins;
22 The Lord said, " Out of Bashan will I bring him,
   Yea, back from the depths of the sea will I bring him;
23 That thy feet thou mayest dash in the enemies' blood,
   And the tongue of thy dogs shall have share."

24 They saw, O God, Thy triumphal return,
   The triumphal return of my God and my King,
      Passing up to His place the most holy.
25 The singers went foremost, behind them the harpers;
   In the midst are the damsels that beat on the timbrels:

26 "Bless the Lord in the choir of the assembly;
   Bless the Lord ye whose fountain is Israel."
27 There is Benjamin the youngest, their ruler;
   In their throng are the princes of Judah,
        With princes of Zebulon, princes of Naphtali.

28 Thy God has ordained that strength shall be thine;
   Then all Thou hast wrought for us strengthen, O God.
29 At Thy royal abode on Jerusalem's height,
   Unto Thee let the kings bring their gifts.
30 Rebuke the wild beast of the reeds, the herd of strong
        cattle,
      And the steers of the peoples,
           That serve basely for ingots of silver;
   He has scattered the nations that delight them in war.
31 The magnates of Egypt are coming,
   And Cush hastens on, with her hands stretched forth
        unto God.

32 Sing unto God, all ye lands of the earth,
   Sound your harps to the Lord, —   [Selah.]
33 To the Rider through the highest heavens of old ;
   Lo, He utters His voice, a voice that has strength.
34 Ascribe might unto God,
   Whose majesty rules over Israel,
        His might in the skies;
35 A God to be feared, coming forth from His Holies;
   It is Israel's God,
        Who gives might and full strength to His people ;
           Blessèd be God!

(1) **God arises, etc.** These opening words are adapted from the language of Moses, when the ark set
forward on its long journey through
the wilderness. See Num. x. 35.
The only change is in the form of
the verbs. What is there prayed for
in the use of the imperative mood:
"Arise, O Jehovah, and let Thine
enemies be scattered," is here set
forth by the graphic imperfect tense,
as in course of present fulfilment.

(4) **A highway cast up.** An ordinary preparation for the march of
kings and their armies through the
pathless wilderness: Is. xl. 1; Mal.
iii. 1. — **The Rider.** Comp. xviii. 10.
"He rode on a cherub, and flew:"
civ. 3, "Who maketh the clouds His
chariot." The deserts through which

the conqueror rides are the extensive steppes, intervening between Palestine and the scene of the recent battles, far away in the north. — **In Jah.** Heb. *Jah.* An archaic abbreviation of the Divine Name Jehovah, first found in the song of Moses, Ex. xv. 2. It is here introduced as a pledge of the gracious exercise of His almighty power on behalf of His people; a reminiscence of Ex. iii. 13–15.

(8) **The skies.** The upper air, the region of clouds and storms. See Judg. v. 4: "The heavens dropped, yea, the clouds dropped water;" Is. xlv. 8.

(9) **A free-flowing rain.** Heb. *géshem n'dābōth, a rain of freewill offerings;* a profuse rain, with possible reference to manna and other Divine gifts.

(11) **When the Lord gives command.** The order for the final onset against the enemy, issued by the Divine Leader of the hosts of Israel.— **The women that herald the tidings.** An allusion to the ancient custom of celebrating a victory by women with song and dance; Ex. xv. 20, 21; 1 Sam. xviii. 6, 7. The three following verses probably give the words in which the joyful news is proclaimed.

(13) **When ye camp midst the sheepfolds.** We find in the song of Deborah, Judg. v. 16: "Why sattest thou among the sheepfolds?" It is an expostulatory question, addressed to those who remained at home in indifference, when the warriors of the nation went forth against the enemy. We might translate here interrogatively. But there can scarcely be a reproof intended. For when these tidings go forth the victory has been won, and it has been so decisive that they may now without fault enjoy their rest. This seems to be a simple congratulation on the rich spoil that has been taken from the enemy, and the glittering appearance of the encampments of Israel. The gleam of the silver and gold is compared to the brilliant ef-

fect of the sunlight upon the rich metallic colours of the plumage of a dove. Israel is also compared to a dove in lxxiv. 19.

(14) The reference to snow upon Zalmon is obscure. Zalmon was probably some well-known eminence on which the effects of a snowstorm could be seen far away. The thought may be that the spoils dropped by the vanquished army in its headlong flight were like the snowdrifts on Zalmon, or that the whitened bones of the slain shall be like the snow. More probably Zalmon was an exposed projecting height over which the wind raged with peculiar fierceness, and the poet refers to the snow as driven during the storm, leaving its summit always bare and black. The name Zalmon means *black.* The mention of the kings as *scattered by the Almighty,* in the preceding line of the parallelism, favours this as the point of comparison. It is not unlike the description of the enemies of God as driven like smoke in ver. 2.

(15–18) The army must now return to Zion, the city of the great King, in order that the glorious victory may be appropriately celebrated. The immediate reference to the mountain range of Bashan confirms the conjecture that the poem is to be connected with the war between Israel and the various Syrian nations from beyond the Euphrates, recorded in 2 Sam. x. 15, 19. The battle was fought at Helam, near the Euphrates, belonging to the half tribe of Manasseh, to which Bashan had been assigned as part of its territory. The lofty mountain range of Bashan was therefore in sight of the army on its homeward march. It is called "a mountain of God," as conspicuous among the works of God. The personification of these great mountains as full of envy, when the triumphant host passed them by, and went by preference to the little hill of Zion, is superb. These may be referred to as an emblem of the hostile powers east of the Jordan, or more widely, of the world and its powers as threatening the people of God (Delitzsch).

(18) **Leading captive the captives Thou receivedst as gifts among men.** The familiar rendering, "Leading captivity captive," yields no meaning whatever, except by understanding that the abstract noun *captivity* is used by metonymy for the concrete *captives*. In order to be intelligible to most readers, it should have been so rendered by the O. T. Revisers. In the above rendering the following line is treated as a defining relative clause, but with the relative pronoun omitted, which is frequent in Hebrew as in English. The clause states how these captives were acquired. Thus treated all these lines, the second as well as the first and third, refer to persons, and not to the ordinary spoil of war. The gifts taken from men are themselves *men*, who have yielded to Divine power, and who may be regarded as tribute to the Great King. Tribute in money, though enforced by superior power, is spoken of as a "gift" or present in 2 Sam. viii. 2, 6. In Eph. iv. 8 ff. this passage is cited as having its fulfilment in the triumph of the Redeemer, who is there said to have received gifts *for* men. Yet, as Moll well says, "from the standpoint of fulfilment, the conqueror has not taken to himself these gifts, which constitute his spoils, for his own enrichment, but for the benefit of men." In the mind of the Apostle these "gifts for men" are *men*, the captives of Divine grace, of whom "He gave some to be apostles and some prophets," etc.; Eph. iv. 11. The subordinate clause might be rendered, "Thou receivedst gifts *consisting of* men," or more freely, "Thy trophies are men." See the use of the same preposition after a similar verb in Job xxxix. 17: "nor hath he imparted to her *of* understanding."

(21) **The hairy crown.** A head with luxuriant growth of hair is a sign of youth and power (Del., Hupf.), here of defiant power. The context

shows that the two following verses relate to proud enemies who had been conquered, and endeavour to hide themselves in the impenetrable forests of Bashan, or in deep gulfs, probably referring to the Dead Sea, about whose unfrequented shores a fugitive might hope for successful concealment; but from whose deepest recesses this malefactor shall be dragged back to punishment.

(24) **Thy triumphal return** Lit. *goings*, repeated in the second line. The word receives its colouring from the following description. It is the stately advance of a triumphal procession celebrating the victory over the enemies of God and His people.

(27) **Benjamin the youngest, their ruler.** This recognizes Saul, the first king of Israel, as belonging to the tribe of Benjamin, and the location of the sanctuary within its borders. — **Judah** follows, the tribe to which the sceptre of Israel had been permanently attached by the prophecy of Jacob in Gen. xlix. 10, confirmed by the promise to David in 2 Sam. vii. 12-16. — **Zebulon** and **Naphtali** had possession on the northern boundary of the kingdom, and are mentioned in the song of Deborah as having distinguished themselves by their valour in the early history of the nation; Judg. v. 18, comp. iv. 6.

(30) **Rebuke the wild beast of the reeds.** This verse has been overloaded with exposition, and the result is somewhat bewildering. The principal exegetical authorities agree that all after this first clause relates to the recent confederation against Israel. — The **strong cattle** (Heb. *'abbírím, strong ones;* see *'abbírē bāshān*, "strong bulls of Bashan" in xxii. 12) are the leaders of the great army combined against Israel, and **the steers** (*young bullocks*) **of the peoples** represent the Syrian tribes that followed them in vast numbers. These last are further described by a participial clause variously interpreted, and the verse

closes with an emphatic reference to the act of God in their dispersion, as already declared in the opening sentence of the Psalm. These successive clauses being so closely combined, all relating to the poet's own time, and to the terrible war he commemorates, "*the wild beast of the reeds*," mentioned first in the series, must have been some distinguished chieftain who had made himself peculiarly obnoxious in the great rising against Israel. Or it may be an ideal impersonation of the spirit of hostility to God, a creation of the poet's own thought. In either case, real or imaginary, it is to be identified with the one spoken of and addressed in verses 21–23. The common assumption that this beast is Egypt is founded solely on the mention of reeds by the rivers and brooks of Egypt in Is. xix. 6, and the designation of Pharaoh as "a broken reed," in Is. xxxvi. 6. The reed may have been a symbol of Egypt, but this is not sufficient to prove a reference to that land here. It is a well-established fact that along most of the rivers throughout Syria, reeds and canes of various kinds are abundant, including with the ordinary cane here mentioned, the Egyptian papyrus, and the bulrush (Heb. *gôme*) of Ex. ii. 3 and Is. xviii. 2. See Dr. W. M. Thomson, *The Land and the Book*, pp. 450–452, in his description of the impenetrable jungle of both species on the marshy shores of Lake Hûleh, the source of the Jordan. The warlike chieftain of the Psalm may have earned his appellation "wild beast of the reeds" by his use of such thickets for con-

cealment when hotly pursued by his enemies. For anciently as now these tangled masses of reed and rush, with other vegetation of larger and smaller growth, were the favourite resort of wild beasts of every kind. This was "the pride of the Jordan," Jer. xlix. 19, l. 44 (Rev. Old Test.), from which lions came forth in search of their prey. The reference here to Egypt seems still less probable when we see that it is mentioned in the following verse by its proper name, in connection with Cush (Ethiopia), the two being ancient enemies of God in the opposite direction to those previously described. — **That serve basely for ingots of silver.** Heb. *letting themselves be trampled upon for bars* (uncoined masses) *of silver.* The verb is the reflexive (*hithpael*) form of *rāphā, to trample upon;* like *hithrappā, to get one's self healed; hithhappēs* (from *khāphas, to seek*), *to conceal* or *disguise one's self,* lit. *to make one's self sought.* It refers to those who render mercenary service in war as guilty of an act of immeasurable baseness, and deserving the utmost contempt. This rebuke was called for by the fact that the great Syrian army was hired by the Ammonites, and fought not for principle but for pay; 2 Sam. x. 6; 1 Chron. xix. 6, 7. The prep. *bêth* is not *with,* but *in exchange for,* the regular formula for mentioning *price* in connection with barter or wages.

(31) **And Cush hastens on, etc.** Lit. *and Cush makes her hands run unto God.* In the connection of this verse with ver. 29, the hands are to be regarded as laden with gifts, rather than stretched forth in supplication.

LXIX.

A SUFFERER FOR RIGHTEOUSNESS' SAKE.

THE authorship of this Psalm is regarded as more doubtful than that of many ascribed by their title to David. Various expressions point rather to Jeremiah (Delitzsch), but objections are made to connecting it with the latter which cannot be set aside (Keil, Kurtz). In its scope and various expressions it is closely related to Ps. xl., and like it must be regarded as typically prophetic of the Messiah. Next to Ps. xxii. it is cited in the New Testament oftener than any other.

1. He describes his sufferings, especially as resulting from his faithfulness to God (1-12). 2. His cry for help becomes more importunate (13-21). 3. He invokes retribution upon his persecutors (22-28). 4. Thanksgiving and confidence (29-36).

FOR THE LEADER OF THE CHOIR. SET TO SHOSHANNIM. BY DAVID.

1 Save me, O God,
   For the waters come in, yea, even to my soul.
2 I sink in the mire of the abyss,
     Where is no place for standing;
   I am come to deep waters,
     And a flood overwhelms me.
3 I am weary with calling, my throat is burned up;
   Mine eyes waste away while I wait for my God.
4 Those that causelessly hate me,
     Are more than the hairs of my head;
   My destroyers are strong, my slanderous foes, —
     That which I robbed not, I then must restore.

5 Thou Thyself, O God, well knowest my follies,
   My faults are not hid from Thy sight;
6 Yet not through me, Lord Jehovah of Hosts,
     Let those hoping in Thee come to shame;
   Not through me, God of Israel,
     Let those seeking for Thee be dishonoured.

7 But for Thee I bear insult,
   And dishonour has covered my face.

 8 I am a stranger to my brethren,
   An alien to the sons of my mother;
 9 Because zeal for Thy house has consumed me,
   Thy revilers' revilings have fallen upon me.

10 When I fasted and wept out my soul,
   It brought me their scoffing;
11 When I put on me clothing of sackcloth,
   It made me their by-word;
12 Of me do they talk while they lounge at the gate,
   And sing while gulping strong wine.

13 But I, O Jehovah, in a time of favour my prayer is to Thee,
       Through Thy great lovingkindness, O God;
   Be Thy faithful salvation mine answer!
14 Pluck me out of the mire, and let me not sink;
   Let me escape from my foes,
       From the depths of the waters;
15 Let not the rush of the waters o'erwhelm,
   Nor the abyss shut me in.

16 Give me answer, Jehovah, for Thy kindness is good;
   In abundant compassions,
       Turn toward me Thy face;
17 And conceal not Thy face from Thy servant,
   For distress is upon me, — come quick at my call;
18 Draw nigh to my soul and redeem it,
   Set me free because of my foes.
19 My reviling Thou knowest, my shame, my dishonour,
   Mine enemies all are before Thee;
20 Their insults have broken my heart and I languish;
   For pity I looked, but in vain,
       For consolers, but none could be found.
21 They provided me gall for my food,
       And vinegar brought me to drink in my thirst.
22 Let their table before them be a trap,
   And their greetings of friendship a snare;
23 Let their eyes become dim that they see not;
   Smite their loins with continual trembling.

24 Pour the heat of Thine anger upon them,
   Let the glow of Thy wrath overtake them.
25 Let their camp be laid waste,
   And let no man inhabit their tents.
26 For they persecute him Thou hast smitten,
   And they tell of the pain of those Thou hast pierced.
27 In their guilt hold them guilty,
   Have Thy righteousness out of their reach.
28 Blot them out of the roll of the living,
   Let their names not be writ with the just.

29 But I, — O my God, in suffering and sorrow,
   Let Thy power to help give me safety;
30 And God's Name will I praise with a song,
   And with thank-offering laud Him.
31 Thus, more than by an ox, will Jehovah be pleased,
   More than by a bullock with horns and with hoofs;
32 Let the suffering behold and rejoice;
   Ye that seek after God, let your heart take new life.
33 For Jehovah gives heed to the needy,
   His prisoners He has not despised.
34 Let the heavens and the earth give Him praise,
   The seas, yea and all that is moving therein;
35 For God is the Saviour of Zion,
        And the cities of Judah He builds,
   And there men shall dwell and possess them;
36 The seed of His servants shall hold them,
   And therein shall those loving His Name have a home.

(4) **That which I robbed not, I then must restore.** Probably proverbial, and illustrative of the injustice of those who charged him with a crime of which he was innocent, and demanded satisfaction to justice. For a similar case see Jer. xv. 10.

(12) **They talk while they lounge at the gate.** "The gate" is mentioned as including the public square for the transaction of business, just within the gate of a city, a general place of resort for its inhabitants. See note on lv. 11. The verb *siahh*, which is only used of light conversation, indicates that the following verb, literally, *they sit*, does not describe the formal sitting of a magistrate or of those engaged in important business, but the careless ease of those who have come merely for gossip and amusement.

(22) **And their greetings of friendship.** Heb. *shelômîm*, the plural of *shâlôm*, oftenest translated *peace*, but in its radical and frequent meaning

it covers the whole conception of soundness, health, prosperity, and blessing. We are to remember here the question *Shālôm l'kā?* "Is it well with thee?" 2 Kings iv. 26, etc., and the common use of the word as a salutation of civility or friendship, which is perpetuated in the oriental *salam.* The rendering "their salams a snare" would be understood by a multitude of readers. "Their table" in the preceding line is the table at which they are entertained in pretended friendship, and "their greetings" here are those which they receive.

LXX.

THE CRY OF A PERSECUTED ONE FOR HELP.

A REPETITION with slight variations of the latter part of Ps. xl., the resemblance of which to Ps. lxix. has already been noticed. This fragment stands in similar relation to both Psalms. Yet it is complete in itself, and therefore suitable for separate use.

FOR THE LEADER OF THE CHOIR. TO BRING TO REMEMBRANCE.

1 O God, haste Thee on to deliver;
　Oh haste Thee, Jehovah, to help me.
2 Let those come to shame and confusion,
　　Who hunt for my life;
　Let those be repulsed in disgrace,
　　Who desire to destroy me;
3 Let those turn away in their shame,
　　That say to me, "Aha!"

4 But all those that seek Thee,
　　In Thee let them joy and be glad;
　All that love Thy salvation,
　　Let them say without ceasing,
　　　"Jehovah be greatly exalted!"
5 And I, in my suffering and need, —
　　Make haste to me, O God;
　Thou art my help and deliverer,
　　O Jehovah, delay not!

LXXI.

THE PRAYER OF OLD AGE FOR DIVINE AID TO THE END.

AN anonymous Psalm, which begins like Ps. xxxi. and closes like Ps. xxv. "The whole Psalm is an echo of the language of older Psalms." Delitzsch regards it as the work of Jeremiah, but his reasons are not conclusive. "There are no sufficient reasons against the Davidic composition of this Psalm at the close of his life. It is as natural to suppose that the aged David should repeat himself in familiar phrases of the Psalms of his younger days as that Jeremiah or any other poet of later times should use the words and phrases of David." — *Briggs*.

It contains: 1. Prayer for deliverance, with thankful acknowledgment of God's goodness from his earliest childhood (1–6). 2. After referring to wonders already wrought as a ground of hope, he supplicates like favour for the present and future (9–13). 3. He resolves to go on in the strength of the Lord (14, 15). 4. Thanksgiving (19–24).

1 In Thee, O Jehovah, I take refuge;
  Let me never come to shame.
2 In Thy righteousness rescue and save me;
  Incline Thou Thine ear and deliver.
3 Become to me a home in the rock for continual resort,
    Thou that gavest commandment to save me;
  For Thou art my cliff and my fortress.

4 My God set me free from the hand of the wicked,
  From the grasp of the man that wrongeth and rageth;
5 For Thou, even Thou, art my hope,
  Thou, Lord Jehovah, my trust from my youth.
6 Upon Thee was I stayed from my birth,
    By Thy help I came from my mother,
  And my praise shall be ever of Thee.

7 I am a wonder to many,
  But Thou art my strong place of hiding;
8 And full of Thy praise is my mouth,
  Yea, full of Thy glory all the day long.
9 Cast me not off in the time of old age,
  And do not forsake me when strength is declining.

10 For mine enemies say,
　　As conspiring together they watch for my life:
11 " Surely God has forsaken him,
　　Press after and take him, for no one can rescue."
12 Be Thou not afar off, O my God,
　　Oh, haste Thee to help me."

13 Let those pass away in their shame,
　　　　That lie in wait for my life;
　　Let those put on clothing of scorn and disgrace,
　　　　That seek to destroy me;
14 As for me, I continually hope,
　　And more, and yet more, will I praise Thee.
15 My mouth Thy righteousness tells,
　　　　And all the day long Thy salvation,
　　For I know not their number.
16 With the mighty acts of Jehovah the Lord do I come,
　　And Thy righteousness praise, yea, Thine only.

17 Thou hast taught me, O God, from my youth;
　　Hitherto I have shown Thy wonderful works:
18 Even down to old age and gray hairs,
　　　　Let me not, O God, be forsaken of THEE?
　　Till I show forth Thy might unto this generation,
　　　　Thy power unto all that shall come.
19 Thy righteousness reaches high heaven, O God;
　　Thou that doest great things, who is like unto Thee?
20 Who hast made us to suffer distress great and sore,
　　　　But wilt give us new life;
　　From the depths of the sea wilt Thou bring us;
21 Thou wilt add to my greatness,
　　And again wilt console me.
22 And I on the lute will extol Thee,
　　　　Thy truth, O my God;
　　Unto Thee will I play on the harp,
　　　　Thou Holy One of Israel.
23 My lips sing with joy while I play,
　　And my soul which Thy grace has redeemed.

24 Yea, my tongue shall speak of Thy righteousness all the
          day long;
      For they are in shame, for they are confounded,
          That seek to destroy me.

(7) **I am a wonder to many.** He is thinking of his remarkable escapes from danger, and of the marvellous vicissitudes of his life. The Heb. *môphēth* often occurs after *'ōth*, of things contrary to the course and order of nature, the miraculous *signs and wonders.* So in the New Test. from the Sept. σημεῖα καὶ τέρατα.

(15) **I know not their number.** That is, of the acts which prove God's righteousness or salvation.

He would declare them, but cannot in their full detail. They are innumerable, and furnish matter for thanksgiving that can never be exhausted. See xl. 5.

(16) **The mighty acts of Jehovah.** Heb. *gebûrōth.* Lit. *powers;* that is, proofs of the Divine power. It is the nearest equivalent to the Greek δυνάμεις, in the New Testament always meaning *miracles.*

LXXII.

PRAYER FOR THE PEACEFUL, PROSPEROUS, UNIVERSAL, AND EVERLASTING DOMINION OF GOD'S ANOINTED ONE.

EVERYTHING here indicates the pen of Solomon, rather than of David. It is a grand prophetic prayer. It relates to himself and his own administration, but upon the basis of the promise to David in 2 Sam. vii. 12–16, which included the whole royal race descended from Solomon in its typical unity, and so culminates in the Messiah and His eternal reign of blessing over the whole race. The apocopate form of the verbs in their succession indicate supplication, and that he was not to his full consciousness a prophet. But nevertheless he was an inspired suppliant, and his utterances are a glorious prophecy of the coming and kingdom of a greater than Solomon.

The kingdom desired and foretold is: 1. Righteous (1–4). 2. Perpetual (5–7). 3. Universal (8–11). 4. Benign (12–14). 5. Prosperous (15–17).

The closing doxology in verses 18 and 19 does not belong to this separate Psalm, but to the Second Book of the Psalter, and also the subscription in verse 20.

BY SOLOMON.

  1 Give Thy justice, O God, to the king,
        To the royal by birth Thy righteousness give;
  2 Let Him righteously govern Thy people,
        With equity rule Thy sufferers;

3 Let the mountains bear peace for the people,
And the hills be fruitful in right;
4 For the suffering people let Him execute judgment,
Let Him save those whose birthright is want;
Let Him crush the oppressor.

5 While the sun shall endure let them fear Thee,
While the moon gives its light,
Throughout all generations:
6 May He come like the rain on the meadow,
Like showers that water the earth;
7 In His days let the righteous man flourish
And welfare abound till the moon be no more.

8 From the sea let Him rule to the sea farthest off,
From the river to the bounds of the earth;
9 Let the wild men come crouching before Him,
And His foes have their mouth in the dust;
10 Let the kings pay Him tribute,
Of Tarshish and shores far away;
Kings of Sheba and Seba bring gifts;
11 Let all kings bow before Him,
And the nations all serve Him.

12 Because he delivers the needy that cries,
The sufferer whom no one can rescue;
13 He pities the wretched and needy,
And the lives of the needy He saves;
14 He redeems them from wrong and from outrage,
Of great price is their blood in His sight.

15 Let Him live ; of the gold of Sheba let them give Him;
For Him let them pray without ceasing,
Yea, all the day long let them bless Him.
16 To the top of the mountains
Abundant be grain in the land;
Let the growth thereof wave
Like the cedars of Lebanon,
And away from the city men flourish
Like plants of the earth.

17 Let His Name continue forever ;
      While the sun shows its face
      Let His Name still endure,
      And men count themselves blessèd in Him ;
   Let the nations all hail Him, the Blest.
18 Blessèd be Jehovah, even Israel's God,
      Who alone doeth wonders ;
19 And blessèd the Name of His glory forever,
      And let the whole earth be filled with His glory ;
         Amen and Amen.

20 The prayers of David, the son of Jesse, are ended.

(1) The king . . the royal by birth. Heb. *the king . . . the son of a king.* The prayer is by Solomon, not for a king and his son, but for a single person, first as a king in fact, and then as of royal descent.

(4) Let Him execute judgment. Not always against culprits, but often in behalf of the injured ; see vii. 8, xxvi. 1. — **Those whose birthright is want.** Heb. *the sons of want;* a common Hebraism.

(7) Let the righteous man flourish. Heb. *burst into blossom.* A figure derived from luxuriant vegetation, and suggested by "the showers" in ver. 6. See note on xcii. 12. — **Welfare.** Heb. *shălōm,* usually rendered *peace.* From the root *shălōm, to be whole, sound.* It comprehends all completeness in condition and relations. See note on lxix. 22. The Greek εἰρήνη, *peace,* through its use in the Septuagint in rendering *shălōm,* brings into the New Test. a much fuller and richer conception of blessing than it has in classical usage.

(8) From the sea ... From the river. This verse describes universal dominion geographically. "The river" and "the sea," meaning the river Euphrates and the Mediterranean, were the eastern and western boundaries of Solomon's kingdom. and are the starting-points in this description. Beyond the great sea it was imagined that another sea might exist, and this the absolute limit of the world. The parallelism requires that the western sweep of the Messianic kingdom should be as extensive as the eastern.

(10) Pay Him tribute. Lit. *bring again gifts.* The verb *shûb* expresses repetition, and indicates regular payments to a conqueror, as in 2 Kings iii. 4, xvii. 3, etc. — **Of shores far away.** Heb. *'iyyīm,* usually rendered islands, means *coast-lands ;* places reached only in ships.

(17) Hail Him the Blest. From *'ăshar,* the verb from which the frequent *ăshrē,* "O *the happiness,*" is derived. See on i. 1. Just before and after we have forms of the verb *bărak, to bless.*

BOOK III.

LXXIII.

THE PROSPERITY OF THE WICKED TRANSIENT.

THIS Psalm and the ten following are attributed in their title to Asaph. The only one of the group that precedes this is Ps. l., where see remarks upon their general character.

The same problems that are discussed in Psalms xxxvii. xlix., and in the Book of Job, are treated here, and with similar solution. But the vindication of God's ways by Asaph is more satisfactory, and the confidence and joy in God are more explicit than we find in Job. Indeed the veil that conceals the heavenly world was lifted before him. Everything seemed bright and clear for the future to one who could say, " Thou wilt guide me by Thy counsel, and thereafter receive me into glory."

I. A problem (1–14). II. Its solution (15–28).

I. 1. His present conviction of God's unvarying goodness to His faithful people, contrasted with his previous disturbance (1–3). 2. The prosperity and pride of the wicked (4–9). 3. The apostasy produced by their example (10–14).

II. 1. In his perplexity the Psalmist turns to God (15–17). 2. The riddle solved (18–20). 3. Thus relieved, he confesses his folly, and God becomes his stay and his hope (21–26). 4. Contrast between the lot of the wicked and his own (27, 28).

A PSALM OF ASAPH.

1 Of a truth God is gracious to Israel,
  To those of pure heart.
2 But my feet very nearly gave way,
  In a moment my steps would have failed.

3 For my jealousy flamed at the boastful,
  I saw how the wicked were prospered;
4 For they suffer no pangs,
  Sound and firm is their strength;

5 They share not the trouble of mortals,
   And are not stricken down with mankind;
6 Therefore pride is their necklace,
   And a garment of outrage enfolds them.

7 From their grossness of heart their iniquity comes,
   The vain thoughts in their mind overflow;
8 They scoff, and wickedly speak of oppression,
   They speak from on high;
9 Yea, their mouth they have set in the heavens,
   Their tongue roves about in the earth;
10 And thitherward, therefore, God's people turn back,
   And full flowing waters they greedily drink.

11 They say, " How can God know?
   Has indeed the Most High any knowledge?
12 Behold, these are the wicked;
   Yet fearless forever they attain to great power;
13 It was surely in vain that I made my heart clean,
   Or my hands in innocence washed;
14 For all the day long was I smitten,
   Every morning my chastisement came."

15 Had I said, " Even thus will I speak,"
   Lo, I then had been faithless to the race of Thy sons.
16 When I pondered, in order to know this,
   It was painful toil to mine eyes;
17 Till I entered the sanctuary of God,
   And considered what end must be theirs;
18 Of a truth Thou hast set them in slippery places,
   Thou castest them down to destruction.

19 How suddenly ruin overtakes them!
   Swept off, made away with by terrors.
20 As a dream when one wakens,
   So, Lord, at Thy rousing,
      Thou wilt scorn their vain show.
21 When my heart became bitter,
   And my soul was in pain,

22 I was brutish and stupid;
Before Thee I became as a beast.

23 But to me it has fallen to be with Thee alway;
Thou hast grasped my right hand:
24 By Thy counsel Thou wilt lead me,
And thereafter wilt take me to glory.
25 Whom have I in heaven beside THEE;
And with Thee as mine own,
In the earth I have nought to desire.
26 My flesh and my heart pass away;
But God is the Rock of my heart,
And my portion forever.

27 For, lo, those afar from Thee perish;
Those that wantonly leave Thee,
Thou destroyest them all.
28 As for me, my great joy is my nearness to God;
In Thee, Lord Jehovah, I hide me,
That so I may tell all Thy works.

(2) **Gave way.** Heb. *nâtâh* (נָטָה), *to bend over*, inclining to a fall; so of a wall, *leaning over*; lxii. 3. — **Would have failed.** Heb. *were poured out*, of footsteps as slipping.

(4) **Pangs.** Heb. *hhartsûbbâh*, 1. *a tightly drawn cord*, Is. lviii. 6; then, *torture*, as by tight constriction; equivalent to the more frequent *hhébel*, *a cord*; 2. pl. *pangs*, convulsions, throes. The clause in the present Hebrew text asserts that the wicked suffer no pain in dying. This cannot be the thought of the poet. If it had seemed to him true, it would not be placed foremost in the description. The difficulty is relieved by a slightly different division of the verse, throwing the two final letters of the first line into the second. So Cheyne, following Del., Ew., Olsh., Hitz., and others.

(5) **Mortals ... mankind**; as in viii. 4, *'enôsh, man* as frail, and *'âdâm, man* generic. The thought of the verse is that these bad men seem to be treated as if they belonged to a superior race, exempt from the suffering of humanity at large.

(7) **From their grossness of heart their iniquity comes.** Lit. *their eyes go forth from* (because of) *fatness.* Olsh., Hitzig, and others prefer the Septuagint rendering on the basis of *'avônâm* (עֲוֹנָם), *their iniquities*, for *'ênâm* (עֵינָם), *their eyes.* "Fatness" is used of a heart full of evil desire. The same general result is reached by taking "*eyes*" in the standing text, in its frequent ethical sense, of inward propensity or desire, good or bad, as expressed through the eyes. This is favoured by the verb *yâtsâ'* (יָצָא), of evil lusts in their activity as *going forth.*

(10) **And thitherward, therefore, God's people turn back.** Heb. *therefore his people turn back hither.* The pronoun *His* certainly refers to God. *Hither* and *thither*,

like *come* and *go*, are relative and easily convertible terms, depending on the position of the speaker. The poet, for the purpose of closer observation and more vivid description, has ideally planted himself in the midst of the men who are enjoying their prosperity and "drinking iniquity like water" (Job xv. 16), but to those at a distance his *hither* is a *thither*. So *pōh v'pōh*, prop. *here and here*, and *shām v'shām*, prop. *there and there;* both mean, by rapid transference from one ideal standpoint to another, *here and there.* Prof. Cheyne adopts a change in the text purely conjectural, which he admits is inconsistent with the use of the conjunction *therefore* (Heb. *lākēn*), "Therefore He satisfies them with bread." The line so read is absolutely unintelligible. — *Therefore* here is co-ordinate with *therefore* in ver. 6. Both are connected with verses 4 and 5, giving two distinct results of the prosperity of the wicked, their own encouragement in all evil, and among the people of God, discouragement and apostasy. — **And full flowing waters they greedily drink.** Heb. *and waters of fulness are drained by them.* The verb *mātsāh* means *to drink greedily,* as in lxxv. 8; Is. li. 17. The meaning *wring out* found in Lev. i. 15 is suggestive of punishment, and cannot be the thought here.

(11) **And they say, How can God know?** etc. These are questionings of the apostates, followed in verses 12 and 13 by the considerations that had induced them to cast in their lot with the wicked.

(19) **Swept off, made away with.** Heb. *sōphū tammū,* two short, sharp verb forms, closely combined, expressive of sudden and irresistible ruin. — **Terrors**; that is, frightful calamities; especially familiar in Job (xviii. 11, 14, xxiv. 17, etc.).

(20) **Vain show.** Heb. *tsélem, a shadow;* then, *an illusion,* referring back to their boasted strength and fearlessness.

(21) **My soul was in pain.** Heb. *I was pricked in my reins.* The *reins* (kidneys) in Heb. psychology as the seat of the passions and of all deep emotions; see on xvi. 7.

LXXIV.

AN APPEAL TO GOD AGAINST THOSE WHO HAVE DESOLATED THE SANCTUARY.

THE title mentions Asaph as the author. But it cannot be the elder Asaph, who was contemporary with David. For the description here given cannot apply to any event earlier than the destruction of the temple by the Chaldeans, recorded in 2 Chron. xxxvi. 19. To this period it is assigned by De Wette, Hengstenberg, Hupfeld, Moll. But in several important particulars it does not correspond with the historic details of the Chaldean invasion, especially in verses 3, 4, 8, 9. Olshausen, Hitzig, and Delitzsch connect it with the atrocities of the Syrian invasion under Antiochus Epiphanes, B. C. 167. The only objection lies in ver. 7, which is taken to mean that the temple was utterly destroyed, which is not in accordance with the historic statement in the Books of the Maccabees. Yet the porch of the temple was burned (2 Macc. i. 8), and the whole interior so thoroughly stripped and desecrated (1 Macc. i. 21-24) that they cried to God in their misery, "Behold, our sanctuary and our beauty and our glory are laid waste, and the heathen have profaned them." 1 Macc. ii. 12.

It is one of the most spirited and graphically descriptive Psalms in the Psalter, and its appeals to God, referring to past interventions of His Almighty power in behalf of Israel, are magnificent.

Like the preceding it consists of two principal parts, 1-11, 12-23. In the former half: 1. An appeal to God's compassion in behalf of His afflicted people (1-3). 2. A description of the desolation that had come upon them (4-9). 3. God is called upon to give aid by an act of judgment (10, 11).

In the second half: 1. The poet recalls past miracles in Israel's great perils (12-17). 2. Thus encouraged, he turns again to prayer, which becomes cheerful and bold (17-23).

A MASKIL OF ASAPH.

1 Wherefore, O God, dost Thou spurn us forever?
    Why riseth the smoke of Thine anger,
        'Gainst the flock of Thy care?
2 Remember Thy people, Thy purchase of old,
    The tribe Thou hast bought for possession,
        And Mount Zion whereon Thou hast dwelt.
3 Let Thy footsteps pass up to the ruin enduring,
    To all wreck of the Holy Place wrought by the foe.

4 Thine enemies roared in Thy place of assembly,
    They set up their symbols for the symbols of God.
5 It seemed as if men with their axe lifted high,
    Were assaulting a thicket of trees;
6 For now the carved work thereof all
    Is smitten with hammer and sledge.
7 To Thy holy fane they put fire,
    They pollute to the earth the abode of Thy Name.
8 They said in their heart, "We will crush them at once,"
    And they burned all the houses of God in the land.
9 We see not our symbols;
    No more have we with us a prophet,
        Nor any that knoweth how long.
10 How long, O Jehovah, shall oppressors revile?
    Shall enemies alway scoff at Thy Name?
11 Oh, why should Thy hand, Thy right hand hold back?
    Let it now from Thy bosom come forth and destroy.

12 Yet God is my King from of old,
   Who worketh deliverance to the bounds of the earth.
13 It is Thou that didst sunder the sea in Thy strength,
   In the deep didst Thou shatter the heads of the dragons ;
14 It is Thou that didst crush Leviathan's head,
   And didst give him for food to wild beasts of the desert.
15 It is Thou that didst cleave the fountain and torrent,
   And dry up the streams ever flowing.
16 Thine is the day, also Thine is the night ;
   It is Thou that preparedst the light and the sun ;
17 And Thou that hast fixed all the bounds of the earth ;
   Summer and winter, it is Thou that hast formed them.

18 O Jehovah, remember how the enemy scoffs,
   A foolish people are blaspheming Thy Name ;
19 Thy turtledove give not to a ravenous brood,
   Forget not forever Thy suffering charge.
20 Oh, look on the covenant ;
   For the land's darkest corners
       Are crowded with violent homes.
21 Let not the oppressed be turned back in dishonour,
   Let the suffering and needy give thanks to Thy Name.
22 Arise, O God, and plead Thine own cause ;
   Remember how all the day long the foolish revile Thee.
23 Forget not Thine enemies' voice,
   The loud roar of Thy foes that ascendeth forever.

(1) **Why riseth the smoke of Thine anger.** Heb. *why smokes Thine anger.* See xviii. 8. — **Of Thy care**; that is, care as a shepherd. The corresponding verb (see on xxviii. 9) means *to be a shepherd, to tend* a flock, and this noun includes the whole conception, and is not confined to pasturage or feeding : lxxix. 13, c. 3 : Jer. xxiii. 1, 2.

(2) **The tribe Thou hast bought.** After the destruction of the northern kingdom tribal distinctions were lost sight of, and "*tribe*" came to be used of the whole people as a race. See Jer. x. 16 and li. 19 in the Rev. Vers.

(4) **Their symbols for the symbols of God.** Heb. *their symbols for symbols ;* that is, false and idolatrous institutions of worship for the true. The latter included the ark, altar, and all appurtenances of the temple. For the former see 1 Macc. i. 45-49. So "symbols" in ver 9.

(5) **It seemed as if men.** Heb. *it made itself known as if men.* See R. V. The Hebrew expresses both the upward motion of the axe, and the penetrative incision.

(8) **Houses of God.** Lit. *meeting-places of God.* There are various reasons for concluding that these

must be the synagogues, of which there are no traces in history till long after the exile.

(13, 14) In connection with the parting of the Red Sea, the poet mentions the destruction of the *tan-nînim*, **dragons**, creatures of enormous length, and of **Leviathan**, by etymology, flexible and gathering itself into folds. The latter is the name given the crocodile in Job xli. 1. Both refer to the emblem of the king and kingdom of Egypt. See Is. xxvii. 1, li. 9. — **To wild beasts.** Heb. *to wild beast people.* See the word *people* used of the ants and rock badgers in Prov. xxx. 25, 26.

(15) **Didst cleave the fountain and torrent.** Here the smiting of the rock so that it became a fountain and the smiting of the Jordan so that its waters rolled back, are combined. See lxxviii. 15 and Josh. iv. 23, v. 1.

(19) **Thy turtle dove.** A symbol of Israel. See lxviii. 13. — **To a ravenous brood.** Heb. *hhavyath néphesh.* The Septuagint has θηρίοις, *wild beasts*, as in Gen. i. 25, ii. 20, etc. But against this may be fairly urged the improbability of this meaning here, when in the following member of the verse it means *life.* No solution can be admitted which does not give the same sense in both lines. Now without question the sing. *hhay-yâh* is used collectively of living creatures, the lower orders as well as the highest. Without more exact definition it will describe animal life

in general. So in lxviii. 10 we have translated, " For there were Thy living ones dwelling." In l. 11 the parallelism shows a reference in both lines to *birds*, as in ver. 10 of the same Psalm, there is a reference in both to *beasts.* Consequently we there translate, " I know every bird of the mountains, and *the brood* (Heb. *life*) of the meadows is with Me." Here (lxxiv. 19) in each line a word in the genitive is added to *hhayyath* for more exact definition. In the first line the defining word is *néphesh, eager desire, greed* for food (see Prov. xxiii. 2, a man of *néphesh;* that is, *a greedy man*), but here of the voracity of vultures or other carnivorous birds for their prey. To them a dove would be a dainty morsel. In the second line also *hhay-yath* has a defining genitive. It is *'aniyyîm*, God's *suffering ones*, who in parallelism with the preceding *turtle-doves* might also be called *a brood*, harmless, helpless, affrighted, and in danger of being torn in pieces and devoured by their natural enemies ; and would warrant the translation, *Forget not forever Thy suffering lives*, that is, living ones. There seems to be a play on the word *life* which is not easily brought out in translation, but which satisfies the exegetical requirement mentioned in the former part of this note. The sense is, Give not up a helpless and harmless life, to be destroyed by a savage brute life.

LXXV.

GOD SITTING IN JUDGMENT UPON PROUD AND DEFIANT WICKEDNESS.

THIS Psalm is probably to be referred to the defeat of the Assyrians under Sennacherib before Jerusalem (2 Kings xix.). Hengstenberg regards it " as the lyrical accompaniment of Isaiah's prophecies in view of

impending destruction by the Assyrians, and as the evidence of the living
faith with which God's people received His promise."

The prophetico-judicial character of the Psalm is strongly suggestive of
Ps. l., the first of the Asaphic group.

*1. The church gives thanks for the near approach of God's revealed presence in the
might of His Name (1). 2. God personally announces Himself as the Judge and
Upholder of all things, with rebukes and warnings (2–5). 3. The church takes up
the strain, expressing its confidence in the fact and impartial equity of God's judgment (6–8). 4. The poet, personating the king, resolves to praise God forever, and to
make the Divine equity the principle and rule of his own acts (9, 10).*

TO THE LEADER OF THE CHOIR. "AL-TASSHETH." A PSALM OF ASAPH.
A SONG.

1 Unto Thee we give thanks — O God, we give thanks;
    Very near is Thy Name;
Thy wonderful works have been told.

(God speaks.)

2 " Yea, I seize the set time;
It is I that in equity judge:
3 When the earth is dissolving with all that are on it,
It is I that set firmly its pillars.   [Selah.]
4 I say to vain boasters, ' Boast vainly no longer,'
To the wicked ' Exalt not your horn ; '
5 Exalt not your horn to high heaven,
And be not of stubborn and arrogant speech."

6 For nought can avail from the east or the west,
And nought from the desert of mountains ;
7 But God is the Judge ;
And one He brings low, but another exalts.
8 For Jehovah has a cup in His hand,
    The wine is brisk and well mingled ;
        Of this He pours out ;
And surely the wicked of the earth
    Shall drain, fully drain, all its dregs.

9 Forever be it mine to proclaim —
To praise Jacob's God on the harp ;
10 All the horns of the wicked will I shatter,
But exalted be the horn of the righteous.

(1) **Very near is Thy Name.** The Name of God is the manifestation of what He is in relation to men. To say that His Name is near, is simply to announce an approaching activity judicial and redemptive. It is mentioned here as a matter of special thanksgiving. — **Thy wonderful works have been told.** The construction is impersonal. *They* (that is, men) *have told.* These works consist of all past wonders of redemption, as encouraging the expectation of glorious results from His appearing as now promised.

(2) **Yea, I seize the set time.** As by a voice from heaven, God announces Himself as now upon the throne of judgment. "The set time" is the time determined in His own wise and gracious purpose. To every fresh Divine activity there is a "fulness of time."

(5) **Exalt not your horn.** Rebuking inordinate pride of power, as now exhibited even against God and His people. In ver. 11, under the same figure, the poet speaks of the exaltation of the righteous to dignity and power as coming from God. This figure, which occurs frequently in the Old Testament, has its earliest suggestion in Deut. xxxiii. 17, and is derived from animals remarkable for power and aggressiveness, that push with their horns. It is thus a standing symbol of power, whether for offence or defence. It often carries with it the accessory idea of confidence and courage, but sometimes, as here, of pride and presumption. It may be used of an individual in humble life, as of Hannah in 1 Sam. ii. 1; much oftener of the power of a king or nation; and even God in His saving power is called "a horn of salvation;" 2 Sam. xxii. 3; Ps. xviii. 2. — **Be not of stubborn and arrogant speech.** Heb. *speak not arrogantly with a stiff neck.*

(6) **From the desert of mountains.** A literal rendering from the Hebrew as in the margin of the Revised Version. The reference is undoubtedly to "the south," as in the English Bible, and to what lay beyond the mountains of Arabia Petræa; that is, to Egypt. The absence of any allusion to the north as a supposable source of aid is probably that Israel is now threatened with destruction by a power that has come from the north (Moll, Delitzsch).

(8) **Brisk.** Heb. *boiling up,* actively effervescing; of wine in sparkling life and potency.

(9) **Forever be it mine.** The pronoun is here emphatic and antithetical.

LXXVI.

GOD'S RIGHTEOUS JUDGMENT IN ITS TRIUMPH.

THIS Psalm follows Ps lxxv. most appropriately. It is the consummation of the judgment there forecast, and throughout bears the impress of the same historic connection. Without this the preceding Psalm disappoints us by its incompleteness. For the self-manifestation of God in the illustration of His glorious Name at important crises in history, when all is lost without the aid of Almighty power, embraces both the announcement and the execution of His righteous judgment. This Psalm follows, as its companion precedes, the destruction of the Assyrian power.

There are four strophes, each having three couplets:

*1. Where God has attained renown (1-3). 2. The victory by which He has sig-
nalized Himself (4-6). 3. The dread which this victory is fitted to awaken (7-9).
4. God is irresistible, and it becomes men to worship and obey Him (10-12).*

TO THE LEADER OF THE CHOIR.   UPON STRINGED INSTRUMENTS.
A PSALM OF ASAPH.   A SONG.

1 In Judah God made Himself known,
  In Israel He won a great Name;
2 Then Salem became His retreat,
  And His home was in Zion.
3 From thence has He scattered
      The lightninglike shafts of the bow,
  The shield, and the spear, and the battle.

4 Bright-shining art Thou,
      And more glorious than the mountains of prey;
5 The men of stout heart are a spoil;
  They sank down in deep slumber;
6 Of the valiant could none find their hands;
  Thy rebuke, God of Jacob,
      Brought a stupour on chariot and horse.

7 Thou, even Thou, art a God to be feared;
  Who can confront Thee when once Thou art angry?
8 Thou proclaimedst Thy sentence from heaven,
  And the earth was fearful and still,
9 When God rose to judgment,
  To save all the meek of the earth.

10 Surely man's wrath shall praise Thee,
   For with mightier wrath dost Thou gird Thee about.
11 Make vows, and fulfil them, to Jehovah our God;
   All ye that surround Him,
       Bring presents to Him ye should fear;
12 He breaketh the spirit of princes,
   He is One to be feared by the kings of the earth.

(1, 2) These opening sentences seem to go back to the first revelations of God's power and grace by which He became established upon His throne in Zion. From Zion as the centre must go forth every new manifestation of His glorious majesty in behalf of Israel, the latest of which is now celebrated in thankful song.

(2) **His home.** Heb. *mā'ôn* (מָעוֹן), *a dwelling-place;* also used of a *lair,* as the noun just before it, properly, *a booth,* or covering made of boughs, might describe *a thicket,* the prowling place of wild beasts. But all thought of God under the figure of a lion coming down from "the mountains of prey" is unsuitable.

(3) **The lightninglike shafts of the bow.** Heb. *the lightnings of the bow,* meaning the arrows in their swiftness and deadly effect (Job xli. 20); "the battle" includes all the weapons that have been used against His people Israel by their assailants. Comp. xlvi. 9.

(4) **More glorious.** Heb. *'addîr;* used in viii. 1, 9 of the Name of God as "transcendent." See the note there. — **Than the mountains of prey.** This is an emblematical designation of the high-handed potentates or world-powers that plunder every one that comes near them (Del.). The prep. *min, from,* is here a particle of comparison.

(10) **For with mightier wrath dost Thou gird Thee about.** The Authorized Version renders this line: "the remainder of wrath shalt Thou restrain." But while the verb *hhāgar* means *to bind around,* it is never used of binding for the purpose of restraint. The Revised Version gives the rendering: "The residue of wrath shalt Thou gird upon Thee." This is after Hupfeld, and it means, as explained by him, that the residue of the wrath (of hostile

men) God will gird upon Him as an *ornament,* or *trophy.* But again, there is no instance of the use of *hhāgar* in this sense; and if there were, it is difficult to understand what residue is intended. In these explanations it is assumed that in the second line of the verse as well as the first, the wrath of *man* was in the poet's mind. The difficulty disappears when we observe that on the contrary, God's wrath in its superabundance is spoken of, as aroused against the feeble and ineffective wrath of man. The word *she'ērîth* is usually *a remainder,* or *surplus.* It implies that there is enough and more than enough for a given purpose; and in this connection, that God's wrath is mightier than man's, and that the latter praises Him by its submission to His superior power, practically confessing its own impotence. As for the verb *hhāgar,* it is used elsewhere of putting around one's loins a girdle for some great exertion. Then, figuratively, a girding with strength, with righteousness, with faithfulness, are expressions familiar to the Hebrew. See Ps. xviii. 32; Prov. xxxi. 17; Is. xi. 5. This surely gives the best sense here, and agrees with the scope of the Psalm. Against all combinations of human wrath, God girds Himself with a wrath that exceeds it, and returns as conqueror, with a residue sufficient for all future need, even if the whole earth should turn against Him.

LXXVII.

COMFORT FOR THE DESPONDING.

THE time to which this Psalm belongs is uncertain. It has a near connection with Habakkuk ch. iii., which seems, in view of the abrupt ending of the Psalm, as if it might have been intended as a continuation. Delitzsch's argument in favour of a connection between the two, and of the priority of the Psalm, is very satisfactory (*Comm. on Hab.*). This would fix its date as not later than the reign of Josiah.

Without reference to the question of historic relation, " it may be said, in general, that the poet flies from the sorrowful present away into the memory of the years of olden times, and consoles himself more especially with the deliverance out of Egypt, so rich in wonders."

The general division is into Complaint (1-9), Consolation (16-20). 1. The sufferer is impelled to unremitting prayer (1-3). 2. Despondent wailings (4-9). 3. He calls to mind God's wonders of old (10-15) 4. He finds special relief in recalling God's mighty acts in the redemption from Egypt (16-20).

1 Unto God I lift up my voice, and will cry ;
  Unto God I lift up my voice, till He hear me.
2 In my day of distress I enquire for the Lord ;
  My hand in the night is stretched forth without ceasing,
      My soul refuses all comfort.
3 Remembering God I must moan,
  When I yield me to thought my spirit grows faint.

4 Thou holdest mine eyes on the watch ;
  I toss to and fro and am speechless.
5 I think of the days of old time,
  Of the years far off in the past ;
6 I remember my song in the night ;
  I commune with my heart,
      And my spirit makes diligent search.

7 Will the Lord forever cast me from Him?
  Will He favour no more?
8 Has His kindness forever passed away?
  Is His promise a failure to all generations?
9 Has God forgotten to be gracious?
  Has He shut up His mercies in anger?

10 And I said, " Mine affliction is this,
   The right hand of the Most High is all changed ; "
11 Yet the deeds of Jehovah I remember,
   Yea, Thy wonders of old will recall ;
12 Upon all Thy works I reflect,
   And Thy glorious deeds will consider.

13　O God, Thou in holiness orderest Thy way;
　　What God is so great as this God of ours?
14　Thou alone art a God that doest wonders;
　　Thou revealedst Thy might midst the nations:
15　With arm lifted high Thou redeemedst Thy people,
　　The children of Jacob and Joseph.

16　O God, when the waters beheld Thee,
　　　　When the waters beheld Thee they writhed;
　　Yea, the depths were in anguish;
17　The clouds poured out water,
　　　　And the skies gave their voice;
　　Yea, Thy darts flashed about,
18　The voice of Thy thunder rolled along,
　　　　The lightnings illumined the world;
　　And the earth was convulsed, and it trembled.
19　In the sea was Thy way,
　　　　And Thy path in great waters;
　　Thy footsteps were not to be traced;
20　Thou leddest Thy people like a flock,
　　By the hand of Moses and Aaron.

(2) **My hand is stretched forth without ceasing.** Heb. *my hand floweth out and is not congealed;* that is, it does not become chilled and sluggish. The hand as extended upward is a symbol of supplication, and it is this, in its persistence and fervency, that is described in the sentence. The figure is very bold, and the language becomes readily intelligible only by substituting other verbs properly applicable to the hand in the attitude of earnest prayer, as in the English Bible, or by substituting *supplication* for *hand,* which would give the more poetical conception of a flowing stream that lies in the Hebrew text.

(4) **Thou holdest mine eyes on the watch.** Lit. *Thou holdest fast the guards of my eyes;* that is, my eyelids, to keep them from closing.

(10) **Affliction** Heb. *sickness;* fig. *grief,* as in Prov. xiii. 12: "Hope deferred maketh the heart to grieve." The precise rendering of the Hebrew is, "and I said, 'My grief is this, the change of (or, the years of) the right hand of the Most High.'" The word *shenôth* may have either meaning. The rendering we adopt is in the marg. of Revised Version. It is that of the Sept. and most of the ancient versions. So Maur., Hitz., Hupf., Perowne. The thought is that the grief of the sufferer is intensified by the contrast between the present withdrawal of God's favour, and His wonderful works of grace and power in the past. Yet he finds his greatest comfort in recalling them, and cherishes the hope that God will be equally gracious in the present sore need.

LXXVIII.

A LESSON FROM THE PAST.

NO historic connection can be determined for this Psalm. It sweeps over the whole period from Moses to David, in order to impress upon the hearts of the Israelites their obligations to God and the danger of rebelling against Him.

1. The warnings of history to be kept ever in mind (1-8). 2. The backslidings of Israel in the wilderness (9-16). 3. Rebellious gluttony, its gratification and punishment (17-31). 4. Deceitful repentance and God's forbearance (32-39). 5. Distinguishing mercies forgotten (40-55). 6. Idolatry in Canaan (56-64). 7. The choice of Judah, David, and Zion in place of Ephraim and Shiloh (65-72).

MASKIL OF ASAPH.

1 Hear my law, O my people;
  Incline your ear to the words of my mouth.
2 I will open my mouth in a poem,
  I will utter the oracles of old.
3 The things we have heard and have known,
  That our fathers have told us,
4 We will not conceal from their children,
      But rehearse to the next generation,
          The praiseworthy deeds of Jehovah,
  His power and the wonders He wrought.

5 He established a precept for Jacob,
      He appointed a law unto Israel;
  Which He ordered our fathers
      To make known to their sons;
6 That the next generation might know,
      Even sons that were yet to be born;
  Who should rise and tell it to sons of their own.
7 That so they might place their reliance on God,
  And should not forget what Jehovah has done,
      But should keep His commands;
8 And should not become like their fathers,
      A race rebellious and stubborn,
  A race that had not established its heart,
      And in spirit unfaithful to God.

9 The children of Ephraim, equipped with the bow,
Turned back in the day of the battle;
10 They kept not the covenant of God,
Were unwilling to walk in His law,
11 And His glorious deeds they forgat,
The wonderful works He had shown them.

12 He did wonders in sight of their fathers,
In the borders of Egypt, the country of Zoan;
13 He sundered the sea and let them pass through,
Made the waters stand up as a heap;
14 With a cloud did He lead them by day,
And all the night through with the light of a fire.

15 He clave rocks in the desert,
And gave them to drink like the depths in abundance;
16 Yea, streams He brought out from the cliff,
And made waters flow down like a river;
17 Yet they still went on sinning against Him,
In the deserts defied the Most High.

18 Tempting God in their heart,
They asked food for their craving;
19 Yea, they spake against God;
They said, " Hath God power
In this wilderness land to prepare us a table?
20 Behold, He smote rock, and waters gushed out,
And streams dashed along;
Can He also provide us with bread,
And find flesh for His people? "

21 Therefore, Jehovah, when He heard it, was wroth,
And fire was kindled in Jacob,
Yea, wrath went up against Israel;
22 For they believed not in God,
Nor trusted His power of salvation.

23 Yet He ordered the skies high above,
And opened the doors of the heavens;

24 He rained on them manna to eat,
    And gave them of grain out of heaven ;
25 The mortal did eat the bread of the mighty,
    Yea, food in abundance He sent them.

26 He led forth an east wind in the heavens,
    And His power was guide to a wind from the south ;
27 And flesh He rained down as the dust,
    Fowl of wing like the sand of the sea, —
28 Let them fall in the bounds of their camp,
    All around their abode ;

29 So they ate and were filled to the full,
    Yea, that which they craved had He brought them.
30 But their craving was still unappeased,
    The morsels were yet in their mouth,
31 When the anger of God rose against them ;
          He slew their most comely,
    The chosen of Israel destroyed.

32 Through all this, they still went on sinning,
    They believed not His wonders ;
33 So their days He made cease like a breath,
    And their years to pass off in dismay.
34 When He slew them they sought Him ;
    They turned back and brake through unto God ;

35 They remembered that God was their Rock,
    Yea, God the Most High, their Redeemer ;
36 They spake fair with their mouth,
    But their tongue was deceitful ;
37 Their heart was not steadfastly with Him,
    They were false to His covenant.

38 Nevertheless, He is full of compassion,
          Forgiving iniquity, He will not destroy ;
    And ofttimes He turns from His anger,
          And arouseth not fully His wrath ;
39 He remembered they were flesh,
    A breath passing forth, and never returning.

40 In the desert how oft they provoked Him,
How oft in the wilderness vexed Him;
41 Again and again they tempted their God,
And angered the Holy One of Israel.
42 His power they kept not in mind —
The day He released them from foes;
43 When He set forth in Egypt His signs,
His wonderful works in the country of Zoan.

44 Their streams from the Nile,
He had turned into blood,
And no more could they drink of their brooks.
45 He sent flies that devoured,
And frogs that destroyed them.

46 To the grasshopper gave He their increase,
And their labour to locusts ;
47 Killed their vineyards with hailstones,
And their fig trees with ice ;
48 Their cattle He gave to the hail,
And their flocks to the lightnings.

49 He let loose His hot anger against them,
Wrath, indignation, and trouble,
An embassy heralding woe.
50 He levelled a path for His anger;
Their soul He withheld not from death,
But their life He gave up to the plague ;
51 He smote all the firstborn of Egypt,
The firstlings of strength in the dwellings of Ham.

52 Then He led forth His people as sheep,
Like a flock did He guide them in deserts ;
53 He led them securely, and freed them from fear,
And the sea overwhelmed their oppressors.
54 To His holy domain did He bring them,
To this mountain His right hand had gained;
55 He drove out the nations before them,
Whose possessions He assigned them by measure,
Making Israel's tribes to dwell in their tents.

56 Yet they tempting rebelled against God the Most High,
    And His ordinance kept not;
57 But, faithless, fell away like their fathers,
    Turned aside like a treacherous bow;
58 For they stirred up His wrath by their worship on hills,
    His jealousy burned at the sight of their idols.

59 God heard, and was wroth,
    And fierce in abhorrence of Israel;
60 He forsook His pavilion at Shiloh,
    The tent He had pitched among men,
61 And His Majesty gave to be captive,
    To the hand of the tyrant He yielded His Glory;
62 To the sword He gave over His people,
    And against His heritage poured out His wrath;
63 The fire consumed their young men,
    And hushed was the song for the maiden as bride;
64 Their priests were cut down by the sword,
    And their widowed ones made no lament.

65 Then the Lord roused up as one that had slept,
    Like a warrior that shouts over wine;
66 He smote back their oppressors,
    Made to bear everlasting disgrace;
67 Yet, rejected the encampment of Joseph,
    And chose not the standard of Ephraim;

68 But the standard of Judah He chose,
    The mountain of Zion that He loved.
69 Like the heavenly heights He builded His Holies,
    Like the earth which He founded forever.

70 He chose David His servant,
    Whom He took from the folds of the sheep;
71 From tending the milk-giving ewes did He bring him,
    As shepherd to Jacob His people,
            To the Israel preserved as His own.
72 Who their shepherd became
            In his soundness of heart,
    And their guide by the skill of his hands.

(44) Their streams from the Nile. Lit. *their Niles.* It is the plural of the Egyptian word *ye'ōr, a river*, but used exclusively of the Nile. It refers here, without question, to the distribution of the waters of the great river by canals for tillage.

(49) Heralding woe. Heb. *messengers* (or *angels*) *of woe.* This seems to be a personification of the Divine displeasure under different aspects.

(61) His Majesty ... His Glory. Designations of the ark of the covenant, the symbol of the majesty and glory of God as revealed to Israel. See especially 1 Sam. iv. 21. The removal of the ark was the withdrawal of God's presence as King and Deliverer.

(64) Their widowed ones made no lament. Heb. *their widows did not weep.* Not to be pressed as if there were no sorrow for the dead. But the slain were so numerous that the public obsequies at their burial, in which according to oriental custom the loud wailing of the nearest relatives was a principal feature, had to be omitted. See Job xxvii. 15, Rev. Vers., and Amos viii. 3: "The dead bodies shall be many; in every place they shall cast them forth with silence."

(72) Their shepherd became. This is to be preferred to the rendering "*fed them.*" The service described by the verb includes much more than feeding. See note on xxviii. 9.

LXXIX.

DEVASTATION, BLOODSHED, AND DIVISION.

IN every respect this is a companion to Ps. lxxiv. The general character and style, the language and historic allusions, all indicate the same time and authorship, with the same doubt and probability as to which of the two great national calamities is referred to.

1. A complaint of grievous misery (1-4). 2. A prayer that God will turn His wrath against the heathen (5-7). 3. A supplication for Divine compassion and help (8, 9). 4. Further entreaty that God will avenge the dishonour inflicted upon His Name and His servants (10-12). 5. A vow of thanksgiving (13).

A PSALM OF ASAPH.

1 Thy heritage, Lord, have the heathen invaded,
    Thy holy palace defiled,
And have laid Jerusalem in ruins.
2 They have given Thy servants' dead bodies
    As food to the birds of the heaven,
Thy favoured ones' flesh to the beasts of the earth.
3 All around Jerusalem,
    Their blood they have poured out like water;
There are none to bury their dead.

4 We are a scorn to our neighbours,
  A scoff and a jest to those round about us.

5 How long as if alway will Jehovah be angry?
  How long shall Thy jealousy flame up like fire?
6 On the nations that know Thee not, pour out Thy wrath,
  On the realms that invoke not Thy Name;
7 For they feed upon Jacob,
  And his pastures lay waste.
8 Recall not against us the guilt of our fathers;
  Let Thy mercies with speed come to meet us,
    We are brought very low.

9 Give us help, our God of salvation,
    For the glory of Thy Name;
  For Thy Name's sake deliver us, and cover our sins.
10 Oh, why should the heathen say, " Where is their God? "
  Let the heathen in our sight know Thy vengeance,
    For their shedding the blood of Thy servants.
11 Let the groans of the captive come before Thee,
  In the might of Thine arm save the children of death;
12 And repay to our neighbours sevenfold in their bosom,
  The reviling, O Lord, wherewith they revile Thee.

13 So we, Thine own people, the flock of Thy care,
    Will forever give thanks;
  Yea, to all generations will utter Thy praise.

---

(2) **Thy favoured ones.** The plural of *hhasid, beloved*, or *loving*. See note on iv 3.

(5) **How long as if alway will Jehovah be angry?** See note on xiii. 1. — **Shall Thy jealousy flame up like fire?** Jealousy of every rival in the regard of His people, in accordance with the favourite representation of their spiritual relation to Him as that of a wife to her husband, and idolatry as unfaithfulness to that relation. Compare Jer. iii. 14, "for I am married unto you." See Deut. xxxii. 21.

(8) **Come to meet us.** Anticipating our need, as in xxi. 3, lix. 10.

(11) Heb. *in the greatness of Thine arm let survive the children of death.* " The children of death " are those in imminent danger, especially, in continuation of the preceding line, through the barbarities of war. They are those whom death seems to have claimed as belonging to his great family, and who may soon say to him, unless God have mercy, "Thou art my father:" see Job. xvii. 14.

(13) **The flock of Thy care.** See note on lxxiv. 1.

LXXX.

A PRAYER FOR THE VINE JEHOVAH HAD PLANTED.

THERE is difference of opinion here, as in the preceding Psalm, about the historic allusion. Delitzsch is probably right in referring it to the earlier part of the reign of Hezekiah, and before the destruction of the northern kingdom, but when the oppression of Syria was resting heavily upon Israel, and Judah saw itself threatened with ruin when this bulwark should have fallen.

The Psalm is divided by a refrain into three parts, consisting of three, four, and twelve verses:

1. An invocation of God to give help in distress (1-3). 2. A lamentation over the deplorable results of God's anger (4-7). 3. The former prosperity of the people as a vine under God's gracious care, contrasted with present desolation (8-13). 4. Prayer for protection and restoration (14-19).

FOR THE LEADER OF THE CHOIR. SET TO "SHOSHANNIM EDUTH."
BY ASAPH. A PSALM

1 Shepherd of Israel, give ear,
    Thou Leader of Joseph, Thy flock;
  Yea, Thou that art throned upon cherubim, shine forth;
2 Before Benjamin, Ephraim, Manasseh,
    Stir up Thy strength,
  And come Thou to save us;
3 Restore us, O God;
  Let Thy presence give light,
    For we then shall be saved.

4 O Jehovah, God of Hosts,
  How long wilt Thou threaten the prayer of Thy people?
5 Thou hast given them weeping for food,
  And for drink they have tears in full measure.
6 Thou hast made us a gibe to our neighbours,
  Our enemies have us their sport.
7 God of hosts, restore us;
  Let Thy presence give light,
    For we then shall be saved.

 8 A vine didst Thou bring out of Egypt,
   Didst thrust out the nations, and plant it;
 9 Before it Thou madest large room;
   Its roots struck deep, and it filled up the land.
10 By its shade the mountains were covered,
   By its branches, the cedars of God;
11 Its boughs it sent out to the sea,
   Its fresh roots to the river.

12 Oh, why didst Thou break down its hedges,
   So that all may pluck it that pass by the way? —
13 Torn up by the boar of the wood,
   Eaten off by the brood of the field.
14 God of Israel, return, we beseech Thee;
   From heaven look down and behold,
        Give Thy care to this vine;
15 What Thy right hand has planted, protect,
   The son Thou mad'st strong for Thyself.

16 Burnt with fire, swept away,
   At the frown on Thy face they must perish.
17 Hold Thy hand over the man of Thy right hand,
   The one born of mankind,
        Over him Thou mad'st strong for Thyself.
18 That from Thee we may not fall away,
   Oh, give us new life,
        And thus on Thy Name will we call:
19 " Jehovah, God of Hosts,
   Let Thy presence give light,
        For we then shall be saved."

(4) **Threaten.** Heb. *smoke against.* See lxxiv. 1, xviii. 8 ; Deut. xxix. 20. " But the figure is bolder here than in the other passages, as it is applied immediately to God *Himself.*" — *Perowne.*

(6) **Have us their sport.** Heb. *make us sport for themselves.*

(15) **The son.** This might apply to the vine, as in Gen. xlix. 22; but more probably the figure is for the moment dropped, as in ver. 17 it is entirely abandoned, and Israel, as the son of God, becomes the subject. The Divine utterance at the time of the transplantation of the vine, which explains both verses, is Ex. iv. 23, " Israel is my son, my firstborn." — **For Thyself.** That is, for Thine own possession and use. The verb *'immêts, mad'st strong,* so followed, includes selection, seizure,

and appropriation, as in Is. xliv. 14. Delitzsch translates it "Thou hast chosen."

(17) **Hold Thy hand over.** Heb. *let Thy hand come to be over.* The connection with ver. 15 indicates the reference to the vine planted *by* God's right hand, rather than *at* God's right hand as a place of high dignity and power, which is elsewhere differently expressed; see cx. 1. The Targum gives here, "over the king Messiah whom Thou didst establish for Thyself." There may be an allusion to Israel, exalted to a place of high privilege and dignity, as the nation from whom one higher than the kings of the earth should descend; but the passage cannot be considered directly Messianic.

LXXXI.

THE FEAST OF THE PASSOVER.

THERE can be no doubt that the feast referred to in ver. 5 is the Passover, as the one which begins with the full moon of the month Nisan, and as connected with the new moon of the same month, which was the first day of the *sacred* new year.

1. A summons to the whole congregation to unite in celebrating the Divinely appointed festival (1–5). 2. A festival address in which God refers to the mercy shown them in Egypt, and reminds them of the solemn charge He then gave them (5–10). 3. The frustration of His purpose by their disobedience and selfwill (11, 12). 4. An earnest wish that even yet they would return and enjoy His blessing (13–16).

FOR THE LEADER OF THE CHOIR. UPON THE GITTITH. BY ASAPH.

1 Shout for joy unto God;
 It is He is our Strength;
Unto Jacob's own God, shout aloud.
2 Raise a psalm, strike the timbrel,
 The sweet harp, with the lute of ten strings;
3 At the new moon blow trumpets,
 With the moon at the full on the day of the feast.
4 For this is a statute for Israel,
 A law Jacob's God had ordained;
5 This He appointed a witness in Jacob,
  When He went through Mizraim's land;

  (*God speaks.*)

 " I heard there the speech of a people I knew not;
6 His shoulder I removed from the burden,
 And his hand was relieved from the basket;

7 In distress didst thou cry, and I freed thee;
   I heard thee from the covert of thunder,
      I proved thee by the waters of Strife.
8 I said to thee, ' Hearken, my people,
      I must witness against thee;
   O Israel, if only thou wilt hear me!
9 Let no god of the alien be with thee,
   Nor worship the foreigners' gods;
10 For I, Jehovah, thy God,
      Brought thee up out of Egypt;
   Thy mouth open wide, — I will fill it.'

11 But My people obeyed not My voice,
   Even Israel refused Me submission;
12 So I cast them away in their hardness of heart,
   To walk as themselves should desire.
13 Oh that My people would hear Me,
   That Israel would walk in My ways;
14 Right soon would I vanquish their foes;
   My hand would I turn to destroy their oppressors.
15 Yea, before them the foes of Jehovah should crouch,
   That so their own time might continue forever."

16 With the finest of the wheat would He feed them,
   And fill them with honey from the rock.

(5) The text here is very difficult. It is condensed, and in some sense elliptical. It is not necessary to suppose anything lost, yet a connecting line between 5 and 6 may possibly have dropped away. The " going forth through the land of Egypt (Heb. *Mitsraim*)," as connected with the preceding reference to the institution of the Passover, must refer to God's going forth through the land on the night of the first Passover, for the destruction of the firstborn. There is then very abruptly, in the middle of verse 5, a change from the third person to the first. We can hardly doubt that it is a Divine utterance, direct and oracular. This is not singular in an Asaphic Psalm. In Ps. l., after introductory sentences by the poet, God Himself speaks, and in Ps. lxxv. 2, His voice breaks in almost as abruptly as here, after a single introductory sentence. The mention of Mizraim is the signal for direct mention of what occurred there, from the lips of the principal actor. It recalls the tones of the voices He heard there, not necessarily at the time specified by the poet, but as that to which He referred when He said to Moses, " I have heard their cry by reason of their taskmasters " (Ex. iii. 7). It is the voice of these taskmasters that He then heard,

representing a people that He knew not, afflicting His people whom He knew. The mention of a tongue other than that of Canaan is very graphic here; for a foreign tongue indicates a foreign people, strangers to Israel, and strangers to God.

(5) **I heard there the speech of a people I knew not.** The word *s'phath, speech,* literally *lip,* is a *construct* form, preceding a genitive clause; that is, a relative clause with the relative pronoun suppressed. See note on xvi. 3, and Ges. Gram. § 116, 3. It is not "*a language that I knew not,*" but "*the language of* (those whom) *I knew not.*" This is the rendering in the marg. of Rev. Version, and the only one grammatically possible. The tense is the imperfect "*I was hearing,*" as if continuously listening to the harsh commands of the taskmasters on the one hand, and the outcries of the suffering Israelites on the other. It tells the whole story, without supplying the particulars to those who knew them so well. There is no reason why another sentence should not immediately relate the whole tale of deliverance, and with equal brevity, — "His shoulder I removed from the burden, and his hand was relieved from the basket."

LXXXII.

THE JUDGE OF ALL THE EARTH.

THIS Psalm has reference to some time of great judicial corruption. "Asaph, the seer, beholds how God, reproving, correcting, and threatening, appears against the chiefs of the congregation of His people, who have perverted the lustre of the majesty He has put upon them, into tyranny." — *Delitzsch.*

1. God comes forward, censuring and admonishing (1-4). 2. He declares the ineffectiveness of correction, and their overthrow and ruin (5-7). 3. The poet prays that the Divine judgment thus expressed may be realized (8).

A PSALM OF ASAPH.

1 God stands in the assembly of the mighty,
  In the midst of the gods He is Judge;
2 " How long shall your judgment be wrongful?
  How long will ye favour the face of the wicked?
3 Let the wretched and orphan have justice;
  Give their right to the suffering and poor;
4 Deliver the wretched and needy,
  Set them free from the wicked man's hand.

5 But they know not, discern not,
    They are walking in darkness;
  The foundations of the earth are all trembling;

6 I Myself have said, ' Ye are gods,
    Ye are all sons of God, the Most High ; '
7 Yet like men shall ye die,
    Ye shall each of you perish like one of the princes."

8 Arise and give judgment, O God, in the earth,
    For by rightful possession all nations are Thine.

(8) **Possession.** The words *in-herit* and *inheritance* are less suitable in connection with God than *possess* and *possession*, and the latter give the primary and proper meaning of the Hebrew words.

LXXXIII.

GOD INVOKED TO TAKE PART IN THE CONFLICT.

THIS is the last of the twelve Psalms of Asaph in the Psalter.   It probably has its historical place before the victory of Jehoshaphat over the allied forces of the Moabites, Ammonites, and their confederates, described in 2 Chron. xx.

1. A cry to God to arise against those who have combined for the destruction of Israel (1-4). 2. The confederates are enumerated (5-8). 3. (Part ii. of the Psalm) An appeal to God to visit them with the same disgrace and overthrow inflicted formerly on such foes (9-12). 4. An entreaty that they may be utterly dispersed and brought to shame (13-16). 5. A wish that in their downfall they may seek Jehovah, and that all the earth may know and adore Him (17, 18).

A SONG.   A PSALM OF ASAPH.

1 O God, keep not silence ;
    Hold not Thy peace, nor refrain Thee, O God ;
2 For, behold, Thine enemies rage,
    And Thy foes lift their head.
3 Against Thine own people they craftily plot,
    They conspire against those Thou hast hid.
4 They say, " Come ; cut them off as a people ;
    Let Israel's name be remembered no more."
5 For they plan with one mind,
    Against THEE, they are in covenant bound ;

 6 The encampments of Edom and Ishmael,
    Of the Hagarenes and Moab.

 7 Gebal and Ammon and Amalek,
    Philistia and the households of Tyre;
 8 Yea, Assyria has joined them,
    Helping forward the children of Lot.   [Selah.]
 9 Do to these as Thou didst unto Midian,
    As to Sisera, and Jabin at the torrent of Kishon;
10 They were smitten at Endor,
    And became as dung for the ground;
11 Make their nobles like Oreb and Zéeb,
    Their princes like Zéba and Zalmun;
12 Who said, "Let us take in possession
    The pastures of God."

13 Make them, my God, like the dust in its whirl,
    Like the chaff that is chased by the wind;
14 As fire burns the forest,
    As mountains are kindled by flame,
15 Even so with Thy tempest pursue,
    With the sweep of Thy whirlwind confound them;
16 Fill their face with confusion,
    That Thy Name they may seek, O Jehovah.

17 Be they shamed and confounded together,
    Yea, abashed and destroyed.
18 Let them know that Thou only,
        Whose Name is Jehovah,
    Art God the Most High,
        That shall rule the whole earth.

(3) **Those Thou hast hid**. That enemy cannot find them. Comp. is, those who are under God's gra- xvii. 8, xxvii. 5, xxxi. 20, xci. 1. cious protection, placed where the

LXXXIV.

LONGING FOR THE HOUSE OF GOD.

THE Psalm is attributed by its title to the Korahite band of Levitical
singers.   It is clearly connected with Psalms xlii. xliii., and like them
it belongs to the flight of David before Absalom.   The poet probably
speaks as from the soul of David (Hengstenberg).   " It is all through a
tender and fervent expression of love for the sanctuary of God, — of love
which yearns in the distance to return to it, and pronounces all that have
their home there happy." — *Delitzsch.*

*1. His personal affection and intense longing for the house and worship of God
(1, 2).   2. The birds find quiet and safety there, and how blest the men whose
privilege of worship is never interrupted (3, 4).   3. The pilgrim band coming from
their distant homes to the yearly festival in Zion (5–8).   4. Prayer and praise with
strong confidence in the power and grace of God (9–12).*

1 How lovely Thy dwellings,
   O Jehovah of hosts !
2 My soul longs, yea, it pants
     For the courts of Jehovah ;
   My heart and my flesh cry aloud
     To the God that has life.

3 Yea, the bird finds a home, the swallow a nest,
     Where she putteth her young,
   At Thine altars, Jehovah of hosts,
     My King and my God.
4 And how blest are all they that dwell in Thy house,
   Who continually praise Thee.   [Selah.]

5 How blest are the men whose strength is in Thee,
   In whose heart are the highways to Zion ;
6 As they pass through the valley of Baca,
     They fill it with fountains ;
   Yea, with blessings the early rainfalls enrobe it.
7 From strength to strength they go forward,
   Till each in Zion appears before God :
8 " O Jehovah, God of hosts, hear my prayer ;
   God of Jacob, give ear."   [Selah.]

9 O God, our Protector, behold,
Yea, look on the face of Thine anointed;

10 For a day in Thy courts is better than a thousand;
I choose rather the threshold in the house of my God,
Than to dwell in the tents of the wicked.

11 For Jehovah God is a sun and a shield,
Jehovah gives favour and glory;
From the blameless in life,
He withholds no good thing.

12 Jehovah of hosts,
How blest is the man whose trust is in Thee!

(2) **Cry aloud**. Heb. *rānan, to utter a clear, ringing sound;* usually, of the voice raised in joyful shouting or singing; but here a cry of suffering and intense desire, as in Lam. ii. 19, "Arise, cry out in the night, lift up thy hands for the life of thy young children." — **The God that has life**. Not merely of God as living, in contrast with dead idols, but of God as having in Himself the absolute potential life, from which all life proceeds, for which he thirsts, and without which he must perish. See xlii. 2, and the note there, also lxiii. 1.

(3) **The bird**. Heb. *tsippôr*. The word is imitative, *a chirper*, or *twitterer*. It is used of birds of every kind; Gen. xv. 10, of doves and pigeons; and more generally in Gen. vii. 14, Lev. xiv. 4-22, and Ps. viii. 9, etc.; even birds of prey in Ezek. xxxix. 4. It refers here to the smaller birds that abound near the habitations of men, but not exclusively, if at all, to the sparrow. — **At Thine altars**. The birds need not be thought of as having access to the interior of the sanctuary. On that subject there are different opinions. The altar, as the most important feature in the mind of the poet, may stand for the whole edifice and its precincts. Hengstenberg and Delitzsch think that actual birds are not intended, but that we have here a bold metaphorical description of the Psalmist and his family, as the bird and its young. But it is not probable that he would so completely bury himself in a figure that not one reader out of ten thousand would discover his meaning. Especially the verb *mātsā* (מָצָא), in the perfect tense, is decisive against the supposition that he refers to himself. For it includes with the finding a home, its present occupation and enjoyment, and such reference is not consistent with his exile and suffering as just described. — "*Thine altars*" is preceded in the Hebrew by the particle *'eth*, which indicates illustrative apposition, and defines the place of building more precisely; as in Deut. i. 22, "that they may bring us word (*'eth haddê'rek*) by what way." This precludes our finding here an exclamation, as if an optative particle preceded, "oh for Thine altars," or a particle of lamentation, "alas for," as several of the older interpreters. Nor need we suppose that important words have been lost from the text, for the supply of which Cheyne, following Mendelsohn, suggests, "(so have I found, even I, a home) at Thine altars" as if the unmutilated text had contained a formal comparison. The poet does not seem to have had in mind either likeness or contrast, as between himself and the birds. There is indeed

underlying the surface a sad consciousness of separation from the place he loves more than all others upon the earth, which might easily burst forth into envy of the birds in ver. 3, and the men in ver. 5. But it is suppressed. He is only seeking some solace in his banishment by calling up before him a picture of his lost joys. The particle *gam*, *yea*, at the beginning of ver. 3 is simply confirmative of his first outcry, "How lovely Thy dwellings!" Even the birds find there a quiet and protected home, where they need fear no rude interruption of their joy. He seems almost to personify these nest-builders, as if they were in sympathy with the strongest feelings of his own heart, in finding a special attractiveness in this favoured spot. He then passes in ver. 4 from the exterior to the interior, — from the bird that cherishes her callow brood in the trees within the sacred enclosure (Perowne), or on the projecting ledges of the sanctuary, to the men, his own former companions, who dwell in God's house and are always praising Him. This is all in contrast with his own forlorn condition. But a direct reference to himself would interrupt the continuity of thought, as he now passes on, and in ver. 5 pronounces those happy who come up annually to the Divinely appointed feasts of Zion.

(6) **The valley of Baca.** The name means *weeping*, and is derived from a species of balsam, from which when wounded a fluid gum issues like tears from the eye. There are several valleys of that name in the Holy Land, in which these trees abound, and which are remarkable for their arid and barren soil. The conclusion of the sentence shows that this feature is referred to, rather than the meaning of the name Baca. Their pathway lies through regions naturally sterile and uninviting. It is not necessary that we should think of any single actual valley known by that name as the one intended. "The words are a figurative expression of the thought that the Divine blessing accompanies them everywhere, and supplies the means by which they are refreshed on their journey, and so strengthened that they become neither faint nor languid, but even stronger as they advance. The valley through which they are advancing becomes green meadows and pastures, and fruitful fields, by springs and rain." — *Moll.*

(9) **Our Protector.** Heb. *our shield.*

(10) **I choose rather the threshold.** The verb form *histophéph*, used only here, is derived from the noun *saph, a threshold*, and means *to put one's self at the threshold*, as a place within God's house, but the most remote and least desirable. The position of doorkeeper in the temple was very honourable, and is expressed by another word.

(11) **The blameless in life.** Heb. *those that walk blamelessly;* the *walk* in Old Test. usage is the life in its activity.

LXXXV.

COME TO US AGAIN, O GOD.

THIS Psalm seems to belong to the period after the captivity in Babylon. Yet this is not certain, for the term "captivity" (or captives) in ver. 1 may be only a figure of some great distress, and God's bringing back the captives, of relief from that distress, as in Job. xlii. 10.

1. A retrospect of former mercy (1–3). 2. Prayer for renewed manifestation of God's favour under present suffering (4–7). 3. The intention declared of listening to what God now shall say (8–10). 4. The certainty of rich blessings in the future is joyfully proclaimed (11–13).

TO THE LEADER OF THE CHOIR. BY THE SONS OF KORAH. A PSALM.

1 Thou, O Jehovah, didst favour Thy land,
  Didst return to the captives of Judah;
2 Didst pardon the guilt of Thy people,
  Didst forgive all their sin;
3 Didst withdraw all Thy wrath,
  And turn from the heat of Thine anger.

4 Our God of salvation, come to us again,
  And let cease Thy grievous displeasure.
5 Wilt Thou alway be wrathful,
  And Thine anger prolong to all generations?
6 Wilt Thou not Thine own self restore us to life,
  That Thy people may be joyful in Thee?
7 Give us sight of Thy merciful kindness, Jehovah,
  And bestow Thy salvation upon us.

8 I will hear what God Jehovah will speak;
  He will surely speak peace to His people, His beloved,
    Not again let them turn unto folly.
9 Yea, indeed, His salvation is nigh them that fear Him,
  That glory may dwell in our land.
10 Lovingkindness and truth meet together,
   Justice and peace have embraced one another.

11 Truth shall spring forth from the earth,
   And justice look down out of heaven;
12 Yea, every good thing Jehovah will give,
   And our land shall yield us its increase.
13 Before Him goeth justice,
   And shall follow the way of His steps.

---

(8) **His people, His beloved.** The connective particle here is *vav* explicative; not *and*, but *even*, exhibiting apposition.

(13) **Shall follow the way.** Heb. *shall set to the way.* The verb *sim, to set*, is probably for *sim lêb, set the mind to, give heed to*, as in Job. iv.

20. The general sense is that righteousness as the principal characteristic of His rule shall precede and follow Him, conspicuously manifested in connection with every Divine activity. There may be some reference to righteousness among men, who shall prepare for His coming by turning to righteousness, and in their righteous deeds shall follow in the footsteps of Jehovah, the Righteous.

LXXXVI.

PRAYER UNDER PERSECUTION.

THE ascription to David in the title cannot be maintained. The structure and style indicate a later origin. It can only be called a prayer of David as expressing the spirit of some of his supplicatory Psalms. It abounds in loosely connected passages out of the book of the law and the earlier Psalms, and is liturgical, rather than poetic.

1. Various invocations and entreaties (1–7). 2. A strain of adoration (8–10). 3. Prayer for direction, which the poet gratefully promises to follow (11–13). 4. Prayer for deliverance from enemies (14–17).

A PRAYER. BY DAVID.

1 Turn Thine ear, and answer me, Jehovah,
  For I am suffering and needy.
2 Preserve Thou my soul, for I am one whom Thou lovest;
  Save Thou, my God, Thy servant that trusteth in Thee.
3 O Lord, show me pity,
  For I cry to Thee all the day long.
4 Give joy to the soul of Thy servant,
  For, O Lord, unto Thee do I lift up my soul;
5 For Thou, Lord, art good, and ready to pardon,
  And of great lovingkindness to all that invoke Thee.

6 O Jehovah, give ear to my prayer,
  Attend to my suppliant cry.
7 In my day of sore trouble I call Thee,
  For Thou givest me answer;
8 With Thee, O Lord, not one of the gods can compare,
  And no works are like Thine.
9 All the nations Thou madest shall come,
    And shall worship before Thee, O Lord,
  To Thy Name giving glory;

10 Because Thou art great and doest wonders;
   Thou, and Thou only, art God.

11 Teach me Thy way, O Jehovah;
      I would walk in Thy truth;
   Unite my heart in the fear of Thy Name.
12 With all my heart do I thank Thee, O God;
   To Thy Name I give glory forever.
13 For Thy great lovingkindness is over me;
   Thou hast rescued my soul
      From the depth of the world underneath

14 The proud rise against me, O God;
   A violent band are seeking my life,
      And have not set Thee before them.
15 But Thou, Lord, art God,
         Gracious and full of compassion,
   Long suffering, abundant in kindness and truth.
16 Oh, turn to me in pity;
   Give Thy strength to Thy servant,
      And save the son of Thy handmaid.
17 Show me a token for good,
   That mine enemies may see, and with shame,
      That Thou, O Jehovah,
         Hast helped and consoled me.

(13) **The depth of the world underneath.** Heb. *Sheol underneath;* not *the lowest Sheol,* as if it were divided into a higher and a lower, but the spirit-world is described as below the surface of the earth. See note at vi. 15.

LXXXVII.

ZION THE BIRTHPLACE OF NATIONS.

WE have here a glorious exhibition of the kingdom of the Messiah, as covering the whole earth, but having its beginning and permanent centre at Jerusalem. The keynote is verse 9 of the preceding Psalm : —

> " All the nations Thou madest shall come,
> And shall worship before Thee, O Lord ; "

which is itself an echo of xxii. 27 in the earlier worship of Israel : —

> " All the bounds of the earth
>   Shall remember and turn to Jehovah ;
> All the families of nations
>   Shall worship before Him."

Several representative nations are mentioned, not as subjugated enemies, but as highly honoured members of the household of God, in fellowship with Israel, and entitled to look with joyful pride to Zion as their birthplace and spiritual home. This is connected with a Divine declaration in verses 3 and 4 that they shall enjoy this great distinction. Its central thought is presented so boldly and concisely that it might be obscure were it not illuminated by other prophecies, especially Is. ii. 2–4, xi. 10–18, xix. 18–25, xlv. 14. The regenerative grace which shall bring all nationalities of the earth into the most intimate and exalting relation with God, is ever represented as issuing from Zion, the city of the Great King.

1. God's love to Zion in view of her glorious future, as secured by His promise(1–3). 2. The promise is given. She represents to the heart of God a redeemed world. Every nation shall trace his birth to her, and has his name upon her register of the sons of God, and this in permanency (4–6). 3. The joy of the nations in her fountains of blessing are celebrated in song and dance (7).

BY THE SONS OF KORAH. A PSALM. A SONG.

1 On His holy hills He laid His foundation;
2 And Jehovah loveth the gateways of Zion,
    More than all the dwellings of Jacob.
3 Glorious things of Thee have been spoken,
    Thou city of our God: [Selah.]

4 " Rahab and Babel I proclaim as my friends;
    Lo, Tyre and Philistia with Cush,
        It is here they were each of them born.
5 Yea, of Zion shall be said,
        That in her they were born, each and all;
    The Most High will Himself keep her firm.
6 Jehovah will count, in enrolling the nations,
    That this one was born there."   [Selah.]

7 And singers with dancers shall greet her,
    " All my springs are in thee."

(2) **The gateways of Zion.** These have special mention because through them, in all the future, the redeemed, whether nations or individuals, shall come before God as His people.—**Jehovah loveth.** The

participle of the verb *'āhab, to love*, is used, as expressing in the Hebrew idiom a permanence which is not conveyed by either tense.

(3) **Have been spoken**, or *promised*. Here also the participial form *m'dubbār*, as concrete, expresses permanence.

(4) **I proclaim**. Lit. *I cause to be remembered;* but it denotes in usage a public and solemn announcement. Here God is the speaker.— **Each of them**. Heb. *this one*, as if pointing them out one by one.

(5) **Each and all**. Lit. *man and man;* a Hebrew idiom for *each and every one.*

(6) **In enrolling the nations.** Compare Is. iv. 3. " Every one that is inscribed unto life."

(7) **Greet her**. Supplied by the translator. The words of the song follow, and unquestionably relate to Zion. The singers and dancers are the leaders in a procession of redeemed Gentiles, representing the peoples mentioned in ver. 4; Egypt, by its prophetic name Rahab (see lxxxix. 10), the world power on the south, and Babylon northward; rich and proud Tyre, warlike Philistia, and Ethiopia, " the land shadowing with wings," more remote than the rest; Is. xviii. These in their turn represent the whole world, as brought into fellowship with the living and true God, through the gracious influences that proceed from His dwelling-place in Zion.

LXXXVIII.

DEEP DESPONDENCY.

THE gloomiest prayer in the Psalter ; even more so than Ps. lxxvii., and in marked contrast with the cheerfulness of lxxxvii. The exhibition of this picture indicates that periods of affliction sometimes occur in human experience during which for an indefinite time the sufferer will accept no comfort. He seems to find his only satisfaction in dwelling upon his misery, as if in love with darkness bordering on despair.

1. Various complaints (1-9). 2. Expostulations, and wrestling with God, showing that hope was not abandoned, but ending in gloom (10-18).

A SONG. A PSALM OF THE SONS OF KORAH. FOR THE LEADER OF THE CHOIR. SET TO "MAHALATH LEANNOTH." MASKIL OF HEMAN, THE EZRAHITE.

1 O Jehovah, my God of salvation,
　　As by day, so I cry in the night-time before Thee ;
2 Let my prayer reach Thy presence,
　　Turn Thine ear to my wailing.

3 For sore evils have sated my soul,
　　And my life draws near to the regions of death :
4 I am counted with those that go down to the pit,
　　And become like a man whose strength is all gone ;

5 Set free with the dead, that lie in the grave,
      Whom no more Thou rememberest, —
With those cut off from Thy hand,

6 In the nethermost pit hast Thou laid me,
  In the abodes of darkness and depths of the sea.
7 I am heavily pressed by Thy wrath,
  And all Thy great waves bear me down.   [Selah.]

8 Away from me far hast Thou put mine acquaintance,
  Thou hast made them abhor me,
      As a prisoner who cannot come forth.
9 Mine eye wasteth through suffering;
  O Jehovah, I call on Thee daily,
      And to Thee do I stretch forth my hands.

10 Shall Thy wonders be wrought for the dead?
   Shall the shades rise and praise Thee?
11 Shall Thy kindness be told in the grave,
   Or Thy faithfulness shown in destruction?
12 Shall Thy wonders be known in the darkness,
   And Thy righteousness told in oblivion's land?

13 But I, O Jehovah, unto Thee do I cry;
   In the morning my prayer comes before Thee.
14 Why, O Jehovah, wilt Thou cast off my soul,
   And why hide Thy face from my sight?

15 From my youth I am wretched and dying;
   I suffer Thy terrors, my senses must fail.
16 Thy hot wrath overwhelms,
   Thy terrors destroy me.
17 All the day long they surround me like waters,
   All at once they come circling about me;
18 Thou hast put far off from me lover and friend,
   Mine acquaintance — I have but the darkness.

LXXXIX.

PLEADING THE PROMISE TO DAVID.

A THOROUGHLY national song. It is probably connected historically with the defeat of Rehoboam (1 Kings xiv. 25 ff.; 2 Chron. xii.
1 ff.) by Shishak (Sheshonk I.).

*Part I. (a) 1. The poet celebrates the covenant with David as faithful and sure
(1-4). 2. The power and faithfulness of God (5-12). 3. The mercy and truth of
God (13-18). (b) 1. He recounts God's promise to David personally (19-28).
2. His promise to his seed after him (29-37). Part II. 1. A dark picture of the
present reverse (38-45). 2. Earnest expostulation (46-51). A Doxology follows,
which does not belong to this particular Psalm, but to the Third Book of the Psalter.*

MASKIL OF ETHAN, THE EZRAHITE.

1 Forever will I sing the lovingkindness of Jehovah,
  And to age after age with my mouth Thy faithfulness tell ;
2 For I say, lovingkindness is built up forever,
  In the heavens, even there,
      Wilt Thou make Thy faithfulness stand.

3 "In the covenant I made with My chosen,
  I sware unto David My servant,
4 'Forever I establish thine offspring,
  And build up thy throne to all generations.'"   [Selah.]

5 Thy wonders, Jehovah, the heavens shall praise,
  And Thy truth, in the assembly of the holy ;
6 For who in the skies can compare with Jehovah,
  Who, with Jehovah, of the sons of the mighty?

7 In the council of the holy, He is God very dreadful,
  To be feared above all that surround Him ;
8 O Jehovah, God of Hosts,
      Who is like Thee, Thou mighty Jehovah,
  With Thy faithfulness all round about Thee?

9 It is Thine to bear rule o'er the pride of the sea,
  When the waves thereof rise, it is Thou that canst still them ;

10 It was Thou didst crush Rahab as one that is slain,
   With Thy mighty arm Thou hast scattered Thy foes.

11 Thine are the heavens, and Thine is the earth,
   It is Thou that hast founded the world and its fulness;
12 The north and the south, it is Thou didst create them,
   Tabor and Hermon exult in Thy Name.

13 Thine is the arm that has power;
   Strong is Thy hand, and Thy right hand is high;
14 The supports of Thy throne are justice and right,
   Lovingkindness and truth stand waiting before Thee.

15 How blest are the people that know the glad sound,
   Who walk, O Jehovah, in the light of Thy presence!
16 All the day long they have joy in Thy Name,
   And Thy righteousness lifts them on high.

17 For Thou art the glory of their strength,
   In Thy favour their horn is exalted;
18 For our shield appertains to Jehovah,
   To the Holy One of Israel, our king.

19 Thou hast once in a vision assured Thy belovèd,
       " I give help to one valiant,
   I have raised to high place one I chose;
20 I found David, My servant,
   And him with My holy oil I anointed.
21 With him My hand shall be steadfast,
   And Mine arm shall furnish him strength.

22 An enemy shall not ensnare,
   Nor a son of injustice oppress him;
23 For I beat down before him his foes,
   And will smite those that hate him.

24 My truth and My love shall be with him,
   In My Name shall his horn be exalted.
25 His hand will I set on the sea,
   His right hand shall rest on the rivers.

26 He shall call to Me, ' Thou art my Father,
   My God and my rock of salvation ; '
27 And I, My firstborn will I make him,
   The Most High to the kings of the earth.

28 For him will I ever retain lovingkindness,
   And with him shall My covenant stand fast ;
29 I will give to his offspring to continue forever,
   And his throne shall endure as the heavenly days.

30 If his children depart from My law,
   In My ordinance walk not,
31 My statutes profane,
   My commandments no longer observe, —

32 I will visit their sin with the rod,
   Their guilt will I punish with stripes ;
33 But from him will I never withhold lovingkindness,
   And My faithfulness will not belie.

34 My covenant I will not profane,
   Nor alter the word that goes forth from My lips ;
35 This one thing have I by My holiness sworn,
   That surely I will not deal falsely with David.

36 His seed shall endure forever,
   And His throne as the sun in My presence ;
37 Like the moon it shall ever be established,
   And faithful is the witness in the sky."   [Selah.]

38 Nevertheless Thou hast spurned us with loathing ;
   Thou art wroth with Thy anointed ;
39 Thou abhorrest the covenant Thou mad'st with Thy servant,
   Thou profanest his crown to the earth.

40 Thou hast broken his hedges all down,
   Thou layest his stronghold in ruins ;
41 He is plundered by all that pass by,
   And his neighbours revile him.

42 The right hand of his foes Thou exaltest,
      And hast made all that hate him rejoice;
43 The edge of his sword Thou hast also turned back,
      And hast not made him stand in the battle.

44 His splendour Thou hast brought to an end,
      And his throne hast cast down to the earth;
45 Thou hast shortened the days of his youth,
      And hast clothed him with shame.   [Selah.]

46 How long, as if alway, wilt Thou hide Thee, Jehovah?
      How long shall Thy wrath burn like fire?
47 Oh, remember how short is my lifetime;
      For what nothing Thou createst the children of men.

48 For who is the man that shall live and not die,
      Delivering his soul from the spirit-world's power?
49 Where are Thy first lovingkindnesses, Lord,
      Those sworn in Thy truth unto David?

50 Remember, O Lord,
          The reviling endured by Thy servants,
      That I bear in my bosom from all the great nations,
51 Wherewith those that hate Thee revile, O Jehovah,
      Wherewith they revile Thine anointed one's steps.

52 Blessèd evermore be Jehovah;
          AMEN and AMEN.

(2) **In the heavens.** A symbol of the unchangeable and enduring, in contrast with the unstable and transient upon the earth.

(9) **The pride of the sea.** As in xlvi. 3, lxv. 7, and xciii. 3, 4, the power of God in stilling the raging of the sea symbolizes His power to subdue the rebellious raging of the nations. Its introduction is fitly followed in the second line of the couplet by the mention of Rahab, a prophetic name of Egypt, and other enemies of God as scattered by His power.

(12) **Tabor and Hermon.** Mt. Tabor represents the east side of the Holy Land, and Mt. Hermon the west side. In connection with "the north and the south," in the preceding line, they fill out the conception of universal joy in the creative and sustaining power of God.

(19) **Hast assured Thy belovèd.** Heb. *hhasidêkā.* See on the word *hhāsîd* at iv. 3. The form here is

plural, referring to Samuel and Nathan, whose prophecies with respect to David are now combined. — **To one valiant.** Heb. *gibbor*, prop. an adjective, *mighty*. When used as a noun it always refers to military prowess, *a warrior* or *hero*. See on xix. 6, xxiv. 8, xlv. 3.

(24) **Shall his horn be exalted.** See note on lxxv. 4.

(27) **The Most High to the kings of the earth.** Heb. *'elyôn*. As appointed by God with the assurance of universal and everlasting rule, and sustained by Divine power, he represents God in the earth.

(46) **How long, as if alway.** See note on xiii. 1.

(48) **The spirit-world's power.** Heb. *the hand of Sheol.*

BOOK IV.

XC.

THE ETERNAL GOD THE ONLY REFUGE FOR MORTAL MAN.

" THE Fourth Book of the Psalms begins with a prayer of Moses, the man of God, which comes out of the dying off of the older generation during the march through the wilderness. There is scarcely any memorial of antiquity which so brilliantly justifies the testimony of antiquity concerning its origin as does this Psalm. Not alone with respect to its contents, but with respect to the form of its language, it is perfectly suitable to Moses. Even Hitzig can bring nothing against this view; for the objection that the author, in ver. 1, glances back upon past generations, whilst Israel was only born in the time of Moses, is removed by the consideration that the existence of Israel reaches back into patriarchal times." — *Delitzsch.*

1. The transitoriness of man's earthly life, contrasted with the eternity of God (1-6).
2.   The frailty and misery of man the result of God's wrath against sin (7-12).
3. Prayer for mercy, and perpetual establishment in God's favour (13-17).

A PRAYER OF MOSES, THE MAN OF GOD.

1 Lord, Thou art a home for us in all generations:
2 Ere the hills were brought forth,
    Or yet Thou hadst formed the earth and the world,
  Through the ages everlasting Thou art God.

3 To the dust Thou restorest the mortal;
  Thou sayest, " Return, ye children of men."
4 For a thousand years in Thine eyes,
  Are like yesterday's passing,
    Or a watch in the night.

5 Thou sweepest them off as a flood, and they sleep;
  They are like grass that springs up in the morning,

6 In the morning springs up, and it blossoms,
  At eve is cut down, and it withers;
7 For Thine anger consumes us,
  By Thy wrath we are dismayed;
8 Our transgressions Thou settest before Thee,
  In the light of Thy presence the deeds we conceal.

9 For all our days turn away in Thy wrath,
  Our years we pass off like a sigh.
10 Threescore and ten are the years of our life,
    Or fourscore if strength should avail;
  Yet their proudest are toilsome and vain;
    For they are soon cut off and we fly.
11 But who has yet learned the power of Thine anger,
  And Thy wrath as measured by the reverence due Thee?
12 So teach us to number our days,
  That our heart may attain unto wisdom.

13 Return, O Jehovah; how long!
  Have pity on Thy servants;
14 At the dawn with Thy kindness so fill us,
  That throughout all our days we may exult and be glad;
15 Make us glad according to our days of affliction,
  The years in which we see evil.
16 Let Thy works be revealed to Thy servants,
  To their children Thy glory;
17 Let the beauty of Jehovah our God be upon us,
  And establish upon us the work of our hands,
    Yea, establish the work of our hands.

---

(1) **Art a home for us.** As to the verb, it is *hāyithā*, properly *Thou hast become;* not of existence, but of manifestation, and of coming historically into gracious relations. See on this verb, in the note upon the Divine Name Jehovah, i. 2. The whole context implies safety from danger. This gives a colouring to the noun *mā'ôn*, prim. a *dwelling-place* of God or man, or even *the den* or *lair* of wild beasts. Here the idea is protection and rest from alarms, as in lxxi. 3, xci. 9.

(2) **Thou hadst formed.** Heb. *Thou hadst given birth to.* — **The earth and the world.** The former of these words (*'erets*) is the earth as *material*, the latter (*tēbēl*), which is used only in poetry, the earth as *productive*, filled with generative organisms, and so perhaps including

all life; but especially, the world, as inhabited by men; see ix. 8, xcvi. 14. In this use it is equivalent to οἰκουμένη, *the world as the abode of men*, in Luke iv. 5; Heb. i. 6, ii. 5, etc. — **Through the ages everlasting**. Heb. *from 'ōlām to 'ōlām*. The reference in the whole verse is to the time during which the power of God carried on the process of creation as related in the first chapter of Genesis; from the first creative act to the advanced stage when the mountains appeared (see civ. 7, 8), and then onward till the work was finished. So the *'ōlāms* by which measurement is made are the great days of creation, successive immeasurable periods. To short-lived man each of them seems an eternity, according to the primary conception of eternity from *'ālam, to hide*, a period the extremities of which are hidden out of sight. In the later Hebrew, the conception passed from that of *time* to things existing in time, the world in its long continuance. See Eccl. iii. 11. This corresponds with the N. T. use of αἰών (from αἰεί), *always, an age*, a very long period, not definitely measured by years. Then of things created as existing in periods, and these in succession. In the αἰῶνες of Heb. i. 3 and xi. 3, we have the same reference to creation in vast periods that we have here in the word *'ōlāmim*. We have no English word that expresses it satisfactorily. The word *age* is limited in ordinary use to the comparatively short spaces into which man's occupation of the earth is divided. The rendering "ages everlasting" is an attempt to convey the meaning without introducing an unfamiliar term. The rendering of the English Bible measures the existence from an eternity in the past to another in the future, which gives a general conception, not wholly inappropriate, but does not at all translate the Hebrew, and loses the fine idea of the poet, who strengthens his heart for the present

and the future by sweeping over the vast periods during which God had already manifested His presence, power, and goodness. He does not present an abstract conception of God's eternal existence, but refers to His creative activities as described in the earliest historic records. See the same expression in xli. 13, ciii. 17, and cvi. 48.

(4) **As yesterday's passing**. Heb. *when* (or *while*) it *was* (or *is*) *passing*. The verb is in the imperfect tense. It describes what is *now* occurring, or *was* occurring, at some assumed time in the past. In the former conception, it may refer to yesterday as we look back, and see it recede from us; in the latter, it recalls the impression it made while its hours were flitting by. It is hard to choose. The A. V. "when it is past," is not far from the former.

(5) The first clause is represented in Hebrew by the single word *zăramtăm*. The verb *zăram* describes a washing away by a volume of water from above, as connected with the noun *zérem, a pouring rain*. It might be translated, *Thou floodest them away*. — **And they sleep**. Heb. *shĕnāh hāyū*. *They become a sleep;* that is, *fall into a sleep;* swept away into the sleep of death.

(9) **A sigh**. Heb. *hégeh*, from *hāgāh*, on which see note at ii. 1. The rendering of the English Bible, "*as a tale* that is told," the translators supplying "*that is told*" in italics, has no foundation in the Hebrew, but was retained by the Revisers because so familiar. Their margin gives, "Or, *a sigh*," which the Am. Rev. Comp. prefer to put in the text. See App. to the Revised O. T. The early English translators were evidently at a loss about the meaning of the word in this connection. They were probably not thinking of one relating the incidents of a story, but of one telling (counting) a tale of numbers, in the older English sense. This was perhaps suggested by the "threescore and ten

or fourscore years " immediately following; a number that soon trips off from lips moving at ordinary speed. The count is soon finished.

(11) **But who has yet learned.** Heb. *who is a knower.* The Hebrew participle is almost uniformly a concrete noun. It is somewhat difficult to express it here, in distinction from either tense form of the verb *to know.* It is one who has attained full knowledge of the matter referred to, by careful and thoughtful observation of the course of God's providence with respect to the punishment of sin, as described in the preceding verses. It is the true wisdom firmly imbedded in the mind and heart, and is prayed for in the following verse. — **Thy wrath as measured by the reverence due Thee.** Heb. *and according to Thy fear* (that is, the fear of Thee) *Thy wrath.* A concise expression of the principle that determines the severity of punishment. The word most important to the sense is the minute particle *as* (Heb. כ), *in proportion to.* God's displeasure, as expressed by penalty, is measured by His high claims to respect and obedience, which the wicked ignore, or even repudiate.

(17) **Establish upon us the work of our hands**; that is, establish in our possession the fruit of our labour — do not take it from us, nor us from it.

XCI.

SAFETY UNDER THE SHADOW OF THE ALMIGHTY.

IT is impossible to decide the authorship. It bears marks of antiquity which entitle it to its place alongside the Psalm stamped with Moses' name, to whom this also was attributed by the Jewish doctors. Great perplexity has been occasioned by the abrupt change of person in passing from verse to verse. From the third person "He" in ver. 1, we pass over to the first person "I" in ver. 2, and to "Thou" in ver. 3. This is maintained till ver. 9, where we again strike the first person "I" in the first line, and then in the following line the second person "Thou." The simplest explanation is the dramatic arrangement of the Psalm, different voices alternating. There are two voices that speak in the first twelve verses, and in the three that follow God speaks (J. D. Michaelis, Maurer, Stier, Olshausen, Delitzsch).

"It is one of the freshest and most beautiful Psalms, resembling the second part of Isaiah in its light-winged, richly coloured and transparent diction."

1. A declaration by the Psalmist, not personal but general (1). 2. A voice heard in soliloquy, expressing trust in Jehovah (2). 3. The Psalmist responds, assuring him of safety in all dangers (3–8). 4. The voice is again heard addressing God with confident trust (9 a). 5. Again the Psalmist responds with additional assurances (9 b–13). 6. God now speaks, confirming the hope of His servant (14–16).

(The Psalmist.)

1 He that dwelleth in secret with God the Most High,
  Shall abide under the shadow of the Almighty.

(A voice.)

2 I say to Jehovah, " My refuge and fortress,
  My God, in whom I will trust."

(The Psalmist.)

3 From the snare of the fowler He will surely protect thee,
  And will save from the plague that destroys;
4 His pinions shall cover, His wings shall conceal thee,
  His truth shall be thine, as a buckler and shield;
5 Thou shalt not be afraid for the terror by night,
  Or the arrow that flieth by day;
6 For the pestilence walking in darkness,
  Or the sickness that wasteth at noonday;
7 A thousand may fall at thy side,
      At thy right side a myriad,
  But it shall not come nigh thee;
8 Thou shalt only behold with thine eyes,
  Thou shalt see the reward of the wicked.

(Again, the voice.)

9 For Thou, O Jehovah, art my refuge —

(The Psalmist.)

Hast thou made the Most High thine abode?
10 Then shall nought that is evil befall thee,
  Nor scourge make approach to thy tent;
11 For He charges His angels about thee,
  That in all thy ways they shall keep thee;
12 On their palms do they lift thee,
  That thou strike not thy foot on the stones.
13 Thou shalt trample on lions and adders,
  Young lions and serpents shalt tread under foot.

(God speaks.)

14 Forasmuch as he lovingly cleaves unto Me,
      I will give him escape;
  I will set him in safety, for he knoweth My Name.

15

15 When he calls I will answer,
        And be with him in trouble;
    I will rescue and bring him to honour.
16 His measure of life will I fill with long days,
        And his eyes shall behold My salvation.

XCII.

THOUGHTS FOR THE SABBATH.

THE character of this Psalm indicates a probability that it was prepared for the Sabbath, in accordance with the tradition embodied in its title. Yet it contains no direct reference to that day. Neither its author nor its age is known.

1. The suitableness of thanksgiving to God for His lovingkindness and faithfulness (1–3). 2. This is supported by the manifestation of His greatness and wisdom in His government and works (4–6). 3. The prosperity of the wicked is transient (7–9). 4. On the contrary, the righteous shall be established in prosperity, beauty, and fruitfulness (10–15).

A PSALM. A SONG FOR THE SABBATH DAY.

1 It is good to give thanks to Jehovah,
    To Thy Name to make melody, O Thou Most High;
2 In the morning to show forth Thy kindness,
    And Thy faithfulness tell in the night;
3 With the lute of ten strings and the lyre,
    With the murmuring sound of the harp.

4 For Thy doings have filled me with gladness;
    I will joyfully sing of the works of Thy hands.
5 How great are Thy works, O Jehovah,
    And deep beyond measure Thy thoughts;
6 A brutish man knows not,
    Nor can this be discerned by a fool.

7 When the wicked sprang up like the grass,
        And they that work evil all flourished,
    Before them lay blasting forever;
8 But Thou, O Jehovah, art ever on high.

9 For lo, those that hate Thee, Jehovah,
    For lo, those that hate Thee shall perish;
    Those that practise iniquity all shall be scattered.

10 But my horn Thou exaltest like horns of wild oxen;
    Freshly pressed is the oil that anoints me;
11 Mine eyes shall behold the defeat of my foes,
    And mine ears hear the fall of my wicked assailants.

12 The righteous spring up like the palm,
    And like cedars of Lebanon grow;
13 They are plants in the house of Jehovah,
    They bloom in the courts of our God.
14 They shall still bring forth fruit in old age,
    Well nourished and thrifty;
15 To make known that Jehovah is upright;
    He is my Rock, there is no wrong-doing in Him.

(3) **The murmuring sound of the harp.** Heb. *higgāyōn*, from the verb *hāgāh*, which is imitative of any low, suppressed sound, and especially applicable to the soft trill of the harp. See note on ii. 1. The English Bible has the rendering "solemn sound," which does not at all represent the meaning of the word.

(7) **Flourished.** Heb. *blossomed.*

(10) **My horn Thou exaltest.** A common figurative expression of the infusion of courage, and increase of power and dignity, as in lxxxix. 17, 24. See note on lxxv. 6.

(11) **Behold the defeat ... hear the fall.** The words "*defeat*" and "*fall*" are not expressed in the Hebrew text. Both verbs are here followed by the preposition *bēth*. This in established usage with this class of verbs, carries with it the idea of seeing or hearing with satisfaction. This is expressed in the English Bible by supplying the words "*its desire upon*" in italics, after both verbs. See note at xxvii. 4 and liv. 7.

(12) **The righteous spring up like the palm.** The following from Delitzsch will surely be appreciated: "Not till the blossoming of the ungodly comes to an end does the blossoming and growth of the righteous rightly make its beginning. *Tāmār* is the palm, and more especially the date-palm. How rich the inflorescence of the date-palm is, appears from the fact that when it has attained its full size it bears from three to four hundred, and in some instances even six hundred, pounds of fruit. And there is no more charming and majestic sight than the palm-tree of the oasis,—this king among the trees of the plain, with its proudly raised diadem of leaves, its attitude as it looks far away into the distance, and gazes frankly into the face of the sun, its perennial verdure, and its vegetative power, which is continually renewing itself from the root,— a symbol of life in the midst of a world of death. From the earliest times the palm-tree has been an emblem of longevity, of fruitfulness and victory, of unity and peace. Along with the palm-tree there stands here the cedar, the prince of

the trees of the mountain, and especially of Mount Lebanon. The most obvious point of comparison is, as the verb *sâgâh, to grow great* (comp. Job viii. 11), implies, its stately and lofty growth, then in general, the intensity of its power of growing, but also the perennial verdure of its foliage, and the fragrance it breathes out. Comp. Hos. xiv. 7."

(13) **They bloom.** Heb. *burst into blossom.* A stronger word than that used of the wicked in ver. 7.

XCIII.

GOD ON HIS THRONE ABOVE THE RAGE AND TUMULT OF MEN.

THIS Psalm, like the two that precede it, goes back to the beginning of history. The subject is Jehovah, the God of revelation, ruling in majesty over all hostile powers, in executing the purposes of His grace. The Theocratic Psalms, beginning "Jehovah is King," are no less Messianic than those commonly so designated, and in the same general direction. In fact they steadily converge toward the event in which they both find their fulfilment, the ascension of our blessed Lord to the right hand of the Father. (Del.)

1. Jehovah is King on a throne eternal and immovable, and in His majesty and power He upholds the world (1, 2). 2. All the raging of human pride, power, and passion cannot obstruct His rule, nor defeat His gracious purpose (3, 4). 3. The truth of His revelation, and the holiness of His house shall endure forever (5).

1 Jehovah is King, and apparelled with splendour,
　　Jehovah apparelled and girded with might;
　So the world stands fast without tottering.
2 Thy throne stands fast from of old;
　From eternity art THOU.

3 O Jehovah, the floods have uplifted,
　The floods have uplifted their voice,
　　The floods have uplifted their roaring;
4 Than the voice of great waters, grand waves of the sea,
　Far grander is Jehovah on high.
5 Very sure are Thy testimonies, Jehovah,
　And holiness becometh Thy house,
　　While the days shall endure.

XCIV.

THE JUDGMENT OF GOD UPON TYRANNY AND OPPRESSION.

THERE is no reliable tradition with reference to this Psalm. It is probably one of the latest.

The first fifteen verses are general, the last eight are personal.

As general : 1. Vengeance is implored upon the wicked (1–3). 2. Their conduct described (4–7). 3. Their folly exhibited (8–11). 4. The happiness of God's people (12–15).

As personal : 1. His comfort under Divine protection (16–19). 2. His assurance that just retribution will overtake those guilty of great wickedness (20–23).

1   God of vengeance, Jehovah,
     God of vengeance, shine forth ;
2   Lift Thee up, Thou Judge of the earth,
     Give the proud their desert.

3   O Jehovah, how long shall the wicked,
     How long shall the wicked exult?
4   They gush out with arrogant speech,
     Those busied in wrong are all boastful.

5   They crush Thy people, Jehovah,
     And Thy heritage sorely oppress ;
6   The widow and stranger they slay,
     And murder the orphan.

7   "Jehovah," they say, "will not see,
     Nor the God of Jacob regard it."
8   Understand, ye brutish of the people ;
     Oh, when, ye fools, will ye be wise?

9   Shall He fail in hearing that planteth the ear?
     Or shall He fail in seeing that formeth the eye?
10 The Corrector of nations shall not He punish?
     He that teacheth man knowledge —
11 Jehovah well knoweth the projects of men,
          That they are breath.

12 How blest is the man whom Thou chastenest, Jehovah,
And shalt teach from Thy law;
13 To quiet him when evil days come,
Till the pit shall be digged for the wicked.

14 For Jehovah rejects not His people,
And His heritage will not forsake;
15 But let judgment return unto justice,
And the upright in heart all pursue it.

16 Who will rise to defend me from those that do evil?
Who will stand on my side against workers of wrong?
17 If Jehovah had not helped me,
How soon had my soul dwelt in silence!

18 When I said, " My footsteps are tottering,"
Thy kindness, Jehovah, sustained me;
19 In the many distractions within me,
Thy comforts give joy to my soul.

20 Shall thrones of injustice be in covenant with Thee,
That frame outrage by statute?
21 They combine against the life of the righteous,
And the innocent blood they condemn.

22 But Jehovah becomes my high tower,
And my God the rock of my refuge;
23 He brings back their ill deeds on themselves, —
Cuts them off in their sins,
Jehovah our God cuts them off.

XCV.

A CALL TO WORSHIP AND OBEDIENCE.

THIS Psalm contains no clue to the time of its composition. It connects with Psalm lxxxix. in calling Jehovah a "rock of salvation."

*1. The church is invited to praise God as the supreme God and Creator (1–5),
and as its own gracious and faithful Shepherd (6, 7). 2. A declaration of God to
His people, which draws its warnings from the history of their march through the
wilderness (8–11).*

1 O come, let us sing to Jehovah,
      Let us shout to our rock of salvation.
2 Let us come with thanksgiving before Him,
      With psalms let us shout to His praise.
3 For Jehovah is God very great,
      Above all the gods the Great King;
4 In whose hands are the depths of the earth,
      And the wealth of the mountains is His;
5 The sea, too, is His, for He made it,
      And His hands have formed the dry land.

6 Oh come, bowing down let us worship,
      Let us kneel to Jehovah our Maker;
7 For He is our God,
            And we are the people of His care,
                  The flock of His hand;
      Oh that to-day ye would hearken to His voice.

8 Do not harden your heart as at Meribah,
      At Massah, the day in the desert;
9 Where your fathers tempted — they tried Me,
      Though they witnessed My work.
10 Forty years was I troubled by that generation;
      " A people," I said, " whose heart goes astray,
            And they know not My ways ; "
11 So I sware in My wrath,
      " They shall surely not enter My rest."

(6) Our Maker. This does not
refer to their creation as men, but to
the Divine formative act by which
they have become His people; as in
c. 3, cxlix. 2; Is. xliii. 21, xliv. 2, etc. ;
Deut. xxxii 6.

(7) Of His care. Heb. *of His
shepherding;* not to be confined to
"pasture" as in the English Bible.
It covers the whole work of the shepherd. See on xxviii. 9. — **Of His
hand.** That is, under His protection.

**(9) Your fathers tempted — they
tried Me.** The use of the two words
together, scarcely distinguishable in
meaning, indicates severe and persistent temptation. — **Though they witnessed.** The particle *gam*, usually

meaning *also*, is here *although*, as in Is. xlix. 15; so *gam ki* in Is. l. 15.

(10) **I was troubled.** Heb. *qút*. The primary meaning is *loathing*. It indicates great disturbance of mind, displeasure, and antipathy.

(11) **They shall surely not enter.** Heb. *if they shall enter*. A common elliptical form of taking an oath. The full form occurs in 1 Sam. iii. 17, "God do so to me, and more also, if aught but death," etc.

XCVI.

THE COMING KINGDOM OF GOD.

THE following remark of Delitzsch is important. It applies to several other Psalms of the same general tenor with those he mentions. "Psalms xcvi.–xcviii. are more Messianic than many in the strict sense of the word Messianic; for the centre of gravity of the Old Testament proclamation of redemption does not lie in the Messiah, but in the appearing (*parousia*) of Jehovah,—a fact which is explained by the circumstance that the mystery of the incarnation remains outside the Old Testament knowledge of salvation."

The theme of the Psalm is found in xcv. 3. "For Jehovah is God very great, above all the gods the Great King."

1. Jehovah revealed as the God of salvation, who manifests His glory in the sanctuary (1–6). 2. On this ground all nations are called upon to worship and fear Him (7–9). 3. The reign of Jehovah as joyful tidings in all the earth, and especially His coming in righteousness and truth (10–13).

1 Oh, sing a new song to Jehovah;
   Yea, sing, all the earth, to Jehovah:
2 Raise your song to Jehovah, and bless ye His Name;
   Proclaim every day His glad news of salvation:
3 Declare in the nations His glory;
   Let the peoples all know of His wonders.

4 For Jehovah is great, and all worthy of praise,
   And above all the gods to be feared.
5 For the gods of the nations are all things of nought,
   But the heavens were made by Jehovah.
6 In His presence are grandeur and glory,
   In His holy place splendour and strength.

 7 Ascribe to Jehovah, ye families of nations,
      Ascribe glory and strength to Jehovah.
 8 Ascribe to Jehovah the glory of His Name,
      Bring an offering and come to His courts.
 9 Oh, worship Jehovah in holy attire;
      All the earth be in anguish before Him.

10 Declare in the nations, " Jehovah is King,"
        So the world stands fast without tottering;
      The peoples He in righteousness rules.
11 Let the heavens be glad, and the earth full of joy,
      The sea, let it roar, and the fulness thereof;

12 Let the field shout in triumph, and all it contains,
      And the forest trees all sing for joy —
13 Before Jehovah, for He comes, —
        For He comes to judge the earth;
      The world will He in righteousness judge,
        And the nations in truth.

(5) **Things of nought**. Heb. '*ali-lim, nothings*. Engl. Bible, *idols*. See the fine contrast in Lev. xix. 4, between these *that are not* and the meaning of the Name *Jehovah, He that is*. So here.

XCVII.

THE KINGDOM HAS COME.

ANOTHER of the Theocratic Psalms, with " Jehovah is King " as its key-note. " It is composed as mosaic work out of the earlier original passages of Davidic and Asaphic Psalms, and out of the Prophets, more especially of Isaiah, and is entirely an expression of the religious consciousness which resulted from the exile."

1. An announcement of the appearing of Jehovah as King and Judge (1-3). 2. His awful majesty in its significance to the whole earth has revealed itself (4-6). 3. The shame of idol-worshippers, and the joy of Israel (7-9). 4. An admonition to fidelity, with the assurance of unbounded blessing to the righteous (10-12).

 1 Jehovah is King, let the earth shout for joy,
      Let the shores far distant be glad;

2 Clouds and darkness are about Him,
Justice and right the supports of His throne;
3 A fire goes before Him,
Consuming His foes round about.

4 His lightnings illumine the world;
The earth sees and it trembles,
5 And the hills melt like wax,
At the face of Jehovah,
At the face of the Lord of all the earth.
6 The heavens proclaim Him the Righteous,
And the nations all witness His glory.

7 Let those that serve images all come to shame,
Those that glory in idols;
All ye gods, bow in worship before Him.
8 Zion hears and is glad,
And the daughters of Judah rejoice,
Because of Thy judgments, Jehovah.
9 For Thou, O Jehovah, Most High,
Art above the whole earth,
Far above all the gods art exalted.

10 Ye that love Jehovah, the evil thing hate;
He preserveth the souls of His saints,
From the hand of the wicked He saves them.
11 For the righteous man, light has been sown,
And gladness for the upright in heart.
12 Be glad in Jehovah, ye righteous,
And give thanks to His holy Memorial.

---

(7) **All ye gods, bow in worship.** The Septuagint has here ἄγγελοι. In connection with the Divine judgment against idolaters and their idols, the poet addresses the powers of nature which the heathen personify, deify, and antagonize to the living God, as if they were possessed of real personal life and intelligence. They are called upon to yield and lie prostrate before Him. It involves a graphic prediction that false worship shall come to an end, and that all His rivals in the homage and obedience of men, whether human or superhuman, existent actually or only in their vain imaginations, shall be forever dishonoured.

(12) **His holy Memorial.** That is, His Name Jehovah; Ex. iii. 17, "This is My Name forever, and this My Memorial to all generations." So in xxx. 4, cxxxv. 13.

XCVIII.

SALVATION REVEALED TO ALL NATIONS.

THIS Psalm agrees very closely with Psalm xcvii. It is the echo of the
same joyful tidings; but here the past tense prevails, as of wonders
already accomplished. It is what Hebrew grammarians call the predictive
future, characteristic of the prophetic parts of the Old Testament.

*1. God's wonderful deeds of salvation are thankfully recalled (1-3). 2. Men are
called upon to celebrate His praise publicly and with suitable musical accompaniment
(4-6).*

1 Oh, sing a new song to Jehovah,
    For marvellous things hath He done;
His own right hand and His holy arm the victory gained.
2 Jehovah made known His salvation, —
His justice revealed in the sight of the nations;
3 To Israel's house He remembered His kindness and
    truth,
And the earth's utmost bounds have seen the salvation
    of God.

4 Shout aloud to Jehovah, all the earth;
Break forth into song, and make melody;
5 With the harp to Jehovah make melody,
With the harp and the sound of the lyre;
6 With trumpets and cornet,
Shout aloud to Jehovah the King.

7 The sea, let it roar and the fulness thereof,
The world and those dwelling therein.
8 Let the streams clap their hands,
All at once let the mountains shout aloud —
9 Before Jehovah, for He comes to judge the earth;
To the world He awards right,
    And to nations just judgment.

XCIX.

PRAISE TO THE THRICE HOLY ONE.

THIS is the third of the Theocratic Psalms, commencing "Jehovah is King."

There are three parts, each ending with a refrain, which is somewhat lengthened in its last repetition :

1. A manifestation of God's majesty and might as enthroned in Zion (1–3). 2. The righteousness of his rule in Zion celebrated (4, 5). 3. A glance at persons and events of time long past, as illustrating God's faithfulness, justice, and mercy (6–9).

1 Jehovah is King, —
    Let the nations be afraid,
And on Cherubim throned, —
    Let the earth be convulsed.
2 Jehovah in Zion is great,
    And above all the nations exalted ;
3 Let them praise Thy great and terrible Name :
    IT IS HOLY.

4 As the strength of the king, and equity loving,
    It is Thine to establish the right ;
Thy doings in Jacob are righteous and just.
5 Exalt ye Jehovah our God,
And bow at His footstool ;
    HE IS HOLY.

6 There were Moses and Aaron, His priests,
    And Samuel, of those that called on His Name ;
On Jehovah they called, and He answered.
7 Unto them did He speak in the pillar of cloud ;
They observed His injunctions,
    The statutes He gave them.
8 Thou, O Jehovah our God, didst answer their prayer ;
They found Thee a God that forgives,
    But One on their deeds taking vengeance.

9 Exalt ye Jehovah our God,
  At His holy mountain worship before Him;
    FOR HOLY IS JEHOVAH OUR GOD.

C.

THE WHOLE EARTH CALLED TO WORSHIP JEHOVAH.

THE last of ten Psalms that are upon the same key with the second part of Isaiah. It strongly resembles Ps. xcv. Yet the invitation to all lands, and the closing assurance are not found there.

" Among the Psalms of triumph and thanksgiving this stands pre-eminent as rising to the highest point of joy and grandeur. No local restrictions, no national exclusiveness, can find place in the contemplation of God as the common Creator and Father of men. Hence it is that no hymn or psalm in any subsequent age can find a readier response than this first appeal to the whole world to unite in worshipping Jehovah on the ground of common sonship and humanity."

FOR THE THANKOFFERING. A PSALM.

1 Shout for joy to Jehovah, all the earth;
2 Serve Jehovah with gladness,
  Come before Him with singing.
3 Know ye that Jehovah is God;
  It is He that hath made us, we are therefore His own,
    His people and the flock of His care.
4 Enter His gates with thanksgiving,
    And His courts with a song;
  Give Him thanks and bless ye His Name.
5 For Jehovah is good;
    His kindness endureth forever,
  And His truth to the uttermost age.

CI.

THE VOWS OF A KING.

" THE Psalm before us belongs to the time when the ark of the covenant was in the house of Obed-Edom, where David had left it through horror at the calamity which befell Uzzah. On that occasion David said: *How shall the ark of Jehovah come unto me* (the unholy one)? 2 Sam. vi. 9. He did not dare to bring the ark of the awful and holy One within his own

house.   In our Psalm, however, he gives expression to his determination as
king, to give earnest heed to the sanctity of his walk, his rule, and the
ordering of his house ; and this determination he brings as a vow before
Jehovah, to whom, having in view the rich blessing which the ark of God
diffused round about it (2 Sam. vii. 11 ff.), he yearningly sighs.   To defend
the sanctity of Jehovah's dwelling-place (ver. 8) in all faithfulness and with
all his might, is what David pledges himself to here." —*Delitzsch.*

The Psalm consists of a series of resolves to act uprightly: *1. In personal
conduct and domestic life (1, 2).   2. With reference to his associates (3-5).   3. In
keeping watch over his subjects, his servants, and the inmates of his house (6, 7).
4. He will exercise his punitive power as king, with reference to the city of Jehovah (8).*

BY DAVID.   A PSALM.

1 I will sing lovingkindness and justice ;
   O Jehovah, unto Thee shall my melody rise.
2 I will heed the way of perfection, —
     Oh, when wilt Thou come? —
  With sound heart will I walk
     In the circle of my house.
3 I will set no base act
     Within sight of mine eyes ;
  Deeds that swerve from the right do I hate,
     They shall not hold me fast.
4 A heart of perverseness shall depart from before me,
     I will know nothing evil.
5 He that slanders his neighbour in secret,
     Him will I destroy ;
  He of arrogant look, and heart proudly swelling,
     I cannot endure him.
6 On the faithful in the land is mine eye,
     To have them about me ;
  He that walks in the way of perfection,
     It is he that shall serve me.
7 None shall dwell in my house,
     That practise deceit ;
  And no liar shall stand
     Where mine eyes can behold him.
8 I will slay every morning
     All the wicked of the land ;
  To cut off from the city of Jehovah
     All workers of wrong.

(8) **I will slay every morning,**
etc. This would be impossible, and
neither David nor any other king of
Israel ever attempted it. There is
no place in Oriental poetry where
hyperbole may not come in. He
speaks as the supreme magistrate of
the land, under special obligation to
guard the Holy City from profana-
tion. He will faithfully and rigidly
execute the Divine law, even where
it requires the infliction of death.

The Psalm breathes intense abhorrence of falsehood, malignity, and
baseness of every kind, but its severest sentences have no tinge of
personal animosity. There is nothing in the life of David to indicate
that he was revengeful and bloodthirsty, but the reverse. He has no
rancour against men, but to the extent of his power would destroy evil
from the house and city of God.

CII.

AN APPEAL TO GOD'S UNCHANGEABLE MERCY.

THERE are internal evidences that this Psalm is not by David. It belongs to the later time assigned to those before it that are in the tone
of the later prophecies of Isaiah. Passages occur in it of the highest poetic
beauty, and even sublimity. It is the cry of an individual sufferer, but
through a considerable part of his song he loses sight of himself in his concern for Zion, and his contemplation of the grace and faithfulness of God.

*1. With earnest prayer he describes his distress (1–11). 2. He expresses his confi-
dence in the unchangeable mercy of God, to restore and glorify Zion, as a centre of
worship and privilege for all nations (12–22). 3. He entreats that he may not perish
prematurely, appealing to God as eternal and immutable, who will establish His servants in His presence forever (23–27).*

THE PRAYER OF A SUFFERER POURING OUT HIS LAMENT BEFORE
JEHOVAH.

1 Hear my prayer, O Jehovah;
 Let my cry come before Thee.
2 Hide not Thy face in my day of distress;
 Bow Thine ear at my call and haste to my rescue.

3 For my days have vanished like smoke,
 And my bones are burned up as by fire;
4 My heart is smitten and withered like grass,
 Yea, the bread I should eat I forget;
5 At the sound of my groaning,
 My bones cleave fast to my flesh.

6 Like a pelican off in the desert,
   Like an owl of the ruins;
7 I am kept on the watch,
   Like a bird all alone on the housetop,
8 All the day long they that hate me revile me;
   Those that rage at me name me in their oaths.

9 For ashes have I eaten like bread,
   And my drink have I mingled with tears,
10 Because of Thy wrath and grievous displeasure,
   For Thou liftedst me up, and hast cast me away.
11 Like a shadow grown long is my life,
   And my substance is withered like grass.

12 But Thou, O Jehovah, art forever enthroned,
   Thy Memorial Name is to age after age.
13 Thou Thyself wilt arise and compassionate Zion,
   For the time to pity her, the set time is come;
14 For even in her stones Thy servants take pleasure,
   And have pity on her dust.
15 So the nations shall reverence the Name of Jehovah,
   All the kings of the earth, Thy glory.
16 For Jehovah has builded up Zion,
   He appears in His glory;
17 He has turned toward the prayer of the needy,
   For their prayer He has not despised.

18 This is written for the next generation,
   A people yet to be created shall give praise to Jehovah.
19 For from His holy height He bent down,
   Out of heaven Jehovah has gazed upon the earth,
20 To hear the prisoner's groans,
   And to loosen the children of death;
21 That Jehovah's Name they may publish in Zion,
   In Jerusalem may utter His praise,
22 When the peoples are gathered together,
   And the kingdoms, for serving Jehovah.

23 My strength He brought down in the way,
   He has shortened my days;
24 I say, O my God, "Do not take me away in the midst of
      my days,
   Thou whose years are to all generations;
25 Of old didst Thou lay the foundations of the earth,
   And the heavens are the work of Thy hands;
26 As for them they shall perish, but Thou shalt endure;
      They all shall wax old like a garment;
   As a robe wilt Thou change them, they surely shall change;
27 But Thou art the same,
   And Thy years shall not end.
28 The children of Thy servants abide,
   Their seed are established before Thee."

(7) **I am kept on the watch.** Sleepless and exhausted.

(8) **Name me in their oaths.** Heb. *swear by me;* that is, they make his name a by-word of execration; invoking upon themselves, if they prove false, the same curse that God has inflicted upon him. See Is. lxv. 15; Jer. xxix. 22.

(11) **Like a shadow grown long.** The lengthening of the shadow indicates that the sun is low, and the night close at hand. — **My substance.** Heb. *I myself*, the emphatic pronoun. That which belongs to, or constitutes myself, as distinguished from its duration, just before mentioned.

(12) **Thy Memorial Name.** Heb. *Thy memorial*, in allusion to Ex. iii. 15, "This is My Name forever, and this is My Memorial to all generations." So in cxxxv., and elsewhere in the Psalms.

(14) **Her stones . . . her dust.** Of her ruins. Comp. Neh. iv. 2, 10.

(19) **From His holy height He bent down.** The verb is *shākaph, to bend over*, especially of one gazing intently at something of absorbing interest below him. See the note on xiv. 2.

(20) **To loosen the children of death.** Those in great peril, and claimed by death as belonging to his great family. See the note at lxxix. 11, where as here the former line of the couplet mentions "prisoners." The loosening, properly, *the opening*, or setting free, implies a binding and holding till the hour of execution.

CIII.

PRAISE TO THE ALL-COMPASSIONATE GOD.

ALTHOUGH the title ascribes it to David, nearly all authorities regard the authorship of this song as doubtful. There is an accumulation of Aramaic forms, such as are found only in the latest Hebrew songs. But there can be no difference of opinion about its beauty and preciousness. Its key-note is God's proclamation of Himself to Moses as "Jehovah, a God full of compassion and gracious, slow to anger, and plenteous in loving-kindness and truth." Ex. xxxiv. 5.

1. The poet stirs up his own soul to bless God for His mercies to himself individually (1-5). 2. He describes God's gracious and fatherly conduct toward the children of men, especially as exhibited toward Israel, and as known and recognized in the light of revelation (6-18).

BY DAVID.

1 Bless Jehovah, my soul,
   And all that is in me His holy Name bless;
2 Bless Jehovah, my soul,
   All His favours forget not;
3 Who forgives all thy sins,
   All thy sicknesses heals;
4 Who redeemeth thy life from destruction,
   And crowns thee with kindness and mercies;
5 Who perfects thy beauty with good,
   And thy youth is renewed like the eagle's.

6 Righteous deeds Jehovah performs,
      And judgments for all the oppressed.
7 His ways He made known unto Moses,
   His acts to the children of Israel.
8 Jehovah is gracious, and full of compassion,
   Long suffering, and plenteous in kindness;
9 He will not always contend,
   Nor keep up His anger forever.
10 He deals not with us according to our sins,
   Nor rewards as our guilt has deserved.

11 As the heavens are higher than the earth,
   His kindness prevails for those that revere Him.
12 As far as the rise of the sun from its setting,
      So far away He removes our transgressions;
13 As a father has pity on his children
   Jehovah has pity on those that revere Him;
14 For He knoweth our frame,
   He remembereth we are dust.

15 As for mortals, their days are as grass,
      Like the flower of the meadows they flourish;
16 When the wind passeth over, it is gone,
      And the place thereof knows it no more.
17 But the kindness of Jehovah to those that revere Him,
            Endures through the ages everlasting;
      To their offspring forever is His righteousness shown;
18 Unto those who are true to His covenant,
      And remember His commandments to do them.

19 Jehovah established His throne in the heavens,
      And His kingdom shall rule over all;
20 Bless Jehovah, His angels,
      Ye mighty in strength, that fulfil His command,
            That hearken to the voice of His word.
21 Bless Jehovah, all His hosts,
      Ye that serve Him, obeying His will;
22 Bless Jehovah, all His works,
            Throughout all His dominion;
      Bless Jehovah, my soul.

(5) **Perfects thy beauty.** Heb. *fills up thine ornament*, or, *that which beautifies thee.* The noun *'adî* (עֲדִי) is difficult. The Septuagint translators render it ἐπιθυμία, *desire*, which seems to be remote from the signification of the Hebrew word. The conjecture is hazarded that they regarded *'adî* here as equivalent to *hhāmûd, an object of desire*, in xxxix. 11, where the English Bible has, "Thou makest *his beauty* to consume away like a moth." They give ἐπιθυμία, as if it were equivalent to the concrete form ἐπιθύμημα, thinking of the fresh and exuberant strength of early life as an ornament. This seems to be the poet's meaning. It is confirmed by the parallelism with "youth" in the following line. The **good** he speaks of has reference to the seasonable supplies by which the grace of God maintains this beauty. — **Thy youth is renewed.** Not meaning a sudden restoration from extreme weakness, but a cont nued impartation of new life; and the comparison with the eagle is an allusion to the long life through which the early fire and force of the royal bird continue undiminished. Delitzsch speaks of the renewing of the feathers of the eagle in his annual moulting, as an emblem of the renewal of one's youth through grace. See Is. xl. 31.

(15) **Mortals.** Heb. *'enôsh*. Man as weak and frail. See on viii. 4.

(17) **Through the ages everlasting.** Heb. *from 'ôlām to 'ôlām;* of time as divided into immense periods. See note on xc. 2. — **To their offspring forever** Heb. *to children's children* Our familiar version is literal, yet misleading. To get the full conception of time it

should be said that the word *bēn, a son,* is used in Hebrew of remote, as well as of immediate, descendants. There is nothing in the expression that limits the reference to two generations. On the contrary, the parallelism with "ages everlasting" in the former line of the couplet, absolutely requires indefinite extension.

CIV.

THE HYMN OF CREATION.

THE subject of praise in this Psalm is God's working in the kingdom of nature, as that of the preceding was His working in the kingdom of grace. "The poet celebrates in his song the present continuance of the world ordained by God, bearing in mind His first creative work recorded in Gen. i. 1–ii. 3, and concludes with the desire that evil may be banished from this fair creation which reveals universally and in profusion His power, wisdom, and goodness." — *Delitzsch.*

The Psalm is a lyric masterpiece, in whose beauty and grandeur the greatest minds have revelled with wonder and praise. Among others Perowne quotes from Von Humboldt, the great naturalist (*Cosmos,* vol. ii. part i.) : " It might almost be said that one single Psalm represents the image of the whole *cosmos.* We are astonished to find in a lyric poem of such limited compass the whole universe, — the heavens and the earth, — sketched with a few bold touches. The contrast of the labor of man with the animal life of nature, and the image of omnipresent, invisible power, renewing the earth at will, or sweeping it of inhabitants, is a grand and solemn poetical creation."

1. The work of the first and second days ; light, the sky, clouds, winds, lightnings (1–4). 2. The original chaotic state, and the separation of land from water on the third day (5–9). 3. The third creative day continued ; the growth of plants and trees, implying irrigation by clouds and streams. Here the poet introduces birds, and creatures of the field and forest, which do not appear in the Mosaic narrative till much later (14–18). 4. The work of the fourth day, the sun and moon, but with special reference to men and animals (19–23). 5. The poet, having already woven into his song part of the work of the fifth and sixth days, now returns to it, and describes the sea with its living creatures, — these with all else, the whole visible creation (ver. 27), in absolute dependence upon God (24–30). 6. He longs to see the bright original restored (31–35).

1 Bless Jehovah, my soul ;
O Jehovah, my God, Thou art greatly exalted,
And with glory and grandeur art clothed ;
2 Who hast robed Thee in light as a mantle,
And spread out the heavens like a tent-cloth ;

3 Who frames in the waters His upper apartments;
 Who takes clouds as His chariots,
     And goes swiftly on the wings of the wind.
4 Of the winds He makes angels,
 Of the lightnings His servants.

5 Who founded the earth on its base,
 That it may not be shaken forever and alway;
6 With the deep as a robe didst Thou cover it,
 And the waters stood over the mountains;
7 But they fled at Thy threatening,
 Made escape at Thy voice in the thunder, —
8 The mountains rose high, and the valleys sank down, —
 Made escape to the place Thou hadst founded;
9 A bound hast Thou set which they may not pass over,
 That they turn not again to cover the earth.

10 Who sends springs into the valleys,
 And they run 'twixt the mountains ;
11 They give drink to all beasts of the field,
 And wild asses thereat quench their thirst.
12 Above them the birds of the air have their home,
 That give voice from the midst of the boughs.
13 From His storehouse on high He waters the mountains,
 The earth is full of the fruit of Thy works.
14 The grass He makes sprout for the cattle,
     And plants for the service of man,
 So that bread may come forth from the earth ;
15 That the heart of weak man may be gladdened by wine,
     That his face may be shining with oil,
 And that bread may strengthen his heart.

16 The trees of Jehovah are filled,
 The cedars of Lebanon that He planted;
17 Where the birds build their nests,
 The stork has its home in the cypress;
18 The wild goats have high mountains,
 And the cliffs are a refuge for badgers.

19 The moon He has made for fixed times,
   And the sun knows the place of its setting.
20 Thou appointest the darkness, and night cometh on,
   When all beasts of the forest are astir.
21 The young lions then roar after prey,
   From God they are seeking their food;
22 With the rise of the sun they retire,
   And lay themselves down in their dens;
23 But man goes forth to his work,
   To his labour till evening.

24 How manifold Thy works, O Jehovah!
   In wisdom Thou madest them all;
      The earth is full of Thy creatures.
25 Yonder sea is great and wide spreading,
   And teeming therein without number,
      Things alive, great and small;
26 And there go the ships,
   And the whales Thou hast formed to gambol therein;
27 All these look intently to Thee,
   To give them their food in its season;
28 That Thou givest they gather,
   Thou openest Thy hand to fill them with good.
29 When Thou hidest Thy face, they are affrighted;
   Thou withdrawest their breath, they expire,
      And return to their dust.
30 Thou sendest Thy breath, they are created,
   Thou renewest the face of the earth.

31 Let the glory of Jehovah forever endure,
   Let Jehovah rejoice in His works;
32 Who looks on the earth, and it trembles,
   When He touches the mountains they quake.
33 While I live will I sing to Jehovah,
   To my God with the harp while my being shall last.
34 Let the flow of my heart give Thee pleasure,
   And let joy in Jehovah be mine.

35 Let sinners be swept from the earth,
    And the wicked be no more ;
  Bless Jehovah, my soul;
    PRAISE YE JEHOVAH !

(2) And spread out the heavens as a tent-cloth. Compare Is. xl. 22 : "That stretcheth out the heavens as a curtain, and spreadeth them out as a tent to dwell in."

(3) Who frames in the waters His upper apartments. Comp. Am. ix. 6, R. V., "It is He that buildeth His chambers in the heaven, and hath founded His vault upon the earth." The "waters" mentioned are those of the firmament, especially as collected in the clouds; Gen. i. 6, 7. "If the lower heaven appears the firm underpart of the heavenly building, so must the bright watery clouds reaching into infinite heights, correspond to the airy lofts or upper rooms of human dwellings. And from these very heights winds and lightnings, as servants of Jehovah, appear to hasten into the lower world." — *Ewald.* Compare xviii. 11, 12. The word *'eliyyāh* here represents the ὑπερῷον of the Septuagint and New Test., *the upper chamber*, which was the highest, and sometimes the largest, room in an Oriental house, and commonly used as a place of retirement and comparative seclusion.

(4) Of the winds He makes angels. That is, He makes use of the winds as angels. The rendering *messengers* cannot be substituted for *angels* without lowering the ruling conception of the Psalm. It is the grand Theophany in nature, celebrating the presence and activity of God in the material universe. In all such manifestations we not only expect the attendance of competent messengers and ministers, indefinite in kind, but in accordance with other Theophanic descriptions, the intelligent spirits whose high privilege it is to abide in His presence, and to accompany Him whenever He appears among men. In Job xxxviii. 7 they are shouting for joy when God lays the foundations of the earth, and in Ps. ciii. 20, they are the "mighty in strength that fulfil His command, that hearken to the voice of His word." But here, apparently, He does not employ them, but the winds and the lightnings instead. This warrants the use of the passage in Heb. i. 7. The writer claims that in this Psalm they are classed with the winds and the lightnings, which God at His pleasure may employ as their substitutes in the kingdom of nature.

(9) A bound hast Thou set which they may not pass over. Compare Job xxxviii. 8–11 in the Revised Version, and especially ver. 10 as preferred by the Amer. Revisers, "And marked out for it my bound, and set bars and doors."

CV.

THANKSGIVING IN CONNECTION WITH THE EARLY HISTORY
OF ISRAEL.

THE first fifteen verses of this Psalm are found in 1 Chron. xvi., as part of the song given by David to Asaph and his brethren to be sung when the ark was carried to its resting-place in Zion. It is there combined with Ps. xcvi. and verses from cvi. and cvii. This proves very clearly that the Psalm there given is a compilation from other sources, and not the original. The Psalm is lyrical rather than didactic. Like Psalm lxxviii. it is a retrospect of the history of Israel, but it comes no further down than the occupation of Canaan.

It resembles the preceding Psalm in ending with " Hallelujah," and is the first of a series which begin with the word *Hhôdû, Give ye thanks.* They are cv. cvii. cviii. and cxxxvi.

1. An invitation to thanksgiving in special connection with God's covenant with Abraham (1-11). 2. Celebration of God's goodness to Israel previous to their settlement in Egypt (12-24). 3. The plagues inflicted on Egypt, and their deliverance from oppression (25-38). 4. Their guidance through the wilderness to their taking possession of Canaan (39-45).

1 Give thanks to Jehovah; call aloud in His Name;
   Make known in the nations His doings.
2 Unto Him raise your song, unto Him strike the harp,
   And rehearse all His wonders.
3 His holy Memorial Name be your boast,
   And all hearts that are seeking Jehovah be joyful.
4 Enquire for Jehovah and His strength,
   Yea, seek ye His face evermore.
5 Remember the marvellous works He hath done;
   His wonders bear in mind,
      And the judgments that fell from His mouth,
6 O ye offspring of Abraham, His servant,
   Ye children of Jacob, His chosen.

7 He, Jehovah, is our God;
   His judgments are through the whole earth;
8 He remembers His covenant forever,
   The word He ordained for a thousand generations;
9 The covenant He established with Abraham,
   And His oath unto Isaac;
10 And confirmed as a statute to Jacob,
   To Israel for a covenant everlasting;
11 When He said, " I will give you the country of Canaan,
   As your heritage measured by line."

12 When as yet they were few in the land,
   Very few, and as strangers therein,
13 And from people to people went about,
   And from kingdom to kingdom passed on;

14 He let no man oppress them,
  And kings He rebuked for their sake:
15 "Do not touch Mine anointed,
  Nor harm ye My prophets."
16 Then He called for a dearth on the land,
  And brake up the whole staff of their bread.
17 He sent one before them;
  Even Joseph was sold to be a slave.
18 His feet they afflicted with fetters,
  Into irons came his soul;
19 Till the time that his word came to pass,
  That spoken by Jehovah which proved him.
20 The king sent and loosed him,
  The ruler of nations set him free, —
21 Made him lord of his house,
  And the ruler of all his possessions;
22 His princes to bind at his pleasure,
  And his elders make wise.

23 So Israel went down into Egypt,
  And Jacob sojourned in the country of Ham.
24 His people He multiplied greatly,
  And stronger than their enemies made them,
25 Whose heart He turned that they hated His people,
  And defrauded His servants.
26 Then He sent to them Moses His servant,
  And Aaron a man He had chosen;
27 Who performed there the signs He commanded,
  And prodigies wrought in the country of Ham.

28 By them He sent darkness, and darkness came on,
  For they did not rebel at His word.
29 The waters He turned into blood,
  And so killed all the fish;
30 The land swarmed with frogs,
  Which came up to the abode of their kings;
31 When He spake there came gad-flies,
  And in all their borders were gnats;

32 For rain He gave hail,
　　While flames flashed about in their land;
33 It smote down their vines and their fig-trees, —
　　Brake asunder the trees of their border.

34 He spake and the locusts came in,
　　Things that fly, without number;
35 That devoured all the plants of their land,
　　That devoured all the fruit of their soil.
36 Then He smote in the land all their firstborn,
　　The firstlings of strength every one;
37 But He brought forth His people with silver and gold,
　　Not a man in His tribes became faint.

38 Their going filled Egypt with joy,
　　For their terror had fallen upon it.
39 He spread for their covering a cloud,
　　And fire to give light in the night.
40 When they asked He brought quails,
　　And filled them with bread out of heaven:
41 He opened a rock and the waters gushed out,
　　And flowed through the wastes like a river;
42 For His holy word He remembered,
　　And Abraham His servant;
43 And He brought forth His people with gladness,
　　With singing He brought forth His chosen;
44 And He gave them the lands of the heathen,
　　They inherit the toil of the nations;
45 That His laws they might keep,
　　His commandments observe;
　　　　PRAISE YE JEHOVAH!

(15) **Mine anointed . . . My prophets.** The former of these words in the Divine utterance has reference to Gen. xvii. 6, 16, where Abraham is consecrated to be the father of peoples, and even of kings, and Sarah to be a princess. They are called *anointed* as Divinely chosen to their high position. The key to the latter designation is in Gen. xx. 7, where Abraham is called *a prophet*, as being the recipient of a Divine revelation for His descendants, a spokesman for God. For the meaning of the word, both in the Old Testament and the New, we go back to Ex. vii. 1, comparing it with iv. 16.

CVI.

A CONFESSION OF NATIONAL UNFAITHFULNESS.

THIS is the first of the sixteen Hallelujah Psalms.   The others are cxi.
cxiii. cxvii. cxxxv. cxli.-cl. It is retrospective like the preceding,
but unlike it, is penitential. It must probably be assigned to the time of
the exile.

*1. A call to thanksgiving, with recognition of God's power and justice, and prayer
for personal favour in fellowship with His people (1-5). 2. A penitent confession
describing the conduct of the fathers in the desert (6-33), and afterward in the Holy
Land (34-46). 3. A prayer for deliverance from the present captivity, followed by
a Doxology attached to this Psalm, as the last in the Fourth Book (47, 48).*

1 PRAISE YE JEHOVAH;
    To Jehovah give thanks, for He is good,
For His kindness endureth forever.
2 Who can rehearse the mighty acts of Jehovah,
Or declare all His praise?
3 How blest are the men that do justice,
Whose deeds at all times are right!
4 O Jehovah, bear me ever in mind,
    With the favour Thou showest Thy people;
Oh, come in Thy might of salvation,
5 That the good of Thy chosen I may see,
    And the joy of Thy nation may hear,
And thus with Thy heritage glory.

6 We have sinned like our fathers;
We are guilty, our deeds have been evil.
7 Our fathers in Egypt observed not Thy wonders,
    And Thy great lovingkindness forgat;
At the Sea, the Red Sea, they rebelled.
8 Nevertheless, for His Name's sake He saved them,
That His strength might be known.
9 He rebuked and dried up the Red Sea;
Through the depths as on a plain did He lead them;
10 He saved them from the enemy's hand,
From the power of the foe He redeemed them;

11 But the waters overwhelmed their oppressors,
     Of these not one was remaining;
12 Then believed they His word,
     And they sang in His praise.

13 Very soon forgat they His deeds;
     His purpose they would not await;
14 In the wilderness, greedy as gluttons,
     In the desert, they tempted their God.
15 So He gave what they asked for,
     But sickness sent into their soul.
16 In the camp they were incensed at Moses,
     And at Aaron, the holy of Jehovah;
17 The earth opened wide and swallowed up Dathan,
     And covered the band of Abiram;
18 A fire then burned up their band,
     A flame consumed the ungodly.
19 They made at Mount Horeb a calf,
     And worshipped the image they cast;
20 And their Glory they bartered,
     For the form of an ox that eats grass;
21 They forgat the God who had saved them,
     Who in Egypt performed so great deeds, —
22 Yea, wonderful works in the country of Ham,
     And terrible deeds at the Sea;
23 And He said He would bring them to an end,
     But Moses, His chosen, in the breach stood before Him,
          To turn back His wrath from destroying.
24 Yea, they lightly esteemed the fair land He had promised,
     They believed not His word;
25 But complained in their tents,
     And obeyed not the voice of Jehovah;
26 Then He sware with His hand lifted high,
     In the desert to fell them;
27 Through the nations to scatter their offspring,
     In the lands to disperse them.
28 They clave to Baal Peor,
     And feasted on sacrifice slain to dead idols;

29 By their deeds they provoked Him,
   And the plague burst upon them.
30 Then Phinehas rose, interceding,
   And the plague was restrained ;
31 And this was to him for righteousness counted,
   To all generations forever.
32 They stirred up His wrath at the waters of Strife,
   And Moses fared ill for their sakes ;
33 They rebelled against the Spirit,
   So that then with his lips he spake idly.

34 They did not extinguish the nations,
   As Jehovah commanded ;
35 But mingled with heathen,
   And practised their works ;
36 They worshipped their idols,
   Which became to them snares ;
37 They sacrificed sons,
   And their daughters to demons ;
38 And so they shed innocent blood,
        The blood of their sons and their daughters,
   Offered up to the idols of Canaan,
        And the land was polluted with blood.
39 Their doings defiled them,
   Their ways were impure.
40 Then against His own people,
        The wrath of Jehovah was kindled ;
   He abhorred His possession, —
41 Gave them up to the hand of the nations,
   And their foes were their rulers ;
42 Their enemies crushed them,
   And made them bow down 'neath their hand.
43 Though often He came to their rescue,
        They rebelled in self will,
   And they fell in their guilt.

44 But He looked on their trouble,
   When He heard their loud cry, —

45 In their favour remembered His covenant,
    And relented in His great lovingkindness;
46 He procured them compassion,
    In the presence of all that enslaved them.

47 Oh, save us, Jehovah, our God;
      Bring us in from the nations,
    To Thy holy Name to give thanks,
      And triumphantly shout in Thy praise.

48 Blessèd be Jehovah, who is Israel's God,
      Through the ages everlasting;
    Let all people say, " Amen!"
      PRAISE YE JEHOVAH.

(32) **The waters of Strife** — as in lxxxi. 7. Heb. *of Meribah.* See xcv. 11, and Ex. xvii. 7.

(48) **Through the ages everlasting.** As in xli. 13, the doxology to the First Book of the Psalter. See note at xc. 2. Heb. *from 'olām to 'olām,* of time as divided into immeasurable periods; Ps. xc. 2 relates to the past, but these doxologies to the future.

BOOK V.

CVII.

SAVED OUT OF MANY DISTRESSES.

THIS Psalm probably belongs to the period of the captivity in Babylon.
Although in some features it resembles the two that precede it, it is
not historical. It describes the perils of various conditions of human life,
and celebrates the power and goodness of God in the deliverance of those
who cry to Him.

*1. The liturgical formula of intercession, as in cvi. 1; in which the returning exiles
are invited to join (1–3). 2. The mercy of God in various deliverances is commemo-
rated; from homeless wanderings (4–9), from imprisonment (10–16), from peril of
sickness (17–22), and from dangers of the deep (23–32). 3. The controlling power
of God in the varying fortunes of men and nations is described (33–42). 4. Men
are urged to consider wisely the whole of God's disposing guidance, as just described.*

1 Give thanks to Jehovah, for He is good;
  For His kindness endureth forever.
2 Let the redeemed of Jehovah thus say,
  Even those He redeemed from the hand of their foes,
3 And brought in from the lands,
  From the east and the west,
    From the north and the south.

4 They roved through the wilds in a desolate way,
  And they found no city to dwell in;
5 Hungry and thirsty,
  Their soul fainted in them;
6 Then they cried to Jehovah in their trouble,
  And He saved them from all their distresses;
7 By right ways did He lead them,
  To go to a city to dwell in.

8 Let them praise Jehovah for His kindness,
   And His wonderful works to the children of men;
9 For He satisfies souls that are longing,
   And filleth the hungry with good.

10 They that sat in the darkness, the shadow of death,
   That were fettered in misery and iron,
11 Because they rebelled at the words of the Almighty,
   And despised the purpose of God, the Most High, —
12 He humbled their soul with sore travail,
   And they stumbled with no one to help.
13 In their trouble they cried to Jehovah,
   And He saved them from all their distresses.
14 Out of darkness, the shadow of death, did He bring them,
   And their bonds burst asunder.
15 Let them praise Jehovah for His kindness,
   And His wonderful works to the children of men;
16 For the gates of brass hath He shattered,
   And bars of iron heweth down.

17 Foolish men, for their course of transgression,
   And because of their guilt had to suffer;
18 Their soul abhorring all food,
   They drew near to the gateways of death;
19 In their trouble they cried to Jehovah,
   And He saved them from all their distresses.

20 He sent forth His word, and He healed them,
   From their pitfalls He gave them escape.
21 Let them praise Jehovah for His kindness,
   And His wonderful works to the children of men.
22 In offering let them bring Him thanksgiving,
   And tell of His works amid shoutings of joy.

23 They that in ships go down on the sea,
   That do business upon the great waters;
24 It is these that have sight of the works of Jehovah,
   And His wonders behold in the deep;
25 He spake and He raised up the blast of the storm,
   Which lifted its billows on high;

26 They went up to the heavens, and down to the depths;
Their soul was dissolved by their trouble.
27 They staggered and reeled like the drunkard,
And all their wise thoughts disappeared;
28 In their trouble they cried to Jehovah,
And He saved them from all their distresses;—
29 Turned the storm into stillness,
And the billows were hushed;
30 Then were they joyful, because they were quiet,
And He led them to the haven they desired.
31 Let them praise Jehovah for His kindness,
For His wonderful works to the children of men;
32 And extol Him in the assembly of the people,
Give Him praise in the council of the elders.

33 He turned streams into desert,
Fountains of water into a region athirst;
34 Fruitful lands into a barren,
For the wickedness wrought by those dwelling therein:
35 But a desert He turned into pools,
Dry land into fountains of water;
36 He made there a home for the hungry,
And they built them a city to dwell in.
37 They sowed fields, planted vineyards,
And gat fruits to enrich them.
38 He gave them His blessing,
And they multiplied greatly;
He let not their cattle become few.

39 And when they decreased, and were brought very low,
Through oppression, and trouble, and sorrow,
40 Then He that pours scorn upon princes,
And in pathless wastes makes them wander,
41 Set the wretched on high from affliction,
And families He gave like a flock.
42 The upright behold and are glad,
And all the unrighteous are silenced.
43 He that is wise will consider these things,
And shall know the kindness of Jehovah.

(8) **Let them praise.** The rendering is literal. The reference is not to men in general, as in the English Bible, but to such as have just been referred to ; so in verses 15, 21, 31.

(17) **For their course of trans-**gression. So Heb. and marg. of the Rev. Version.

(20) **Their pitfalls.** So Heb. and marg. of the Rev. Version.

(27) **And all their wise thoughts disappeared.** Heb. *and all their wisdom is swallowed up.*

CVIII.

MAN CONFIDING AND GOD PROSPERING.

FRAGMENTS of the Davidic Psalms are here brought together; Ps. lvii. 7–11, and lx. 6–12. It is in the highest degree improbable that this would have been done by David himself. There are some variations, especially that in ver. 9, which may indicate adaptation to a later occasion, perhaps a victory over the Edomites.

A SONG. A PSALM OF DAVID.

1 Steadfast, O God, is my heart;
   I will sing and will play, yea, even my glory.
2 Arouse, lute and harp;
   I will rouse up the dawn.

3 Midst the peoples, Jehovah, will I praise Thee,
   And to Thee strike the harp midst the nations;
4 For great o'er the heavens is Thy kindness,
   And Thy truth reaches up to the skies.
5 Even higher than the heavens be exalted, O God,
   And above the whole earth be Thy glory.
6 For the rescue of Him whom Thou lovest,
   Let Thy saving right hand give us answer.

7 It is God in His holiness who promised,
      I therefore will triumph;
   I will portion out Shechem,
      And distribute the valley of Succoth;
8 Gilead is mine, and mine is Manasseh,
      With Ephraim the shield of my head,
   And Judah my sceptre of rule.

9 My washpot is Moab,
     I cast off my shoe upon Edom;
  Over me, O Philistia, shout aloud.

10 Who to the fortified city will bring me,
  Who can conduct me to Edom?
11 O God, hast Thou not cast us off,
  And no longer, O God, wilt go forth with our hosts?
12 Oh, give us Thy help from the oppressor,
  For vain is deliverance by man.
13 Through God we shall conquer;
  It is He that shall stamp on our foes.

For notes on verses 7–9 see on lx. 5–8.

CIX.

THE ADVERSARY JUDGED.

THE Apostle Peter in Acts i. 16, cites this Psalm together with Ps. lxix.
as fulfilled in the treachery of Judas. This indicates that it is typico-prophetical. That it is distinctly Messianic, having reference to the
sufferings of Christ, is less probable.

*1. God is appealed to against the malignant (1–5). 2. An individual enemy is
singled out, upon whom and his family the retributive justice of God is invoked
(6–20). 3. Divine compassion is implored on the ground of personal feebleness and
suffering (21–25). 4. A closing entreaty that God's power and mercy may be shown,
with confident and joyful anticipation of a favourable answer (26–31).*

FOR THE LEADER OF THE CHOIR. BY DAVID. A PSALM.

1 O God of my praise, be not silent;
2 For mouths of wickedness, mouths of deceit,
     Have they opened against me;
  They have spoken against me with slanderous tongues.
3 They beset me with clamours of hatred,
  And against me made war without cause.
4 In return for my love they withstood me,
  Whilst I was all prayer.
5 They reward me with evil for good;
  And for love they give hatred.

 6 Appoint Thou a wicked man over him,
   Let an enemy stand at his right:
 7 When judged, let him go forth as guilty;
       Let his prayer become sin:
 8 Let his days become few,
   And his office be filled by another:
 9 Let his children be orphans,
   And his wife be a widow:
10 Let his sons become vagrants and beggars,
   And seek alms far away from their desolate home.

11 All that he has, let extortioners snare,
   And aliens strip off the fruit of his toil.
12 Let none extend kindness to himself,
   Nor pity his fatherless children.
13 Be the heirs of his body cut off,
   In the next generation their names blotted out.
14 Let Jehovah remember the guilt of his fathers,
   And let not the sin of his mother be expunged;
15 Before Jehovah let it alway continue,
   That their memory may cease from the earth.

16 Because he forgat to show kindness;
   But the suffering and needy and broken in heart,
       He pursued unto death.
17 The cursing he loved, it alighted upon him;
   Since from blessing he gathered no pleasure,
       It removed far away from himself.
18 He clothed him with cursing as raiment,
   And it entered his substance like water,
       And like oil it coursed in his bones.
19 Let it be like the coat he puts on,
   Like the belt which he ever girds about him.
20 This is the wage of my foes from Jehovah,
   Of those that plan harm to my life.

21 But thou, O Jehovah, the Lord,
       For Thy Name's sake, come help me;
   Forasmuch as Thy kindness is good, give me rescue.

22 For I am suffering and needy,
  And my heart is sore wounded within me.
23 Like a shadow grown long I pass off;
  I am driven away like the locust;
24 My knees falter through fasting,
  And my flesh falls away from its fulness.
25 I am become their reviling,
  When they see me they fling up their head.

26 Give me help, O Jehovah, my God,
  In Thine own lovingkindness, oh save me ;
27 Let them know, too, that this is Thy hand,
  That Thou, O Jehovah, hast done it.
28 For cursing is theirs, it is Thine to give blessing ;
  When they arise, Thou wilt put them to shame,
    And Thy servant will triumph.
29 Be mine enemies clothed with disgrace,
  Yea, enwrapped in their shame like a mantle ;
30 And thanks great and loud will I give to Jehovah ;
  In the midst of the throng will I praise Him.
31 He stands at the right of the needy,
  To save him from those that give doom to his soul.

(4) **I was all prayer.** Heb. *and I prayer;* meaning *I was absorbed in prayer*, or did nothing but pray.

(6) **Let an enemy stand at his right.** This is not the position of an accuser, but of one who aids, or resists, the most effective employment of the right hand; in the one case to strengthen and help, in the other, as here, to paralyze and hinder. For the former see xvi. 8, cx. 5, for the latter Zech. iii. 1. In this last instance, as here, we find the Hebrew *sâtan;* but there, as a personal designation, Satan; here, in the more general sense, *an adversary.*

(10) **Their desolate homes.** Heb. *their ruins.*

(21) **Come help me.** Heb. *act with me;* that is, *in my behalf*, or *assisting me.*

(23) **Like a shadow grown long I pass off.** (Heb. *I go*); that is, as a shadow lengthens when the sun is declining and the night is at hand. See on cii. 11.—**Like the locust;** as driven by the wind. See Ex. xx. 13, 19.

CX.

PRIEST AND KING AT THE RIGHT HAND OF GOD.

THE words of our Saviour recorded in Matt. xxii. 41-46, Mark xiii. 35-37, Luke xx. 41-44, preclude any other view than that this Psalm is a direct prophecy of Himself. In accordance with these words there is no reference here to David, or to any king of Israel, as a type of Christ. The Psalm is thus raised to a higher plane than most other Messianic Psalms. There is indeed a typical groundwork in the two offices held by men Divinely appointed under the Old Testament, and especially by Melchisedek, king of Salem, and priest of the Most High God, but in the Psalm Christ only is addressed or described.

1. A call of Jehovah upon David's Lord to a place at His own right hand (1), and grounded upon this a twofold assurance: (a) Of a triumphant extension of His kingdom, out of Zion (2); (b) Of the accession of an army of youthful warriors who have consecrated themselves to His service (3). 2. A further declaration of Jehovah that this king is a priest forever, not after the Levitical order, but conformed to an older type, more expressive of the Divine purpose to be hereafter realized (4). 3. An assurance of his final victory and triumph over all enemies (5, 6).

A PSALM OF DAVID.

1 Jehovah said to my Lord,
  " Sit enthroned on My right,
 Till I make those that hate thee,
  A stool for Thy feet.
2 Thy sceptre of power,
  Will Jehovah send forth out of Zion;
 Have dominion in the midst of Thy foes."

3 Thy people will come as gifts of free will,
  On the day Thy forces assemble;
 Thine are Thy youth in holy attire,
  Like the dew that is born of the dawn.
4 Jehovah hath sworn and He will not repent:
  " Thou art ever a priest,
 Melchizedek's order Thy type."

5 At Thy right hand the Lord
 Has smitten down kings in the day of His wrath.

6 He judges the nations,
    They are filled with the dead;
    He has smitten down heads over wide-spreading lands;
7 He drinks of the brook by the way,
    And therefore He lifts up His head.

(1) **Jehovah has said.** Heb. *ne-'um Yehovah* (נאם יהוה), lit. *oracle of Jehovah*, the usual opening, in the prophetical Books, of the immediate utterance of God Himself. See note on xxxvi. 1.—**Sit enthroned on My right.** A seat at the right hand of Jehovah is not merely a place of high honour, but of association in royal majesty and rule, as indicated in all that follows. — **Till I make.** The particle עַד (*until*) does not indicate that at the time specified what is referred to shall cease, but the contrary, as in cxii. 8; Gen. xlix. 10. Yet it may point to entrance upon new conditions, dependent upon what shall then have occurred. See Acts iii. 21; 1 Cor. xv. 25.

(2) **Thy sceptre.** The whole context shows that this is not a rod of chastisement as in ii. 9. but a symbol of royal rule. See, for the same word, Jer. xlviii. 17; Ezek. xix. 11-14.

(3) **Will come as gifts of free will.** Heb. *are free-will offerings.* See the same word in lxviii. 9, of a heavy shower watering the earth profusely; *géshem n'dáboth*, lit. *a rain of free-will offerings.* See the corresponding verb, in the reflexive form, Judg. v. 2. — **On the day Thy forces assemble.** Heb. *in the day of Thy power*, or *forces.* The word *hháyil*, prop. *strength*, is often used of an army; Ex. xiv. 28; 1 Kings xx. 25, etc. — **In holy attire.** Lit. *in holy ornaments.* So in marg. of R. V. and preferred for the text in Am. Revisers' Appendix. Holy attire is a symbol of consecration to the service of the Messiah in bringing the world under His rule. For clearness' sake the order of the Hebrew has been somewhat changed:

In holy attire out of the womb of the dawn, to thee (thine) *is the dew of thy youthful ones.* The young men who have consecrated themselves to this service are compared to the dew which descends upon the king, as if the innumerable drops were children of the dawn (Delitzsch). There may be some reference to the dew as refreshing and beautiful, but principally to its profuseness, the immense multitude of drops. See 2 Sam. xvii. 12.

(4) **Melchizedek's order Thy type.** Heb. *'al dibráthi Malkizédek. after the description of.* In Heb. vii. 15 we find the alternative expression κατά τήν ὁμοιότητα, *according to the likeness of*, which is the exact meaning, the writer there claiming that Christ was "made like to Melchizedek," that is, that the priesthood of Melchizedek was a Divinely instituted prophetic figure or type of the priesthood of Christ, especially in its combination with his royal dominion. He is not descended from Levi, but from Judah, and is a king on the throne of David, yet He is a priest, a high-priest in the temple of God. See the important parallel passage, though Melchizedek is not mentioned, Zech. vi. 12, 13. There are other typical resemblances exhibited in the Epistle, in reply to Jews who questioned whether Christ, as descended from Judah, could be a priest; principally that Melchizedek's name, parentage, birth, and death were not to be found in any priestly genealogy, and that he owed his position to direct Divine appointment on personal grounds, and not to descent from an hereditary line; and further that he had no successor in his priesthood, but held it till

the object of his appointment was accomplished. The writer proves in this and other ways, not only that Christ was truly a priest, but that His priesthood was superior to that of Aaron ; and still further, that the introduction, under the Divine promise and oath, of a priest after the prophetic similitude of Melchizedek, and not of Aaron, proves the insufficiency of the latter, supersedes and annuls it, and so virtually abrogates the whole Levitical law, which was founded upon the priesthood, and could not subsist without it ; Heb. vii. 11–19. There is no mystery connected with Melchizedek or his priesthood. The Rev. Ver. has rendered an important service in substituting "without genealogy" for "without descent" in vii. 3. The sole meaning of the verse, which seems to describe Melchizedek as a supernatural person, is that no priestly register contains a record of his parentage, birth, and death, which the Jews thought indispensable, and yet he is proven by Old Test. history and prophecy to be truly a priest, the honoured prototype of the Messiah.

(5) **The Lord**. Heb. *'Adonāy*.

This form of the plural is never used except as a Divine name. It is now Jehovah who goes forth at the right hand of His anointed King to support and strengthen it against all opposing evil. See xvi. 8, "Jehovah is at my right hand."

(6) **He has smitten down heads**. Heb. *māhhats rôsh*. Lit. *to smite through*, or *crush heads ;* also in lxviii. 22 ; Hab. iii. 13, of inflicting deadly injuries. Literally understood all this seems very terrible, and inconsistent with the spirit of the Gospel. Under such figures the triumphs of grace are often exhibited. The sword of the Spirit does not destroy men, but saves them. It is their enmity that is slain. The victory of the Son of God is over their stubborn hearts. Those who have been in arms against Him, yield to His gracious rule.

(7) **He drinks of the brook by the way**. "The victorious leader, wearied with the battle, and the pursuit of his enemies, stops for a moment on his way, to refresh himself by drinking of the torrent rushing by, and then 'lifts up his head.' With new vigour he continues his pursuit." — *Perowne*.

CXI.

A SONG OF PRAISE TO GOD.

THIS Psalm and the following are twins in form and in subject. The former celebrates the glory, might, and lovingkindness of Jehovah in the circle of the "upright;" the latter celebrates the glory and blessedness that flow therefrom to the "upright" themselves.

Both Psalms are alphabetical. Each consists of twenty-two lines with the twenty-two letters of the Hebrew alphabet at the beginning. In both, the first eight verses have two lines each, and the last two have three each, and the accentuation is identical. This indicates a probability, in view of the musical value of the accents in the poetical books, that they were intended to be sung continuously. There are also various coincidences of thought and expression.

1 PRAISE YE JEHOVAH!
    With all my heart I give thanks to Jehovah
In the council and assembly of the upright.
2 Very great are the works of Jehovah,
Sought out by all that take pleasure therein.
3 In His work there is glory and splendour,
And His righteousness standeth forever.
4 A memorial He ordained for His wonders,
For Jehovah is gracious and full of compassion.
5 He gives food unto those that revere Him,
Remembering His covenant forever.
6 He showed His people the power of His works,
That to them He might give what the nations possessed.
7 The works of His hands are justice and truth,
All His precepts established.
8 They stand fast forever and alway,
They are wrought in equity and truth.
9 Redemption He sent for His people,
    And commanded His covenant forever —
How holy and fearful His Name!
10 The fear of Jehovah is the beginning of wisdom;
A good understanding have all that obey Him;
    Forever His praise shall stand fast.

(4) **A memorial He ordained for His wonders.** Referring undoubtedly to the sacred feasts, and especially to the Passover, and the feast of unleavened bread that accompanied it. See Ex. xiii. 9, where this ordinance is spoken of as *a memorial*, using *zikkārōn*, a slightly different form of the word used here.

(10) **That obey Him.** Heb. *that do them;* that is, His precepts mentioned in verses 7 and 8.

CXII.

THE BLESSEDNESS OF THE UPRIGHT.

1 PRAISE YE JEHOVAH!
    How blest is the man that feareth Jehovah,
That greatly enjoys His commandments.
2 His seed becomes mighty on the earth,
The race of the upright is blessèd.

3 In his house are riches and wealth,
   And his righteousness standeth forever.
4 Light in the darkness shall rise for the upright,
   The pitiful, compassionate, righteous.
5 It is well with the man that shows pity and lends,
   His cause he maintains in the judgment;
6 He surely shall never be shaken ;
   The righteous are held in remembrance forever.
7 He fears no tidings of evil,
   His heart is steadfast, its trust in Jehovah;
8 His heart is established, it is not afraid,
   Till he sees his desire on his foes.
9 He scatters abroad, he gives to the needy,
        His righteousness standeth forever;
   His horn shall be exalted with honour.
10 The wicked man sees, and is vexed,
        He gnasheth his teeth and melteth away;
   The desire of the wicked shall perish.

(8) **Sees his desire**.   See note on liv. 9.   (9) **His horn**.   See note
on lxxv. 5.

CXIII.

THE LOWLY EXALTED.

" IN the Jewish Liturgy the so-called *Hallel* (Ps. cxiii.–cxviii.), also called
the Egyptian Hallel, as distinguished from the Great Hallel (Ps.
cxxxvi.), begins with this Psalm. . . . This first Psalm of the series continued to be sung while the temple stood, and is still recited in Palestine
eighteen times a year, apart from its customary, though not legal use, at the
new moon. Outside of Palestine it is now yearly recited twenty-one times,
on account of the addition of three great feast-days. At the family celebration of the Passover, Psalms cxiii. and cxiv. were sung before the emptying
of the second cup, and Psalms cxv.–cxviii. after the meal, and after the filling of the fourth cup (comp. the expositors on Matt. xxvii. 30 ; Mark xiv.
26). This Psalm is the Old Test. *magnificat*." — *Moll.*

*1. God's Name to be praised forever and over the whole earth (1–3). 2. Though
infinitely exalted, He looks graciously upon the lowly (4–6). 3. He exalts, blesses,
and gladdens the feeble, the despised, and the mourning (7–9).*

1 PRAISE YE JEHOVAH!
   , Praise, O ye servants of Jehovah,
   Praise ye the Name of Jehovah;
2 Blessèd be the Name of Jehovah
   Henceforth and forever!
3 From the rise of the sun to its setting,
   Let the Name of Jehovah be praised.

4 Jehovah is high, far above all the nations,
   His glory is higher than the heavens.
5 Who can compare with Jehovah, our God,
   Whose throne is exalted on high,
6 But who looks far below
   On the heavens and the earth? —
7 He that raises the poor from the dust,
   From the dunghill the needy lifts high,
8 To sit with the princely,
   The princely of His people, —
9 Makes the barren to dwell in a home,
   The glad mother of children;
     PRAISE YE JEHOVAH!

(6) **Who looks far below.** Heb. *who makes low for looking;* a participial clause, usually to be rendered with the relative pronoun, and expresses not single acts, but the habitual and characteristic. So the participles in verses 7 and 9, " Who raises," " Who makes." This first participle, *mashpil, making low,* is not reflexive, but causative. It qualifies the *looking* adverbially, as in our rendering, a construction very common in Hebrew. See Ges. *Heb. Gr.* § 142, Rem. 1. The verb *to look,* is followed by the prep. *beth,* implying deep interest and satisfaction, as delighting in opportunity to gratify His gracious nature. See note on xcii. 11. The grammatical object immediately follows, "the heavens" and "the earth," as parts of a whole. It is not, however, a general interest in the material creation that attracts this absorbing attention, but He looks through the material heavens to the underlying earth on account of His sympathy with the suffering. The expression here borders very closely upon the *bending over* to look on the earth in Ps. xiv. 2, where see the note. Especially see in cii. 19, 20, a mention of God as bending down to behold the earth that He may hear the groaning of the prisoner. It is strikingly similar to the expression here, including the explanatory clauses in the three following verses.

(8) **To sit.** Heb. *to make him sit,* or *dwell.*

CXIV.

THE EARTH IN COMMOTION BEFORE GOD.

"THIS is perhaps the most beautiful of all the Psalms that touch on the early history of Israel. It is certainly the most graphic and the most striking in the boldness of its outlines. The following remarks may perhaps illustrate the conception and plan of the poem: 1. In structure it is singularly perfect. We have four strophes, each of two verses, and each of these of two lines, in which the parallelism is carefully preserved. 2. The effect is produced, as in Ps. xxix., not by minute tracing of details, but by the boldness with which certain great features of the history are presented. 3. A singular animation and dramatic force are given to the poem by the beautiful apostrophe in verses 5, 6, and the effect of this is heightened to a remarkable degree by the use of the present tenses. The awe and the trembling of nature are a spectacle on which the poet is looking. The parted sea, through which Israel walks as on dry land; the rushing Jordan arrested in its course; the granite cliffs of Sinai, shaken to their base, — he sees it all, and asks in wonder what it means. 4. Then it is that the truth bursts upon his mind, and the impression of this upon the reader is very finely managed. The *Name* of God, which has been entirely concealed up to this point in the poem . . . is now only introduced after the apostrophe in verses 5, 6." "The reason seems evident and this conduct necessary, for if God had appeared before, there could be no wonder why the mountains should leap and the sea retire ; therefore that this convulsion of nature may be brought in with due surprise, His Name is not mentioned till afterwards ; and then, with a very agreeable turn of thought, God is introduced at once in all His majesty." — Perowne: *Spectator*, (No. 461).

1 When Israel went forth out of Egypt,
  The house of Jacob from people of strange tongue,
2 His sanctuary was Judah,
  His dominion was Israel.

3 The sea saw it and fled,
  The Jordan turned back ;
4 Like rams sprang the mountains,
  The hills like the young of the flock.

5 What ails thee, O sea, that thou fleest?
  O Jordan, why turnest thou back?

6 Why spring ye like rams, O ye mountains,
   Ye hills, like the young of the flock?

7 Be in anguish, Thou earth,
        At the presence of the Lord,
   At the presence of the Lord God of Jacob;
8 Who turns rocks into pools,
   Flinty rock into fountains of water.

CXV.

THE LIVING GOD IN CONTRAST WITH IDOLS.

1. God is called upon to manifest His glory, and to silence the unbelieving scoffs of the heathen (1, 2). 2. The contrast between the living God, enthroned in heaven, and dead images (3–8). 3. Those who fear Jehovah may depend on His faithful care for aid, protection, and blessing (9–14). 4. He who made all things has given the earth to the children of men, that they may bless Him forever (15–18).

1 Not unto us, O Jehovah,
        To Thy Name, and not unto us, be the glory,
   Because of Thy kindness and truth.
2 Why should the nations say,
        " Where is their God? "
3 But our God is in heaven;
   He has done whatsoever He pleased.

4 Their idols are silver and gold,
   The work of men's hands;
5 They have mouths, but they speak not,
   They have eyes, but they see not ;
6 They have ears, but they hear not,
   They have noses, but smell not ;
7 They have hands, but they handle not,
        They have feet, but they walk not,
   And no sound can come from their throat.
8 They that make, become like them,
   Even so all that trust them.

9 O Israel, trust thou in Jehovah,
   He is their help and their shield ;

10 House of Aaron, trust ye in Jehovah,
  He is their help and their shield;
11 Ye that reverence Jehovah, trust ye in Jehovah,
  He is their help and their shield;
12 Jehovah remembers and will bless —
  He will bless the house of Israel,
    He will bless the house of Aaron;
13 Those that reverence Jehovah will He bless,
  Both the small and the great.

14 Jehovah will add to you more, and still more,
  To you and your children.
15 Ye are blessed by Jehovah,
  The Maker of the heavens and the earth.
16 The heavens are Jehovah's,
  But the earth has He given to the children of men.
17 The dead bring no praise to Jehovah,
  Nor any that go down into silence;
18 But we, Jehovah will we bless,
  Henceforth and forever;
    PRAISE YE JEHOVAH!

CXVI.

THANKSGIVING FOR DELIVERANCE FROM DISTRESS AND PERIL.

ONE who by God's mercy has escaped from death, and whose heart has been penetrated by the tenderest gratitude and affection, here acknowledges his obligations, and with thankful vows publicly consecrates himself to the service of God as long as he lives. As the Psalm progresses, thoughts of his great trouble and the signal mercy shown him accumulate, and develop greater intensity of feeling, richness of expression, and earnestness of purpose, as again and again he reiterates his vow in the presence of Jehovah and His people.

The Psalm evidently belongs to the period after the exile, but has freely borrowed from earlier Psalms, principally from David. It exhibits a power and depth of spiritual life not exceeded in any part of Israelitish history. This has been appreciated in the Christian Church, and has made the Psalm very precious to those who have had like experience of suffering and relief.

 1 I love Jehovah for He heareth
   My loud supplications;
 2 Yea, His ear He bent toward me,
   And on Him will I call as long as I live.
 3 The cords of Death were about me,
       The tortures of Sheol had seized me,
   I found anguish and sorrow;
 4 Then I called on the Name of Jehovah,
   " O Jehovah, I pray Thee, deliver my soul."

 5 Full of pity is Jehovah, and righteous,
   Our God has compassion.
 6 Jehovah preserveth the simple;
   I was brought very low, and He helped me.
 7 Return, O my soul, to thy rest,
   For Jehovah dealt graciously with thee.
 8 For my soul Thou deliveredst from death,
   Mine eyes from tears, and my footsteps from failing.
 9 I shall walk in the presence of Jehovah,
   In the land of the living.

10 I have faith when I speak, —
   I, who was greatly afflicted,
11 I, who found in my peril
   That all men were false; —
12 What shall I render to Jehovah,
   For all His benefits toward me?
13 I will take the cup of salvation,
   And call on the Name of Jehovah;
14 My vows will I pay to Jehovah,
   If I may, with Thy people all present.

15 Of great price in the sight of Jehovah,
   Is the death of those whom He loves.
16 Oh, hear me, Jehovah, for I am Thy servant,
   Thy servant, the son of Thy handmaid;
       Thou hast loosened my bonds.

17 I bring my thanksgiving, the sacrifice due Thee,
   And call on the Name of Jehovah.
18 My vows will I pay to Jehovah,
   If I may, with His people all present;
19 In the courts of the house of Jehovah,
   In the midst of thy walls, O Jerusalem;
   PRAISE YE JEHOVAH!

(10) **I have faith when I speak.** Heb. *he'emantî kî 'adabbēr.* The former of these verbs is in the perfect tense, which, however, does not indicate past time, but firmly established and permanent confidence, in distinction from transient emotion. Lit. *I believe when I speak.* The second verb in the imperfect tense, expressing a passing present, with reference to what he is now saying about the goodness of Jehovah in his great trouble. No two translators quite agree in their rendering of the tenth and eleventh verses, and no rendering yet given exhibits clearly their relation to the context before and after. The failure seems to result from not observing that the emphatic pronoun *I* (Heb. *'anî*), in 10 *b* and repeated in 11 *a*, is in both cases in apposition to the subject of the preceding verbs, and that both clauses are virtually relative, giving a reason for his confidence. He learned to trust God's faithful grace, not from the testimony of others, but from his own personal experience of anguish and sorrow, as described in verses 3 and 4. In his danger and alarm he had looked to men for sympathy and aid, and had to testify that all their promises were falsehood. The contrast between man's treachery and God's faithfulness as thus personally tested and attested is very striking, and would be much less effective in the absence of the emphatic pronoun.

(11) **In my peril.** Heb. *hhophzî,* prop. *my alarm* in view of danger; never of *haste,* as in speaking. The R. V. has *alarm* in the margin, and the American Revisers prefer it for the text. This is an improvement, but the poet is not referring to *imaginary,* but to *real* danger, in which he had appealed for help, and it is important to express this.

(14) **If I may,** and again in ver. 18. Heb. *nâ* (נא), the particle of entreaty, usually translated *I pray;* sometimes strengthening an imperative, but it never means *now,* as a particle of time. Occasionally, as here, humbly asking permission, as well as expressing desire.

CXVII.

THE NATIONS INVITED TO PRAISE JEHOVAH.

" THIS is the shortest of all the Psalms, — a Hallelujah addressed to the heathen world. In its very brevity it is one of the grandest witnesses of the might with which, in the midst of the Old Testament, the world-wide mission of the religion of revelation struck against or undermined the national limitation. It is stamped by the apostle in Rom. xv.

11, as a *locus classicus* for the participation of the heathen, in accordance with God's gracious purpose, in the promised salvation of Israel." — *Delitzsch.*

   1 Praise Jehovah, all ye nations,
       Give Him glory, all ye peoples;
   2 For His kindness over us is mighty,
       And the truth of Jehovah endureth forever;
         Praise ye Jehovah!

CXVIII.

A FESTAL DAY IN THE TEMPLE OF JEHOVAH.

VARIOUS books connect this Psalm with the return from exile, indicating that it was either intended to be used at the dedication of the second temple, Ezra viii. 15 (Delitzsch), or in the first complete celebration, according to legal ceremonies, of the feast of Tabernacles (Stier, Perowne), probably the latter. In the Jewish Liturgy it is the last Psalm of the *Hallel*, which begins with cxiii.

Martin Luther says of it: This is my Psalm, which I love. Although the whole of the Psalter, and of Holy Scripture itself, which is my only consolation in life, are also dear to me, yet I have chosen this Psalm particularly to be called and to be mine; for it has often deserved my love, and helped me out of many deep distresses, when neither emperor, nor kings, nor the wise and prudent, nor saints, could have helped me.

The following account of its contents is from Delitzsch : *The Psalm falls into two divisions. The first division (1-19) is sung by the festive procession which is led up by priests and Levites, and which goes up to the temple with sacrificial animals. With ver. 19, the procession stands at the entrance. The second part (20-27) is sung by the body of Levites who receive the festive procession. Then ver. 28 is the answer of those who have arrived, and ver. 29 the concluding song of all of them.*

   1 To Jehovah give thanks, for He is good,
       For His kindness endureth forever;
   2 Let Israel now say,
       That His kindness endureth forever;
   3 Let the household of Aaron now say,
       That His kindness endureth forever;
   4 Those that reverence Jehovah, let them say,
       That His kindness endureth forever;

5 From sore straits I called on Jehovah;
And He answered in setting me free.
6 With Jehovah on my side, I shall not be afraid,
What can man do to harm me?
7 With Jehovah on my side as my helper,
Even I, undismayed, can look on my foes.
8 To hide in Jehovah is better
Than trusting in man;
9 To hide in Jehovah is better
Than trusting in princes.

10 Let all nations surround me,
In the Name of Jehovah will I verily destroy them;
11 Let them surround me, yea, let them surround me,
In the Name of Jehovah will I verily destroy them;
12 Let them surround me like bees,
Like a fire of thorns are they quenched;
In the Name of Jehovah will I verily destroy them.

13 Thou hast thrust at me sore for my downfall,
But Jehovah gave me help.
14 Jehovah is my strength and my song;
He is become my salvation.
15 The cry of rejoicing and safety
Is heard in the tents of the righteous;
How mighty are the deeds of Jehovah's right hand!
16 The right hand of Jehovah is exalted,
The right hand of Jehovah does valiantly.
17 I shall not die, but shall live,
And shall tell of the works of Jehovah;
18 Very sorely Jehovah chastised me,
But gave me not over to death.
19 Let the gates of righteousness open before me,
I will enter and give thanks to Jehovah.

20 This is the gate of Jehovah,
The righteous may enter therein.

21 I thank Thee because Thou hast heard me,
   And become my salvation.
22 The stone which the builders rejected,
   Is now the chief stone of the corner.
23 From Jehovah this comes;
   In our eyes it is wondrous.
24 This is the day that Jehovah has made,
   And therein let us joy and be glad.

25 Jehovah, O save, we beseech Thee,
   Oh prosper us, Jehovah, we beseech Thee.
26 Blessèd be he that comes in the Name of Jehovah,
   From the house of Jehovah, we bless you.
27 Jehovah is God, He has given us light;
     The festival offering bind ye with cords,
   Even up to the horns of the altar.
28 Thou art my God, and I thank Thee;
   As my own God, I exalt Thee;
29 Give thanks to Jehovah, for He is good,
   For His kindness endureth forever.

(5) **In setting me free.** Heb. *in a broad place.* *Narrowness* and *breadth*
often exhibit figuratively great distress and relief; see on xviii. 19, xxxi. 8.
(10, 11, 12) **Verily.** *ki* ('כִּ), emphatic.

CXIX.

THE LAW OF JEHOVAH MORE PRECIOUS THAN GOLD.

IT is agreed by most authorities that this is one of the latest Psalms in
the Psalter. It contains 176 verses, almost every one of which has
reference to the word of God in its excellence and value. It is divided
into 22 parts, every one of the eight verses in each part beginning with the
same letter and the letters following in the order of the Hebrew Alphabet.
We have no knowledge of the author, or the circumstances under which it
was composed, except such as may be gathered from its contents. It seems
to be the work of a comparatively young man (vv. 9. 99, 100), in great
trouble, surrounded by wicked men and persecutors. Delitzsch, following
Hitzig, suggests it as probable that it is the work of one in imprisonment
who whiled away his time by weaving together his complaints and his con-
solatory thoughts. It certainly indicates surrounding hostility to the worship and service of the true God, and suffering for righteousness' sake, and

as furnishing the necessary conditions, it is thought to have been written either in the time of the Maccabean princes (Hitzig) or in the closing period of the Persian supremacy (Moll).

It is aphoristic and artificial in form, yet characterized by a lofty spirit of loyalty to God and to truth, a fervour of religious affection and aspiration, a bold maintenance of conscientious convictions before princes and kings, and an unwavering confidence in God and His word, such as gives it great value in the domain of spiritual life and culture. With all this its literary character is by no means despicable. There is considerable variety and force of expression, and a charm even in its monotony and simplicity. Those will be found to love it most who know it best.

CONTENTS. — The following from Delitzsch will be found helpful at least in calling attention to some prominent idea in each one of its divisions : "After the psalmist has sounded the praises of faithfulness to God's word (ALEPH) and has characterized it as the virtue of virtues which becomes a young man, and which he himself cultivates (BETH), he prays in the midst of scorning and persecuting companions for the grace of enlightenment (GIMEL), confirmation (DALETH), preservation (HE), appropriate and joyous confession (VAU) ; God's word is his continual study (ZAYIN), he attaches himself to them that fear God (HHETH), and while he acknowledges that his humiliation is wholesome for him (TETH), still he stands in need of comfort (JOD), and sighs : how long ! (KAPH). If it were not for the eternal, stable, and potent word of God, he should despair (LAMED) ; in his trying situation this is his wisdom (MEM) ; he has sworn fidelity to it, and has shown faithfulness even as one persecuted (NUN) ; he abhors and contemns the apostates (SAMECH). He is oppressed, but God will not suffer him to be overwhelmed (AYIN) ; he will not suffer the godless ongoings, which wring streams of water from his eyes, to have dominion over him (PE) ; over him, the small (still youthful) and despised one, whom zeal, because of the prevailing forgetfulness of God, consumes (TSADE). Oh that God would hear his crying by night (QOPH), that He would speedily quicken him with His helpful compassion (RESH) ; for, although he is persecuted by princes, he nevertheless cleaves firmly to Him (SHIN). Oh that He would seek him, the little sheep that goes astray and is exposed to such great danger (TAU)."

ALEPH.

1 How blest are the men whose pathway is blameless,
   Who walk in the law of Jehovah ;
2 How blest those that honour His statutes,
   Who to seeking Him give their whole heart.
3 Yea, they do no injustice,
   They walk in His ways.
4 Thou hast ordered Thy precepts
   With diligence kept ;
5 Oh that my ways were established
   In keeping Thy statutes ;

6 I then without shame,
 Should look unto all Thy commands;
7 With an upright heart would I thank Thee,
 When I learn Thy righteous decisions;
8 Yea, Thy laws will I keep;
 Do not wholly forsake me.

BETH.

9 How may a youth cleanse his path?
 By seeing it accords with Thy word.
10 With all my heart have I sought Thee;
 From Thy laws let me not go astray.
11 Thy word have I hid in my heart,
 That I might not sin against Thee.
12 Blessèd art Thou, O Jehovah;
 Teach me Thy statutes.
13 With my lips I rehearse
 All decrees of Thy mouth.
14 I rejoice in the way of Thy statutes,
 As possessing all wealth.
15 I will think on Thy precepts,
 Intently will look to Thy paths.
16 I delight in Thy statutes;
 Thy words shall not pass from my mind.

GIMEL.

17 Deal well with Thy servant, — let me live,
 I will then give heed to Thy word.
18 Take the veil from mine eyes, — let me see
 What wonders there are in Thy law.
19 I am a stranger in the earth;
 Do not hide Thy commands from my sight.
20 My soul is crushed by its longing
 At all times for Thy righteous decisions.
21 Thou rebukest the proudly defiant,
 The accursèd that forsake Thy commands.
22 Roll away from me insult and scorn,
 For I observe Thine injunctions.

23 Yea, princes assembled, conspiring against me,
   But Thy servant gives thought to Thy statutes;
24 Yea, and more, I delight in Thy precepts,
   From these have I counsel.

DALETH.

25 My soul cleaves to the dust;
   Give me life, as Thy promise assures.
26 My ways I rehearsed, and Thou gavest me answer;
   Teach me Thy statutes.
27 Instruct me in the way of Thy precepts,
   That so I may speak of Thy wonders.
28 My soul melts away in its sorrow;
   Give me strength as Thy promise assures.
29 The way of falsehood remove from me far,
   And graciously grant me Thy law;
30 In the way of faithfulness have I my choice,
   I set Thy judgments before me.
31 I cleave to Thy statutes;
   O Jehovah, let me not come to shame.
32 I will speed me in the way of Thy precepts,
   For Thou my heart dost enlarge.

HE.

33 Teach me Jehovah, the way of Thy statutes,
   I will keep it to the end.
34 Give me understanding, Thy law will I keep;
   With all my heart will I observe it.
35 Help me on in the path of Thy precepts,
   For therein I delight.
36 Turn my heart to Thy statutes,
   And not to despoiling.
37 Turn mine eyes from beholding delusion,
   And give me new life in Thy way.
38 Confirm to Thy servant Thy promise,
   Which tends to Thy fear.
39 Turn away the reviling I dread;
   For Thy statutes are good.

40 Lo, I long for Thy precepts;
   In Thy righteousness give me new life.

VAU.

41 Let Thy kindnesses come to me, Jehovah,
   Thy saving power, as Thy promise assured;
42 I will then have an answer for him that reviles me,
   For I trust in Thy word.
43 Take not out of my mouth all the words of Thy truth,
   For I hope in Thy judgments;
44 So will I continually heed Thy commands,
   Yea, forever and alway;
45 And in freedom shall walk,
   For Thy precepts I seek.
46 Before kings will I speak of Thy statutes,
   And shall not be ashamed;
47 I delight me in Thy precepts,
   Which also I love;
48 And I lift up my hands to Thy law, which I love,
   And will think on Thy statutes.

ZAYIN.

49 Remember Thy word to Thy servant,
   For in this Thou hast made me to hope.
50 This is my comfort in suffering,
   That Thy word gives me life.
51 The proud held me greatly in derision,
   Yet I turn not aside from Thy law.
52 I remember Thy judgments of old, O Jehovah,
   And take to me comfort.
53 Indignation has seized me because of the wicked,
   Who depart from Thy law.
54 I sing of Thy statutes,
   In the house of my pilgrimage sing;
55 I remember Thy Name in the night, O Jehovah,
   And Thy law will I heed;
56 For this is now mine,
   That I keep Thy commands.

HHETH.

57 Jehovah is my portion;
I resolved to give heed to Thy words.
58 With all my heart I entreat for Thy favour;
Have pity upon me according to Thy promise.
59 I thought on my ways,
Turned my feet to Thy statutes,
60 Made haste and delayed not
To keep Thy commandments.
61 The cords of the wicked are about me,
But I have not forgotten Thy law;
62 At midnight I rise and give thanks,
Because of Thy righteous decisions.
63 My companions are those that revere Thee,
That obey Thy commands.
64 The earth, O Jehovah, is full of Thy kindness;
Teach me Thy statutes.

TETH.

65 Right well hast Thou dealt with Thy servant,
As Thou, O Jehovah, hadst promised.
66 Teach me good judgment and knowledge,
For I believe Thy commandments.
67 Before I was afflicted I went astray,
But now I give heed to Thy word.
68 Thou art gracious, and graciously dealest;
Teach me Thy statutes.
69 The proud have forged falsehood against me,
But with all my heart I give heed to Thy precepts.
70 Their heart is gross and unfeeling,
But I in Thy law find delight.
71 For me it is good that affliction has come,
For thus Thou hast taught me Thy statutes.
72 Better to me is the law of Thy mouth,
Than thousands of silver and gold.

JOD.

73 By Thy hand was I made, and was fashioned,
Give me discernment to learn Thy commands.

74 Those that fear Thee shall see and be glad,
   For I hope in Thy word.
75 I know, O Jehovah, Thy judgments are righteous,
   And because Thou art faithful, my affliction has come;
76 Let Thy kindness, I pray, give me comfort.
   As Thou saidst to Thy servant.
77 Let Thy mercies come in, that my life may continue,
   For Thy law is my pleasure.
78 Let the proud be ashamed, for with lies they destroy me,
   But I will give thought to Thy precepts.
79 To me let those that revere Thee return,
   Those taught in Thy law.
80 Let my heart in Thy statutes be blameless,
   That I come not to shame.

KAPH.

81 For Thy saving power my soul pines away;
   In Thy word do I hope.
82 Mine eyes pine away for Thy promise,
   Saying, " When wilt Thou come with Thy comfort? "
83 I become like a wineskin dried up in the smoke,
   Yet forget not Thy statutes.
84 How few are the days of Thy servant,
   Oh, when wilt Thou judge my pursuers?
85 The proud have digged pits for my life, —
   Those not in accord with Thy law.
86 Thy commands are all faithful;
   When with lies they pursue me, oh, give me Thy help.
87 They had almost consumed me in the land,
   Yet I have not forsaken Thy precepts.
88 In Thy merciful kindness give me life,
   That thus I may heed what Thy mouth has enjoined.

LAMED.

89 Forever, Jehovah,
   Thy word has its stand in the heavens ;
90 Thy faithfulness lasts unto all generations,
   Thou mad'st the earth firm, and it stood ;

91 They stand to this day as Thou hast ordained;
  For all things must serve Thee.
92 If Thy law had not been my delight,
  I then should have perished in suffering;
93 Thy precepts I will never forget,
  For in them Thou gavest me new life.
94 I am Thine, oh deliver me,
  For I search out Thy precepts.
95 When the wicked lie in wait to destroy me,
  I consider Thy statutes.
96 I have witnessed a limit to all that is perfect;
  Thy commandment is broad beyond measure.

MEM.

97 Thy law, how I love it!
  I think of it all the day long.
98 Thy commands make me wiser than my foes,
  For they are ever within me.
99 I have more understanding than all my instructors,
  For I think on Thy law.
100 I know more than the aged,
  Because I regarded Thy precepts.
101 I held back my feet from all paths that are evil,
  That thus I may keep Thy commands.
102 I turn not aside from Thy judgments,
  For Thou, even Thou, art my teacher.
103 How sweet to my taste are Thy words,
  Yea, sweeter than honey to my mouth.
104 Through Thy precepts I have understanding,
  And therefore I hate every way of deceit.

NUN.

105 Thy word is a lamp to my feet,
  And a light to my path.
106 I have sworn and fulfilled it,
  To heed Thy righteous injunctions.
107 I am greatly oppressed;
  Give me life, O Jehovah, as Thy promise assured.

108 Accept Thou, Jehovah, my mouth's willing offerings,
And teach me Thy judgments.
109 I ever hold my life in my hand,
Yet forget not Thy law.
110 The wicked laid snares for my feet,
Yet I go not astray from Thy statutes.
111 Thy precepts I take in possession forever,
For these are the joy of my heart.
112 My heart I incline to perform Thy behests,
Forever, yea, even to the end.

SAMECH.

113 The double-minded I hate,
But Thy law do I love.
114 Thou art my refuge and shield,
And I hope in Thy word.
115 Depart from me, all evil doers,
Let me keep the commands of my God.
116 Uphold me, according to Thy word, that thus I may live,
And let me not blush for my hope.
117 Hold me up, I then shall be safe,
And will always observe Thy commands.
118 Thou wilt spurn all that stray from Thy statutes,
For by lies they are deluded.
119 All the wicked of the earth Thou rejectest like dross,
And therefore I love Thine injunctions.
120 My flesh quivers, for I fear Thee;
I tremble because of Thy judgments.

AYIN.

121 My deeds have been righteous and just,
Thou wilt not give me up to mine oppressors.
122 Be surety to Thy servant for good;
Let the proud not oppress me.
123 For Thy saving power mine eyes pine away,
For Thy promise in righteousness given;
124 Deal with Thy servant in Thy merciful kindness,
And teach me Thy statutes.

125 I am Thy servant, oh, give me discernment,
    That I may know Thine injunctions.
126 It is time for Jehovah to work,
    For Thy law they make void.
127 Therefore I love Thy commandments
    More than gold, more than gold well refined.
128 I therefore esteem all Thy precepts as right,
    And every false way do I hate.

PE.

129 Thy precepts are marvellous,
    My soul therefore keeps them.
130 The unfolding of Thy words giveth light,
    To the simple it giveth discernment.
131 I open wide my mouth and I pant,
    For I long for Thy precepts.
132 Oh, turn to me in pity,
    As is right to those loving Thy Name.
133 Establish my steps in Thy word,
    And let no iniquity rule me.
134 Set me free from the oppression of man,
    And so will I observe Thy behests.
135 Make Thy face to shine on Thy servant,
    And teach me Thy statutes.
136 Streams of water run down from mine eyes,
    Because they observe not Thy law.

TSADI.

137 Thou art righteous, Jehovah,
    And upright are all Thy decisions.
138 Thine injunctions Thou commandest in justice,
    And in faithfulness boundless.
139 My zeal has consumed me,
    For my foes have forgotten Thy word.
140 Very pure is Thy word,
    And Thy servant therefore loves it.
141 I am young and despised,
    But forget not Thy precepts.

142 Thy justice forever is right,
    And Thy law is the truth.
143 Sore trouble and anguish have found me,
    But Thy law gives me joy.
144 Thine injunctions forever are right;
    Oh, give me discernment, that thus I may live.

QOPH.

145 With all my heart do I call Thee,—Jehovah give answer;
    Thy commands will I keep.
146 When I cry to Thee, save me;
    I will heed Thy behests.
147 I am up before dawn, and cry for Thy help,
    For I hope in Thy word.
148 Mine eyes forestall every watch in the night,
    In deep thought on Thy word.
149 Hear my voice in Thy merciful kindness,
    And give me new life, O Jehovah, as Thou hast ordained.
150 Those intent on base plots are approaching,
    Who are far from Thy law;
151 But THOU, O Jehovah, art near,
    And all Thy commandments are truth.
152 Of old have I known of Thy statutes,
    That Thou laid'st their foundation forever.

RESH.

153 Oh, look on my sufferings and save me,
    For I have not forgotten Thy law.
154 Contend for my right and redeem me;
    Give me life as Thy promise assures.
155 Salvation is far from the wicked,
    For they seek not Thy statutes.
156 Thy compassions are many, Jehovah,
    Give me new life, as Thou hast ordained.
157 There are many that pursue and oppress me,
    Yet I turn not aside from Thy laws.
158 I beheld the treacherous with loathing,
    Because they observed not Thy word.

159 Behold how I love Thy commandments,
    O Jehovah, in Thy kindness give me life.
160 The sum of Thy word is the truth;
    And each of Thy righteous decisions everlasting.

SHIN.

161 Without cause have princes pursued me,
    But my heart stands in awe of Thy word.
162 Thy word makes me glad,
    As one finding great spoil.
163 Speaking lies I hate and abhor,
    But Thy law do I love.
164 Seven times in the day do I praise Thee,
    Because of Thy righteous commands.
165 Those loving Thy law have great peace,
    And nothing shall cause them to stumble.
166 I have hope, O Jehovah, in Thy power to save,
    And I obey Thy commandments.
167 My soul gives heed to Thy statutes,
    I exceedingly love them.
168 I observe Thy precepts and statutes,
    For all of my ways are before Thee.

TAU.

169 Let my cry, O Jehovah, come before Thee;
    Give me understanding according to Thy word.
170 Let my suppliant cry come before Thee;
    Remembering Thy promise, deliver me.
171 Songs of praise gush forth from my lips,
    That Thou wilt teach me Thy statutes.
172 Let my tongue sing aloud of Thy word,
    For all Thy commandments are righteous.
173 Let Thy hand be ready to help me,
    For I have chosen Thy precepts.
174 I long for Thy salvation, Jehovah,
    And delight in Thy law.
175 Give life to my soul, that it praise Thee,
    And let Thy behests give me help.

176 I go astray as a lost sheep, but seek Thou Thy servant,
For I do not forget Thy commandments.

(2) **Who to seeking Him give their whole heart.** The Hebrew *lêb* is broader than our English word *heart* in its ordinary use. The former includes all the faculties of mind and will, as well as the emotional nature. Especially the phrase "*with all my heart*" only means *sincerely and ardently*, and not *in the use of all my powers*, which is the thought here. So in verses 10, 34, 58, 69, 145.

(21) **The proudly defiant.** The adjective *proud* is too feeble as an expression of the Hebrew *zêd*. The primary conception is that of boiling over with insolent wickedness, and so of sins called *presumptuous* in the English translations of xix. 13, exhibiting rampant rebellion against the Divine law. So in verses 51, 69, 78, 85, 122. Attention should have been called to this in xii. 3, xxxi. 23, xl. 4, lxxxvi. 14, xciv. 2, and ci. 5. It explains the extreme severity with which *these* proud ones are denounced. There is a pride exhibited by men which is offensive and evil, but not seriously harmful, and not at all described by this strong word. — **The accursèd.** We follow the Septuagint and Syriac Versions in their different punctuation, transferring this word into the second line of the couplet. For important reasons it is much better.

(25) **As Thy promise assures.** Heb. *according to Thy word.* In this form of expression, which occurs several times in this Psalm, as in fact often elsewhere, God's *word* is spoken of with reference to some special Divine utterance, a promise of help and blessing; so verses 28, 38, 41, 107, 116, 123, etc.

(83) **A wineskin dried up in the smoke.** A leathern bottle no longer used, and hung up, until blackened and shrivelled, and utterly worthless. Oriental dwellings of the ruder sort were without sufficient outlet for the smoke.

(96) **A limit to all perfection.** The Hebrew substantive *qêts* is not always *an end* in time, but is sometimes used of local boundary. The verse exhibits a contrast between the measurable perfection of things that belong to man's earthly existence and needs, and the immeasurable perfection, the surpassing breadth, of the law of God as the expression of His excellency, — between finite and infinite perfection.

CXX.

A CRY OF DISTRESS AGAINST THE CRAFTY AND CONTENTIOUS.

THIS is the first of fifteen Psalms, called in the Rev. Old Test. *Songs of Ascents*, a literal translation from the Hebrew. The most probable account of the name is that it refers to the journey of pilgrims from all parts of Palestine, going up to Jerusalem as required by the law, to celebrate the three sacred feasts.

A SONG OF THE PILGRIMAGES.

1 To Jehovah in my anguish,
   I called, and He answered;
2 " O Jehovah, deliver my soul from the lying lips,
   From the treacherous tongue."

3 What shall He give thee,
     Yea, what more shall He give thee,
   Thou treacherous tongue?
4 The sharp darts of the warrior,
   With hot coals of the broom.

5 Woe unto me, that I sojourn in Meshech,
   That I dwell by the encampments of Kedar;
6 Too long has my soul had her dwelling
   Beside him that hates peace;
7 As for me, I seek peace,
   But they, when I speak, are for war.

(4) **Sharp darts . . . hot coals.** This seems to be an answer to the question in ver. 3, mentioning a punishment suited to the sin. It is true that the evil tongue is itself compared in the Old Test. to a sharp sword (lvii. 5) and to a deadly arrow (Jer. ix. 8), and in the New Test. to a fire (Jas. iii. 6); so that we might find here a further designation of the slanderer, and the question would be unanswered. But the former view is more probable. See lxiv. 4 and cxl. 10, where "burning coals" are part of the punishment upon lying lips. — **The broom.** The roots of the *réthem, the broom-tree* (not the *juniper*), furnish the best wood-coals in the opinion of the Arabs. (Robinson *Bib. Researches,* I. p. 336.) They retain the glow longest, and therefore, along with sharp arrows, are a suitable figure for this connection.

(5) The poet compares his enemies to the savage hordes of the Caucasus or of the Arabian desert. The regions mentioned are so far apart that it would be impossible to dwell in both at the same time. This indicates that the historic conditions that furnished the background of the Psalm have been idealized.

CXXI.

JEHOVAH THY KEEPER.

THIS song is a charming expression of confidence in the unfailing protection of God. The change from the first person to the third, in
passing from ver. 2 to ver. 3, as if some one else were addressing the original speaker, reminds us of the alternation of voices in Ps. xci. But here,
after the change, the third person is maintained throughout. Delitzsch
regards the poet as here speaking to himself, promising himself comfort,
by unfolding the joyful prospects involved in the hope in Jehovah with
which the song begins. But as intended for use by the company of pilgrims, the first two verses may have been sung by one band of singers, and
the remainder by another in response. It would be appropriate for morning or evening worship when they were approaching the mountains of
Jerusalem. See cxxv. 2.

A SONG FOR THE PILGRIMAGES.

1 I lift up mine eyes to the mountains;
   From whence comes my help?
2 From Jehovah is my help,
     The Maker of the heavens and the earth.

3 He will not suffer thy feet to give way;
   He that keeps thee will not slumber;
4 Lo, He that keeps Israel
     Neither slumbers nor sleeps.

5 Jehovah is thy Keeper;
   Jehovah is thy shade on thy right;
6 The sun shall not smite thee by day,
     Nor by night shall the moon.

7 From all evil Jehovah will keep thee,
   Thy soul will He keep;
8 Jehovah will keep thy going and coming,
     Henceforth and forever.

CXXII.

BLESSINGS UPON JERUSALEM.

THERE is good reason for questioning the correctness of the title of this Psalm in ascribing it to David. It seems to be a reminiscence of a visit to the Holy City, probably at the time of one of the great feasts, after it had been restored, and the tribes of Israel again flocked to it for worship. There is every indication that it was intended to be sung by a band of pilgrims on their arrival at Jerusalem and entrance within its gates.

A SONG FOR THE PILGRIMAGES. BY DAVID.

1 I rejoiced when they said,
  " Let us go to the house of Jehovah."
2 Our feet came to stand
  In thy gates, O Jerusalem, —
3 Jerusalem, thou that art builded
  As a city that is compact together ;

4 Whither the tribes journeyed up,
  The tribes of Jehovah, who gave precept to Israel,
    To give thanks to the Name of Jehovah ;
5 For there, thrones of judgment were set,
  The thrones of the lineage of David.

6 Pray for the peace of Jerusalem ;
  They that love thee shall prosper.
7 In thy strongholds, Jerusalem, be peace ;
  In thy castles, prosperity.
8 For the sake of my brethren and companions,
  Let me speak of thy peace.
9 For the sake of the house of Jehovah, our God.
  Will I seek for thy good.

CXXIII.

SCORNED BY MEN, BUT STILL HOPING IN GOD.

A SONG FOR THE PILGRIMAGES.

1 Unto Thee will I lift up mine eyes,
O Thou, that art throned in the heavens;
2 Behold, as the eyes of a servant,
On the hand of his master,
As the eyes of a maid
On the hand of her mistress,
Even so, on Jehovah our God, are our eyes,
Until He shall pity us.

3 Pity us, Jehovah, oh pity us,
For we are filled to the full with contempt;
4 Yea, filled to the full is our soul,
With the scorn of the careless,
The contempt of the proud.

CXXIV.

JEHOVAH ON OUR SIDE AND WE ARE SAFE.

THERE is great beauty here, as in several of these Pilgrim Songs, in
the poet's way of weaving together the several lines or couplets, and
at the same time giving emphasis, by catching up one or more words, for
repetition in new relations.

A SONG FOR THE PILGRIMAGES. BY DAVID.

1 " If Jehovah had not been on our side,"
Let Israel now say,
2 " If Jehovah had not been on our side
When men rose to destroy us,

3 Then alive had they swallowed us up,
  When their anger was kindled against us;
4 Then had the waters overwhelmed us,
  The torrent had gone over our soul;
5 Then had gone over our soul,
        The proud swelling waters.

6 Blessèd be Jehovah,
  Who gave us not up as a prey to their teeth;
7 Our soul like a bird has escaped
        From the snare of the fowler;
  The snare is broken and we have escaped;
8 We have help in the Name of Jehovah,
  The Maker of the heavens and the earth."

CXXV.

JEHOVAH ROUND ABOUT HIS PEOPLE FOREVER.

A SONG FOR THE PILGRIMAGES.

1 Like Mount Zion are they that trust in Jehovah;
  It cannot be shaken, but forever abides.
2 Jerusalem, — mountains surround her,
  And Jehovah surroundeth His people,
        Henceforth and forever.
3 For not on the lot of the righteous
        Shall the sceptre of wickedness rest,
  Lest the righteous stretch forth
        Their hands unto evil.

4 Do good, O Jehovah, to the good,
  To the upright in heart;
5 But those that turn off in their tortuous ways,
        Jehovah thrusts forth
        With the workers of wrong;
  Upon Israel be peace!

CXXVI.

THE HARVEST OF JOY AFTER SOWING IN TEARS.

A SONG FOR THE PILGRIMAGES.

1 When Jehovah returned to the captives of Zion,
    We were like them that dream;
2 Our mouth was then filled with loud laughter,
        Our tongue with glad shouts;
    Then they said in the nations
        " For these the deeds of Jehovah are glorious,"
3 Yea, for us the deeds of Jehovah were glorious;
    We became very glad.

4 Return, O Jehovah, to our captives,
    As the streams in the South;
5 Those sowing in tears,
    Shall reap with glad shouts;
6 One goes forth and may weep all the way,
        Bearing seed for the sowing;
    But he comes all the way with glad shouts,
        For he beareth his sheaves.

CXXVII.

ALL IN VAIN WITHOUT JEHOVAH.

THE sentiment of the Psalm seems to connect it with the rebuilding of
the temple. Professor Cheyne exhibits its scope most satisfactorily :
" The leaders of the renascent Jewish community are like 'builders' and
'watchmen.' They are tempted (like those that take part in more modern
revivals of spiritual life) to overestimate the importance of routine work.
Our poet recalls them to a 'wise passiveness;' this doubtless is what he
means by 'sleep.' To those who cherish this jewel of the soul, God grants
those things for which the worldly wise often toil in vain. For instance,
those for whom the prophet speaks in Isa. xxvi. 18, were uneasy at the

scanty population of Judea. Our poet, in the second half of the psalm,
reminds them that a numerous progeny of sons is a blessing from Jehovah
(comp. Ps. cxxviii.).   Labour as they may, they cannot do as much for the
defence of the state as the ' joyful mother of her sons ' (cxiii. 9)."

A SONG FOR THE PILGRIMAGES. BY SOLOMON.

1 Let Jehovah build the house,
  Or in vain toil its builders;
 Let Jehovah keep watch,
  Or in vain wake the watchmen;
2 And for you it is vain that so early ye rise,
  Going late to your rest,
  And in toil eat your bread;
 For as well while they sleep,
  He gives unto those that He loves.

3 Behold, sons are a gift from Jehovah,
  The fruit of the womb a reward;
4 Like darts in the hand of a warrior,
  Are the sons of one's youth;
5 Happy the man that hath filled his quiver therewith;
 They shall not come to shame,
  When they speak with their foes in the gate.

CXXVIII.

THE HAPPY HOUSEHOLD.

A SONG FOR THE PILGRIMAGES.

1 How happy is he that feareth Jehovah,
  That walks in His ways!
2 For the labour of thy hands thou shalt eat,
  Happy art thou and good shall be thine.

3 Thy wife like a vine with its fruit,
  In the innermost rooms of thy house;
 Thy children like sprouts from the olive,
  Surrounding thy table;

4 Lo, the man is thus blessed,
   That feareth Jehovah.

5 Jehovah send thee blessing from Zion;
   Behold thou Jerusalem's welfare,
      All the days of thy life;
6 Yea, behold thou the children of thy children:
      Peace be upon Israel!

CXXIX.

ISRAEL HARASSED, BUT DELIVERED.

A SONG FOR THE PILGRIMAGES.

1 " From my youth have they greatly oppressed me,"
      Let Israel now say,
2 " From my youth have they greatly oppressed,
   Yet prevailed not against me.

3 The ploughmen have ploughed on my back,
   And made their long furrows;
4 But Jehovah is righteous,
   He sundered the cords of the wicked.
5 Let them all come to shame and confusion,
   That hold Zion in hatred.

6 Let them be like the grass on the housetop,
   That withers when not yet full grown;
7 With which none that reaps fills his hand,
   His bosom no bearer of sheaves ;
8 And they that pass by shall not say,
      ' Jehovah's blessing be upon you;
   In the Name of Jehovah we bless you.' "

CXXX.

DE PROFUNDIS; THE PATIENCE OF HOPE.

A SONG FOR THE PILGRIMAGES.

1 Out of the depths do I cry to Thee, Jehovah;
2 Lord, hear Thou my voice;
Let Thine ear be attent to my loud supplication.

3 If Thou, O Jehovah, keep before Thee our guilt,
Lord, who would be able to stand?
4 But with Thee is forgiveness,
That so men may fear Thee.

5 I look for Jehovah, for Him my soul looks;
In His word do I hope;
6 My soul looks for the Lord,
More than watchmen look for the morning,
More than watchmen for the morning.

7 Be thy hope in Jehovah, O Israel;
For Jehovah has mercy,
And with Him is abundant redemption;
8 He is Israel's Redeemer
From all his iniquitous deeds.

CXXXI.

CHILDLIKE SUBMISSION AND TRUST.

A SONG FOR THE PILGRIMAGES.

1 O Jehovah, my heart is not haughty,
Mine eyes are not lofty;
I do not concern me with matters too great,
And too wonderful for me.

2 Surely I calm and quiet my soul,
  As a child that is weaned by the side of its mother —
      My soul within me, as a child that is weaned.
3 Be thy hope in Jehovah, O Israel,
  Henceforth and forever.

CXXXII.

THE HOUSE OF GOD AND THE THRONE OF DAVID.

THE allusions in this Psalm to David and to the promises God made him are all retrospective, and in view of ver. 10, it could only have been written by some other than himself. But it must belong to a time in which the throne of David was still standing and before the ark was irrecoverably lost. Delitzsch favours the view of De Wette, Tholuck, and others, that it was composed by Solomon when the ark of the covenant was removed into the newly built temple, referring in support of this to the circumstances as related in 2 Chron. v. 5, and to some points of similarity in Ps. lxxii.

1. David's vow (1-5). 2. The ark found, and God's entrance into His temple, and blessing upon His people (6-10). 3. God's oath to David, conditioned on the obedience of his descendants (11, 12). 4. His promise to dwell in Zion, blessing His people, and establishing the throne of David forever (13-18).

A SONG FOR THE PILGRIMAGES.

1 O Jehovah, remember for David
      All that he endured;
2 How he sware to Jehovah,
      To Israel's God made a vow;
3 " Not again will I enter the tent that I dwell in,
  Nor go up to the couch that I lie on;
4 I will not give sleep to mine eyes,
  Nor slumber to mine eyelids,
5 Till I find out a place for Jehovah,
  A house for the Mighty One of Jacob."

6 Lo, it was, so we heard, in Ephratah,
  In the fields of the forest we found it.
7 Let us enter His dwelling,
  Let us bow at His footstool.

8 Arise, O Jehovah, to the place of Thy rest,
 Thou, and the ark of Thy strength.
9 Let Thy priests be in righteousness robed,
 And the men of Thy love shout for joy.
10 For the sake of Thy servant, of David,
 Turn not away Thine anointed one's face.

11 Jehovah has sworn unto David in truth,
  And He will not turn from it;
 "Of the fruit of thy body
  Will I set on thy throne.
12 If thy children will honour My covenant,
  And My laws that I teach them,
 Their children forever
  Shall after thee sit on the throne."
13 For Jehovah made Zion His choice;
 He wished it His dwelling.

14 He said, "This is forever the place of My rest;
 Here will I dwell for I wished it.
15 I will abundantly bless her provision,
 And her poor fully furnish with bread;
16 Her priests will I clothe with salvation,
 And her loved ones shall joyfully shout;
17 There a horn unto David I cause to shoot forth,
 And prepare Mine anointed a lamp;
18 I will put on his enemies clothing of shame,
 But on him shall his diadem flourish."

CXXXIII.

GRACIOUS FELLOWSHIP.

"IN this Psalm David brings to the consciousness of the Church the glory of the long-lacked fellowship of the saints, the restoration of which had begun with the setting up of the ark in Zion." — *Hengstenberg.*

A SONG FOR THE PILGRIMAGES.

1 Behold how goodly and pleasant it is,
    That brethren in unity dwell.
2 Like the goodly oil on the head,
        Flowing down on the beard,
    On the beard of Aaron,
        Flowing down on the skirt of his robes;
3 Like the dew of Mount Hermon,
        That descends on the mountains of Zion;
    For there has Jehovah commanded His blessing,
        Even life evermore.

CXXXIV.

A HOLY GREETING AND ITS ECHO.

THE greeting in verses 1 and 2 is probably by the congregation of Israel to the priests and Levites who had charge of the temple at night (1 Chron. ix. 33). The response in ver. 3 is a form of priestly benediction, which has its counterpart in cxxviii. 5, "Jehovah send thee blessing from Zion," and its root in Num. vi. 24, "Jehovah bless thee, and keep thee." It is addressed to the church, and to every individual enrolled in it, and thus forms a suitable conclusion for the whole collection of Pilgrim Songs.

A SONG FOR THE PILGRIMAGES.

1 Behold, bless ye Jehovah,
        All ye servants of Jehovah.
    Ye that stand by night in the house of Jehovah.
2 To the holy place, lift up your hands,
        And bless ye Jehovah.

3 Jehovah, who created the heavens and the earth,
        Out of Zion send thee blessing.

CXXXV.

JEHOVAH, THE GOD OF ISRAEL, THE TRUE GOD.

THIS Psalm is among the latest.   It is almost wholly made up of passages from the Psalms, with extracts from the Law and the Prophets.
Delitzsch compares it to a piece of mosaic, resembling in this respect Psalms
xcvii. and xcviii., although its material is gathered from other sources.

It contains thrice seven verses : —
In the first seven : *1. Calls to praise Jehovah* (1–3). *2. The reasons given* (4–7).
In the second seven : *1. Wonders in Egypt* (8, 9).   *2. Conquest of nations*
(10–12). *3. God's kindness to His people* (13, 14).
In the third seven : *1. The impotence of idols* (15–18). *2. God's servants called
upon to bless Him* (19–21).

1 PRAISE YE JEHOVAH!
        To the Name of Jehovah give praise ;
    Praise Him ye servants of Jehovah,
2 That stand in the house of Jehovah,
    In the courts of the house of our God.
3 Praise ye Jehovah, for Jehovah is good,
    Strike the harp to His Name ; it is gracious.
4 For Jehovah chose Zion for Himself,
    And Israel to be His possession.

5 For I know that Jehovah is great,
    That our Lord is above all the gods ;
6 Whatsoever He pleases, He does,
    In the heavens and the earth,
        And in all the deep gulfs ;
7 He makes vapours ascend from the bounds of the earth ;
    For the rain He makes lightnings,
        And the wind He brings forth from His storehouse.

8 It is He that smote down all the firstborn of Egypt,
        From the man to the beast ;
9 Into the midst of thee, Egypt,
        He sent tokens and wonders,
    Upon Pharaoh and all those that served him ;

    10 Who smote many nations,
           And slew mighty kings;
    11 With Sihon, the Amorite's king,
           And Og, king of Bashan,
         All the kingdoms of Canaan;
    12 And their land He bestowed for possession,
           A possession for Israel His people.
    13 O Jehovah, Thy Name shall endure evermore,
           Thy Memorial, Jehovah, to all generations;
    14 For Jehovah awards right to His people,
           And relents over His servants.
    15 The idols of the nations are silver and gold,
           The work of men's hands;
    16 They have mouths, but they speak not,
           They have eyes, but they see not;
    17 They have ears, but they hear not,
           And they have no breath in their mouth;
    18 They that make, become like them,
           Even so all that trust them.

    19 House of Israel, bless ye Jehovah,
           House of Aaron, bless ye Jehovah;
    20 House of Levi, bless ye Jehovah,
           Bless ye Jehovah, ye servants of Jehovah;
    21 Blessèd be Jehovah out of Zion,
           He that dwells at Jerusalem;
               PRAISE YE JEHOVAH!

CXXXVI.

GIVE THANKS TO JEHOVAH.

HERE *Hhōdū* (*give thanks*) occurs in the first line of each of the first three verses, after which the Psalm recites the wonders of God's grace to Israel in twenty-three verses, which are attached to the Divine Name Jehovah at the beginning, by the relative pronoun, so in fact making a single complete sentence of the whole. In every one of these twenty-six couplets, the second line is a refrain like the responses in the Litany, "For His kindness endureth forever."

In Jewish liturgical use it is called the "Great Hallel," although this term is sometimes used more broadly of the whole group cxx.–cxxxvi. See at Ps. cxx.

1 Give thanks to Jehovah, for He is good,
For His kindness endureth forever ;
2 To the God of gods give ye thanks,
For His kindness endureth forever;
3 To the Lord of lords give ye thanks,
For His kindness endureth forever.

4 Who alone does great wonders,
For His kindness endureth forever ;
5 Who by wisdom made the heavens,
For His kindness endureth forever ;
6 Who spread out the earth on the waters,
For His kindness endureth forever.

7 Who made the great lights,
For His kindness endureth forever ;
8 The sun to rule the day,
For His kindness endureth forever;
9 The moon and stars to rule the night,
For His kindness endureth forever.

10 Who smote down the firstborn of Egypt,
For His kindness endureth forever ;
11 Who brought Israel forth from the midst,
For His kindness endureth forever;
12 His hand in full strength and His arm far extended,
For His kindness endureth forever.

13 Who cut the Red Sea into parts,
For His kindness endureth forever;
14 And made Israel to pass through the midst,
For His kindness endureth forever ;
15 But Pharaoh and his host he overthrew in the sea,
For His kindness endureth forever.

16 Who led forward His people in the desert,
    For His kindness endureth forever ;
17 Who smote mighty kings,
    For His kindness endureth forever;
18 And slew kings of renown,
    For His kindness endureth forever.

19 Sihon, the Amorites' king,
    For His kindness endureth forever;
20 And Og, king of Bashan,
    For His kindness endureth forever;
21 And gave up their land for possession,
    For His kindness endureth forever;
22 For a possession to Israel, His servant,
    For His kindness endureth forever.

23 Who bare us in mind in our lowly estate,
    For His kindness endureth forever;
24 And let us break away from our foes,
    For His kindness endureth forever;
25 Who gives food to all flesh,
    For His kindness endureth forever;
26 To the God of high heaven give thanks,
    For His kindness endureth forever.

CXXXVII.

THE RIVERS OF BABYLON.

AFTER the Psalms of praise and thanksgiving, we have a subdued and
plaintive melody relating to the time when Zion lay in ruins, and the
cheerful songs of the Levite choir were hushed. It is the reminiscence of
one who had recently returned from the captivity, recalling the taunts of the
oppressor. It is beautiful in expression, and although tender and elegiac,
especially at the opening, is spirited and pictorial, and becomes at last
almost terrible. See Introductory Essay, page xvi.

1 By the rivers of Babylon, there we sat down,
  Yea, we wept, remembering Zion;
2 On the willows in the midst thereof,
    We hanged up our harps.

3 For our captors there asked for the words of a song,
    Our tormentors asked gladness;
  They said, " Sing us songs of Mount Zion."

4 How can we sing the songs of Jehovah,
    On the soil of the alien?
5 If I ever forget thee, Jerusalem,
    Let forgetfulness seize my right hand,
6 And my tongue, let it cleave to the roof of my mouth,
  If I choose not Jerusalem above my chief joy.

7 Remember, Jehovah, to the children of Edom,
    The day at Jerusalem,
  When they cried, " Lay it bare, lay it bare,
    Even down to its base."

8 O daughter of Babylon, doomed to destruction,
  Blest is he that requites thee,
    That does unto thee as thou didst unto us;
9 Blest is he that shall seize and dash down
    Thy babes on a rock.

CXXXVIII.

THE FAITHFUL AND GRACIOUS JEHOVAH, TO BE PRAISED AND TRUSTED FOREVER.

IN the opinion of Delitzsch and others, although this Psalm is ascribed to David in the title, he is not its author in any direct sense. Yet it is closely related to 2 Sam. vii. and, in its sentiment and expression, one that he might have written when he gave God the glory of all his deliverances and successes, and resolved to build a temple to His holy Name. There seems to be no sufficient reason for questioning that David wrote it.

*1. Thanksgiving to Jehovah for special favour and help in great need (1-3).
2. Prediction that all kings will worship and serve Him (4-6). 3. Confident hope
for all the future (7, 8).*

BY DAVID.

1 With all my heart do I thank Thee,
  And confronting the gods unto Thee strike the harp;
2 Toward Thy holy palace bowing down,
    I give thanks to Thy Name,
      Because of Thy kindness and truth;
  For above all Thy Name, Thou exaltest Thy word.
3 In the day that I called didst Thou answer,
  And with strength in my soul mad'st me bold.

4 All the kings of the earth, O Jehovah, will thank Thee,   ·
  On hearing the words of Thy mouth;
5 They will sing of the works of Jehovah,
  For the glory of Jehovah is great.
6 For Jehovah is high, yet He looks on the lowly,
  But the proud He knows afar off.
7 If I walk amidst trouble, Thou wilt hold me in life,
  Against the wrath of my foes wilt put forth Thy hand,
    And Thy right hand will save me.

8 Jehovah will perfect His work,
    In all that concerns me;
  O Jehovah, Thy kindness endureth forever,
    Forsake not the work of Thy hands.

CXXXIX.

JEHOVAH IS OMNISCIENT AND PRESENT EVERYWHERE.

THIS Psalm abounds in Aramaic expressions. But for the title probably no one would have supposed David its author. Its profound and
sustained philosophic thought, too, have hardly a parallel in the recognized
Psalms of David. Yet on either ground it cannot be pronounced impossible that he should have written it. We can only say that it is apparently
the product of a later age.

Whoever the author, the Psalm is a magnificent exhibition of the perfections of Jehovah in relation to men. It is not speculative, but eminently

practical in its bearing on the life and responsibilities of man. "In loftiness of thought and expressive beauty of language, the Psalm stands preeminent, and it is not surprising that Aben-Ezra should have pronounced it to be 'the crown of all the Psalms.'"— *Perowne.*

1. The omniscience of God (1–6). 2. His omnipresence (7–12). 3. The grounds of this profound conviction in the poet's personal experience, observation, and reflection (13–18). 4. His abhorrence of the wicked, with an earnest prayer for a right heart, and for Divine guidance in the way everlasting (19–24).

FOR THE LEADER OF THE CHOIR. BY DAVID. A PSALM.

1 O Jehovah, Thou hast searched me and knowest —
2 Thou knowest my sitting and rising,
    Thou discernest my thought afar off;
3 Thou hast winnowed my path and my couch,
    And with all my ways hast Thou made Thee acquainted.
4 For a word is not yet on my tongue,
    When, behold, Jehovah, Thou knowest it all.
5 Behind and before Thou art close round about me,
    And down over me puttest Thy hand.
6 Too great is this knowledge, too wonderful for me,
    So high that I cannot attain it.

7 Whither shall I go from Thy Spirit?
    Or whither shall I flee from Thy presence?
8 If I ascend into heaven, Thou art there;
    If I lie down in Sheol, behold, Thou art there.
9 If I lift up the wings of the dawn,
    And alight at the sea's utmost bound,
10 Even there would Thy hand be my guide,
    And Thy right hand would grasp me.
11 If I say, "Let only the darkness enwrap me,
    And the light round about me be night;"
12 Not too dark is the darkness for Thee,
    But the night shines as clear as the day;
        The darkness and light are alike.

13 For Thou didst create mine innermost being,
    And weave me together before I was born.
14 I am fearfully distinguished, and thank Thee;
    That Thy working is wondrous, my soul knows right well.

15 From Thee was my frame not concealed,
     When fashioned in secret,
   I was skilfully wrought in the depths of the earth.
16 Though imperfect my substance, Thine eye was upon me;
     In Thy book were all written,
   Days already shaped out, when not one had yet come.
17 How precious are Thy thoughts to me, O God,
   And how vast is their sum.
18 When I count them, they are more than the sand;
   I awake, and I still am with Thee.

19 The wicked, if Thou only wouldst slay them, O God;
   Men guilty of bloodshed, oh, leave me!—
20 Who profane Thy Name in their plotting,
   It is taken in vain by Thy foes.
21 O God, do I not hate those that hate Thee,
   And abhor those that rise up against Thee?
22 With perfect hatred do I hate them;
   I count Thine enemies mine.

23 Search me, O God, and know Thou my heart,
   Prove me, and know Thou the thoughts that distract me;
24 And see if Thou find there ways ending in sorrow,
   And lead me in the way everlasting.

The opening verses assert the most comprehensive and exact knowledge of the individual man in all the conditions and activities of his outer and inner life.

(3) **Thou hast winnowed my path and my couch.** Heb. *Thou hast sifted my path and my lair;* as if every particle of material, on which he treads by day, or has lain through the night, were subjected to the most searching scrutiny. Perchance it may have received some impression by which his character and life may be more thoroughly known.

(5) **Thou** art close round about me. Heb. *tsartani* from *tsûr, to press upon;* generally used in a hostile sense; but the context before and after shows that it is here to be understood only of such pressure as brings God into immediate contact with him at every point, as closely as the atmosphere which so presses the whole surface of his body; yet not in the way of hostile and painful besetment and restriction. Also, *the putting the hand upon* is here not punitive or afflictive, as in Job xxxviii. 7, but describes the close investment as being also from above; every point at all times touched, felt, and perfectly known by the omnipresent and all-pervading God. "In Him we live, and move, and have our being."

(8) **Heaven** and **Sheol** here represent only the highest and lowest points conceivable. God is everywhere.

(9) **The wings of the dawn.** The earliest rays of the sun; as if on these he were borne westward with the speed of light to the extreme limits of space beyond the Great Sea.

(13) **Mine innermost being.** Heb. *my reins, kidneys;* regarded in the Semitic psychology, as the seat of the desires, affections, and all the deeper emotions that distinguish man's spiritual nature. See note on xvi. 8, "*My longings.*" The interior parts of the body represent the points through which, in one direction, the immortal spirit was supposed to express itself outwardly, and in the opposite direction, to be wrought upon by the Spirit of God. This reference lifts the whole following description above any gross material conceptions, as if the Psalmist were glorifying the wisdom and power of God, as exhibited in his physical constitution. It is not in the possession of a skilfully wrought body, with members adapted to his life on the earth, that man is "fearfully distinguished." The man and the beast are alike in having the heart, the reins, and all other material organs, performing their several functions with admirable perfection and fidelity. But this is the marvel of God's workmanship and the chief glory of man, that his perishable body is the seat and throne of spiritual and Divine endowments, and that the two diverse elements in his nature are woven together as one.

There is wrapped up in the embryonic condition of man, not merely a body to be developed into wondrous symmetry, strength, and adaptation to temporary purposes, but an eternity of thought, feeling, fellowship with God, and spiritual activity and enjoyment. It is a fine thought of Hupfeld, that the "imperfect substance" (Heb. *a rolled up mass,* ver. 16), "is the yet undeveloped course of life, the days of which, in their continuity, are the thread, rolled up as in a ball, which is unwound as life goes on." Yet it is not his own thought, but that suggested by the most literal translation of the words of the Hebrew poet.

CXL.

PRAYER FOR PROTECTION FROM THE MALIGNANT AND CRAFTY.

THERE is much in the style and language of this to confirm its ascription to David, and nothing to the contrary. It finds a suitable historic background in the rebellion under Absalom, and bears a strong resemblance to Psalms lviii. and lxiv., which belong to that time.

FOR THE LEADER OF THE CHOIR. A PSALM OF DAVID.

1 Deliver me, Jehovah, from the wicked,
Preserve me from men of foul deeds;
2 Who plan evil deeds in their heart,
And daily excite wars.

3 They sharpen their tongue like a serpent,
And have in their lips the poison of adders.   [Selah.]

4 Keep me, Jehovah, from the hands of the wicked,
    Preserve me from men of foul deeds,
Who think from my footing to thrust me;
5 For the proud have hid for me nooses and snares,
By my path they spread nets and set traps.   [Selah.]

6 I say to Jehovah, " Thou art my God,
Give ear to my suppliant cry;
7 Jehovah, O Lord, the stronghold that saves me,
In the day of the battle Thou protectest my head.
8 Grant not, Jehovah, the desires of the wicked;
Let their plots come to nought,
    That they be not exalted."   [Selah.]

9 The head of my assailants,
    Let the ill of their lips overwhelm;
10 Let hot coals come quivering against them;
    Into the fire be they hurled,
Into gulfs whence they cannot arise.
11 Let not the slanderer stand fast in the land;
And the men of foul deeds,
    Let evil hunt down to their ruin.

12 I know that Jehovah upholds the sufferers' cause,
The right of the lowly;
13 The righteous shall surely give thanks to Thy Name,
The upright shall dwell in Thy presence.

CXLI.

EVENING SONG IN THE TIME OF ABSALOM.

THIS Psalm, like the last, is best explained by David's persecution during Absalom's rebellion. It was used by the ancient church as the evening Psalm, as Psalm lxiii. was the morning Psalm.

A PSALM OF DAVID.

1 Unto Thee do I call; O Jehovah, come to me quickly;
  When I call Thee, give ear to my voice.

2 Let my prayer come as incense before Thee,
  My hands lifted high as the evening oblation.

3 Set a watch, O Jehovah, on my mouth,
  A guard at the door of my lips;

4 Incline not my heart to any thing evil,
    To practise foul deeds of injustice
      With men busy in wrong;
  And let me not feed on their dainties.

5 "Let a righteous man smite me," in derision they say;
    "Let him kindly correct me;
    Such oil for my head, let my head not refuse;"
  But e'en yet, (and while they do wickedly, this is my prayer,)

6 When their judges are hurled down the sides of the cliff,
  They will hear my words, for they are gracious.

7 As one ploughing and cleaving the soil,
  They have scattered our bones,
    At the mouth of the pit.

8 But to Thee are my eyes, O Jehovah the Lord;
  In Thee do I hide;
    O yield not my soul unto death.

9 Keep me safe from the snare they have laid,
  From the traps of those busy in wrong;

10 Let the wicked fall down in their net,
  So that I thereupon may escape.

(5, 6) By common consent the Psalms contain no passage more difficult than this. Prof. Cheyne pronounces it "hopeless in the present state of the Hebrew text." He says, "the most plausible way out of the difficulty is Bickell's. But it is bold in the extreme. This is his rendering of the corrected text: 'For while my prayer rose at their wicked deeds, down from the crag were hurled their rulers, and the pious heard (concerning) my words that they had been pleasant in the ears of Jehovah.' He finds in this an allusion to some unknown event which the Psalmist regarded as a Divine interposition in answer to prayer." This being all that the most advanced textual criticism can do for us, it may be well to enquire whether nothing more can be accomplished by exegesis.

The whole difficulty does not lie in the parts of these verses that are condemned as corrupted and impracticable, but extends equally to the former part of ver. 5, which is accepted as sound. Perhaps complete relief may result from leaving out of view all that follows, and pressing to an answer a question which does not seem hitherto to have been asked: What motive can be discovered in the scope or context for a reference to personal ill-doing, and the smiting of the righteous? An answer may be obtained by weighing supposable hypotheses.

One of these is that the poet, expressing in ver. 4 his horror at surrounding wickedness, and praying to be kept from it, contemplates nevertheless a possibility that he may be led into sin, and further, that some good man may rebuke him, and declares that he will welcome such rebuke as a kindness. But, where present trouble and need were so absorbing, the introduction of thoughts so far removed from the actual is highly improbable.

The occasion and scope of the Psalm suggest another possibility. It may be supposed that the poet, shocked by what he saw and heard, had remonstrated with the evil-doers, but his words had been unheeded or resented; and that thereupon he declares how differently he would himself have acted under like circumstances. But however probable such rebukes, this meaning must have been indicated by some contrastive allusion, if only by emphasis on a pronoun, implying that their spirit was different from his own.

Looking at the context we find a clue to something more satisfactory at the close of ver. 6: "They will

hear my words, for they are gracious." The verb is in the perfect tense, but surely it is the well-known predictive future. As often elsewhere, future events are seen with prophetic certainty as accomplished facts. See xxxvi. 13. This suggests a contrast in the mind of the poet between a *hereafter*, when, judgment having fallen upon the wicked rulers, the mass of the people shall return to their right mind, and receive meekly his gracious admonitions, and the *present*, in which they mock at his counsel, and will none of his reproof.

This illuminates the whole passage. For it indicates that we are to find the *protasis* in this contrast in ver. 5, as containing not his own words, but the derisive reply of the wicked to his earnest protest against their wickedness: "Let a righteous man smite me," etc. A precisely similar case occurs in xxii. 8, where as here, the explicative "*they say*" is wanting before the jeering words addressed to the sufferer. Also in ii. 3, there is no word to indicate that the cry "Let us tear off their fetters, and their bonds cast away" is from the conspirators, and not from the poet. So lix. 7, and for similar omission before a Divine utterance, cv. 15. Everything now falls into place in the phrase,

$$\text{כִּי־עוֹד וְהִפַּלְתִּי בְּרָעֹתֵיהֶם :}$$

ki (כִּי) is for *ki 'im* (כִּי אִם), *but ;* as often after a negative clause, whether expressed or implied. For the latter see xliv. 22, xlix 10, cxxx. 4.

The particle *'od* (עוֹד), *yet*, carries the mind forward to ver. 6, "they will hear my words," and is nearly equivalent to *hereafter*, as in xlii. 5, xliii. 5, "I shall *yet* praise Him;" Hab. ii. 3, "The vision is *yet* for an appointed time."

The conjunctive *and* (ו) connects his prayer, continuing through "their wickedness," with that future, as the consummation of his desire.

The prep. *in* (ב) is temporal, *in the*

time of, and the following verbs describe the overthrow of the rulers who have personally and officially encouraged and maintained the worst practices, as an accomplished fact, which shall result in the recovery of the people from their folly. " Down by the sides of the cliff " may be an allusion to an ancient mode of punishment, by casting a criminal from a precipice. But more probably it has reference to their exalted position in which they imagine themselves safe. Throughout the Psalms a *cliff* (סֶלַע, *séla*) is a symbol of elevation and security. Here the Rev.

Vers. has, " For even in their wickedness shall my prayer continue. Their judges are thrown down by the sides of the rock ; and they shall hear my words, for they are sweet : " with the marg. or, *For still is my prayer against their wickedness.* As to the former, "*even*" is an inadequate translation of '*ōd* (עוֹד); and in the latter, "prayer *against*" would certainly not be expressed so weakly as by the prep. *beth* (בְּ) *in.* We should have at least '*al* (עַל), *upon, concerning,* and after verbs that involve the idea of opposition, *against.*

CXLII.

A LATER CRY FROM THE CAVE.

IT is impossible to determine whether the cave referred to in the title is the cave of Adullam, connecting the Psalm with 1 Sam. xxii., or the cave of Engedi, with its dark passages and chambers, mentioned in 1 Sam. xxiv. Probably like Ps. lvii. it is connected with the latter.

1. Petition (1, 2). 2. Description of distress (3, 4). 3. Entreaty for deliverance (5-7).

MASKIL. A PRAYER OF DAVID WHEN HE WAS IN THE CAVE.

1 With loud voice I cry to Jehovah,
  With loud voice to Jehovah I make supplication.
2 Before Him I pour out my plaint,
  I spread my sore trouble before Him.

3 When my spirit is fainting within me,
    Unto Thee my path is well known ;
  In the way that I go, they hid snares to entrap me.

4 O look to the right hand and see,
    There is none that regards me ;
  Refuge has failed me,
    There is no man that cares for my soul.

5 Unto Thee, O Jehovah, I cry,
      I say, "Thou art my refuge,
         In the land of the living, my portion."

6 Oh, heed Thou my wailing,
         For I am weak, very weak;
      Deliver me from all my pursuers,
         For they are stronger than I.

7 Bring my soul out of prison,
         To give thanks to Thy Name;
      And in me the righteous shall glory,
         That Thou hast dealt graciously with me.

CXLIII.

THIS Psalm has the same reference to Absalom's persecution as the two preceding. Its prevailing tone is that of despondency, connected with a deep consciousness of sin, which distinguishes the Psalms of this period from those that had their origin in David's persecution by Saul, and on this account it was chosen as the last of the seven Penitential Psalms.

1. Complaint (1-6). 2. Prayer founded upon the complaint (7-12).

A PSALM OF DAVID.

1 Hear my prayer, O Jehovah;
      Give ear to my suppliant cry;
   In Thy faithfulness answer,
      And thus be Thy righteousness shown;
2 And bring not Thy servant before Thee in judgment,
   For no living man can be just in Thy sight.
3 For the enemy pursuing my soul,
      And crushing my life to the earth,
   Has made me to dwell in dark places,
      Like the dead of the far away time.
4 Therefore my spirit within becomes faint,
   Yea, deep within me my heart is benumbed.

5 The days of old I remember,
        I ponder on all Thou hast done,
    The work of Thy power I consider.
6 Unto Thee I stretch forth my hands;
    Like thirsty land my soul turns to Thee.
7 Answer me speedily, Jehovah,
        For my spirit is failing;
    Oh, hide Thou not from me Thy face,
        Lest I be like those that go down to the pit.
8 Thine own lovingkindness may I hear at the dawn,
        For in Thee do I trust;
    Let me know the way in which I should walk,
        For to Thee do I lift up my soul.
9 Give me escape from my foes, O Jehovah,
    For in Thee do I hide.

10 The doing Thy will, wilt Thou teach me,
        For Thou art my God;
    Thy good Spirit, in an even path let Him lead me.
11 For Thy Name's sake, Jehovah, let me live;
    In Thy justice deliver my soul from sore pressure;
12 And in Thy lovingkindness bring death to my foes;
    Those oppressing my soul, let them all be destroyed,
        For I am Thy servant.

CXLIV.

SEEKING HELP BEFORE BATTLE.

THIS Psalm, to the close of ver. 11, is made up of the fragments of other
Psalms. Most frequently it borrows from Ps. xviii. It is probable
that it can only be called David's, as culled from his writings. This would
be more likely to be done by another than by himself. The sections after
ver. 11 are very different in thought, language, and style, and attached very
singularly and inexplicably by the relative pronoun or conjunction, *'asher*,
followed by a series of participles. It is thought by some to be part of
another Psalm, of which nothing is known.

1. *A king praises* God for past help, especially in view of man's feeble and perishing nature **(1-4)**. **2.** He prays for victory over powerful and treacherous enemies **(5-8)**. **3.** *He promises* thankful songs in remembrance **of God's** glorious dealings with David, *repeating the previous* description of *his enemies as a refrain* (9-11). **4.** The *prosperity of a people whose* God is Jehovah **(12-15)**.

BY DAVID.

1 Blessèd be Jehovah, my rock,
    Who traineth my hands for the battle,
  My fingers for war;
2 Who deals with me kindly, and gives me protection,
    My tower and deliverer;
  He is my shield and in Him I take refuge,
    Who subdues my people to my rule.
3 What is man, O Jehovah, that for him Thou shouldst care,
  The son of a mortal to be heeded by THEE?
4 As for man he is like breath,
  His days are a shadow that passes.

5 Bow Thy heavens, Jehovah, and come down,
  Touch the mountains that they smoke.
6 Flash out lightnings and disperse them,
  Shoot Thine arrows and confound them.
7 Snatch and deliver me out of great waters,
    From the hand of the alien;
8 Whose mouth speaketh lies,
  And their right hand is falsehood.

9 I will sing a new song to Thee, O God;
  Unto Thee will I play on a harp of ten strings;
10 Who givest deliverance to kings,
  And David Thy servant didst snatch
    From the death-dealing sword.
11 Oh, snatch me and deliver,
    From the hand of the alien,
  Whose mouth speaketh lies,
    And their right hand is falsehood.

12 When our sons are like trees
    Grown great in their youth;

> Our daughters, the embellished cornices
>> Wrought for a palace;
> 13 Our garners are full,
>> Having store of all kinds;
> Our flocks in our pastures,
>> Bearing thousands, yea, myriads;
> 14 Our oxen increase;
>> And no breach, and no exile,
> And no cry of want in our streets.
> 15 How blest is the people with whom it is thus!
> How blest is the people whose God is Jehovah!

(8) **Their right hand is false-hood.** The right hand, as elsewhere, is power in its greatest activity. In the Hebrew there is an emphatic repetition: "their right hand is a right hand of falsehood." Every activity is possessed, directed, and controlled by falsehood as the spirit that inspires it, the opposite of the description in Ps. xv. 2: "the thought of whose heart is the truth." This occurs again in ver. 11.

(12–15) **When our sons, etc.** The different key in this and the following verses does not necessarily indicate that this is a fragment from an unknown Psalm, which has become attached to this one in some inexplicable way. Such contrasts occur often, and are most artistic and effective. A "radiation of gloom" persistent and sustained to the end, like that in Ps. lxxxviii., is very rare. As another example of the opposite, notice the sudden transition from the wailing cry of a sufferer to the glad shout, "Thou hast answered my prayer," in Ps. xxii., in the middle of verse 21, and continuing in the same key of exultation from that point to the close. See also the closing paragraph in notes to Ps. xxxvi., where the same theory of the accidental coherence of parts of different Psalms has been projected. Among various opinions about the connection, that expressed in the Revised Version seems most probable, *at what time*, or *when*, as *asher* in cxxxix. 15: 1 Kings viii. 9, etc. It does not elsewhere occur in this sense except with the praeter, but there is nothing to forbid the use of the participle where the writer is referring not to an act, but to a settled condition of affairs. He here exhibits the result in the future of the Divine aid and blessing so fervently implored.

(12) **As trees.** Heb. *as plants;* that is, *things planted* of whatever kind, and not limited to the smaller vegetation. The participle *grown great* shows that *young trees* are intended. — **The embellished cornices wrought in a palace.** Heb. *k'zāviyyōth m'hhuttābōth tabuith hēkāl.* It is difficult to identify the precise meaning of the two leading words. The former of them is used in O. T. only of the *corners* of the altar in Zech. ix. 15. The following word occurs elsewhere only at Prov. vii. 16, of the decoration of a bed with *variegated cloths* from Egypt. Its verb-root is used only of cutting sticks for firewood, and never of carving or sculpture. The thought of *carved pillars* or sculptured female forms on the exterior of a building, supporting the entablature, is abandoned as a myth. Everything here points to female shapeliness of form, as enhanced by the use of stuffs of beautiful colours, like

the hangings and other tasteful ornamentation of a palace. The word *tabnîth*, the third in the clause, from *bānāh*, *to build*, is the architectural *plan* or *pattern*, including all details of arrangement and decoration, as in Ex. xxv. 9, 40. As so followed, the leading noun seems to mean some ornamental feature of a palace in which the skill of the architect and decorator are combined. It could scarcely refer to *projecting* corners, boldly challenging admiration; rather, *retreating* corners, in the remote angles of the room, as more suitable to the graceful modesty of Oriental maidens. The only question remaining is, whether in palace-building these were distinguished by any special features of beauty. The answer lies in the cornice with which the corners in a large reception-room were filled. So Dr. J. G. Wetzstein in Delitzsch: "Cornices with variegated carved work are found even in the present day in the reception-room of all handsome houses in Damascus (comp. Lane, *Manners and Customs of the Modern Egyptians*, vol. i. p. 37). An architectural ornament made up with much good taste and laborious art of wood-carvings, and glittering in gold and brilliant colours, covers the upper part of the corners, of which a *ka'a* may have as many as sixteen, since three wings may abut upon the square with the marble basin. This decoration, which produces an exceedingly pleasing effect upon the eye, sets off to great advantage rooms that are from two to three stories high, and is evidently meant to lighten up the darker angles near the ceiling for the length of from six to nine feet, gradually becoming narrower as it descends. It is broadest above, so that there it also covers the horizontal corners formed by the walls and the ceiling. If we might assume that this crowning of the corners goes back into Biblical antiquity, then the Psalmist would have used them (the corners) as a simile to mark the beauty, the gorgeous dress, and the rich jewelry of the women; perhaps also because they are not only modest and chaste (comp. the Arabic *mesturat*, a veiled woman, in opposition to *mesmusat*, one shone on by the sun), but because, like the children of respectable families, they are hidden from the eyes of strangers, — for an Arabic proverb says, 'Treasures are hidden in corners;' and the superscription to a woman of position runs, 'May it kiss the hands of the guarded lady and the hidden jewel.'"

(14) **And no breach.** That is, no breach of the walls, and consequent capture by an invading army. —**No exile.** Heb. *no goings forth;* captivity following upon surrender. See Ezek. xii. 4: "Thou shalt go forth at even in their sight, as they that go forth into captivity."

CXLV.

PRAISE TO THE ALL BOUNTIFUL KING.

THIS is the last of the Alphabetical Psalms. Each verse begins with a letter of the Hebrew alphabet, *nun* only being omitted. It is the only Psalm that has *t'hillāh, praise,* in its title, and this is its keynote. It has great breadth, extolling the goodness of God to every living thing. It was used in the ancient Church at the mid-day meal, and ver. 15 at the Passover.

A SONG OF PRAISE. BY DAVID.

1 My God, O King, I will extol Thee,
  And forever and alway Thy Name will I bless.
2 Every day will I bless Thee,
  And forever and alway Thy Name will I praise.
3 Jehovah is great, and most worthy of praise,
  There is no searching out of His greatness.
4 One generation shall praise to another Thy works,
  Shall declare Thy mighty achievements.
5 Thy majesty glorious in splendour,
  And Thy wonderful works will I sing;
6 That others may publish the might of Thy terrible acts,
  I will tell of Thy greatness.
7 They will pour forth the fame of Thy goodness abundant,
  And Thy righteousness joyfully sing.

8 Jehovah is gracious, of tender compassion,
  Slow to anger, and of great lovingkindness;
9 Jehovah is good unto all,
   Over all His works His compassions abound.
10 All Thy works, O Jehovah, give Thee thanks,
   And those whom Thou lovest adore Thee;
11 They tell of the glory of Thy kingdom,
   And speak of Thy power,
12 To make known to the children of men
         His mighty achievements,
   And the glorious splendour of His kingdom.
13 Thy kingdom is a kingdom everlasting,
   Thy dominion endures throughout all generations.
14 Jehovah upholds all that fall,
   And all the bowed down He lifts up.

15 The eyes of all are looking to Thee,
   And Thou givest them food in due season;

16 Thou openest Thy hand,
   To fill the desire of all things that live.
17 In all His ways Jehovah is righteous,
   And in all His works He is gracious.
18 Jehovah is gracious to all that invoke Him,
   To all that invoke Him in truth;
19 He fulfils the desire of those that revere Him,
   He hears their cry and will save them.
20 Jehovah preserves all that love Him,
   All the wicked He destroys.
21 Let my mouth proclaim the praise of Jehovah,
   And His holy Name let mortals all bless,
         Forever and alway.

CXLVI.

HALLELUJAH TO THE ONE TRUE HELPER.

THE opening and the close connect this with the Hallelujah Psalms,
cxi. and after.   In the Liturgy of the second temple, Psalms cxlvi.-
cxlix. formed a special *Hallel*, which is referred to the Prophets Haggai
and Zechariah.   It describes a depressed condition of the people, and its
language, style, and scope connect it with the period after the exile.

*1. A warning against trusting in princes (1-4).   2. Jehovah, the God of Israel,
exhibited as the Almighty Creator, the Judge and Deliverer of the helpless, and the
Eternal King (5-10).*

1 PRAISE YE JEHOVAH!
  Praise Jehovah my soul;
2 O Jehovah, while I live will I praise Thee;
  Melodious strains will I raise to my God,
        While my being endures.
3 Trust not in princes,
  In the earthborn from whom no salvation can come.
4 When his breath goes forth, he returns to his earth;
  In that very day his devices all perish.

5 How blest is the man that has Jacob's God for his help,
    And that hopes in Jehovah, his God;
6 In the Maker of the heavens and the earth,
        Of the sea and all that is in them,
    Who forever keeps truth;
7 Who redresses the oppressed,
        And deals bread to the hungry;
    Jehovah looses the bound;
8 Jehovah opens the eyes of the blind;
        Jehovah cheers the depressed;
    Jehovah loveth the righteous;
9 Jehovah preserveth the stranger,
        Sustaineth the orphan and widow,
    But the way of the wicked overturns.
10 Jehovah forever shall reign,
    Thy God, O Zion, to all generations;
        PRAISE YE JEHOVAH!

CXLVII.

JEHOVAH THE BUILDER OF JERUSALEM.

IT can scarcely be doubted that this Psalm has special reference to the restoration of Jerusalem after the captivity in Babylon, and it was probably used at the celebration of that joyful event recorded in Neh. xii. 27–43.

From beginning to end the poet connects God's special goodness to Israel, as now manifested, with His infinite power, wisdom, and goodness in the natural world.

1 PRAISE YE JEHOVAH!
        It is good to sing to our God with the harp,
    Yea, pleasant and comely are hymns to His praise;
2 Jehovah rebuildeth Jerusalem,
    And gathers the outcasts of Israel;

 3 He healeth the broken in heart,
    And relieveth their sorrows ;
 4 He numbers the stars,
    And all of them calls by their name.
 5 Great is our Lord, and abundant in power,
    Understanding unmeasured is His.
 6 Jehovah upholdeth the weak,
    But the wicked casts down to the ground.

 7 Praise Jehovah with songs of thanksgiving :
    Let strains of the harp ascend to our God ;
 8 The heavens He covers with clouds,
        Prepares rain for the earth,
    And grass He makes sprout on the mountains ;
 9 He gives to the cattle their food,
    To the brood of the raven when they call ;
10 It is not in the strength of the horse He has pleasure,
    And He has no delight in the power of a man.
11 Jehovah has pleasure in those that revere Him,
    In those that hope in His mercy.

12 O Jerusalem, glorify Jehovah ;
    O Zion, give praise to Thy God ;
13 For He strengthens the bars of thy gates,
    He has blessed thy children within thee ;
14 He makes peace in thy borders ;
    With the best of the wheat He has filled thee.
15 He sends forth to the earth His commands,
    His word runneth swiftly.
16 He gives snow-flakes like wool ;
    The hoar frost He scatters like ashes.
17 His ice He casts forth like morsels of bread,
    In the face of His cold, who can stand ?

18 He sends out His word and dissolves them,
    He puts forth His breath, and the waters flow off ;
19 His word He has shown unto Jacob,
    His statutes and judgments to Israel ;

20 Not so has He blessed any nation,
His statutes and judgments no other has known;
PRAISE YE JEHOVAH!

(10) **Power.** Heb. *legs*, with special reference to foot soldiers in an army, as the preceding line to cavalry. Neither the strength of his steed, nor his own muscular power will secure victory to the warrior, apart from the help and blessing of God.

CXLVIII.

LET THE HEAVENS AND THE EARTH PRAISE JEHOVAH.

THIS Psalm abounds in the boldest personifications. It not only celebrates the Almighty rule of God over all the creatures He has made, but calls upon them all to utter His praise. Delitzsch, following many others, finds within the meaning of this Psalm a transformation in the visible creation, connected with moral transformation wrought by Divine grace upon men, — that "creation will become at last the clear mirror of the Divine glory and a veritable thousand-voiced hymn," and he refers to certain descriptions of the prophet Isaiah, and especially to Rom. viii. 18-22 as of similar import. It may be questioned, however, whether this were in the mind of the poet here. There is no intimation of present discord or depression in the sphere of nature. These striking apostrophes rather suggest that all the works of God obey Him, exhibit His perfections, and so in their dumb way praise Him, and set an example to man, who only is remiss.

There are two parts ; the first (1-6) relating to heaven, the second (7-14) to earth. The order is reversed, descending from the highest to the lowest in heaven, but ascending from the lowest to the highest on the earth.

1 PRAISE YE JEHOVAH!
From the heavens give praise to Jehovah;
Give Him praise in the heights;
2 Give Him praise, all His angels;
Give Him praise, all His hosts;
3 Give Him praise, sun and moon,
And let all the bright stars give Him praise;
4 Praise Him, O heaven of the heavens,
And ye waters that are higher than the heavens.

5 Let them praise the great Name of Jehovah,
  For He gave the command, and they came into being,
6 And He fixed them forever and ever,
  He made a decree which they cannot transgress.

7 Praise Jehovah from the earth,
  Ye monsters of the sea, and all depths;
8 The fire and the hail,
  The snow and the vapour;

9 All ye mountains and hills,
  Fruitful trees and all cedars;
10 Beasts and all cattle,
  Reptiles, and birds that have wings;

11 The kings of the earth, and all nations,
  Princes and all judges of the earth;
12 Both young men and maidens,
  Old men and children;

13 Give praise to the Name of Jehovah,
    For His Name is exalted, His only,
  And His majesty higher than the earth and the heavens.

14 And He lifteth a horn for His people,
    As a praise for all His belovèd;
  For the children of Israel, a people very near Him;
    PRAISE YE JEHOVAH!

CXLIX.

A VICTORIOUS NATION GLORIFYING JEHOVAH.

THIS Psalm, like the three preceding (see cxlvi.), is entirely appropriate to the circumstances of the Jewish people immediately after the Babylonish captivity. They regarded their deliverance as a signal proof of Divine favour, and joyfully anticipated for the chosen nation the glory described in the most glowing predictions of the prophets. This is well expressed by Perowne: "The old days of the nation, and the old martial spirit are revived. God is their king (ver. 2), and they are His soldiers, going forth to wage His battles, with His praises in their mouth and a two-edged sword in their hands. A spirit which now seems sanguinary and revengeful had, it is not too much to say, its proper function under the Old Testament, and was not only natural but necessary, if that small nation was to maintain itself against the powerful tribes by which it was hemmed in on all sides. But it ought to require no proof that language like that of verses 6–9 of this Psalm is no warrant for the exhibition of a similar spirit in the Christian Church."

1 PRAISE YE JEHOVAH!
   Sing a new song to Jehovah,
Hymns of praise when His loved ones assemble.
2 Let Israel rejoice in his Maker,
Let the children of Zion exult in their King;
3 His Name let them praise in the dance,
From the timbrel and harp, to Him let their melody rise.

4 For Jehovah has joy in His people;
The meek He adorns with salvation.
5 Let His loved ones exult in their glory,
Let them joyfully sing on their beds,
6 Lofty praises of God in their mouth,
And a double-edged sword in their hand;

7 On the heathen to execute vengeance,
To punish the nations;
8 To bind up their sovereigns with chains,
Their nobles with fetters of iron;
9 To execute on them the sentence recorded,
This honour have all His belovèd;
    PRAISE YE JEHOVAH!

CL.

HALLELUJAH.   THE CLOSING DOXOLOGY

1 PRAISE YE JEHOVAH!
  In His holy temple praise God:
  Give Him praise in the sky spread out by His power.
2 Give Him praise for His mighty achievements,
  Give Him praise in His manifold greatness;
3 Praise Him with blasts of the trumpet,
  Praise Him with lute and with harp;
4 Praise Him with timbrel and dance,
  Praise Him on strings and the pipe;
5 Praise Him with clear sounding cymbals,
  Praise Him with cymbals loud clashing;
6 Let all that have breath praise Jehovah;
  PRAISE YE JEHOVAH!

THE END.